A City in the Making

A City in the Making

Aspects of Calcutta's Early Growth

RANABIR RAY CHOUDHURY

NIYOGI
BOOKS

Published by
NIYOGI BOOKS
D-78, Okhla Industrial Area, Phase-I
New Delhi-110 020, INDIA
Tel: 91-11-26816301, 49327000
Fax: 91-11-26810483, 26813830
email: niyogibooks@gmail.com
website: www.niyogibooksindia.com

Editor: Sucharita Ghosh
Design: Nabanita Das

ISBN: 978-93-85285-28-8
Publication: 2016
Reprint: 2025

Printed at Niyogi Offset Pvt. Ltd., New Delhi, India

For Mimi,
our shaft of sunlight

Contents

SECTION THREE: **A TIME FOR PLANNING**

Introduction

This is a study of the physical growth of Calcutta (Kolkata)—essentially the regulation of space—from the last decade of the seventeenth century till the commencement of the work of the Lottery Committee in October 1817. The period, stretching for 127 years, covers just about half the history of British Calcutta, from the time Job Charnock set foot in it for the third time in 1690 till 1947 when India gained its Independence. Charnock's decision to make Calcutta the base of the East India Company's operations in the Bay area triggered the evolution of a hitherto nondescript village on the eastern bank of the river Hooghly into a bustling metropolis of the British empire which once came to be described as its 'second city'. The most important phase of the development work was done in the nineteenth century under the guidance of the Lottery Committee which made way for the Fever Hospital Committee in 1836. The basic contours of the physical shape in which we find Calcutta today is a direct product of this specific phase of the city's development, which may be cited as evidence of the lack of any fresh initiative (apart from the work done by the Calcutta Improvement Trust) on its further growth in the twentieth century. To take just one example amongst many that are available, it is only now that the city's splendid riverfront is being given a serious facelift which promises literally to catapult that part of the city from the early years of the nineteenth century directly to the twenty-first. The inference here is that, apart from the addition of memorials like the Prinsep's Ghat (1841) and the Gwalior monument (1847) and the erection of a string of warehouses later in the nineteenth century, the eastern bank of the river has remained basically unaltered for nearly two centuries following the development of Strand Road in the 1820s.

The Lottery Committee itself was the successor to the town-development effort initiated by Lord Wellesley during his Governor-Generalship (1798–1805) the first step being the setting up in 1803 of the Committee for the Improvement of the Town of Calcutta. Considering the growth of Calcutta from the earliest days till it became the centrepoint of the British empire in the East, the point can be made that it was Wellesley who first introduced the tool of planning in the efforts to develop the city which, within the next one hundred years, enabled the city to attain its coveted position in the subcontinent. The East India Company official John Shore (later Lord Teignmouth), Wellesley's immediate predecessor as Governor-General (1793–1798), was essentially a staid and conservative revenue official, his life's work being to put the permanent settlement in place under Lord Cornwallis (whom he succeeded) during the latter's first stint as Governor-General from 1786 to 1793. Archival records indicate that in his time he did nothing epochal for the development of the rapidly expanding town. Whatever he achieved in this direction was not any the more special than what his predecessors had achieved since Robert Clive and Admiral Watson retook Calcutta from Shiraj-ud-Daula in January 1757. Even so, the process of 'importing ideas and procedures relating to landed property that were not the same as those of the nawabs' had already begun which later became 'the basis of property rights in Calcutta and also of the regulation of space in the city (rules about public and private land, markets, encroachment, preservation of roads, ghats, etc)'. These new rules and regulations were meant to enhance the security of the Europeans, 'but it had a major effect on Indian inhabitants too'.[1]

The attribute which distinguished Wellesley from his predecessors was his proactiveness regarding the town's physical and civic development. It is not known whether the Governor-General arrived in Calcutta with his ideas on the subject already formed and ready for implementation. There is little in the published material on Wellesley's pre-India days which throws light on the subject. What we do know is that he was sufficiently impressed with what he saw of the town as he came up the river. Writing to his wife Hyacinthe on 5 June 1798, within a week of his arrival in Calcutta, the Governor-General wrote:

> Nothing could equal the magnificence of my approach to this town. For nearly 3 miles the river, which is as large as the Thames in London, is bordered by lovely well-built country houses with porticos and colonnades. The town is a mass of superb palaces in the same style, with the finest fortress in the world – all this is, as in Rome, mixed up with miserable huts and gardens. The green of the lawns surpasses anything you can ever have seen – an extraordinary effect in so hot a country. The trees are more beautiful, their foliage more luxuriant, than in any European country.[2]

It is more than probable that the decision to 'revamp' the town in its broadest sense was taken soon after he set foot in it, the first step in this direction being the move to build the impressive pile of a Government House, today's Raj Bhavan. That he had taken the decision to build his palace within a couple of months after his arrival is indicated by the fact that the ground on which the house was built was bought 'about the middle' of 1798. Construction commenced without any fanfare, one might even suggest surreptitiously, in February 1799 when the Governor-General was away in the south pursuing the Mysore campaign.[3] Although it was 'quite well-staffed',[4] Wellesley perhaps did not like what he saw of Buckingham House which was then the official residence of the Governor-General. After all, it was not in too good a shape as indicated by Shore's letter to his wife in early 1794.[5] That the new Governor-General stepped on the toes of his employers back in London in the way he went about constructing the house is an engaging story in itself, which left its footprint on his tenure in India.

It may be argued that Wellesley deliberately went out of his way to focus attention on improving the town of Calcutta in an effort to deflect criticism that he was wasting the East India Company's resources on his own, very private, predilections. Among other things, one of the 'unpleasant' things he set out to accomplish was to 'restore the post of Governor General to its due consequence'.[6] This view would hold that the development of Calcutta was actually an afterthought which, however, took on a life of its own with the passage of time. The same charge can in fact be levelled against the Governor-General regarding his intention to set up an experimental farm and menagerie at Barrackpore in 1804 and 1805, a spot which he had already set his heart on as the location for a country retreat. Since he knew that he was 'forever in the public eye and Richard Wellesley attached great importance to example,' it was at Barrackpore that the Governor-General partook of recreational activities which were considered a bit out of place in his palace in the heart of town.[7] Thus, first, a good house fit for him had to be built on the bank of the river with 'a park worthy of a Governor-General'[8] and, secondly, an avenue had to be constructed from Calcutta to the retreat, both of which would be costly propositions. And all this was in addition to the upcoming Government House in Calcutta which had already raised a hornet's nest antagonising the Court of Directors as far as their chief representative in the East was concerned.

Perhaps with the objective of camouflaging his real intentions, Wellesley advanced the cause of an experimental farm and menagerie at Barrackpore which, as he saw it, would justify the expenditure not only on the road to the place but also on what was being spent on the house which he had already begun to plan there, one where he would have to reside to keep a close watch on the proposed scientific proceedings.[9] The allegation is strengthened when it is known that his interest in the completion of the extension of Circular Road—

Baitakhana Road in those days—northwards from Shyambazar was based primarily on how soon he could use the new road to travel to Barrackpore. This may or may not have been true—probably it was because it was reported by Richard Blechynden, the surveyor of roads, in the voluminous diary he kept (1791–1822) during the years he was in Calcutta—but the fact remains that, whatever the basic motivation, Wellesley was the first Governor-General to take a holistic view of the state of the town on his arrival and to engage in a many-faceted exercise to transform the town's future into a better one.

The work begun by Wellesley was continued by his successors Lord Minto (1807–1813) and the Earl of Moira, later Lord Hastings (1813–1823), both retaining the overall administrative framework of the development effort in the shape of a general committee for improving the town and, more importantly, extending all the support they could muster to assist it in its work. This latter point suggests that those at the very top of the Company's administration were aware of the fast-growing contradiction between the old civic and infrastructural arrangements, such as the drains, roads, health, etc., that had marked Calcutta since the early days of the establishment of the British settlement and the demands of a rapidly expanding town, a contradiction which had reached a point of crisis. This explains why there was a uniformity of response on the part of the three Governors-General, which also strengthens the view that Wellesley would in all probability have initiated the era of town-planning for Calcutta even if there was no need for him to camouflage the huge spending on his Government House and the Barrackpore extravaganza by widening the expenditure canvas.

It is within this broad framework governing the planned development of Calcutta that the suspension of Wellesley's committee for improvement of the town at the end of his tenure, on the grounds of a shortage of financial resources, has to be seen. The reason cited for the suspension of the committee was in fact to be expected. 'Resource-shortage' had become a refrain which the Court of Directors in London had resorted to almost continually during the entire period of Wellesley's Governor-Generalship barring the first two years. The important thing to note is that despite the focus on a shortage of resources, the need to continue with the development effort was proposed strongly by the officials who had taken up the reins of the East India Company's affairs in the East during the period following the sudden death of Lord Cornwallis at Ghazipur on 5 October 1805 and Minto's arrival in July 1807.[10] It was left to these officials to suggest that the funds raised by public lotteries could be set aside for city development work generally as opposed to the prevailing practice of financing specific projects like the Town Hall, a proposal which, as the records indicate, was accepted by London grudgingly.

The funds problem being settled for the time being, both Minto and Hastings extended full support to the job of cleaning up the town and improving its civic facilities leaving untouched the formal structure of the development effort, at the apex of which was the committee for improving the town. Since the time of Wellesley and earlier, a serious problem facing the Company administration was the prevention of the fires which broke out in the town regularly especially in the hot summer months. Over-crowding of highly inflammable huts was one reason behind the occurrences, but there was little that the officials could do to check the menace. In fact, the flow of natives into the town was facilitated by the official policy of encouraging 'construction work and domestic service' so much so that 'early attempts were made to enforce labour contracts and to attract labour from elsewhere'.[11] The systemic arrangements in place continued till it was realised that another big push was needed which resulted in the setting up of the Lottery Committee by Lord Hastings in October 1817. The work of this committee, encapsulated in the volumes of its proceedings, and that of its successor the Fever Hospital Committee, as reflected in the latter's voluminous report and appendices, was nothing short of seminal for the development of Calcutta's physical infrastructure and civic profile, which makes this phase of the city's development a subject fit for separate treatment.[12]

The reports drawn up by the special committees set up in Wellesley's time are perhaps the only official documents extant which provide us with an idea of the poor state in which the expanding city of Calcutta found itself at the turn of the eighteenth century. As already stated, one reason for this lack of activity on the town-development front was the absence of a proactive approach by the authorities of the time in toning up the town's infrastructure. This, however, does not mean that no work was done in these specific spheres by the successive administrative official committees, such as the Calcutta Committee of Revenue, the Committee of Revenue, and the Board of Revenue. On the contrary, the records indicate that the committees had their hands full in dealing with problems—mainly in the shape of complaints and petitions sent to the Government of the day—which arose on a day-to-day basis all of which were tackled discreetly by the officials concerned with, at least on the face of it, 'bureaucratic' thoroughness.

It has been argued that 'corruption' and 'exploitation' of every hue—racial, economic, social—were rampant in the Company's administration in India in these years and later, and that the facade of natural justice imported from Britain was deliberately erected to hide the real state of affairs, which was sordid to say the least. This may have been so considering the fact that public opinion back home in Britain at the time, conditioned by political imperatives and the introduction of a new set of values in moral philosophy, was alert and averse to any acts of 'injustice' committed by Englishmen anywhere. The focus on trading companies was perhaps to be expected in an evolving Indian situation where the master at that point of time was an English company under royal charter the avowed commercial policy of which was to squeeze the last penny from a resource-endowed Asiatic populace. In fact, these people had been exploited for centuries by those who had controlled successively the levers of power in the society to which they belonged.

Essentially, the subject matter was not 'exploitation' *per se* but the further fact that the new players had white skin and had come from afar in big ships from across the seas. These were white-skinned outsiders who did not belong to the land from which sprang the habitually exploited. But there was one big difference in the two situations of exploitation which perhaps made all the difference to those whose lot till then had been to be subjugated from time immemorial. The flow and nature of the petitions seeking redress addressed to the various government committees from the 1770s onwards suggest that the native petitioners had come to enjoy a sense of 'security' which was missing in earlier times, a sentiment which emboldened them to approach the authorities with their problems in larger numbers. Admittedly, the official records reflect only the surface-picture without providing any idea what lay underneath both as regards the rulers and the ruled. But having said this the point needs to be made that the evolution of the quality and volume of complaints and petitions made to the government of the day should be seen as a pointer to the 'improvement' that was taking place in the quality of East India Company governance from the last quarter of the eighteenth century onwards.

During the period between Charnock's arrival in 1690 and the fall of Calcutta in June 1756 the Bengal Council was concerned not so much with responding to the pressure of an increasing population (there is firm evidence that Sutanati grew exponentially even before the seventeenth century had bowed out) as with making the three villages comprising the settlement—Sutanati, Calcutta and Gobindapur—'livable' primarily from the point of view of the newly arrived sahibs. This was a period when repeated efforts were made to keep 'the Town Wholesome and free from the Offensive Smels and Ditches and Holes' which was 'indicative of the beginning of public responsibility for environmental conditions and civic improvement in Calcutta, in conjunction with private effort'.[13] Even though the white community comprised just a handful of people when compared with the local inhabitants who had lived in the area for centuries, the official records indicate that in the early days the East India Company was not keen on taking steps to improve the living conditions of the natives. When such measures were in fact contemplated by the Bengal Council, the Directors made it clear that they had to be financed by the natives as well, the consistent view of the Court being that the generality of the inhabitants had to foot the bill for town improvements made for their benefit (this point is discussed in some detail later). The principle of charging money for every 'benefit' sold was operative here which is not difficult to understand given the core commercial basis of the East India Company's operations in the East at the time. The principal objective was an increasing revenue, as is made clear in the following passage from a letter written by the Court to the Bengal Council in November 1700:[14]

> … as we are willing to be at any Charge for your and our peoples Security within your bounds So we rely on you to turne every Stone to raise a Standing Revenue [an idea proposed an year earlier; see later] to bear it and in due time to pay us Interest for Our Money which that the Inhabitants may be enabled the more cheerfully to contribute unto we would have you encourage all People especially handicrafts to Reside there and Employ them in whatever they can make fitt for Europe although you give them rather more than others.

It is instructive to note the further point that there were occasions—such as when the building of wharfs was ordered to control the Hooghly which was eating into its eastern bank—when native merchants refused to toe the Company's line on local contributions, the Council using its zamindari fiat to have its way. Perhaps, it was the 'Impartiality and Mildness of the English Government' which led enterprising natives to adopt a firm stand on the issue, the one certain fact being that their activities or persons would not be threatened or harmed beyond a point because of such perceived acts of insolence on their part.

During this period one comes across diverse and discrete official initiatives such as strengthening the banks of the river, cutting down trees, freeing roads from encroachment, cleaning drains, filling up holes in which stagnant water accumulated posing a threat to the health of the settlement, building a hospital, a church, a town hall and a jail. Following the growing pressure of population, there was also an effort to expand the town southwards and eastwards towards the salt lakes not because of any sustained planning in this direction but for the simple reason that these were the only areas in which the settlement could expand most easily. Though clogged with vegetation and water bodies, the area only had to be cleared for habitation because it was for the most part vacant land. A survey of Bazar Calcutta, Town Calcutta, Sutanati and Gobindapur was ordered in 1705 (the report being submitted in 1707) which provided the authorities with an idea of the topographical and economic profile of the areas concerned. But there is little evidence in the records to suggest that the survey resulted in the framing of any specific targets or that policies were framed and implemented subsequently keeping a firm objective in mind.

In the closing years of the seventeenth century and the early years of the eighteenth (till around 1703), there was no control on, or inventory of, building activity in Sutanati and Calcutta with the result that houses sprang up in all directions in the process diluting severely the fort's military utility. The Directors were simply not aware of this weakness in the defence arrangements perhaps because of the steady stream of reports emanating from Calcutta that the fort had been made strong enough to stave off a 'Revolution or Rebellion in the kingdome of Bengall'. This is suggested by a letter written to the Council in early 1706 asking it to plan the streets in such a way 'that the ffort Guns may be brought to bear on [them] to beat out an Enemy that should gett into them'. The Council was also asked to ensure that the houses around the fort 'may be at such a Distance … as not to prejudice any part of it in Case by accident or design they should be sett on fire'.[15] But of course the suggestions arrived too late, for the damage had already been done. Alternatively, the authorities in Calcutta could do little to rectify the situation because most of the houses around the fort were owned and tenanted by important people who were not too happy with the suggested changes. As far as native housing was concerned, it was only a matter of time before an effort would be made by the authorities to regulate the property profile and develop a proper administrative record of the existing situation which, among other things, would be of help in future revenue assessment and collection. Thus, in 1704 the Bengal Council wanted 'all the black inhabitants, who have no writing for their tenements, ... to give them writings, they paying the Company *salami*, and he (the English zamindar) causing their ground to be measured'.[16] It needs to be mentioned that in the absence of any other equally reliable resource, C.R. Wilson's archival work on the old Fort William and that on the early annals of the English in Bengal have been drawn on heavily to plot the official measures taken in this direction.

Another engaging subject is the tightrope-walking which the Court of Directors in London resorted to, especially before the death of Aurangzeb in March 1707, between the military imperative of strengthening the fort and the need to pursue the strategic line of not arousing the suspicion of the local ruler regarding the longer-term implications of such a step. The records indicate that the Company was extra-cautious in pursuing this line—thereby adding to the problems of the Bengal Council which pressed for implementation of the defensive measures as quickly as possible—because it was aware that, in the event of an assault by the nawab's forces in the very early years of the settlement, it simply would not have been able to defend the settlement effectively. In fact, it is clear that the level of ambition as far as the defensive preparedness of the first Fort William was concerned was limited. In December 1699 the Court was writing to the Council:

> We desire to follow Our Trade and mind our busyness, and doe never want a fort, but only as it may prove a safe Retreat from Threatened Danger a Security against open Violence, or to make our Servants put on such a face of Power as to discourage every Upstart Neighbouring Governour from daring to affront them.

Fourteen years later, in 1713, the Council was told unambiguously that the fort was to be made strong enough to take care of 'sudden Insults of Rebels or mutinuous Partys', but certainly the objective was not to turn it into 'a Fortress to withstand a Royal Army',[17] which is precisely what happened in 1756 when Shiraj-ud-Daula attacked the fort and took it for six months.

There are strong indications in the official records that, even before the seventeenth century had rung itself out, the East India Company, in the capacity of a zamindar reporting to the nawab, had begun to see itself as a fledgling sovereign power. There was certainly no misunderstanding of the technical position of the Company as a zamindar in an eastern setting. It was probably the innate arrogance of the white man which made it difficult for the Company to observe both in letter and spirit the limitations set on its activities by its position as a zamindar. The tone adopted in its letters to the Bengal Council, in the first flush of acquiring the zamindary rights in November 1698, gives the impression that the Court of Directors saw in the transfer a tectonic shift in its position vis-a-vis the ruling power in Bengal. In November 1699, the Court asked the Council to get on with strengthening the fortifications there 'without fear of giving Umbrage to the Moors, because they cant pretend to make an inquisition in a Place where they have nothing to do withall'.[18] A year later, the expression 'Our ffortifications and Dominion in Bengall' is used by the Court, which provides an insight into how the Court of Directors in distant London viewed the way events were unfolding in Bengal. During the next four decades the Company gained in confidence to such an extent that in 1748 it was instructing its officials in Calcutta that, in the event of the nawab raising any hackles with regard to new defensive works undertaken by the English, it was to let him know that the 'King of England' was ready to 'support the Company in whatever they may think fit to do for their future Security'.[19]

As we have seen, in Wellesley's time, the Directors in London repeatedly drew attention to a shortage of financial resources whenever any spending was suggested on civic development by their Government in Calcutta. The adoption of this position may have been justified at the time but there can be little doubt that the policy was a long-standing one as far as the Company's affairs in Bengal were concerned. Thus, in the early years, we come across a number of occasions when the Court of Directors impressed on the Bengal Council the need to curtail costs and, where expenditure could not be curbed, to make the people pay for the improvements effected. The policy when practised by the Council was described approvingly as 'good management' by its masters in London. The earliest instance of the policy being pursued is to be found in 1704 when the subject of repairing the few roads in existence at the time came up. Recourse was had to the 'petty fines from the black inhabitants', the 'moral justification' for such a step being found in the link between the expenditure and the objective of making 'the town more wholesome and convenient'.[20] Initially, the Council had gently objected to the policy which it felt would add to the hardship of the local populace, both native and European. But the Company had its way and, by the early 1750s, the policy was given concrete shape with the Court of Directors writing to the Council that, as it saw 'no reason why the Expence of Publick Works should not be defrayed at the Expence of the Inhabitants', it was empowering its officers 'for the future in Cases of the like Nature, to raise Money by way of Duty, Contribution or otherwise as you shall think will best answer that purpose'.[21] As the Company saw it, protection was being offered to those residing within its zamindary from the rapacity of local zamindars and the nawab's men, a service for which payment in some form had to be made by the beneficiaries; hence, the imposts.

One upshot of this was that even if the Bengal Council was keen on building a 'new Calcutta' and making it 'more regular' as early as 1706,[22] there were limits to what it could do in view of the tight resource situation and the Company's stand on spending. Seen from the perspective of the Directors, they probably found their hands tied. After all, they represented a trading outfit and in the historical stage in which the company found itself at the time the surplus generated from ongoing trading operations was simply not enough to look after expenditure on town development. Even so, as noticed earlier, the Court did not hesitate to tell the Council that one of its main objectives was to keep the people living within its zamindari happy because it felt that such contentment would ultimately lead to an increase in its revenue. In December 1699 the Directors wrote to Charles Eyre in Bengal:[23]

> You know we have been at great Charge in our ffortifications there [Calcutta], and are desirous You should omitt nothing which may make that ffort tenable and your Selves secure against any Attempts of the Moors and being so strong and able to afford Protection it necessarily Occurs, That the protected should pay an Acknowledgment to their Defenders; Protection being the true ffoundation on which all Pretences for raising Customs Subsidies and other Taxes are originally built, ffor this it is Tenants swear ffealty to their Lords, and All Subjects owe Allegiance to their Princes, and on this Ground, and to Reimburse Us our great Charge We recommend to you the raising a standing Revenue by the Methods above mentioned, or any other you shall observe more adapted to the Genius and Custome of the Inhabitants, well knowing that when they shall find the Impartiality and Mildness of the English Government, They will be easily induced to betake themselves to your Protection, and in a short time render the Territory within your late Grant the most fflourishing Spott of Ground in Bengall.

A month earlier, on 21 November, after the villages of Sutanati, Calcutta and Gobindapur had been given to the English as their zamindari, at the cost of 'a large hole [being made] in our Cash' (Rs 1,300), the Directors had written, 'We shall now expect to see an Instance of your Zeal and Skill for our Service by the Advancement of our Revenues there, well knowing that due Care and a kind Treatment of the Natives will make those Towns flourish under the mild Government of the English'.[24] Progress was made, for in 1719 the Court was writing to the Council[25]

> It is a great satisfaction to Us to read that exact Justice is administer'd to all under you and that it shall be continued. We know (of) no better way to People your Towns nor any better proof of it than the increase of useful Inhabitants who to be sure will resort where they may best be secured from oppression or secret or open Squeezings, and treated with humanity. The more such Inhabitants there are the more will our Revenues encrease besides other benefits to the Place.

Since 1690, till the fort fell into the hands of Shiraj-ud-Daula, the little that was done by way of town development was effected in the part of the settlement populated by Europeans.[26] This is proof, if proof was required, that in the minds of the sahibs there was the inevitable dichotomy between white and black people, which necessarily influenced the actions they took on the ground. Not only was the discrimination a direct consequence of being the foreign ruler in a sea of natives, but the colour of the skin and the vastly different cultures which confronted each other also added to the pressure of segregation,[27] which was only natural in the circumstances. There was of course a measure of mutual dependence among the two peoples, more so on the part of the outsiders who had no alternative but to depend on the services provided by the natives in the prosecution of their daily lives. Over time, this was bound to lead to a situation where some 'mixing' would take place, not in the social sphere but certainly in a physical, topographical sense. In the first flush of settling down in a new place this gradual co-habitation was probably not noticed, and even if it was there was not much anyone could do about it. But with some sort of social stability emerging in the new environment, the Europeans had no choice but to become increasingly aware of the growing physical proximity of the natives, an unnatural and unwanted phenomenon which was bound to be taken note of in official circles.[28]

Thus, the Bengal Public Consultations of June 1745 tell us that

> Several Black people having intermixed themselves among the English Houses, and by that means occasion Nuisances and disturbances to Several of the English Inhabitants … Ordered That the Jemindar do make enquiry there and lay before us an Account of such Houses as are Inhabited by them in order for them to quit, and remove to proper places in the Town …'[29]

The use of the word 'proper' is significant because it tells us that the sahibs considered it 'improper' for the natives to get close to them physically, which again is not surprising in the prevailing social and temporal circumstances. Three years later, the Court was writing to Bengal that houses 'belonging to our Servants or any English must not be sold to Moors or any Black Merchants whatsoever',[30] which clearly points to the early development of the contours of a black and white town. By 1753 the concept of the white town had entered officialese: the Bengal Council was writing that the 'Houses belonging to Europeans and others in the *white* [emphasis added] Town sell from ten to twelve thousand Rupees each, bearing upper rooms, and the Repairs thereof, are usually so large as to afford little advantage to the Proprietors'.[31]

Following the retaking of the town from the nawab in early 1757, the English authorities focused attention on strengthening the town's defences. As we have noted earlier, the old fort was an apology in terms of military utility one reason for which was the sensitivity of the Court of Directors not to be seen to be strengthening military arrangements which would annoy the nawab. This policy no longer applied after the retaking of Calcutta by the English, an opportunity being presented to the Company to construct an effective fort which would be free of civilian encumbrances, as was the case with the earlier fort. For about a decade, the focus of all energy devoted to the town's affairs was directed at this activity, which included settling issues relating to compensation to be given to those who had to be shifted from Gobindapur where the new Fort William was coming up. The official records of this period suggest that the Government of the day did not quite do its homework in working things out in the way it should have. Consequently, the failing led to complications which in some cases resulted in legal suits being filed. One point which emerges is the unwillingness of Warren Hastings to force the issue, which would have put a large number of natives—moved out of Gobindapur and Kidderpur to Jorabagan—to great trouble for no fault of their own. Looking back, it would appear that the Governor-General refused to take peremptory action, even in a situation where revenue collections were being affected adversely, because he was aware that the Government itself was to blame for shifting people to an area which already belonged to someone else, namely, the Setts. This trait of Hastings, erring on the side of humanity in a fast-evolving imperial setting, is also discernible in the way he tackled the issue of clearing the ground on which the Barrackpore cantonment came up in the 1770s. Despite pressure from the military authorities to evict landowners summarily from the ground required for the cantonment, the Governor-General cautioned patience and laid emphasis on due process for resolution of the problem, which included giving a fair hearing to the affected natives.[32]

Another major sphere of official activity relating to the town during this period was demarcation of the limits of the ground cleared to form the esplanade of the new fort.[33] The issues thrown up by the controversy enable us to form a clearer idea of the physical lay of the land involved as also of the play of human relationships spawning not only the native-European divide but also the civil-military clash of ambition. The maidan today is a distinctive physical feature of Calcutta which marks it out from other comparable Indian cities which still holds out the hope that it can grow into a better-looking metropolis than it is today. That the expanse of ground has been able to survive relatively unscathed through the past couple of centuries, barring the work done by the city's metro railway project and some construction work on the fringes to its south-west, is wholly due to the constant alertness of the Indian military authorities under whose jurisdiction the maidan falls. The revenue and judicial records indicate that official vigilance regarding prevention of encroachment of ground has a long history and that it began immediately following the formation of the esplanade in the 1770s.

This was also the period which saw building activity in the Chowringhee area reach a frenetic pace which, in later years, gave the city its appellation of being a city of palaces. Here one comes across specific decisions taken by the authorities on what some historians would choose to describe as mundane, inconsequential issues which have left their footprint on the past two centuries, one such issue being the 'angular' meeting point of modern-day Park Street (the Burial Ground Road of the past) with J.L. Nehru Road (Chowringhee Road). The specific configuration of the two roads in question and the problem it led to found a place in official documents at the turn of the eighteenth century following the frequency of accidents taking place at the spot. Despite the unlimited executive powers available to the authorities concerned nothing drastic was done to solve the problem, such as altering the alignment of the old Burial Ground Road thereby reducing the sharpness of the angle of the meeting point with the Chowringhee Road. Instead, the offending corner was merely rounded off so as to mitigate to an extent the cause of the accidents with the result that the configuration of the two roads remains much the same today as it was more than two centuries ago, the only significant change since being a substantial increase in the width of the two roads which has had the effect of reducing the number of road mishaps at the spot. It may be argued that, from the point of view of the study of History, this particular 'footprint' of the late eighteenth century is not important because it does not contain any 'lessons' left behind for posterity, nor does it tell us anything about the complex processes involved in the unfolding of contemporary events involving the human mind and social categories. This may or may not be so, but for our limited purposes here the fact of the angular meeting point of the two roads in question is of interest for the simple reason that it has come down to us two centuries later, and that itself is a point worthy of notice.

In September 1786 Lord Cornwallis took over from John Macpherson who had played the role of pro tem Governor-General following the departure of Hastings at the beginning of February 1785. Though this was the beginning of a period of debate and controversy regarding Hastings' brand of governance, the important thing to note is that the tradition of 'fair administration' left behind by the departing Governor-General, especially among officials working at the grassroots level, was followed under the new dispensation almost seamlessly. One particular case which bears this out is that relating to the Government's treatment of the claim of a 'poor, old, infirm' native to land 'north of Park Street' roughly where the Asiatic Society stands today, which had been set aside for a riding school, a project dear to the heart of the cream of the town's European society. There was some uncertainty whether the man, Ahmed Sodial, had been compensated for his land—given to him during the time of Henry Vansittart (1760–1764)—which had been acquired later by the authorities to set up the sepoy barracks, an important landmark in the area. The important point was that the collector involved, the Board of Revenue as well as the Governor-General in Council kept harping on the theme that Sodial's claim to the land could not be brushed aside just because he had not asserted his claim earlier. In the end *pattas* to the land were given both to the riding school and the petitioner which suggests that there was a serious effort to implement at the ground level the English principles of fairness and equity codified by East India Company officials following the precepts then in vogue back home. Later, in Wellesley's time, the sanctity of private property—irrespective of whether it belonged to natives or Europeans—was put on a pedestal, which often had the effect of slowing down implementation of development plans for the town.

A recurring feature of the last three decades of the eighteenth century was the disputes involving bazars in certain areas of the town in which both Europeans and natives were involved, in some cases European fighting against a fellow European, in others native against native, and in yet others native against European. Here too one finds little hesitation on the part of natives to take their grievances to the rulers for a settlement even if the opposing party was a sahib.[34] The dispute between Jagannath Sarkar and Charles Wyatt at Kidderpur is a prime example of this, the record of the case providing us with, among other things, an idea of the topography of the Watgunje area as far as competing bazars were concerned and also the play of politics within native society, in this case between a so-called upstart hailing from a low caste and members of the 'ruling' strata.

This book is a purely descriptive effort at unfolding some facets of the story of early Calcutta's development, in the course of which light is thrown on how precisely the authorities went about the business of governance in a situation where a settlement was rapidly evolving into a town and then a city. Given the nature of the sources relied on for the narrative, it is inevitably a warped view of the proceedings covered. But then, during the period covered by the volume, the official records form the only repository where the issues and controversies of the day have been preserved for posterity. It is true that there is a strong element of subjectivity involved here for inevitably, human judgment and choice determined which issues of the day were to be discussed in Council and which to be ignored and thus not put on record. Also accounted for is the observation that the East India Company 'turned a blind eye to rule violations, petty and vast, except when transgression was formally brought to its attention, a very serious step for anyone to take'.[35] G.R. Elton writes:

> The historian does not just 'select' facts; he employs them in controlled reconstruction of that past of whose reality he knows them to be evidence. Nor does the critic seem to be well acquainted with the manner in which evidence comes into existence, for that which is deliberately preserved by observers is a drop in the bucket compared with that which is left behind by action and without thought of selection for preservation purposes.[36]

Further, one is aware of the criticism that the documents have been allowed 'to speak for themselves in a far too literal sense',[37] which subsumes the broad trends of societal movements within the perspective of the actors themselves, thereby reducing the entire effort into a simple story-telling exercise without any value for later generations. This has been done deliberately, emphasis being put on how 'contemporary reality' played itself out during the times in focus rather than trying to fit the comments and actions of the protagonists within a preconceived pattern of human thought and action. To quote Elton once again: 'Preconceived notions are a much greater danger to historical truth than either deficiency of evidence or error in detail, and nothing entrenches them so deep as the approval of some other form of study which seems to rest on independent thought'.[38]

Notes

1 Professor Peter Robb, of the School of Oriental and African Studies, University of London, in a private communication to the author.

2 Iris Butler, *The Eldest Brother* (London: Hodder & Stoughton, 1973), p. 134.

3 Ranabir Ray Choudhury, *The Lord Sahib's House* (Kolkata: Wild Strawberries Books, 2010), pp. 100 and 116, note 6.

4 Wellesley to his wife, 5 June 1798 (Butler, p. 135).

5 See chapter 'A Time for Planning'.

6 Peter Robb, *Useful Friendship: Europeans and Indians in Early Calcutta* (New Delhi: Oxford University Press, 2014), p. 28.

7 Butler, *The Eldest Brother*, p. 220.

8 Ibid., p. 221. Wellesley's letter to his wife dated 6 March 1800.

9 For the two minutes see *The Asiatic Annual Register*, 1807, Miscellany Section, pp. 110–114. See also Ray Choudhury, *The Lord Sahib's House*, p. 176ff.

10 Though Wellesley had left office on 30 July, he remained in Calcutta till the end of August 1805.

11 The author is indebted to Professor Robb for drawing attention to this point.

12 There is a debatable contrary opinion which holds that despite the fact that the Lottery Committee was set up to effect improvements, 'no bold and comprehensive plan was carried out' (Robb, *Sentiment and Self: Richard Blechynden's Calcutta Diaries, 1791-1822* [New Delhi: OUP, 2011], p. 246).

13 Professor Robb, in a private communication to the author.

14 C.R. Wilson, *Old Fort William in Bengal,* vol. 1 (London: John Murray, 1906), p. 48.

15 Wilson, *Old Fort William,* vol. 1, pp. 49 and 61.

16 C.R. Wilson, *The Early Annals of the English in Bengal,* vol. 1 (London: W Thacker & Co., 1895), p. 250.

17 Wilson, *Old Fort William*, vol. 1, pp. 46 and 91. See also Partha Chatterjee, *The Black Hole of Empire* (Ranikhet: Permanant Black, 2012), pp. 7–8.

18 Wilson, *Old Fort William*, vol. 1, p. 44.

19 Ibid, vol. 1, p. 208. See Chatterjee, *Black Hole*, pp. 33–39 for an analysis of the probable factors determining the attitude of the East India Company when dealing with its Mughal hosts.

20 Wilson, *Early Annals*, vol. 1, p. 252.

21 Wilson, *Old Fort William,* vol. 1, p. 230.

22 Ibid., p. 61.

23 Ibid., p. 47.

24 Ibid., p. 44.

25 Ibid., p. 106.

26 Wilson's work throws little light on the development of the native parts of Sutanati and Calcutta.

27 Mental segregation—the human sentiment from which springs the description of a native as a 'Blackie'—as opposed to physical segregation had always been there right from the time Charnock landed in Calcutta and even earlier.

28 Many years later, in the 1860s, a manifestation of the white man's wish to keep his distance from natives is to be found in the then

Lt-Governor of Bengal, Cecil Beadon's view that should natives be allowed to buy property close to Belvedere, the residence of the head of the Bengal Government, the place 'would be no longer a fit residence for the head of the Bengal Government' (Revenue Proceedings [West Bengal State Archives], June 1867, No. 6, pp. 4–5).

29 Wilson, *Old Fort William*, vol. 1, p. 183.

30 Ibid., p. 205.

31 Ibid., p. 252.

32 See Governor General in Council Proceedings (Revenue Department), 14 April and 6 May 1784 (West Bengal State Archives). This touches on the much-debated issue of whether the rule of Warren Hastings in Bengal was an 'enlightened' one. In his essay on Hastings, Macaulay speaks of the 'just and humane government' of the English which successfully effaced the earlier brazen rule of the 'band of English functionaries, daring, intelligent, eager to be rich'. This period of 'brazen rule', he writes, saw its zenith during the administration of Henry Vansittart who found himself at the head of 'a new and anomalous empire'. On the one side was this band of Englishmen, on the other 'a great native population, helpless, timid, accustomed to crouch under oppression'. It was a struggle between unequals, the inequality being reinforced by the attribute of the rulers who represented 'the strength of civilisation without its mercy'. In Macaulay's words, '... against misgovernment such as then afflicted Bengal it was impossible to struggle. The superior intelligence and energy of the dominant class made their power irresistible. A war of Bengalees against Englishmen was like a war of sheep against wolves, of men against demons. The only protection which the conquered could find was in the moderation, the clemency, the enlarged policy of the conquerors.'

This brief interregnum of 'enlarged policy' was initiated by the government of Hastings, its reflection being found in the way various episodes of conflict and confrontation between the rulers and the ruled which figure in this book were resolved.

33 The name 'esplanade' exists even today but, in the public mind, refers only to the north-east corner of the vast expanse which constituted it in the eighteenth and nineteenth centuries.

34 For more details see Soumitra Sreemani, *Anatomy of a Colonial Town Calcutta, 1756 – 1794* (Calcutta: Firma KLM Pvt Ltd, 1994).

35 Robb, *Sentiment and Self*, p. 5.

36 G.R. Elton, *The Practice of History* (Collins-Fontana, 1974), p. 118.
37 Ranajit Guha, *The Small Voice of History*, ed. Partha Chatterjee (Ranikhet: Permanent Black, 2010), p. 121.
38 Elton, *The Practice of History*, p. 52.

SECTION ONE

Around the Old Fort

1

Just Another Village

What was Sutanati like when Job Charnock landed there for the third time in August 1690, blissfully unaware that he was beginning a journey for Englishmen in the region which would, after many triumphs and fewer vicissitudes, come to an end two-and-a-half centuries later? What is certain is that there was nothing distinctive about the place, or the two other villages, Kalikata and Gobindapur, which explains why hardly any English visitor in the seventeenth century, or Portuguese and Dutch, has left any descriptive account of the place.[1] On the other hand, Hooghly figures frequently in the diaries and travelogues as does the small Dutch settlement of Baranagar, the Portuguese town of Bandel, and Muckwa Tannah[2] fort located on the western bank of the river Hooghly, possibly on the site of the superintendent's house of the present-day Botanical Gardens.

The town of Hooghly was the focus of European interest at the time because, among other things, it was the centre of trade. Thomas Bowrey, who visited these parts in the 1670s, writes:[3]

> This Kingdome of Bengala ... is replenished with many faire and pleasant Rivers, the most famous and much admired of which is the great River Ganges, one of the four principall rivers in the world, and is Supposed to runne up Paradise or the garden of Eden. The Other brave and Navigable Rivers are for the most part onely branches of this.

> One of the most admirable of which arms is Hugly river. Up and downe the Same a very Considerable Merchandize is drove, and very beneficiall, Especially to the English and Dutch Nations, havinge Excellent conveniences for carrying theire European Commodities up into the inland towns and Cities, and the like for bringinge downe the commodities purchased in this or some other Kingdoms.
>
> This River is soe named from the great towne of Hugly Scituated Upon the banks of it, neare 150 miles up from the Braces or Shoals that lye at the Entrance thereof. The towne or Citty of Hugly is a famous and Sumptuous place, adorned with many fine Structures, and very populous, and what addeth to the beauty thereof, it is well furnished with gardens, fine groves, a very large Bazar or markett place, one of the finest Chowlteries (or free lodgeinge houses for all travellers) that is contained in this Kingdome, and, more Especially, the 2 fine European Factories, namely the English and Dutch ....
>
> The towne is not very Uniforme, but is a very good and pleasant place, inhabited with Some of the richest Merchants of the Kingdome; and all sorts of Commodities that Orixa, Bengala, and Pattana doe afford are here dayly to be bought and Sold in the publicke Bazar, commonly called the great Bazar, by reason there are many where onely Cotton, course Calicoes, provisions, &c. are to be Sold.

It is of interest that while coming up the river, Bowrey does not have anything to say on the eastern bank of the Hooghly. In 1676 when Streynsham Master[4] made the same trip on his way to Kasimbazar, he mentions Tanna[5] and 'little Tanna', the latter probably being the Metiabruz of today where he ordered the burial of one of the Englishmen accompanying him who had died. Sailing up the river, at seven in the morning on 13 September 1676, he passed by 'Barnagur where the Dutch have a place called the Hogg Factory, and I was informed they kill about 3,000 hogges in a yeare, and salt them up for their shipping.' The Dutch chief at Balasore, Van Helyn, came to see Master here. Further up the river, Master even mentions 'a large spot of ground which the French had laid out for a factory', the editor of the *Diaries* identifying the place as modern-day Chandannagar.[6] Two months later, when Master was returning to Balasore, he mentions Chanock, or modern-day Barrackpore, and then Tanna once again where his ship anchored. On Tanna, which was 'distant from Hugly about 40 miles by water and twenty miles by land', Master wrote that

> ... there stands an old Fort of mud walls, which was built to prevent the incursion of the Arracaners, for it seemes, about ten or twelve yeares since, they were soe bold that none durst inhabit lower downe the river then this place, the Arracaners usually takeing the People off the shoare to sell them at Pipley [modern Pipli].

On 15 September 1679, on his second trip up the Hooghly, Master even supped at Tanna, the clear inference being that the other side of the river held no attractions at all ('little Tannah' is mentioned in the extract).[7]

Just eight years before Charnock landed at Sutanati for the last time, William Hedges had sailed up the river. He too does not mention the three villages on the east bank of the Hooghly despite the fact that the new agent sent to manage the Company's affairs in the Bay stopped almost opposite them at Muckwa Tanna. In fact, the years immediately following were unsettling as far as the English presence on the Hooghly was concerned, with many comings and goings, both from Fort St George and London. Even so, there is no description anywhere of what our three villages looked like, or their topography generally, which lends some support for the point of view that but for Charnock's personal predilection for Sutanati the future metropolis of the British empire in India would, if established at all, have been founded elsewhere.[8]

Among the earliest descriptions of the English at Sutanati, we have the jaundiced view of Fort St George. On 25 May 1691, it wrote to the East India Company's Court of Directors:[9]

> They (in Bengal) ... live in a wild unsettled condition at Chuttinuttee, neither fortifyed houses nor goedowns, only Tents, hutts, and boats, with

> the strange charge of near 100: soldiers, guardship, etc, for no business, and a doubtfull foundation , wholly depending on the good Nabob's Stay and favour ..... The King's promised Phyrmaund being not yet sent them from Surratt.... (The President had advised delay till the phyrmaund was received etc) but the Bengall gentlemen being in hast to return to their sweet plentyes which sandy Madras could not please them in.

A note is appended which says that the letter was signed only by the president, Eluhi Yale, who was not on the best terms with his Council, the Council secretary writing that, 'the Council refuses to sign or give their reasons for it.' Given the fractiousness of the Council at Fort St George at this point in time, the refusal of the rest of the Council to endorse Yale's views does not mean that what the president wrote to the Court about Bengal was untrue. Even so, the editor of *Hedges' Diary* adds, 'It is odd to find presidential jealousies expressed at so early a date.' If jealousy it was, it is possible, perhaps even likely, that the portrayal of conditions in Bengal was also coloured by the sentiment.

What is clear from the literature available on the subject is that, apart from its location down the river—which was important for a maritime power such as Britain giving it proximity to the high seas—there were no other purely topographical features which could have drawn Charnock to Sutanati.[10] Even so, the agent had set his heart on the place as the site for an English presence in the Bay.[11] The first mention of Sutanati ('Chuttanuttea') appears in a letter written by Charnock and his Council to Sir John Child at Surat on 31 December 1686, Charnock having made the small village his temporary base after leaving Hooghly.[12] He returned towards the end of 1687 and remained there for as long as a year, the editor of *Hedges' Diary* commenting that he could find 'no particulars whatever' of this period.[13] Within the next two years the choice of place for an English factory and settlement had narrowed down to Uluberia,[14] the island of Hidgelee, and of course Sutanati. On 30 September 1689, the Bengal Council based in Madras was writing to the Court that it had chosen Sutanati instead of Uluberia because the former was 'the best and fittest (place) up the River on the Maine', the problem with Hidgelee being that 'it would have been the most proper and most commodious place in all Bengall both foe Shipping and Traide'[15] had it been a more healthy place.

For the third time, and following the Heath episode, Charnock landed at Sutanati in August 1690, this time, as events turned out, for the continuous occupation of the place till 1947 when India gained its independence from the British. The point of interest for us is: how did the English pursue their lives at Sutanati in the years immediately following Charnock's arrival at the place? Unfortunately, the official records do not tell us much on this aspect; neither have any of the early protagonists left any descriptions of the place which could serve as reference points for us three centuries later. The only snippet of information we have on how Charnock and his men lived their lives at Sutanati, when they stayed there for about a year in 1687–1688, was that 'the factors and soldiers lived in huts until they could provide proper habitations'.[16] There is a similar famine of information on this specific aspect for about the first three years after Charnock landed at Sutanati in 1690. Within three months of Charnock's arrival at Sutanati, Fort St George was writing to the Court that it was

> ... a defenceless place ... where he [Charnock] continues contrary to all reason, or consent of the Government, who will neither permit building or Factory, nor merchants to settle or trade with them, but offer a more convenient place for it, two miles below Hughley, but that he will not hear of.[17]

The most substantive portrait we have of Sutanati following the advent of Charnock is that drawn by Sir John Goldsborough, the 'Superviser, Commissary Generall, and Chief Governour in East India,'[18] who wrote to Charles Eyre from Sutanati on 30 September 1693:[19]

> When I came hither I found your Agent and Council had been Remiss

> in not marking out a place whereon to build a factorie on, if we should hereafter be Libertized to setle here, and by that omission of theirs noebody knew where, or how to build, but everyone built straglingly where and how they pleased, even on the most properest place for a factorie, and have dug holes and tancks that will cost the Company mony to fill up agen, and the longer they Run, the worse would be the Evill. Therefore I though fitt to order the Inclosing a peece of ground with a Mud wall, whereon to build a factorie when we have a perwanna for it, which I mean to goe in hand to inclose in a day or two. This is all I know of this matter. Further upon the Walshes[20] house, bought for the Company, I intend to build above Staires upon the 2 Tarresses 4 Rooms or Chambers, that I may bring in the Accomptants and Secretaries, and the books and papers in their Charge, within this brick house, which now Ly scattering abroad in thatched houses Lyable to the hazzard of fire every day....

But, clearly, even though we do not find any substantive description of the stretch of the river bank where Charnock landed, it is safe to assume that the place had its fair share of open spaces, human habitation and vegetation, generally. Orme, in his *Historical Fragments of the Mughal Empire* (1805), includes a native version of Charnock's flight from Sutanati in early 1687 where the point is made that the agent 'took possession of Calcutta, which, after clearing of the jungles, he fortified'.[21] Although such narratives are usually wanting in veracity, there is little doubt that Charnock had to do some 'cleaning up' before his men could settle down, no matter for how short a period.

Available literature tells us that the site of the village known as Gobindapur—where Fort William now stands and its adjacent area—was once upon a time covered by dense jungle. Writing for the 1901 Census of India, A.K. Roy says that in the second decade of the eighteenth century—about thirty years after Charnock arrived in Sutanati—the expanse of ground which later became the esplanade of the new fort was 'a jungle not yet cleared, "interspersed with a few huts and small pieces of grazing and arable lands".' Sutanati was to the north of Chandpal Ghat, and we are told that to the south of the ghat, 'which was then the southern boundary of "Dhee Calcutta"'—where, as Reverend Long writes, 'a few weavers' sheds stood'[22]—'extended a forest, which was afterwards removed by degrees'.[23] Citing the authority of William Blaquiere, the Calcutta magistrate who first set foot in the town 'a fortnight after the execution of Nandakumar' on 5 August 1775 and was described in 1852 as being its oldest living resident,[24] Long writes that, in the 1770s, the maidan was 'a rice field', implying that the ground had been cleared to some extent. But the process must have been slow and halting, perhaps reflecting the tardiness in the expansion of the settlement southwards, for he writes that, at the time he was putting his thoughts down (1852), there were

> … two residents in Calcutta, who remember Sir W Jones and Warren Hastings, who have heard the tiger roar adjacent to the spot where now a noble cathedral and episcopal residence rear their heads,[25] who remember the period when Chauringi was out of town, when shots were fired off in the evening to frighten away the *dakaits*, and when servants attending their masters at dinner parties in Chauringi left all their good clothes behind them, lest they should be plundered in crossing the maidan ….[26]

Reverend Long says that in 1682 'an ancient forest' covered the spot occupied today by Fort William and the maidan, and that by 1756 the area was occupied by 'native huts, the property chiefly of the Mittre family, and by salt marshes, which afforded fine sport to buffalo hunters.'[27] If indeed there was a forest there was it an uninterrupted expanse or was it punctuated by open spaces populated by villages and markets and crop-bearing ground, the riverside providing enough place for such settlements? Long does not adduce any source for the view that the Mitra family owned land in Gobindapur which, however, is not a proposition difficult to accept in view of the economic clout of Gobindaram Mitra. The very fact that the 'black zamindar' made such investments implies that the region was not without economic potential. It also suggests that commercial activity was already rife in the area.

By the time Charnock settled down at Sutanati, it would seem that Gobindapur was already a busy place in its own right, the activity being fuelled by the business acumen of some of the oldest mercantile families of the area. In the words of Gaur Das Bysack, himself a scion of the Basak family:[28]

> Some centuries ago, when the river Saraswati, at Satgong, showed incipient signs of silting up,[29] some of the people of that place, especially the mercantile and trading classes, felt the necessity of removing elsewhere. Hughli then was becoming an important mercantile town; but, among the great merchants, five opulent families, one of Sett and four of Bysacks, emigrated to and colonised Calcutta. They arrived at the site of Govindpur, and having cleared the jungle, settled at the place, excavated tanks, built houses and other structures, among which was the shrine of their tutelary deity, Govindjee, to commemorate whose name they called the new settlement Govindpur. They established also a cloth market, which was named Sutanati *Hat* – a mart for the sale of skeins of thread and woven cloth – and from this the village in which it was situated was called Sutanati.

Writing in 1891, Bysack says that the emigration from Saptagram took place 'nearly 425 years ago', that is, around 1466, which would mean that at the time the English arrived in Sutanati the village of Gobindapur was already well settled. He also writes, without citing any source, that at the time of the original settlement in the fifteenth century, Gobindapur was 'a belt of jungle, infested, as it was at the time, with all kinds of wild beasts'. Sutanati too was 'a regular jungle, till the Setts and Bysacks gradually cleared it'. But why did they choose Gobindapur and not some other place with better basic infrastructure for trading purposes?

C.R. Wilson suggests that the advent of the European traders with their big ships was largely responsible for Sutanati emerging as a cloth-trading depot, which may have drawn Charnock to stop there in the first place. He writes:[30]

> The capital of British India did not, as some seem to think, spring up, like Jonah's gourd, in a single night. Calcutta, or at any rate that portion of the Hugli where Calcutta now stands, has a history, and the city is the growth of many centuries. At first the place was merely a group of villages to all appearance, not distinguishable in any way from hundreds of other riverside places. There was, however, this difference, that at the point where these villages stood in the 16th century, the stream became much shallower and less accessible to sea-going vessels. As long as the local trade was carried on in small boats, this was of little importance, and Satgaon, on the Sarasvati, near the modern Hugli, was the great centre of commerce. But when the Portuguese began to frequent the river, about 1530, this difference made itself felt. The foreigners did not care to risk their galliasses in the shallow waters, but sent their goods on to Satgaon in small boats. Meanwhile their ships lay at anchor in Garden Reach, and an important market sprang up on the west side of the river at Betor, close to Sibpore. This foreign market attracted native traders and merchants to the spot, and in particular, four families of Bysacks and one of Setts, leaving the then rapidly declining city of Satgaon, came and founded the settlement of Govindpore on the site of the present Fort William, and established the Sutanati market, on the north side of Calcutta, where they did business with the Portuguese. Soon after this the Portuguese themselves going higher up the river abandoned Betor, and the whole of the trade was thus transferred to the east side of the river, from Betor to Sutanati.

It was into this typically pre-modern, Oriental setting that, in a manner of speaking, the English were injected, and where, as Sir John Goldsborough tells us, they went about building thatched and *pucka* houses in a most disorganised manner. One reason for this could be that there was no point in investing in houses and godowns at Sutanati till the Bengal nawab permitted them to do so, and it was not until late 1695 that such 'connivance' on the part of the nawab surfaced although it was still a far cry from 'open approbation'.[31] There were some, like Walsh—whose house was bought by the Company in 1693—who took the risk to build brick houses, possibly on the assumption that, unlike as in the past, the English would not once again leave Sutanati in a hurry. However, as noted earlier, not much information is available on the situation prevailing in Sutanati immediately following Charnock's arrival[32] apart from the official papers exchanged between the East India Company's representatives in Bengal and its head office in London, which means that one has solely to depend on the Consultations to get an idea of the developments in the area around the old fort, the kernel so to speak of the future capital of the British empire in the East. What follows is a reconstruction of this picture, as reflected in the myriad issues placed before the Bengal Council and the decisions taken to settle them. All of these different strands taken together formed the building blocks of Calcutta's evolving topography as the early English settlement took its baby steps into the eighteenth century.[33]

Notes

1 As is well known, Calcutta figures in the account by the late fifteenth-century Bengali poet Bipradas of Chand Sadagar's voyage down the Hooghly to the sea, as also does Chitpur, and Betor on the west bank of the river, but not Sutanati or Gobindapur. There is also a passing reference to the shrine of Kalika at Kalighat which indicates that the old channel of the Hooghly (the Adi Ganga) was at the time a navigable waterway making its way down south to rejoin the Hooghly above Khejuri (Kedgeree).

2 See note 5 below.

3 Thomas Bowrey, *A Geographical Account of Countries Round the Bay of Bengal, 1669-1679*, ed. R.C. Temple (Cambridge, 1905), pp. 165–168.

4 Streynsham Master was sent out by the Company as '"a fit and able person" to bring order out of chaos in the Company's factories on the Coromandel Coast and in the Bay of Bengal.'

5 R.C. Temple, ed., *The Diaries of Streynsham Master, 1675-1680,* vol. 1 (London: John Murray, 1911), p. 322. The editor writes in a note that Tanna was known as 'Great Thana' where, in Master's time, 'there was a Muhammadan fort constructed against the river pirates'. William Hedges calls the 'village' Great Tanna in his diary entry of 23 July 1682 [R. Barlow and Henry Yule, ed., *The Diary of William Hedges,* vol. 1 (London, 1887), p. 32]. The village standing on this spot was known as Makhua where there was a 'police station', or *thana*, under the *faujdar* of Hooghly (ibid., vol. 2, p. xcix).

6 *The Diaries of Streynsham Master, 1675-1680,* vol. 1, pp. 324–325.

7 Ibid., vol. 2, pp. 66, 240.

8 *Hedges' Diary,* vol. 2, p. lxxv. Court's letter dated 15 February 1688–1689. The operative passage is, '... and since he [Charnock] likes Chuttnauttee so well, we are content he should build a ffactory there, but with as much frugallity as may be'.

9 Ibid., p. lxxxvii.

10 The Court's letter to Fort St George dated 11 September 1689, that is, before Charnock arrived at Sutanati for the third and last time, lays out in some detail the reason why London felt that Sutanati was a better proposition for the English to settle down in compared to Balasore, at a time when the ill-fated Heath episode was casting its shadow on the Company's affairs in the East (Wilson, *Old Fort William*, vol. 1, p. 5). As regards the 'Heath episode', not being happy with the situation prevailing in the Bay at this time and suffering from the disadvantage of a severe paucity of information for over a year in a fluid political scenario, the East India Company had in early 1688 sent out a 'hot-headed, wrong-headed, capricious, and futile, feather-brained skipper', Captain William Heath, 'armed with an extraordinary commission, which in fact superseded Job Charnock in his chief command of the forces in the Bay' (*Hedges' Diary,* vol. 2, p. lxxvi). Among other things, he was ordered to take of all places Chittagong—which was construed by the Company to be 'on the Ganges'—where it was intended to shift the Bengal establishment. The project fell through, a consequence of which was 'the loss of the results of half a century's painful toil and effort' [P.E. Roberts, *History of British India* (Oxford, 1921), p. 45]. On 22 March 1689 Charnock and the other members of the Bengal Council, then in Madras, wrote in a fit of anger and desperation that the captain, 'tripping from Port to Port without effecting anything, hath not only rendered our nation Ridiculous, but hath unhinged all

treaties, by which means the trade of Bengall will be very difficult to be ever regained' (*Hedges' Diary*, vol. 2, p. lxxxv).

11 Alexander Hamilton writes in *A New Account of the East Indies*, vol. 2 (London, 1744), p. 5, that Sutanati was chosen by Charnock 'for the sake of a large shady Tree', probably the one located at what was then called Baitakhana, roughly where Bow Bazar Street meets Circular Road today. This may or may not have been the case, but it does suggest that the tree was visible from the river, the inference being that the view from the river was unobstructed. In 'Calcutta in the Olden Times' (*Calcutta Review*, July-December 1852, pp. 276–277), Long repeats this story, probably basing his account on Hamilton, but also says that Cossaitala—or the area traversed by the modern-day Bentinck Street, to the east of Old Court House Street—was in 1757 'a mass of *jangal*, and even as late as 1780, it was almost impassable from mud in the rains' (ibid., p. 291). If this was the scene during Charnock's time, and there is no reason why it should not have been so, it stands to reason that the Baitakkhana tree was hardly visible from the river. This, however, does not rule out the possibility of Charnock having heard about the uses the 'great tree' was put to by traders visiting the area—after all, Charnock was not new to Sutanati—which to him may have been important from the view of the trade-potential of the place.

12 *Hedges' Diary*, vol. 2, p. lix. According to the editors of the *Diary*, the earliest mention of 'Calcutta' in the English records is said to be that found in a document penned by Captain William Heath in early 1689 (ibid., p. lxxix, fn. 2). P.T. Nair [*Calcutta in the 17th Century* (Calcutta: Firma KLM, 1986), p. 305, note 23] says, however, that the first mention of 'Calcutta' is to be found in a letter written by Charles Eyre and Roger Bradyll from Dhaka to Charnock on 22 June 1688. Importantly, Nair asserts that this mention and another featuring in a letter written by the same writers on 9 July 1689, along with the mention of the place made by both Heath and Charnock himself (the latter on 22 March 1689), 'cannot be rejected as copyists' mistakes and show that Calcutta [instead of Sutanati] was the place where Job Charnock [settled] in 1687'.

13 Ibid., p. lxxvi.

14 The Court had once hoped that this place would become 'a famous and well-governed English colony'. It wrote to Bengal in a letter dated 27 August 1688, 'Your town of Ulabarreah we understand hath Depth of water Sufficient to make Docks and conveniences for the repairing

of any of our biggest ships, and is a healthfull place, and therefore we have added a Paragraph to our letter to our Generall [John Child in Surat] .... that if he can obtain a Phirmaund from the Mogull for our holding that place fortifyed with the same immunities and privileges we hold Fort St George, we will be therewith content, without looking further or being at any new charge in contending for any other fortifyed settlement in Bengall'—*Hedges' Diary*, vol. 2, p. lxxv.

15 Ibid., p. lxxxvi.

16 Ibid.,vol. 2 , p. lxxii. Gaur Das Bysack, writing in *The Calcutta Review* (vol. XCII, January 1891, pp. 305–327), cites family tradition to say that 'Job Charnock's successors removed to Govindpur, because they found it more convenient for the transaction of their business with the Setts and Bysacks who resided there, and easier to get at the Bazar for supplies and necessaries of life [an entry in the Bengal Council Consultations dated 18 September 1704 says that a market had been "ordered at the town of Govindpur, by which the Company will receive a considerable benefit in time"—Wilson, *Early Annals*, vol. 1, p. 258]'. Bysack continues: 'Sutanuttee, in the earliest days, was, with the exception of a small clearance (where the *hat* or mart used to be held, since called Hatkhola Ghat), a regular jungle, till the Setts and Bysacks gradually cleared it, improved the place, and turned it into their Suburban gardens – Sett Bagan; Jora Bagan, established (by a) brother Sett; Kala Bagan; Goa Bagan. They likewise established bazars in places as they came to be inhabited [such as Barabazar, Bowbazar, Lalbazar and Laldighi, Baghbazar, and Sobhabazar].'

17 *Hedges' Diary*, vol. 2, p. lxxxviii. Letter dated 2 November 1691.

18 Ibid., p. clvi.

19 Quoted in ibid., vol. 2, p. xciv. Charnock had died on 10 January 1693 (*Hedges' Diary*, vol. 2, p. lxxxviii).

20 Possibly, the Walsh who negotiated the zamindari rights for the three villages of Sutanati, Calcutta and Gobindapur with the emperor's representatives in Bengal in 1698 (Wilson, *Old Fort William*, vol. 1, pp. 34–38).

21 *Hedges' Diary*, vol. 2, p. xcviii.

22 *Calcutta Review*, July–December 1852, p. 276.

23 A.K. Roy, *A Short History of Calcutta* (Calcutta: Rddhi-India, 1982; first published in 1902), p. 204. On Chandpal Ghat, Roy writes (ibid., p. 245) that it was named after '... one Chandra Nath Pal who, in

those olden times, when the maidan was a dense forest, interspersed with a few weavers' sheds, and the river was scarcely frequented, kept hereabouts a *mudi's* shop for way-worn pedestrians and *manjees* (or boatmen) plying up and down the river. When the new fort was erected and the intermediate space to it was into the Respondentia Walk, the Chandpal Ghat became the landing place where "the Governor General, the Commander-in-Chief, the Judges of the Supreme Court, the Bishops and all who were entitled to the honours of a salute from the ramparts of Fort William, first set foot in the metropolis". At this spot India welcomed and bade farewell to her rulers.'

Roy cites no source for this derivation of the name Chandpal Ghat. This apart, the idea of a retinue of English governors-general landing at a grocer's ghat to take up the reins of a burgeoning empire is also not without some interest.

24 William Blaquiere was just thirteen when he arrived in Calcutta with his father Jacob, Superintendent of Piece Goods, on the *Seahorse* which also brought various notables like Richard Plowden and Edward Wheler among others (information made available to the author by Professor Peter Robb of the School of Oriental and African Studies, London).

25 St Paul's Cathedral and the Bishop's Palace on Chowringhee.

26 *Calcutta Review*, July–December 1852, pp. 275, 315. A.K. Roy writes that it was not till 1746 that Europeans began to move into Chowringhee. See *A Short History of Calcutta*, p. 204.

27 *Calcutta Review*, July–December 1852, pp. 304–305. The 'Mittre family' was none other than that of Gobindaram Mitra, the 'black zamindar', who remained in that office for long years and was charged with fraud and embezzlement of funds on a massive scale by John Zephaniah Holwell. Mitra's defence was that every deputy of the English Collector 'was allowed similar privileges, and that he could not from his wages keep up the equipage and attendance necessary for an officer of his station'. See Holwell's *India Tracts* (London, 1764), pp. 174–202.

28 'Kalighat and Calcutta' in *Calcutta Review*, vol. XCII, January 1891, pp. 305–327.

29 Note in original article: 'Satgong stood on the banks of the Sarasvati. It lost its commercial importance, which it enjoyed from the most ancient times, when the river silted up, in 1520, or 1530.'

30 Wilson, *Early Annals*, vol. 1, pp. 127–128.

The following description of a journey from Orissa to Bengal, made by Caesar Frederich around 1563, was published in *Bengal Past and Present*, vol. 2 (1908), pp. 383–384: 'I departed from Orisa to Bengal, to the harbour Piqueno [Saptagram], which is distant from Orisa towards the east a hundred and seventy miles. They go as it were rowing along the coast fifty and four miles, and then we enter into the river Ganges: from the mouth of this river to a city called Satagan, where the merchants gather themselves together with their trade, are a hundred miles, which they row in eighteen hours with the increase of the water in which river it floweth and ebbeth as it does in the Thames, and when the ebbing water is come, they are not able to row in it, by reason of the swiftness of the water, yet their barks be light and armed with oars like to foistes, yet they cannot prevail against that stream, but for refuge must make them fast to the bank of the river until the next flowing water, and they call these barks Bazaras and Patvas; they row as well as a Galliot, or as well as ever I have seen any. A good tides rowing before you came to Satgaon, you shall have a place which is called Buttor [modern Betor], and from thence upwards the ships doe not goe, because that upwards the river is very shallow and little water. Every year at Buttor they make and unmake a village with houses and shops made of straw, and with all things necessary to their uses, and this village standeth as long as the ships ride there, and till they depart for the Indies, and when they are departed, every man goeth to his plot of houses, and there setteh fire on them, which thing made me to marvel. For as I passed up to Satagan, I saw this village standing with a great number of people, with an infinite number of ships and bazars, and at my return coming down with my Captain of the last ship, for whom I tarried, I was all amazed to see such a place so soon raised and burnt, and nothing left but the sign of the burnt houses. The small ships go to Satagan, and there they laid.'

31 Wilson, *Old Fort William*, vol. 1, p. 3.

32 *Hedges' Diary*, vol. 2, p. lxxxvii.

33 The subsequent depiction of the growth of the settlement in the early years is based on volumes 1 and 2 (Part 1) of C.R. Wilson's *Early Annals* (1895 and 1900) and the two volumes of the same author's *Old Fort William* (1906), which, along with Reverend James Long's *Selections from Unpublished Records of Government, 1748 to 1767* (1st edition 1869; 2nd edition: edited by Mahadevaprasad Saha,

Firma K.L. Mukhopadhyay, Calcutta, 1973), are the only published collections of selected Consultations of the Bengal Council relating to early British administration in the region, apart from the original records held in the India Office Records now held in the British Library, London, and also at the National Archives of India, New Delhi.

2

A Citadel Hemmed In

On arriving at Sutanati, on 24 August 1690, Charnock wrote:[1]

> On board the *Maddapollam*. This day at Sankraul [Sankrail, on the west bank of the river below Sutanati] order'd Capt. Brooke to come up with his Vessell to Chutanutte where We arrived about noon but found the place in a deplorable condition nothing being left for our present accommodation, and the Rains falling day & night, We are forced to betake ourselves to boats, which considering the Season of the yeare is very unhealthy Mellick burcoordar (Malik Barkhurdar, the Nawab of Dacca's representative sent to Hooghly to discuss matters with the English) and the Country People at our leaveing this place burning downe and carrying away what they could.

However, not everything was destroyed. The Consultations of 28 August 1690 indicate that there were still standing the ruins of a couple of structures which could be repaired and recommissioned into service.[2] We have no idea of where these structures were precisely located but it is clear that the English had to start from scratch as it were. Since a magnificent expanse of riverside was there to be exploited, plans were drawn up to put up houses on the bank having mud walls and thatched roofs, a list being made for the early building works.[3] These were a warehouse, a dining room, a room to sort cloth in, a kitchen, a house for the Company's servants, a house for Francis Ellis, and a guard room. Three structures still standing but which could be put to use only after repairs were carried out were the Secretary's office and the houses of the Agent and Jeremiah Peachie.[4] Clearly, these were the Company's buildings. But it is apparent from Goldsborough's September 1693 letter to Charles Eyre that private houses had also come up during the preceding three years, built wherever their owners chose to do so.

To those interested in the early history of English-settled Calcutta, the story of the building of the fort cannot but be of some interest, not merely because of the tortuous course it took—being 'completed' well after 1710—but also because it reveals the heightened sensitivity of the East India Company's Court of Directors to the reaction and response of the nawab and his principal officers to the prospect of English military infrastructure being created in the region as opposed to buildings geared to the pursuit of purely trading operations.[5] Suffice it to say that it took a while to get the construction work on the fort started in right earnest, the rebellion of Sobha Singh of Burdwan acting as a catalyst. In fact, it was only after the nawab allowed the European traders to fortify their factories and trading outposts against the rebel zamindar (late 1696 to the end of 1697)—the nawab being actively assisted in his campaign against Sobha Singh—that the Dutch, French and the English in the region took the opportunity to arm themselves and protect their settlements.

Goldsborough had marked out the ground for the fort on the eastern bank of the Hooghly, on the precise spot occupied today by the General Post Office, the Calcutta Collectorate, the Reserve Bank of India building and the Fairlie Place railway offices in the western part of Dalhousie Square (BBD Bagh). Our study of the layout of the topography of the early settlement will, therefore, be made with the help of this reference point. Among other things, we are told that, in the very early years of the settlement, that is, just five years after Charnock had landed, the English factors and writers lived not within the compound of the fort as marked out by Goldsborough but were scattered around it. Since they lived in thatched houses, the Calcutta weather ensured that their abodes were routinely flattened by 'the Southerly storms which causes often repairs'. Not surprisingly, special importance was given to the 'cookroom' of the factory with the result that in October 1697 it was decided to move it inside the fort compound and be made of brick.[6] This apart, as the Council noted in March 1695, since they were all living around the fort, the agent could not keep an eye on the young factors and writers 'as youth ought to be'. This must have developed into a serious enough problem because the Council decided that, within three months, 'half a dozzen Chambers of brick and mudd be built on the Northside of the Compound for them to live in'. By the end of January 1698 the Bengal Council was reporting that all factors and writers were living within the factory compound.[7]

But this could have been only a temporary solution because by September 1705 the Bengal Council was again looking around for premises outside the fort where its officials could reside.[8] The Consultation of 6 March 1718[9] says that every single room in the fort was taken by the Company's officers 'who live two and Three together'. In September 1755, since there was no room within the fort for 'the young Gentlemen lately come out in the Service', premises were being rented outside it for their accommodation.[10] On 11 February 1756 the Court asked the Council to build if required 'apartments' for the accommodation of the young writers 'in the most Frugal Manner … having a particular regard that they be as near the respective Offices for Business as possible'.[11] By October 1759, nearly three years after the retaking of Calcutta by the English, the problem of accommodation 'for the Junior Servants and Officers' had arisen once again, this time because of the 'number of houses which have been destroyed for the Fortifications', the Council ordering the construction of 'Matt Bungaloes on the long Row and Cottah Godowns in the Factory'.[12] The Bengal Council told the Court on 29 December the same year that this was a time when there was 'a great Scarcity of houses in the Settlement'.[13]

As the fort came to be built, the sahibs began to build their houses to the north and south of it and also to the north-east, the south-east being taken up by a water body (today's BBD Bagh tank), the antiquity of which is unclear. What is probable is that the English did not dig the tank because if they did there would have been a reference to it in the official records. Amongst the earliest references to the tank which we find in Wilson's works is that contained in the Consultation of 28 February 1709 which tells us about a decision being taken by the Bengal Council to lengthen and deepen it so that the settlement could continue to get a supply of 'good water'. This improvement was undertaken under the heading 'drains', the Court having given the Council the 'liberty and directions to make drains and necessaries for the Fort'. The tank was said to have been a perennial source of potable water, especially in March and April when the river water turned 'brackish'.[14] On the antiquity of the tank, A.K. Roy cites the 'family traditions' of the Sabarna Chowdhurys to say that *Laldighi* (the native name for the tank), Lalbazar and Radhabazar all derived their name from the festival of Holi related to Shyam Roy (the original Vishnu) and his spouse Radha in the course of which 'a vast quantity of red powder (*kumkum*) used to be sold and scattered in and around their *cutchery* tank'. For our purposes, what this means is that the tank predated the arrival of the English, Roy citing the claim that, 'it was the *hat* and bazar round their idols and their *pucka zamindari cutcherry* west of the tank that gave Calcutta its original importance.'[15]

Some light is thrown on the antiquity of the zamindari *kachari* to the west of the BBD Bagh tank by the Consultation of 9 August 1711[16] which says that the 'thatch house in the Honourable Company's garden being very rotten was lately blown down to the ground' and that the *bakshi* had been ordered to rebuild it. It stands to reason that, at this stage of the settlement's history, the Company's fledgling garden must have been the one immediately to the east of the fort, around the Laldighi tank, portrayed in the painting attributed to George Lambert (1730). If it was just a thatched house the English may not have put it up, the inference being that it was there for some years perhaps even going back to the days of Charnock, which could explain why it was in a 'very rotten' state. The question arises, who set it up? Was it the Sabarna Chowdhurys who ran the zamindari of the three villages when Charnock first set up camp in 1690? The thatched house in question may have belonged to people who mattered at the time which may be a reason why the English left it standing when they were turning the area around the tank into a garden. However, one cannot wholly rule out the possibility that the English themselves may have put up the thatched house in question. After all, they did not hesitate to construct similar facilities for use as 'godowns for naval stores' in the Bankshall Yard which, when they were discovered to be in a wretched state and susceptible to fire, were demolished and replaced by a 'brick and *pucca*' godown.[17] Besides, immediately after Charnock's arrival in Sutanati in 1690, the first 'houses' set up by the English for habitation were thatched establishments, the inference being that the thatched house to the west of the tank may also have been set up at this time.

A.K. Roy[18] maintains that the 'zamindari *cutchery*', west of the Laldighi tank, was a pucka construction and not otherwise. He claims that the old kachari office was none other than the factory house itself inside the fort, which was demolished in 1706. H.E.A. Cotton[19] too says that the kachari of the Sabarna Choudhurys was a 'masonry building' in which Charnock 'lodged the Company's official staff and the records'. Cotton's book first appeared in 1909 and it is possible that he may have sourced this point from Roy—whose *Short History* was first published in 1902 as part of the 1901 Census—who had written[20] that before Charnock died, in January 1693, he had 'acquired the jagirdar's *pucka cutchery*' which formed 'the first *pucka* lodgement of the Company's official staff and of its records'. But did Charnock in fact do so? John Goldsborough wrote to Charles Eyre from Sutanati on 30 October 1693 that on top of Walsh's house, which had been bought for the Company, he intended to build four rooms so that 'I may bring in the Accomptants and Secretaries, and the books and papers in their Charge, within this brick house, which now Ly scattering abroad in thatched houses Lyable to the hazard of fire every day'.[21] What this implies is that, at the time Goldsborough was writing to Eyre, the 'books and papers', or 'records', were still lying around in thatched houses, the inference being that Charnock, who had died nine months earlier, had done nothing to shift the documents to a pucka place. If the old kachari was among the thatched houses where the records were kept then Roy is mistaken in claiming that the house was a pucka construction. We are told in May 1733[22] that the 'old *Catcherry*' built 'of all Bamboo and Straw' had once more fallen down, and since a lot of money was being spent on it every year on repairs it was decided that a new one be built of brick 'for the Jemindars Business'.

The area around the fort was peppered with water bodies. Like the one to the east of the fort, in 1695 there was one also to the north of it which had to be filled up not only because it was 'very offensive' but also because a need had arisen to 'enlarge the Compound to the Northward where the chambers for the factors and Writers are to be built'. The Consultation of 18 March[23] tells us that this tank was 'near the ffactory-gate', which would place the gate to the north of the fort and not to the east where early paintings have indicated it was located. Does this mean that in the very early days the fort had a northern gate as well which was closed after some time? The same Consultation adds that a trench dug around the chosen ground for the fort under Goldsborough's orders, 'to drain the water from the higher ground as a means to keep the place wholesome', had become choked by mud since the rains, and that, consequently, it was deepened 'to carry the raine water into the river'.[24] In 1699 we again read of a 'large tank near the passage way coming to the Northward of the ffactory which is very Offensive', which was filled up by orders issued on 28 September of that year. Giving us some idea of what the housing scene was like to the north of the fort at the turn of the seventeenth century, the 15 July 1703 Consultation says that there was at least one house, that of Henry Moore, which was 'over against the north-east point of the garrison, that is, the site of the north-east bastion'.[25]

The situation was no better in the north-west where too the fort had come up against houses, one of which belonged to John Beard, the former president of the Bengal Council.[26] The Consultation of 3 June 1707 says:

> Having occasion for one-third of President Beard's (deceased) compound to build the north-west bastion upon, and to keep the Fort clear from any building, and since it will not be very much prejudice to the dwelling-house and warehouse for which, as well as the whole compound, he has a lease for 31 years, paying a quit-rent for the same, agreed that the trustees for the deceased's house and compound be allowed 300 rupees to repair the damages, rebuild the wall, etc., and what ground is taken away, so much quitt-rent as is in proportion to the whole to be deducted out of the yearly payment.[27]

What emerges is that the fort, small as it was when it came into full bloom decades later with warts and all, was even smaller in the early years. This suggests that, at the very beginning, the English had accorded a low priority to the defence capabilities of such an establishment, which was set up keeping the protection of their business interests foremost in mind. Another reason for the unimpressive dimensions of the fort could have been the initial overriding concern of the Court in London not to arouse the ire of the nawab or his satrap at Hooghly.[28]

From the very beginning, therefore, the fort was crippled by the proximity of houses and warehouses, the situation becoming worse with warehouses being set up against the fort's southern wall with the passage of time. In the early years the eastern side of the fort too had its share of problems: the Consultation of 17 August 1710 tells us that there were huts and trees right up against the wall. The entry reads:

> The Fort being very much choaked up and close set with trees and small country thatched houses and standing pools of stinking water, which having maturely considered, we are of opinion that clearing them away and filling the holes to level ground will contribute very much to the making of the town wholesome and healthful. … Therefore, we order the *Buxie* to open the way directly before the Fort, continuing the present walk already made further into the open field, filling up all the holes and cutting small trenches on each side to carry the water clear from the adjacent places into the large drains.[29]

The church, St Anne's, had already come up in 'front' of the fort (that is, if we take the fort's gate to the east as its main gate), to the south of which was the old water body, a decision to deepen which had been taken in February the previous year. So where exactly was the 'open field' which the Consultation mentions? Probably it was to the south towards which a 'walk' had already been made, which by the 1750s, if Robert Orme is to be given credence, had become 'a broad road which passed along the eastern side of the fort'.[30]

1 St Anne's church in 1756 at the time of the nawab's assault on Calcutta.

A 23 June 1704 entry in the Consultations says that a Dr Warren[31] had been given a lease for land (two *bighas* and eighteen *kathas*) 'out in the fields', the annual rent for which was Rs 8-11-3. Where were 'the fields' fourteen years after Charnock settled down in Sutanati? One would imagine that there was hardly any open space of ground answering to the description of 'the fields' to the north where the native settlement was located. There is little evidence of any open ground existing in the east which stretched away to the salt lakes. The earliest records pertaining to the English settlement indicate that its southern limit was the creek running eastward from the Hooghly to the salt lakes, roughly along the present alignment of Hastings Street (renamed Kiron Shankar Roy Road), down Government Place North, along Waterloo Street, through Chandney, along Creek Row (which is said to draw its name from this fact), across Circular Road, and onward to the vast salt-water swamp lying to the east of the town.

The 'fields' then were probably located to the south or to the south-east of the fort[32] and Warren's ground may have been located on the northern or north-eastern fringe of today's maidan which, in earlier times—certainly in Charnock's—was covered by vegetation? If there was a jungle in the area when Charnock landed it must have been there for a long time before 1690. Taking us back to the fifteenth century, Gaur Das Bysack writes[33] that the area known as Gobindapur was 'a belt of jungle, infested, as it was at the time, with all kinds of wild beasts'. Sutanati too was 'a regular jungle, till the Setts and Bysacks gradually cleared it' to set up their weaving establishment and market. The early Englishmen must have begun to clean up the immediate neighbourhood of their settlement shortly after their arrival, and it is probable that within fifteen years of Charnock's arrival, the mass of trees, or at least that part of the jungle contiguous to the settlement, had been cleared for the area to answer to the description of being a field.

Could Warren have been given land to the east of the maidan, that is, on the eastern side of what was then the old Pilgrims' Road (today's Chowringhee Road), which linked the Chitteswari temple at Chitpur to Kalighat?[34] This, especially in the early years, appears to be a remote possibility because of the inhospitability of the area to human habitation, especially 'genteel' English habitation. Writing in 1880, an anonymous contributor to the *Calcutta Review* says that the 1756 plan of Calcutta shows the site of the present fort to have been 'a jungle, and the ground now occupied by the fashionable and imposing line of buildings along Chowringhee road was then covered with bamboo bush jungle, or paddy field swamps'.[35] However, even if it were so, there are flattering descriptions of the settlement penned by visitors coming up the river in the early years of the eighteenth century. In the winter of 1712, an 'adventurer' visiting Calcutta wrote that, having passed

> … Tana [Muckwah Tannah where the Moghul *choukey* was located], a great town to the larboard side of the river, having for its defence a large brick fort to the river, with four round bulwarks …. we opened [sic] Calcutta our desired port; it gratifying us with a most agreeable prospect which when we were come its length we dropt anchor before the fort, saluting the garrison with 7 guns, who returned us the like compliment.[36]

This, incidentally, is one of the earliest descriptions of the settlement we have from the river, such accounts being routinely favourable to the town in the eighteenth century and later. However, the flattering nature of the description is not remarkable if one considers the general scenery presented to the visitor as he sailed up the river in these times. In the early days, one can imagine that the view was marked by a rush of greenery, not in the shape of well-kempt gardens or rolling fields coming up to the water's edge—as was the case with, say, Garden Reach from the late eighteenth century onwards—but by dense growth punctuated by human habitation taking the shape of clusters of thatched huts complemented by open spaces where crops were being cultivated. In 1712, the settlement flaunted St Anne's church, with or without its spire at this point of time, the fort, some nondescript houses with gardens, and an excess of thatched huts along the river. The visitor's perception of an 'agreeable prospect' probably measured the difference between the English settlement and the typically eastern and native scenes which he had encountered on his way up the river. It was certainly not something which stood out, as was the case a century later when the new Fort William had come up, the maidan had taken shape, and the buildings on Esplanade Row, including Wellesley's splendid Government House, were proclaiming loud and clear the advent of a rising English colonial town in the East.

Before we move on, let us consider for a moment St Anne's church which, along with the fort, must have been an important landmark of the English settlement as one came up the river. The Reverend H.B. Hyde[37] does not give a date when the steeple was completed but merely says that it was completed before 1724 when it was recorded to have been hit by lightning. When completed the spire was 'the most conspicuous ornament of the town'. The Consultation of 21 September 1724[38] says that the church was severely damaged by a lightning hit, specially the steeple 'which is all cracked, and the Beams of the Belfry almost all broke which makes it very insecure and in Danger of falling'. Further, we know that the church was located in front of the fort's east gate. The records indicate that the first site selected for the church lay elsewhere. The Consultation of 6 November 1704[39] says that a site for a church for the settlement had been selected on 'Broad Street ... next or pretty near to Captain Wallis' his house, between that and Mr Soames's, and that a broadway be left on the side next the river fully sixty feet broad clear from the Church'. But, in the first place, where was Broad Street at a time when there were not many broad streets in the settlement? Was it today's Council House Street, opening out in the south on to the creek where, according to the old maps, there was a bridge across it, and to the north going past the old fort (the Netaji Subhas Road of today or erstwhile Clive Street)? But the street did not exist as a road at this point of time, being completed in 1721. A.K. Roy[40] says that in the first half of the eighteenth century today's Bentinck Street was known as Broad Street. If so the proposed site for the church could not have been near the river which, however, is what the 6 November 1704 Consultation implies it was. Since the proposed site of the church was on the banks of the river, it could only have been to the north of the fort because, to the south of it, as a reference to old maps will indicate, there was simply no space for the accommodation of two houses with grounds and also a church, not to speak of the graveyard adjoining the creek. But all this is pointless conjecture for the Consultation of 22 December 1704 tells us that, owing to opposition from 'many inhabitants', the site was shifted to 'opposite ... the (east) curtain at a convenient distance from the wall of the Fort'.[41]

As a matter of fact, however, the distance was hardly 'convenient' for the defence of the fort because the place of worship which, as Orme wrote,[42] commanded 'the whole of both the Northern and Eastern ramparts' of the fort, was, according to Governor Drake, a mere 'thirty yards distant from our front gate'.[43] Given its location, the church ought to have been totally destroyed in the course of the fighting. In fact in March 1757 the Court was writing to the Bengal Council that the old theatre to the east of the great tank (on today's R.N. Mukherjee Road, erstwhile Mission Row) could, 'with a little Expense be converted into a Church or Publick Place of Worship' the cost being met from the Company's funds.[44] But it is possible that the church escaped total destruction because we find that efforts were made to 'repair' it and the churchyard.[45] Perhaps the intended repairs were not successful in view of the fact that services were not resumed in the old edifice. The Consultation of 24 March 1760[46] says the premises being then used for worship—the Portuguese church at Murgihatta—were 'unwholesome and damp' and that the Surveyor of the Works, Bartholomew Plaisted, should tell the Council of the expense necessary to turn 'the remains of the Gateway in the Old Fort'—opposite the *ruined* [emphasis added] St Anne's—into 'a tolerable Chapel till such time as the Chapel design'd to be built in the New ffort be erected'. Following Plaisted's report, the Council ordered the repairs to be undertaken so that the growing settlement could get a temporary chapel of its own, the latter being declared ready for use on 17 July 1760.[47]

Five years later, the chapel was still there but it had become too small to accommodate the settlement's congregation, there being space for only one half of it.[48] On 28 November 1766 the Bengal Council was writing to the Court that while it would certainly abide by the instruction to postpone 'the building a Church until every other Building be completed',[49] it wished that permission was accorded to construct 'a convenient place of Publick Worship which we think essential towards a Reformation of the Morals of the Individuals of the Settlement'. By the end of 1766 the makeshift chapel provided accommodation for only a quarter of the town's worshippers.[50] The writer of the letters in *Hartly House,*[51] Sophia Goldborne, described the chapel thus:

> It is situated at the Old Fort, and consists solely of a ground-floor, with an arrangement of plain pews; nor is the Governor himself much better accommodated than the rest; and of course the Padra, as the clergyman is called, has little to boast of; the windows are, however, verandahs, which are pleasing to me in their appearance, independent of the blessing of air enjoyed through that medium.

To return to the 'open fields' and Dr Warren, assuming the latter had but one house in the settlement at the time, he was probably given ground south of the fort near the river.[52] The important thing for us here is to understand that the use of the word 'fields' suggests that there was open ground beyond the immediate vicinity of the fort, the critical inference being that the wooded area, especially to the south of the settlement in these years, was not uniformly so. In fact, following the establishment of the fort, the first such open space to be developed by the English was the ground to the east of the fort where the great tank was located. In early 1728 the Bengal Council decided to '(enclose) the plain before the Fort', which may be seen as one of the early acquisitive moves by the English in furtherance of town-development.[53] George Lambert's portrayal of Fort William from the east[54] provides an idea of what this 'plain' was like, rather picturesque and idyllic, to say the least. Making an allowance for painter's licence, the point to be noted is that the ground was not enclosed at the time, which means that either the decision to enclose it was implemented after the painter had applied brush to canvas, that is, around 1730, or that the canvas was created sometime before 1728 assuming that the

2 William Baillie's view of Tank Square from the east, 1794

3 James Baillie Fraser's view of the west side of Tank Square, 1819

enclosure was made in the course of the year itself. But the fenced-in enclosure had come to stay in the area, coming down to our own times. William Baillie's view of Tank Square (BBD Bagh) from the east, created more than sixty years later in 1794, shows the ground enclosed by a railing with a gateway. Lambert's painting cited above shows the recreational dimension of the area in the 1720s. Nearly a century later (1819), James Baillie Fraser has left us evidence of the fact that the dimension was still extant at a time when the Lottery Committee was working overtime to usher in improvements.[55]

Notes

1 Wilson, *Old Fort William*, vol. 1, p. 6.

2 Ibid., p. 7.

3 The decision not to put up brick houses, except for a warehouse and godown, was taken keeping in mind the strategy of not doing anything in the new settlement except for 'what is of necessity for your Honours business untill wee have the Nabobs and Duans Perwanna for a firm Settlement here'. (Bengal Council to the Court, 14 December 1694: Wilson, *Old Fort William*, vol. 1, p. 15.)

4 The agent's house, where Charnock lived in his time followed by Francis Ellis, was located at 'a considerable distance from the ffactory'. It was burnt down in an accidental fire ignited by the carelessness of peons on the night of 19 December 1694. The 8 April 1695 Consultation tells us that it was sold by outcry for Rs 575 when it was discovered that the cost of rebuilding it with 'brick for security', namely, Rs 400 rupees, had exceeded estimates. (Wilson, *Old Fort William*, vol. 1, pp. 15–16, 18.) Peachie and Ellis were members of the Bengal Council, the latter succeeding Charnock as agent only to be replaced by Charles Eyre on the orders of John Goldsborough.

5 We will have to skirt this absorbing subject as it is beyond the scope of the volume.

6 Wilson, *Old Fort William*, vol. 1, pp. 17, 30. Consultation of 11 March 1695 and 7 October 1697.

7 Ibid., p. 34.

8 Ibid., p. 60.
9 Ibid., p. 103.
10 Ibid., vol. 2, p. 27.
11 Ibid., p. 43.
12 Ibid., p. 151.
13 Ibid., p. 155.
14 Wilson, *Old Fort William*, vol. 1, p. 77. About 130 years later, the potability of the tank's water was attested to by R. Scott Thomson, whose medical shop standing to the east of Government House (Raj Bhavan), on the spot occupied today by the Esplanade Mansions, gave the place its almost iconic name, Scott Thomson's Corner. Answering questions put to him by the Fever Hospital Committee (on 10 May 1838) on the quality of the water of the BBD Bagh tank, Scott Thomson said: 'I have been resident in the neighbourhood of Tank Square for the last twelve years, and have been in the constant habit of employing the Loll Dighee water for all domestick purposes, as well as for the manufactory of Soda Water. From the facilities I possess in being enabled to keep up a large supply of the Loll Dighee water in a purified state, I have never had occasion to complain of it as injurious during the whole year, either as … drinking water, or employing it for culinary purposes.'

Upon being asked when the water of the tank was at its purest, Scott Thomson said: 'I would except the periods when the Tank is filled from the river, at which times it must necessarily contain many impurities, but I have generally found that ten days or a fortnight was sufficient to render it available to the inhabitants as a (sic) pure drinking water, and perfectly wholesome.'

He added: 'I have had frequent occasions to supply the Loll Dighee water to persons proceeding to sea, and have known it to keep in perfect purity during a voyage to England. One lady who took a stock of it with her on the homeward passage, wrote to me from Liverpool that she had produced a bottle of it at that port some time after her arrival in comparison with the drinking water there, and it was not surpassed in either sweetness or transparency' (Report of Committee upon the Fever Hospital and Municipal Improvements, 1839, Appendix F, Calcutta, pp. 79–80).
15 Roy, *Short History*, pp. 22–23. Reverend Long writes (*Calcutta Review*, July–December 1852, pp. 293–294): '*When* this tank was dug, we have never been able to ascertain'.

16 Wilson, *Early Annals,* vol. 2, p. 20.
17 Consultation of 2 May 1712 (Wilson, *Early Annals,* vol. 2, p. 50).
18 *Short History*, pp. 22–23, 42.
19 *Calcutta Old and New* (Calcutta: General, 1980 edition; first published in 1909), p. 9.
20 *Short History*, p. 38.
21 *Hedges' Diary*, vol. 2, p. xciv.
22 Consultation of 7 May (Wilson, *Old Fort William*, vol. 1, p. 139).
23 Ibid., p. 17.
24 This trench may have been the location of a ditch made later around the fort which was filled up in 1766. See chapter 'Natives Dig a Ditch'.
25 Wilson, *Old Fort William*, pp. 43, 56.
26 The Consultation of 5 September 1704 (Wilson, *Early Annals,* vol. 1, p. 233) says Beard moved out of the fort premises in March 'to make more room for the "Manager's servants"'. He was given a monthly house rent of fifty rupees.
27 Ibid., vol. 1, p. 283.
28 This is in fact a fascinating subject of study, particularly the extent to which the East India Company went to keep the local powers in good humour, at times showing its teeth (Wilson, *Old Fort William*, vol. 1, p. 76) but failing to persist with such an attitude when the ground conditions turned a bit too hot for comfort. It can be argued that but for this built-in constraint the fort at Calcutta, despite its inherent drawbacks, could have become a much stronger defence establishment with consequences which could possibly have led to the negation of the 'black hole of empire'. There are contemporary accounts following the fall of Calcutta in June 1756 which suggest that Shiraj-ud-Daula embarked upon the assault on the town following reports of defence works being put up by the foreign traders (ibid., vol. 2, pp. 68–69).
29 Wilson, *Early Annals,* vol. 1, p. 340. On 7 January 1712 the Council was writing to the Court that the job of levelling the ground around the fort had been completed (Wilson, *Old Fort William,* vol. 1, p. 87).
30 Ibid., vol. 2, p. 171. The present-day alignment of this path is marked by BBD Bagh West and Council House Street.
31 William Warren, Surgeon to the factory at Calcutta, who was described as 'a man of most pernicious principles and debauched manners'. See Wilson, *Early Annals,* vol. 1, pp. 201–202.
32 Wilson (ibid., vol. 1, p. 208) says that to the east of the fort there existed a field, a 'green', which extended right up to the Rope Walk of

those times, that is, today's Mission Row, adding that 'to the south of the green, before the fort, there are plenty of eligible sites for building'.

33 *Calcutta Review*, vol. XCII, January 1891, p. 312n.

34 Reverend Long, *Calcutta Review*, July–December 1852, p. 308. He writes that Chitpur Road, the part of the Pilgrims' Road to the north of today's Bentinck Street, took its name from the goddess Chitteswari 'who had a splendid temple here, where human sacrifices were formerly offered'. He says that the road is 'the oldest road in Calcutta, forming a continuation of the Dum-Dum road, which was the old line of communication between Murshidabad and Kali Ghat'. But where was the temple to Kali located in the eighteenth century and earlier? Did it stand on the banks of the Adi Ganga (Tolly's nullah of later times) or was it situated in Gobindapur, the present-day maidan, at a spot where the Victoria Memorial Hall stands today (see chapter 'The Temple on the Maidan')? Admittedly, a 1754 Consultation (Wilson, *Old Fort William*, vol. 2, p. 2) refers to a spot of ground 'Scituated within the Creek [the Adi Ganga] that runs from Surmans Bridge *to Callygat* [emphasis added]', but this 'Callygat' could have been the ghat leading to the temple which at the time was perhaps located on the maidan, the ghat (or landing stage) perhaps being situated where the Alipore Bridge stands today. In the early days, the Pilgrims' Road may just as well have followed the alignment of today's Chowringhee and Cathedral Roads, veering west from the point opposite today's Ho Chi Minh Sarani (earlier Harrington Street). Upjohn's map of the early 1790s shows such a road branching off westward from the road to Russapuglah. There is nothing in the records to suggest that it was not an old road, or that it was made after the English arrived on the scene.

35 'The City of Calcutta and its Municipal Constitution', *Calcutta Review*, vol. LXX, 1880, p. 480.

36 Wilson, *Early Annals*, vol. 2, p. 384.

37 *The Parish of Bengal* (Calcutta: Thacker, Spink & Co., 1899), p. 35.

38 Wilson, *Old Fort William*, vol. 1, p. 115.

39 Wilson, *Early Annals*, vol. 1, p. 264.

40 *Short History*, p. 99.

41 Wilson, *Early Annals*, vol. 1, p. 265.

42 Wilson, *Old Fort William*, vol. 2, p. 74.

43 Ibid., p. 70.

44 Ibid., p. 138.
45 Ibid., p. 136.
46 Ibid., p. 158.
47 Ibid.
48 Ibid., p. 173.
49 Court's letter dated 24 December 1765; Wilson, *Old Fort William*, vol. 2, p. 175.
50 Wilson, *Old Fort William*, vol. 2, p. 181.
51 *Hartly House Calcutta: A Novel of the Days of Warren Hastings* (Calcutta: Thacker, Spink and Co., 1908, with Notes by John Macfarlane; reprint of the 1789 first edition which was published anonymously its author being revealed later as Phebe Gibbes), pp. 23–24; Wilson, *Old Fort William*, vol. 2, Note, p. 183.
52 There is a reference in the Consultation of 23 June 1710 (Wilson, *Early Annals*, vol. 1, p. 335) to Dr Warren having built a house on the bank of the river, which could mean that the land given to the doctor in 1704 was to the extreme south of the fort, perhaps near the mouth of the creek. See Chapter Three.
53 Letter from Bengal Council to Court dated 28 January 1728 (Wilson, *Old Fort William*, vol. 1, p. 123).
54 See J.P. Losty, *Calcutta City of Palaces* (London: The British Library, 1990), Plate 2, opposite p. 32.
55 On the park at Tank Square, see Ray Choudhury, *The Lord Sahib's House*, pp. 337–339.

3

The Town Surveyed

The survey[1] ordered by the Council in July 1705—and submitted in 1707—of Sutanati, Calcutta and Gobindapur throws some light on, among other things, the extent of open space in the settlement. It gives us a picture of the topography of the three 'towns', indicating the scope for development in the years ahead. The first point is a comparison of the sheer size of the different divisions of the settlement the total area of which was found to be 5,076 bighas 18¾ kathas. Of this, Bazar Calcutta accounted for 488 bighas 9¾ kathas, Sutanati 1,692 bighas 12 kathas, Gobindapur 1,178 bighas 7 kathas, and Town Calcutta 1,717 bighas 10 kathas. In terms of human habitation measured by the ground covered by huts/houses, Bazar Calcutta—the smallest component in terms of area among the four sections—was the most crowded accounting for an area of 401 bighas 10¾ kathas (82 per cent) against 248 bighas 6 kathas for Town Calcutta (14.4 per cent), 134 bighas 4 kathas for Sutanati (7.9 per cent) and just 57 bighas 9 kathas for Gobindapur (4.8 per cent). Expectedly, Gobindapur had the smallest number of houses because it was sparsely populated, but it had the largest area designated as wasteland, namely, 169 bighas 12 kathas against 27 bighas 3 kathas in Town Calcutta, the survey indicating that there was no wasteland in Bazar Calcutta and Sutanati. Tobacco cultivation was widespread in the region with Gobindapur accounting for 139 bighas 16 kathas, Town Calcutta 38 bighas 7 kathas, Sutanati 8 bighas 6 kathas, and Bazar Calcutta a mere 11 kathas.

Reverend Long has written that, at the time of Charnock, the area to the south of Calcutta was covered by a dense forest. If true, the 1705 survey suggests that within fifteen years the green cover had more or less thinned in the Gobindapur area (83 bighas 14 kathas), being far thicker in Town Calcutta (363 bighas 15 kathas) and Sutanati (487 bighas 1 katha). Long has also written that the esplanade of the new fort was covered by paddy fields in the 1770s and earlier. The survey tells us that in 1705 more land was under paddy in Sutanati (515 bighas 6 kathas) than in Gobindapur (510 bighas 11 kathas) and Town Calcutta (484 bighas 17 kathas). For a sparsely populated area such as was Gobindapur just 18 bighas were covered by grass while the corresponding figures for Town Calcutta and Sutanati were 15 bighas 9 kathas and 11 bighas 16 kathas respectively. The statistics given above are summarised in the table below:

	Bazar Calcutta	**Gobindapur**	**Town Calcutta**	**Sutanati**
Houses	401b 10¾k	57b 9k	248b 6k	134b 4k
Gardens	19b 3k	59b 2k	70b 1k	147b 7k
Brahmins	26b 8¾k	57b 16k	109b 15k	111b 3k
Padee (Paddy)	-	510b 11k	484b 17k	515b 6k
Wasteland	-	169b 12k	27b 3k	-
Jungle	-	83b 14k	363b 15k	487b 1k
Tobacco	11k	139b 16k	38b 7k	8b 6k
Grass	-	18b	15b 9k	11b 16k

Source: C.R. Wilson, *Early Annals*, vol. 1; b – bighas, k – kathas

As regards the revenue situation in the early years of the eighteenth century, the accounts for October 1703 show income from 'rent of houses and land' from Bazar Calcutta—that is, the area corresponding roughly to the present Bara Bazar—as being 359 rupees 6 annas and 3 pies (Rs 359-6-3) against Rs 224-5-6 from Town Calcutta, Rs 177-0-0 from Gobindapur and Rs 147-9-9 from Sutanati. The accounts for June 1711 are instructive because they show how the four areas were undergoing change regarding human habitation and their comparative revenue earning capacity (see table below). Thus, perhaps not unexpectedly, we see a decline in rent collected from houses in Gobindapur, from Rs 177-0-0 (in 1703) to Rs 136-9-6, suggesting that people were moving out of the area and settling down in other parts of the settlement, especially Sutanati and Town Calcutta. In Sutanati, receipts from house rent had gone up from Rs 147-9-9 to Rs 400-0-0 while in Town Calcutta the corresponding figures were Rs 224-5-6 and Rs 434-4-0, indicating that a larger number of people had come to reside in the two areas in 1711 compared to 1703. As regards Bazar Calcutta, one would expect a decline in the house rent receipts from the area during the period, which is precisely what the figures show: a decline from Rs 359-6-3 to Rs 160-15-3. However, reflecting the increasing importance of Bazar Calcutta in the economic scheme of things, we see a sharp rise in total receipts from the area from Rs 392-8-9 to Rs 1,073-7-5 during the eight-year period. Sutanati and Town Calcutta too show an increase in total receipts, from Rs 279-6-6 to Rs 697-14-0 in the first case and from Rs 285-14-3 to Rs 567-8-1 in the second, which (particularly for Town Calcutta) roughly corresponds to the increase in the house rent proceeds in the two areas. In Gobindapur, keeping pace with the decline in the house-rent receipts, total receipts declined from Rs 272-7-3 to Rs 173-4-3, indicating a sharp decline in the economic importance of the area to the English Government.

	1703 October	**1711 June**
Town Calcutta house rent	224-5-6	434-4-0
Town Calcutta total receipts	285-14-3	567-8-1
Bazar Calcutta house rent	359-6-3	160-15-3
Bazar Calcutta total receipts	392-8-9	1073-7-9
Sutanati house rent	147-9-9	400-0-0
Sutanati total receipts	279-6-6	697-14-0

Gobindapur house rent	177-0-0	136-9-6
Gobindapur total receipts	242-7-3	173-4-3

Source: C.R. Wilson, *Early Annals,* vols 1 and 2. Figures in rupees, annas, pies

The table above confirms that, barring Gobindapur, revenue growth was underway in the English settlement from the last decade of the seventeenth century itself.[2] With this growth came a territorial expansion of the settlement and along with it the need for greater resources to look after civic requirements of the expanded area. This aspect of growth was exclusive of the trading establishment, and yet without looking after the civic needs of the expanding settlement the very objective of increasing the profits from trading activity would suffer. The Court of Directors was acutely aware of this link, as is clear from its letters to the Bengal Council, its prescription for raising revenue being laced by the sentiment of keeping the natives within the Company's jurisdiction happy and contented. On various occasions in the second decade of the eighteenth century, the Court wrote to the Bengal Council harping on the following theme:

> Let your ears be open to complaints and let no voice of oppression be heard in your streets. Take care that neither the broker, nor those under him, nor your own servants use their patron's authority to hurt and injure the people. Go into the different quarters of the town and do and see justice done without charge or delay to all the inhabitants. This is the best method to enlarge our towns and increase our revenues.[3]

Six years later, in 1719, the Court wrote to the Council[4] that it was happy to note that everything was being done to increase the revenues 'without oppressing the People', a policy-line which was perhaps at that point of time not sullied by disingenuousness. In the same letter, the Court amplified on the theme thus:

> It is a great satisfaction to Us to read that exact Justice is administer'd to all under you and that it shall be continued. We know no better

way to People your Towns nor any better proof of it than the increase of useful Inhabitants who to be sure will resort where they may best be secured from oppression or secret or open Squeezings and treated with humanity. The more such Inhabitants there are the more will our Revenues encrease besides other benefits to the Place.

In fact, the Court of Directors had begun harping on this theme within a decade of Charnock's arrival in Sutanati as it began to recognise that the revenue from the fledgling settlement had to increase if its profits were to be protected and enhanced. On 29 November 1699 it had written to the Bengal Council, 'We shall now expect to see an Instance of your Zeal and Skill for our Service by the Advancement of our Revenues there, well knowing that due Care and a kind Treatment of the Natives will make those Towns flourish under the mild Government of the English'.[5] Was this the Dutch model of setting up trading outposts in the East? After all, a decade earlier, on 11 September 1689, the Court was coaxing Fort St George to 'govern yourselves in the Settlement and [collect] our Revenue after the same manner as the Dutch do in those townes which they possess in that Countrey'.[6] In other words, the East India Company, as far as its India operations were concerned, was prepared to emulate the successful Dutch model of trading being followed in distant parts of the globe in which the focus was on territorial and revenue control if the factories established for trade purposes were to function effectively.

The official correspondence of the English reveals clearly that the objective of bringing in additional areas under the control of the Bengal Council was to increase the revenue. Within four years of Charnock setting foot in Sutanati, the Bengal Council was writing to London (on 14 December 1694):[7]

Wee have endeavoured to farm 2 or 3 Towns Adjacent to us (Chutanutte included) the rent whereof will amount to about 2,000 or 2,500 Rupees yearly which is a means to Increase your Honours Revenues in youre

> Towne of Chutanutte for allthough wee doe make some Matter out of your Buzar by Grain, fines etc yett wee cannot lay any Impositions on the people, though never [ever?] soe reasonable, till such time as wee can pretend a Right to the place, which this farming of the Towns Adjacent will soon cause, and procure us the liberty of Collecting Such Duties of the Inhabitants as is Consistent with our own Methods and Rules of Government and this is the only means wee can think of till wee can procure a Grant for our firm Settlement.

This then was the essential springboard of the desire of the English to get under their wings the adjacent villages of Calcutta and Gobindapur, which they acquired in 1698. In 1697 the Court was directing the Council 'to hire of the Jemmidar of that Countery 3 or 4 Miles circumjacent to your ffactory at the rent of 800 or 1000 Rupees per Annum.' So certain was the Court of increasing revenue in the future that it told the Council that, if necessary, they could double the rent paid for the additional ground.[8]

In their quest for higher revenue, in 1714 the English drew up a list of a further thirty-eight villages the zamindari of which they wanted in addition to the existing three, which was granted by Farukshiyar to the John Surman embassy in 1717. When the emperor's approval came, the Court exhibited characteristic circumspection in taking over the villages, which sprang mainly from a desire to operate in the region with as little risk as possible to the continuance of what it already had in Bengal. Writing to the Bengal Council on 3 February 1720, the Court said that, despite the fact that the Council saw 'great advantage' if all the villages were taken over, it felt that it would be sensible 'to have only so many of them (when you can purchase them) as lye contiguous to our Three Towns above and below them and those on the other side of the River within about the same extent of Ground as the Towns when purchased reach on your side.' The Council was advised to give more importance to defence issues, the Court maintaining that it would prefer to have

> ... only such of them as lye on or within about two Miles of the Bank of the River because if there should ever be a necessity of defending them from the Inroads of some neighbouring Petty Governour our Souldiers may not be harrast by long Marches to defend our Bounds.[9]

Notes

1 Wilson, *Early Annals,* vol. 1, pp. 284–286.

2 This growth was expected by the Court of Directors as also the consequent impact on the growth of revenue (Wilson, *Old Fort William*, vol. 1, p. 38). By the end of January 1699 Bengal was reporting to the Court that 'Chuttanuttee was very much increased within these 5 years' (ibid., p. 3).

3 Wilson, *Early Annals,* vol. 2, p. lxix. This apparent streak of 'conscientiousness' on the part of the East India Company may be interpreted as the benevolent, exterior face of pre-imperial Western exploitation of the East, rooted in the habits of thought and action prevalent in their own social milieu. It may be argued that the route chosen was the direct result of giving priority to political considerations. It may have been so, but the end result, provided the policy was executed appropriately, was more humane treatment of the native population which could be said to represent 'progress' in a feudal, pre-modern social and economic environment.

4 Wilson, *Old Fort William,* vol. 1, pp. 105–106. Letter of 9 January.

5 Ibid., p. 44.

6 Ibid., pp. 5–6.

7 Ibid., p. 15.

8 Ibid., p. 23. Court's letter to Bengal dated 16 April 1697.

9 Ibid., p. 109. The Consultation of 4 May 1714 (Wilson, *Early Annals,* vol. 2, pp. 172–174) gives a list of the thirty-eight villages sought by the English (with the rent expected from them) which, as hindsight shows, was a harbinger of the Greater Calcutta of today.

Villages	Parganas	Rs As Pie	Expected Rent: Rs As Pie
Salica	Borow	61-11-0	
	Paican	216-3-3	277-11-3
Harirah	Borow	237-5-4	

	Paican	145-13-5	283-2-9
Cassundeah	Borow	129-14-4	
	Paican	0-8-7	138-5-4
Ramkissnopoor	Borow	89-3-8	
	Paican	80-11-0	169-14-8
Batter	Borow	351-13-0	
	Raican	229-1-9	580-14-9
Dackney pack parra	Ameriavad	-	145-2-2
Belgashia	Calcutta	304-6-9	-
	Paican	13-10-0	318-0-9
Dackney Dand	Calcutta	37-8-9	
	Paican	12-0-3	
	Ameriabad	376-0-0	425-9-0
Hogulchundey	Paican	-	137-11-3
Ultadang	Calcutta	194-1-6	
	Paican	120-12-9	314-14-3
Similiah	Manpoor	-	81-15-5
Macond	Manpoor	-	118-12-8
Comorparrah	Calcutta	-	63-10-9
Cancergassiah	Paican	37-7-0	
	Nodiah	170-15-8	208-6-8
Bagmarrey	Calcutta	-	49-7-8
Arcooly	Manpoor	-	22-11-9
Mirsapoor	Calcutta	57-15-9	
	Paican	115-13-9	173-13-6
Sealda	Calcutta	-	118-9-10
Cooliah	Calcutta	127-6-8	
	Paican	445-3-9	572-10-5
Tangarah	Calcutta	62-11-6	
	Paican	166-1-9	228-13-3
Sundah	Calcutta	62-0-4	
	Paican	586-11-8	648-9-3
Badsundah	Calcutta	-	40-8-0
Shekparra	Calcutta	-	41-6-6

Doland	Calcutta	111-6-8	
	Paican	195-1-0	306-7-8
Bergey	Calcutta	22-6-2	
	Paican	213-10-1	
	Nodiah	1-14-0	
	Ameriabad	45-15-2	283-13-5
Tiltola	Calcutta	31-11-0	
	Paican	175-3-5	206-14-5
Topsiah	Calcutta	73-8-0	
	Paican	217-2-9	290-10-9
Sapgassey	Calcutta	-	211-3-0
Chobogah	Calcutta	-	37-4-0
Cherangy	Calcutta	14-13-5	
	Paican	74-14-0	89-11-5
Colimba	Calcutta	270-3-3	
	Paican	113-4-10	283-8-1
Gobra -	Paican	-	100-1-6
Baddockneydand	Paican	-	125-8-4
Sicampoor	Calcutta	11-7-6	
	Paican	95-3-7	
	Amierabad	20-8-0	127-2-10
Jola Colimba	Calcutta	-	114-3-8
Gendalparah	Calcutta	31-9-2	
	Paican	70-4-4	101-13-6
Hintaley	Calcutta	61-9-10	
	Paican	167-8-8	229-2-6
Chittpore	Amierabad	-	252-8-0
			6,571-8-2

4

A Wayward River

The river was the lifeline of the English in the early days providing them with, among other things, the comforting thought that if ever there was a siege of the settlement they could always use the waterway to get away or receive help. Yet, it was the river that was proving to be difficult for the English because of its waywardness especially with regard to the eastern bank, which was being eroded by the strong current. In 1766 the Bengal Council was under pressure to protect the spot where the new Fort William was coming up because of 'encroachment of the River', a threat which was averted by spending around six lakhs Arcot rupees on a scheme to protect the fortifications.[1] In fact, this particular section of the river bank had been a source of concern for the English from the very early days of their presence in Calcutta. Towards the end of 1724, Henry Cave, the Master of Attendance (a position which later came to be known as Master Attendant), reported that the river 'had greatly gained' on the *ganj* at Gobindapur and that there was 'great reason to fear' that if the erosion was not checked in time it would 'prove very detrimentall to the whole Town'. The Council asked the commanders of East Indiamen present in town to take a look at the area and suggest how the menace could be tackled. One of them, Captain Joseph Tolson, wrote back to John Deane, president of the Council, that he had surveyed the area 'before the Great Bazar' (the Gobindapur market) and had found it to be

> … very defective, and of necessity to be repair'd, the Bazar not only being in Danger, but a large Tract of Land in the Honourable Company's bounds, which lyes considerably lower than the Bank, and liable to be entirely overflowed which may prove of prodigious ill consequence not only by the Loss of [the] said Ground but likewise the prejudice the Navigation of the River may receive thereby.

Tolson said that about 850 feet of the bank would have to be repaired which would cost Sicca Rs 2,500 if the work was done immediately 'before the Bank receives any further Damage'.[2]

Notwithstanding this resolve, the river continued to trouble the authorities and six years later Thomas Snow and John Aloffe (Oliffres) were asked to survey the river bank at Gobindapur, their alarming conclusion being that the river 'had gained so much, that it will be necessary to move the high Artificial Bank ten or twenty yards further in in some places where the Tide rises with the greatest force, Which We apprehend will be the most likely means of preserving the whole.'[3] Another survey followed three years later, and in their report dated 30 April 1733 Thomas G. Warren and Oliffres said that 'the Rapidity of the Ebb and Flud' of the river at 'Govindpore Point' had led to a great part of the bank being eaten away and the only way of protecting 'the Gunge from being carryed away in the Rains' was 'by making a bank some distance within the Old bank'.[4] Whether or not the steps suggested were taken is not recorded, but twenty years on the problem surfaced once again with the Council being told by the zamindar that 'by the Encroachments of the river at Govindpoor that space where the market was kept is 3/5 washed away'. Permission was sought from the authorities to buy ground 'from the Proprietors in the Neighbourhood to reastablish the markett that the Company may not lose the Annual advantage of that Farm.'[5]

While the river was eating into the eastern bank at some places it was also shifting its channel westward, a result of which was that a lot of land on the eastern bank was being reclaimed. This is of interest in view of the fact that, at that point of time, the land on which the Strand Road of today is built was under water.[6] One of the reasons for the shift in the channel could be that in the early days, when Sutanati had become a major calling point for the Europe ships, all the ballast which these vessels had necessarily to carry on their long voyage out was dumped in the river while they were anchored opposite the settlement on the eastern bank. The situation had in fact become so untenable that it figured in the Council's deliberations, the Consultation of 6 March 1699 quoting the river pilots as saying that 'one main reason why the road of Chutanutte is so Shallow, and almost Spoilt is the Masters of Particular Shipping, flinging their Ballast of their Shipps and Vessells over board into the River.' Turning the situation to its advantage, the Council ordered that the sand ballast be flung

> … above the Bank of the River from whence all the Inhabitants may convey it away as their Occasions Require, by which means the Road will be cleared and the ways in the town amended, by Strowing sand in those muddy places where people can hardly have Passage in the Rainy Season.[7]

Cleaning up the river bank was one of the earliest steps taken by the English after they landed at Sutanati in 1690. The Bengal Council had written to the Court asking for 'stones to mend the banks' of the river, the Court's 3 January 1694 reply being that burnt bricks would be better given the cheapness of wood.[8] By December 1708 work on the 'great bank by the Fort' was completed projecting for the first time ever a totally different view of the fort from the river.[9] Two years later, the Bengal Council was taking up the Court's suggestion to build a wharf 'before the Fort' which the former felt would be 'a great security to the banks and a strengthening thereto'.[10] A dry dock was also on the cards the Council, on 23 June 1710, agreeing to Samuel Blount's proposal, in lieu of ground rent, to build such an establishment on 'the small piece of ground that lies between Mr Russell's warehouse and the house built by Dr Warren.'[11]

The Consultation of 24 January 1717[12] tells us that there were 'small thatch Hutts standing on the Rivers edge' and that it was the job of the zamindar[13] to clear them 'as far as Prann's House a little short of Capt Seaton's Compound formerly called the Facquier's Ground.'[14] There are two points of interest here: first, that there were huts along the river which was perhaps to be expected, and which could just have been the case when Charnock set foot in Sutanati in 1690. But the huts could also have been put up subsequently to cater to house those employed in the building of the fort and also other works which were in progress at the time. Secondly, there was a bit of ground on the river bank to the north of the settlement known as the Fakir's Ground, the inference being that a *fakir* (or a Muslim *sanyasi*) was associated with the plot at, or more likely before, the time Charnock landed. We do not know who this fakir was but we do know, thanks to the Consultations, that he lived on the river bank north of Calcutta and probably had little or no dealings with the English when they arrived.

During the time when Anthony Weltden was president of the Council, which lasted less than eight months—till 7 March 1711—the fourth side of the fort was completed, that is, the western side fronting the river. Wilson writes that one of Weltden's accomplishments during the brief period he occupied the hot seat was the commencement of 'the construction of some buildings on the waterfront,' the completion of the fort's riverside facade being a result of this. But apart from such productive work, the governor was also engaged in financial activity for which charges of irregularity were levelled against him which were taken up 'in full Council'.[15] The building work which Wetlden began was completed by his successor, John Russell.[16] Wilson says that Russell 'completed a range of buildings begun by Weltden which served both for warehouses and for a curtain between the two river side bastions'.[17] Outside the fort, Russell bought 'a large house and gardens for the Company which was to be used for the reception of distinguished visitors but which afterwards', as Wilson surmises, became the Governor's residence. The Consultation of 3 October 1712 says:[18]

> There being in this Town a very large new Pucker brick built house, with Warehouse, etc., Necessarys Offices, and a large Garden, Cost Rupees 12,000, And Mr James Williamson and Capt. Hornett, the Attorneys of Mr March, the Owner of Said House, Offering it to Sale for 6,000 Madrass Siccaes, Agreed that we Purchase it, being in great want of a Place to Entertain any of the Government when here.

The Consultation of 2 September 1712[19] tells us that the Persian ambassador, who was in Calcutta at the time, was put up in a house 'provided for him in this town'. Given the status of the occupant, who was on his way to meet the emperor, the house ought to have been an impressive one. But where precisely was it located in a town which at the time did not have many houses answering to that description? Was it the March house that was bought for the use of the ambassador, and which later became the Company's House—as marked out in Wells' 1753 map where some governors of Fort William put up in later years;[20] or was it, as Wilson says,[21] at the corner of Lalbazar and Mission Row which later was taken over for sittings of the Mayor's Court? In fact, on the occasion of the envoy's visit in 1712, a number of houses were set aside for him and his retinue, the total rent for which came to Rs 805-8-0, which was of course borne by the East India Company. The rent-free accommodation for the envoy was in response to the desire 'of the Mogull that Embassadors from Persia have free quarter everywhere in his Dominions, as his also has in Persia, and we judge it might be an injury to the Company's affairs now much Embroyled in Persia if we Should be Less Complesant then is Customary to the Persian Embassador'.[22]

Focusing on the early days of the English saga in Bengal, no description of the eastern bank of the river can be complete without a mention of the Octagon, which enjoyed a strategic position on the river as it wound its way past the three villages of Sutanati, Calcutta and Gobindapur towards the Bay. But whether the Octagon was a pleasure spot or a lookout on the river is not known. It is also not known as to who built it: the English probably did not because if they did they would have left a record of the event in the official papers. None of the diaries of the early travellers to the region mentions it. The Company's men in Bengal were, however, quick to appreciate its strategic value and record it in their official deliberations. Thus the Consultation of 14 November 1717 refers to 'the Octagon built on a point of Land near Chuttanuttee from which the River bends towards Hugly,' its strategic position being underscored by the fact that it commanded a view of the river 'up and down a great way'. This is why the 'Collector of Hugly Customs' had tried to get control of it so that he could establish a *chowkey* there, 'which would greatly incommode all the Affaires both Publick and Private at this Place'. The Bengal Council felt that this could not be allowed to happen, which is why it decided to buy the place for 400 Madras rupees. The price was thought to be reasonable because, first, it was less than the cost of the building which was 'strong and well built' and, secondly, because 'the Ground belonging to it is nearly worth that money'. While discussing the controversy over the regulation of private trade by the Company's servants (Consultation for 17 December 1717) the Council suggested that, 'the Octogon on Chuttanuttee Point is the most proper place of any within our bounds above us, to keep an out Guard at, for thence all boates passing up and down may be seen a great way.'[23]

Busteed[24] provides a map entitled 'Calcutta 1756-57' which shows 'Kelsall's Octagon' just to the north of Perrin's Point, the inference being that at that point of time it was owned by Henry Kelsall, senior merchant who had arrived in the settlement in August 1743. The 14 November 1717 Consultation implies that the structure did not belong either to the nawab or to his governor at Hooghly and that it was owned, perhaps also built, by moneyed private people. Who could these people be, especially at a place like Sutanati? If the Setts and the Basaks were involved, the connection would almost certainly have been known to the English with whom these traders worked closely. Did the Dutch or the Portuguese build it sometime before the English arrived so as to keep watch over the river passage, not merely from a military point of view but also from a trading perspective, later disposing of it to some local satrap as their influence in the area waned? Also of interest is the point made by Francis Drake, governor of the settlement at the time of the nawab's assault on Calcutta, that 'an Octagon built at Mr Kelsall's garden' reportedly figured as one of the reasons for Shiraj-ud-Daula's annoyance with the English for putting up defensive military establishments at the place, which finally provoked him to launch his assault in June 1756.[25]

The early maps show the Great Tank to be the one in the middle of today's BBD Bagh. Close to the southeast there was another water body, marked as the Little Tank in Wells' map, the rough location of which would correspond today with that of the nineteenth-century Dead Letter Office with its distinctive campanile—diagonally across the road from the iconic but (at the time of writing) mutilated Currency Office in BBD Bagh owing to earlier attempts at demolition—and perhaps a part of the building between it and the head offices of the United Bank of India. Wells' map shows that this tank was directly to the east of the establishment of the calicoe printers,[26] which itself was located to the east of the sizable premises occupied by Reverend Gervais Bellamy (to the south of present-day BBD Bagh).[27] A letter from the Bengal Council to the Court[28] tells us that the tank—one of two—was made in the early years of the eighteenth century, the earth excavated from it being used to fill up the 'pits' in the area.[29] With time the 'great tank to the southward of the park' became an eyesore for the Bengal Council which recorded in its Consultation of 12 May 1755[30] that it was 'so damaged and wore [worn] away that the Houses now inhabited by Messrs Becher, Collett and Nixon[31] [have] become greatly endangered.' Given the potential of the tank becoming 'a Great Ornament to the Settlement' and also

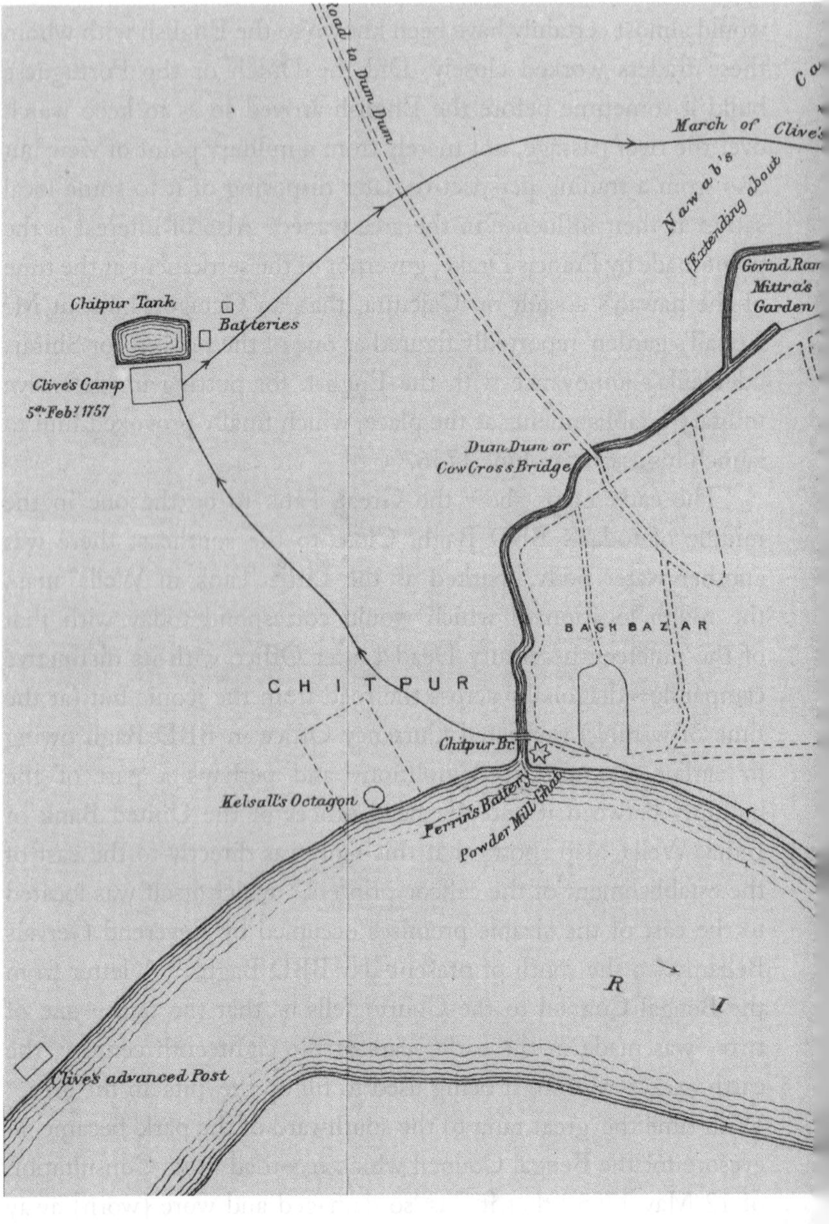

Road to Dum Dum
March of Clive's
Nawab's
(Extending about
Govind Ram
Mittra's
Garden
Chitpur Tank
Batteries
Clive's Camp
5th Feby 1757
Dum Dum or
Cow Cross Bridge
BAGH BAZAR
CHITPUR
Chitpur Br.
Kelsall's Octagon
Perrin's Battery
Powder Mill Ghat
R
I
Clive's advanced Post

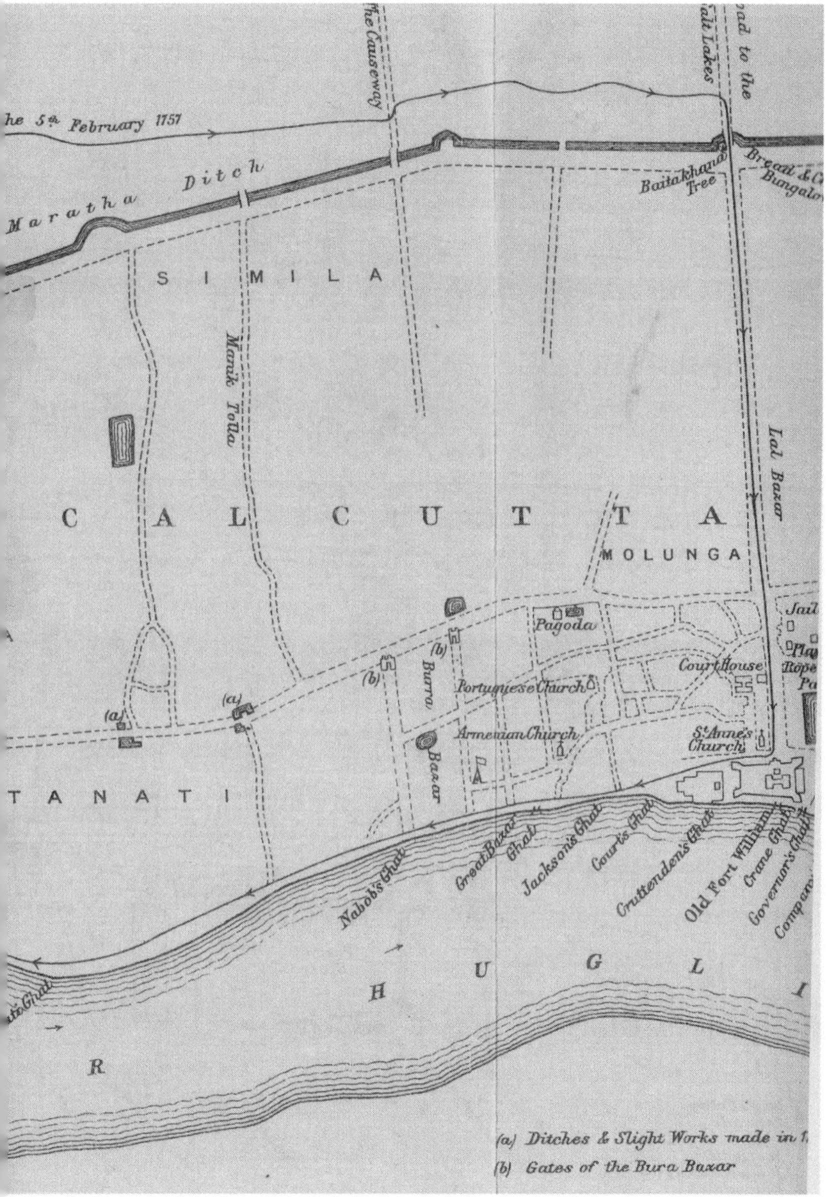

4 Kelsall's Octagon, shown in a map of the town as it was in 1756–1757

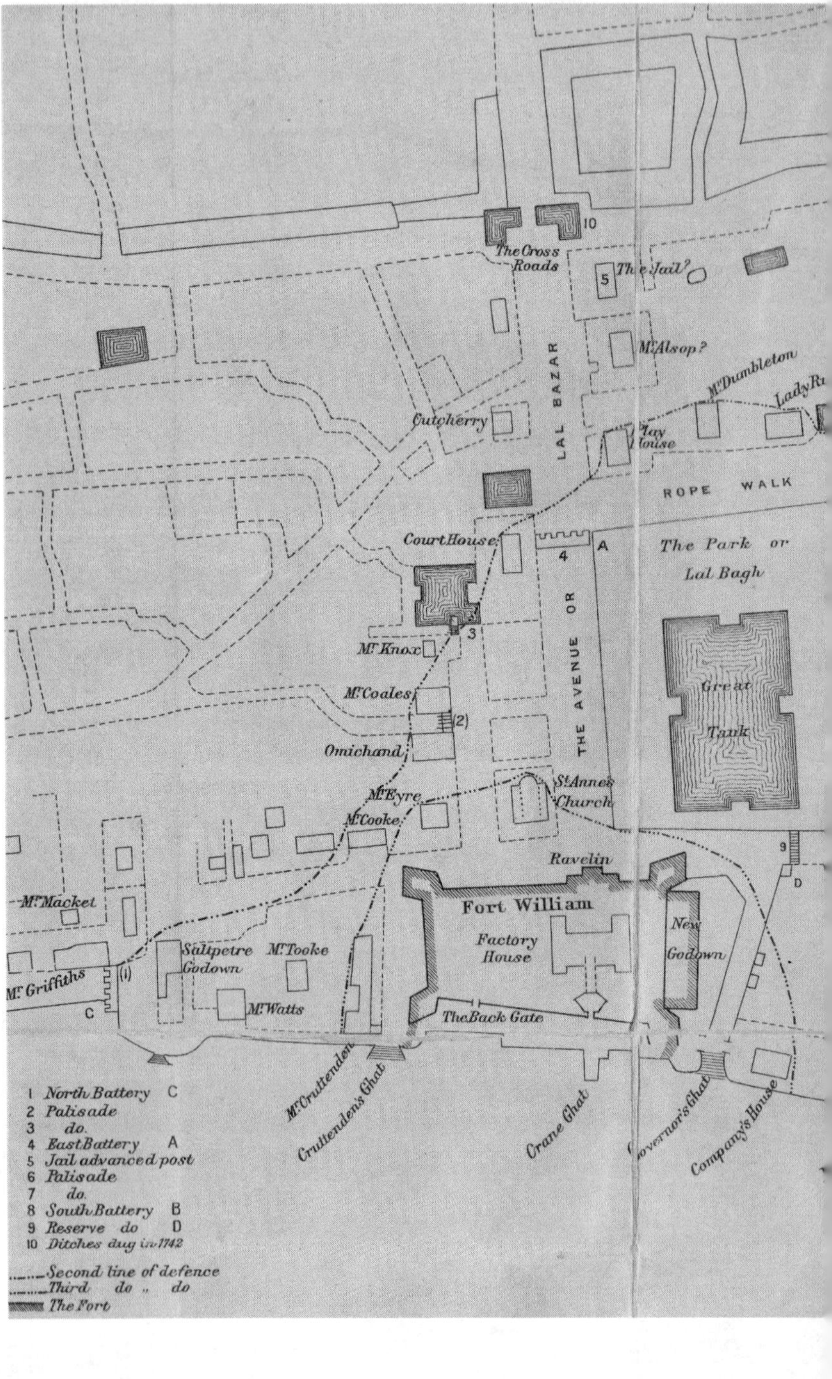

The Cross Roads
10
5
The Jail?
Mr. Alsop?
Mr. Dumbleton
Lady Ru
LAL BAZAR
Cutcherry
Play House
ROPE WALK
Court House
4
A
The Park or Lal Bagh
3
THE AVENUE OR
Mr. Knox
Great Tank
Mr. Coales
(2)
Omichand
Mr. Eyre
St. Anne's Church
Mr. Cooke
9
Ravelin
D
Mr. Macket
Fort William
New Godown
Factory House
Saltpetre Godown
Mr. Tooke
Mr. Griffiths
(1)
C
Mr. Watts
The Back Gate
Mr. Cruttenden
Cruttenden's Ghat
Crane Ghat
Governor's Ghat
Company's House
1 North Battery C
2 Palisade
3 do.
4 East Battery A
5 Jail advanced post
6 Palisade
7 do.
8 South Battery B
9 Reserve do D
10 Ditches dug in 1742
Second line of defence
Third do „ do
The Fort

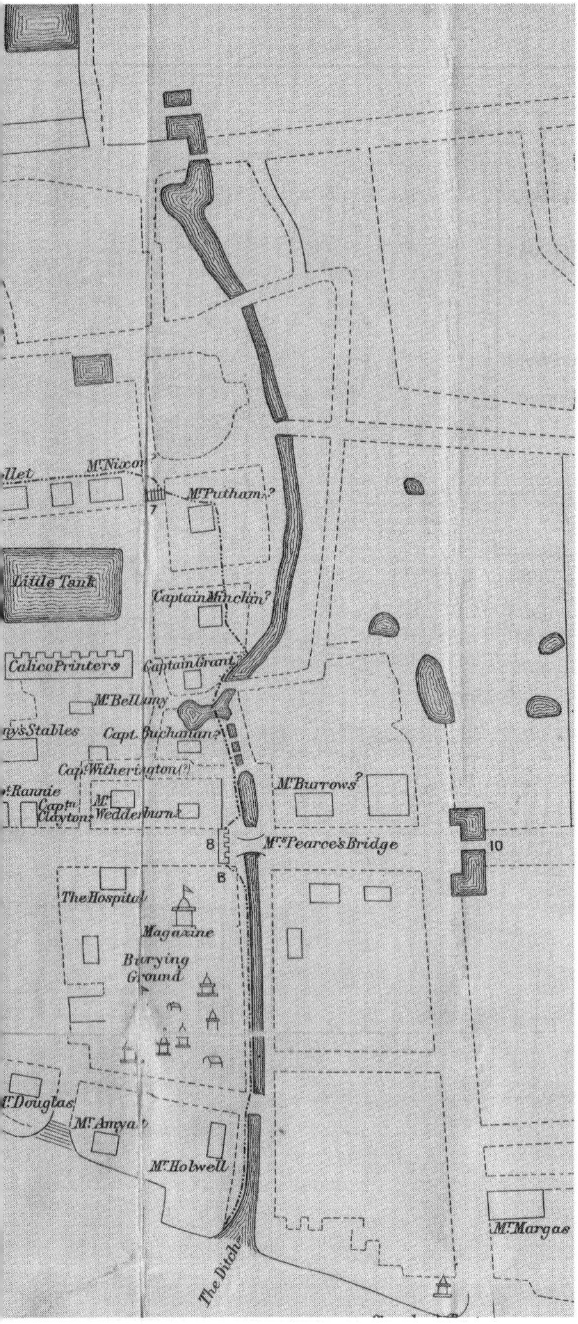

5 The environs of Fort William

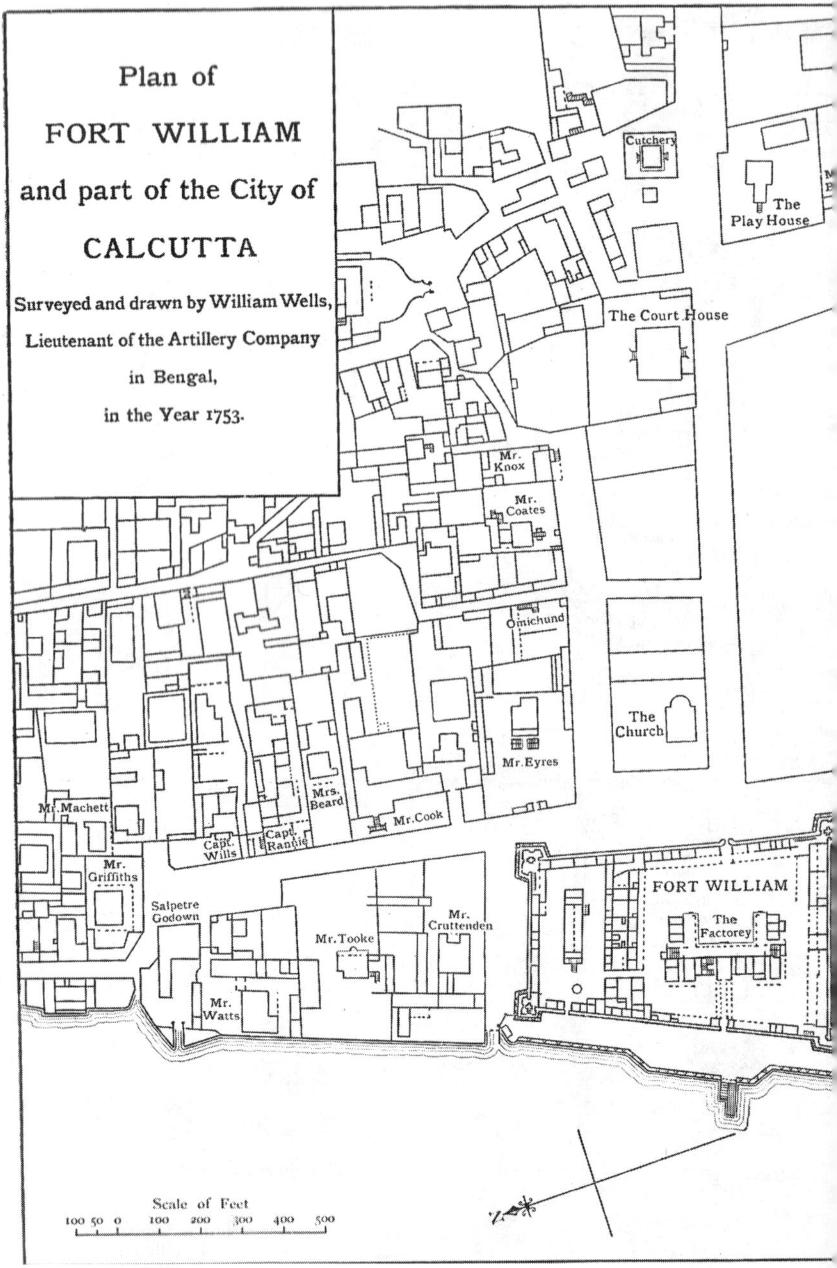
Plan of
FORT WILLIAM
and part of the City of
CALCUTTA
Surveyed and drawn by William Wells,
Lieutenant of the Artillery Company
in Bengal,
in the Year 1753.
Cutchery
The Play House
The Court House
Mr. Knox
Mr. Coates
Omichund
The Church
Mr. Eyres
Mr. Machett
Mrs. Beard
Mr. Cook
Capt. Wills
Capt. Rannie
Mr. Griffiths
Salpetre Godown
Mr. Tooke
Mr. Cruttenden
Mr. Watts
FORT WILLIAM
The Factorey
Scale of Feet
100 50 0 100 200 300 400 500
N

6 William Wells' map of 1753 showing Amirchand's house to the north of Writers' Buildings

'a most useful Reservoir of Water for the Poor the Year Round,' the zamindar sought permission to put a stop to the washing of horses and bathing of people and also to enclose it, which was granted.

Orders were also issued to 'stake and turf' the dock 'by the Storehouses and Workyard' which would look after the facility for a year more and would also cost 'but little money'. In fact, so great was the erosion by the river of the eastern bank that a deliberate policy was adopted very early on to strengthen the bank by building wharfs along the major part of it. At the end of 1718,[32] several merchants had been persuaded to set up wharfs in front of their houses in the hope that the rest would be prevailed on 'by degrees ... to prevent the Rivers gaining on the town'. On securing the river bank at Sutanati, on 17 February 1727 the Court was writing to Bengal that the sooner the work was done the better.[33] Ruing the delay in tackling the menace, it said that preventive measures should have been taken when the erosion was

> ... first discover'd ... for no one knows what may be the Consequence of a neglect in not stopping the first approaches of Water breaches, and what will be the charge if not taken in time. Therefore you will do well at all times to guard securely against such impending Evils at the first appearance, and to repair substantially whatever stands in need of it.

Three years later, in April 1730, Thomas Snow and John Oliffres recommended that

> ... for the preservation of that part of [the town] towards Chuttanuttee ... a Bridge [be made] across the Road between Seats' [Setts'] Garden and Perrin's[34] by which means great quantity of Water will be carried to the back of the town which otherwise will endamage much of the Banks and many Houses.[35]

A point of topographical interest is the precise location of 'Seats' Garden'. One indication is found in the discussion on placement of batteries to counter an assault by the Marathas, Wilson writing[36] that the suggestion to set up 'a battery at Seats Garden' presumably referred to the garden of the Setts at *Zura Bari Bag* (*jora bari bagh*, or garden of the two houses) which features in the Forrestie and Oliffres 'Plan of Calcutta and the Adjacent Country in 1742' in the British Museum. 'Jorabagan' in modern-day Calcutta is probably the result of the etymological evolution of Zura Bari Bag through Zura Bag. It is common knowledge that the Setts were important native traders with whom the English had close dealings. A pointer to the exalted place they enjoyed in the scheme of things overseen by the Bengal Council is the following arrangement made to keep an important road in repair. The Consultation of 11 September 1707[37] states:

> In consideration that Jonundan [Janardan] Seat [Sett], Gopaul Seat, Jadoo Seat, Bonarsy [Banarashi] Seat, and Jaykissen will keep in repair the highway between the Fort's landmark[38] to the norward on the back side of the town, we have thought fit to abate them 8 annas in a bigha of their garden rent, which is about Rs 55 in the whole less than it is ordered in Consultation the 12th of June last, and they being possessed of this ground which they made into gardens before we had possession of the towns, and being the Company's merchants and inhabitants of the place.

Wilson[39] identifies the 'highway' as Chitpur Road 'which the Company's broker, Janarddana Seth, planted with trees'. Half a century later, the gardens figured in disputes between the Setts and those who had been given settlement rights in the area by the authorities in exchange for land at Kidderpur which had been taken up to build Watson's docks.[40]

By the time Shiraj-ud-Daula took over Calcutta the economic standing of the Setts was firmly on the downtrend as indicated by the following report on the value and specific ownership of their gardens. The 22 October 1759 entry in the Consultations[41]—focusing on the report sent in by J. Brohier and Bartholomew Plaisted on the 'Value of the Gardens belonging to the Bussendass Seat's family'

PLAN OF CALCUTTA

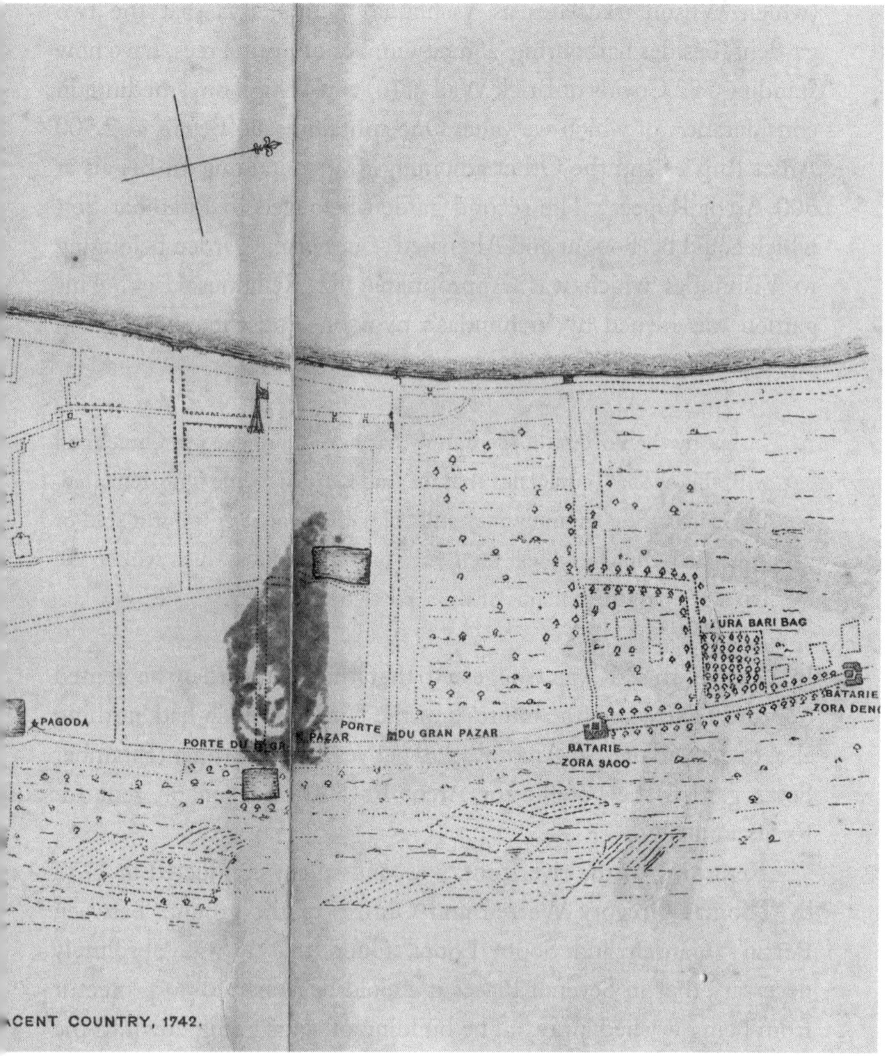

7 A French map dated 1742 (Forrestie and Oliffres Plan) showing the location of Captain Lloyd's Battery (No. 6)

(which Wilson translates as Vishnudas Seth)—says that the two gardens, besides harbouring 'a great number of Fruit Trees, have now standing 752 Covids of Brick Wall of (6) covids high on a medium in consideration of which we value One containing 66 Begais at 2,500 Arcot Rupees and the Other adjoining to it containing 16 Begais at 500 Arcot Rupees'. The second garden belonged to Pitambar Sett which could be 'bought and Alienated', but not the garden belonging to Vishnudas which was 'Appropriated for Religious Uses'. This garden was owned by Vishnudas's two sons and Pitambar Sett in equal proportion,

> ... but by the Poverty of the Family has been mortgaged to Omichund with this special Indulgence that the said Garden, while Only tenanted, Bussendass Seat's ffamily may still enjoy the benefit of it but if sold or Alienated Omichund will then seize on the produce which will be the Utter Ruin of the remains of Bussendass Seat's family.

In view of this, it was suggested that the first garden be rented to protect the economic interests of the family—which had 'nothing else' to depend on—at Arcot Rs 250 per year and the other (Pitamber Sett's garden) be bought for Arcot Rs 500 or taken on rent for Rs 50 annually.

Returning to the riverfront, a second survey conducted in 1732 by Thomas Gregory Warren and Oliffres of the ground 'between Perrin's Garden and Soota Loota' found that it was 'absolutely necessary that in Severall Places it should be Wharfed' to protect it from being washed away.[42] The building of stairs going down to the water's edge from the bank, as depicted in some paintings of the time, was another stratagem used to control the damage done by the river's swirling current. Apart from the well-known ghats set up by native personages, most of these facilities were made by the Company for use by the people. The Consultations of 6 March 1727 say that, 'The Town being Wharfing along shore and there being Severall places for Stairs belonging to the Honourable Company', it was ordered

8 Thomas Daniell's view of stairs at Fort Ghat, 1787

that stairs be made 'along shore'. In that year Rs 3,000 was spent on making such stairs along the river bank, the estimated expense for the following year being an equal sum which the Court of Directors found to be 'considerable'. Work on the stairs and wharfs along Sutanati was completed by the middle of 1732.[43]

Clearly, however, the Company relied on private expenditure mostly to tame the Hooghly, an 'imperial' inclination to make the inhabitants pay for necessary civic measures. Importantly, the practice was extended to organised town planning and development which, as we shall see later, was taken up in right earnest in the opening years of the nineteenth century. In 1749 the link between river taming and a development impost was boldly underscored when the Bengal Council ordered the Sutanati market wharf to be rebuilt at the cost of 'the Merchants who live thereabouts in proportion to their Ground'. The natives, however, were not willing to be pushed around by the new rules without a fight. The Council was duly informed that the merchants were not willing to contribute the money required whereupon the zamindar was asked 'to repair the same and debit the Merchants Accounts for the Amount'. This was music to the ears of the Court in distant London which had a clear penchant for being both pound and penny wise: it complimented the Council for asking the natives to finance the wharf's repair. But the Court did not stop there. It issued a carte blanche to Calcutta to apply this method of payment in future, which can be interpreted as a consolidation of the business approach to tackling cost issues arising from investment with a purely social connotation ('publick works').[44]

A year later, on 16 January 1752, with regard to the cutting down of trees in the southern part of the settlement, cleaning the drains, and doing 'whatever else may be necessary for preserving the Healths of the numerous Inhabitants', the Court told the Bengal Council that since this was

> ... an Affair of general and Publick Utility, some part of the Charges ought to be borne by the Inhabitants, the Richer Sort at least, and ... We leave it to you to make a reasonable Assessment upon them for those purposes, and pay the Remainder out of our Cash.

A year earlier, however, after issuing the usual warning that the cost must be kept within the estimate given, the Court had agreed to let the Council pay for the building of the church steeple ('at our expence') which had been destroyed in the great storm of 1737.[45] Not surprisingly, there were variations on this theme depending on which religious denomination was involved. More than seventy years later, in 1813, when the need arose to repair 'the cross lane from Russah to the temple at Colly Ghaut,' the Governor-General in Council of the day, presided over by Lord Minto, declared that while the magistrate concerned, John Eliot, had done the right thing by making it 'convenient' for 'the Hindoo part of the population' by widening the road to the temple, it could not agree to sanction 'so large an expense as would appear to be required for the completion of the work in the mode proposed by you'. Eliot was told that 'it appears to Government that in cases of this nature, the opulent Hindoos must themselves adopt some means of repairing the roads leading to their places of worship or that they must submit to the inconvenience arising from the want of the necessary repairs.'[46]

The Company's policy of making the people pay for measures taken to improve living conditions in the town emerged as early as 1704, the Consultation of 12 June of that year stating that 'all petty fines from the black inhabitants [would] be put to the use of mending the highways and filling up the holes to make the town more wholesome and convenient'.[47] With time the ambit of the policy was widened, the natives being asked to pay for setting up the jail and the Town Hall the latter, to begin with, being accommodated in the Ambassador's House for want of a proper place. Wilson writes that the Mayor's Court began its proceedings in the Ambassador's House in December 1727, the records however indicating that a firm decision was taken only in January 1729 to shift the court to the house.[48] The 'Company's House called the Ambassadors' was 'bought' for Rs 6,480[49] for which a tax was levied which also covered the setting up of a jail. What this probably means is that, since the house was already the Company's property but because it was now being appropriated for a court, the inhabitants of the settlement would have to pay the Company for the use of it. Inevitably, there were objections, the Bengal Council telling the Court two years later, on 10 February 1731,[50] that the inhabitants had not yet paid for the house. The relevant extract from the general letter from the Bengal Council to the Court reads:

> No assessment as yet made for the Town Hall, Company not as yet paid for the Embassador's House as such it being old and weak, the Justices having order'd the Inhabitants to be assessed for to build a Gaol and Townhall it shall be paid for, the Inhabitants think it a hardship to bear the whole Burthen and the Company bear no Share, desisted as yet from assessing for that Reason, if necessary for the Company to bear a part, hope it will be approv'd.

The tone of the passage above suggests that the Council was gently goading the Court to bear a part of the tax burden. But Leadenhall Street would have none of it. The Court responded on 11 February

1732[51] stating that the inhabitants would have to foot the bill for the Town Hall not least because the books at the Mayor's Court had shown that 'they are so fond of bringing all manner of Causes thither, as not to end any by Arbitration, nor to have them decided by the Jemindar as formerly,' and this specially at a time when the revenues of the Company were decreasing. In other words, since litigation was the preferred route chosen by natives to settle disputes they would have to pay for the associated infrastructure. The Company then lifted the veil and bared its teeth invoking its position as 'the Lords Proprietors of the Land' and decreed that no part 'of the said Expence should be placed to Our Account'.[52]

It is instructive to note the show of independence on the part of the Council and the apparent fact that it had a mind of its own, so much so that even when faced with such a firm stand on the part of the Court it did not hesitate to cite the resentment of the inhabitants to put off placing the burden on their shoulders. It wrote to the Court on 16 January 1733 that 'the assessment on the black Inhabitants for the Townhall and Gaol has made them uneasy as they contributed largely to the Roads and Bridges; have therefore been obliged to do that this year at the Company's expence'.[53] It is equally instructive to note that the Court softened its stand suggesting on 29 January 1734 that instead of the natives bearing the full burden, the 'white inhabitants' could share a part it. The Council was asked to 'find out some method to ease Us of that and all other Burthens, which ought to be [borne] by those who reside under our Protection'.[54] In other words, the message was that since the Company was providing protection to a people much harassed by the country powers, the inhabitants would do well to pay for the development works initiated by their protectors.

Finally, of course, the Court had its way the Council informing it on 24 January 1735 that both natives as well as white inhabitants had been assessed for the cost of building the Town Hall and the jail. The justification for the assessment, according to the Bengal Council, was the building of the roads which 'are of great use for the better

Convenience of Cattle bringing provisions to the Markets'.[55] Fifteen years later, the obligations of governance had not yet been accepted by the Company as is clear from the suggestion made to the Council in early 1750 that the inhabitants pay partly for the expansion of the town's defences made under the supervision of Benjamin Robins, the 'Engineer General of all our Settlements in India … either by a voluntary contribution or easy duties', because it would be 'as much to the Advantage and Defence of the Inhabitants as the Company'.[56]

Notes

1 Long, *Selections*, pp. 565–566.

2 Consultation of 16 and 23 November 1724 (Wilson, *Old Fort William*, vol. 1, p. 116).

3 Ibid., pp. 132–133.

4 Consultation of 30 April 1733 (ibid., p. 139).

5 Consultation of 22 August 1754 (ibid., vol. 2, p. 12).

6 In 1820 the committee set up to report 'upon the best mode of appropriating the Government lands on the banks of the river' stated in no ambiguous terms that 'by taking measures for gradually raising the ground between high and low watermarks, sufficient ground for a road along the banks of the river could be obtained with little or no interference with private rights'. The committee's report was accepted by the Government of the day, the Lottery Committee being given responsibility for the project (Proceedings of the Lottery Committee, 4 May 1820, Victoria Memorial Hall, Calcutta).

7 Wilson, *Old Fort William*, vol. 1, pp. 42–43.

8 Ibid., p. 14.

9 Ibid., p. 78.

10 Consultation of 9 Feb 1710 (ibid., pp. 81–82).

11 Wilson, *Early Annals*, vol. 1, p. 335.

12 Ibid., vol. 2, p. 261.

13 Henry Frankland, father of William Frankland (ibid., p. 260). On William Frankland, see Long, *Selections*, Notes section, p. 17.

14 Wilson interprets Prann's as Paran's, which means that the house by the river belonged to a native (Wilson, *Old Fort William*, vol. 1, p. 101). The December 1703 Consultations mention a Parransow (Pran Saha?—query by Wilson), who was at that point of time arranging for

the Company's timber supplies at Jessore (Wilson, *Early Annals*, vol. 1, p . 220).

15 Wilson, *Early Annals*, vol. 2, pp. 10, 15, 42.

16 Russell's mother, Frances, was 'the youngest and favourite daughter of Oliver Cromwell' (ibid., vol. 2, p. xvi).

17 Ibid., p. xxxv.

18 Ibid., p. 85.

19 Ibid., p. 76.

20 See Ray Choudhury, *The Lord Sahib's House*, pp. 5–10.

21 Wilson, *Old Fort William*, vol. 1, p. 119fn.

22 Consultation of 23 November 1713, *Early Annals*, vol. 2, p. 146.

23 Ibid., pp. 283, 301.

24 H.E. Busteed, *Echoes from Old Calcutta* (Shannon: Irish University Press [1972 reprint of 1908 edition], first edition 1882), between pp. 4 and 5.

25 Wilson, *Old Fort William*, vol. 2, p. 68.

26 The 'calicoe printers' came into being in August 1729. The Consultation of 4 August (ibid., vol. 1, p. 130) tells us that the Bengal Council resolved to buy 'a parcell of Buildings offer'd for Sale for seventeen hundred rupees, which are not only cheap but proper for that Purpose'. The premises were to be bought for want 'of a convenient place for making of Chints [chintz]'.

27 Bellamy arrived in Calcutta from England in 1726 to take over the chaplaincy of the parish of Bengal, perishing in the 'black hole' in 1756. See Hyde, *The Parish of Bengal*, pp. 33–35.

28 13 September 1716. An abstract of the letter is to be found in Wilson, *Old Fort William*, vol. 1, p. 99.

29 A detail of interest here is that, as the Bengal Council wrote to the Court, the excavation unearthed the remains of ancient trees at a level of thirty feet which, incidentally, was also the case when the Laldighi was excavated, and also when the Dhurrumtollah Tank was deepened (*Asiatick Researches* [London, 1818], vol. 12, p. 547). Boring operations at Fort William in 1837 reported the discovery of 'decayed wood' at a depth of 381 and a half feet (*The Journal of the Asiatic Society of Bengal*, vol. 6, part 1, p. 498). F.P. Strong, Surgeon to Suburbs of Calcutta, wrote in 1829 (*Calcutta Keepsake*, ed. Alok Ray [Calcutta: Rddhi-India, 1978], pp. 127–128): 'Of the existence of an ancient forest, all now covered by earth, there is no doubt whatever, as almost every where about 20 feet deep, large timber trees are found in a state

more or less of decomposition …' Closer to our time, decomposed trunks of *sundari* trees were found opposite Park Street when work was in progress on the north-south metro line nearly forty years ago.

30 Wilson, *Old Fort William*, vol. 2, p. 23.

31 Collett's house is shown in Wells' 1753 map.

32 Wilson, *Old Fort William*, vol. 1, p. 104.

33 Ibid., vol. 1, p. 120.

34 Perrin's garden—the 'only' garden house which belonged to the Company in 1729 (Wilson, *Old Fort William*, vol. 1, p. 129) and the town's promenade for genteel society in the early eighteenth century—was sold to J.Z. Holwell in 1752 for Current Rs 2,500 (ibid., p. 243). The Consultation of 6 September 1708 (ibid., p. 73) says that Captain Charles Perrin's house and compound were disposed of by outcry for Rs 2,822-8-5. The Company appears to have bought the property and retained it till it was sold to Holwell. In March 1759 the Company once again acquired Perrin's property so as to make the existing neighbouring gunpowder-making establishment more efficient (*Old Fort William*, vol. 2, pp. 147–148). It was only after this acquisition that the northern part of the garden, 'which is all open', was enclosed at a cost of Current Rs 3,255. H.E.A. Cotton (*Calcutta Old and New*, pp. 34–35) writes that as late as 1793 the memory of Perrin's garden 'stood preserved in Upjohn's map by Old Powder Mill Bazar and Road, the latter marking the starting point of the embankment alongside the Mahratta Ditch'.

35 Wilson, *Old Fort William*, vol. 1, pp. 132–133.

36 Ibid., p. 158, fn.2.

37 Wilson, *Early Annals*, vol. 1, p. 289.

38 The Consultation of 16 October 1699 (Wilson, *Old Fort William*, vol. 1, p. 43) says that landmarks were set up to the 'Northward, Southward and Eastward side of the factory' so as to prevent any disputes 'that may futurely happen between the Right Honourable Company and the Jemidars next us about the Ground granted us by the Prince', the landmarks being pyramids made of brick and mud and covered with *chunam* or lime.

39 Wilson, *Old Fort William*, vol. 1, p. 67.

40 See Board of Revenue Proceedings, 29 December 1786 (West Bengal State Archives).

41 Wilson, *Old Fort William*, vol. 2, pp. 152–153.

42 Ibid., vol. 1, p. 137.

43 Ibid., pp. 122, 123 and 138.
44 Ibid., p. 214fn; Court to Bengal Council, 23 January 1751 (ibid., p. 230).
45 Ibid., p. 230.
46 Judicial Criminal Proceedings, 27 March 1813 (West Bengal State Archives). See chapter 'A Flurry of Proposals'. John Eliot here emerges as an official eager to do his duty as an administrator even where the beneficiaries were Hindus. But there was another, 'bigoted imperialist', side to him which is brought out in the diaries of his contemporary Richard Blechynden, the road surveyor (Peter Robb, *Sentiment and Self*, pp. 197–198).
47 Wilson, *Early Annals*, vol. 1, p. 252.
48 Wilson, *Old Fort William*, vol. 1, pp. 127–128.
49 The language used in the 2 February 1729 letter from the Bengal Council to the Court is: 'giving 6,480 rupees for it as it stands on the Company's Books'.
50 Wilson, *Old Fort William*, vol. 1, pp. 133–134.
51 Ibid., p. 136.
52 Why was litigation 'the preferred route chosen by the natives to settle disputes'? Peter Robb (*Sentiment and Self*, pp. 88, 92–93) discusses this question albeit pertaining to a later period when the East India Company's governance mechanism had become more refined than in the 1730s. Even so, as with the later period, perhaps it was 'triumph of hope over experience' that drove natives to have recourse to British law, the white man having already been successful in projecting the view that his rule was less arbitrary than that of the zamindars who acted, not infrequently rapaciously, on behalf of the absentee nawab.
53 Wilson, *Old Fort William*, vol. 1, p. 138.
54 Ibid., pp. 140–141.
55 Ibid., p. 141.
56 Ibid., p. 227.

5

Natives Dig a Ditch

The Court had settled views on what development schemes the inhabitants of the settlement should pay for and what they should not, the general policy being to get such expenses off its back in the interests of economy. The ditch built around a part of the town at the time of the Maratha scare of 1742 is a case in point. No eyebrows were raised in London despite the project being a sizable one in terms of cost because the bill was met by the natives of the town.[1] The digging of it commenced in 1743, the Consultation of 31 March 1743[2] telling us that,

> The Several Merchants and Inhabitants of Calcutta propose to the Board at their own Expence to dig a Ditch Twenty one *Covids* wide from the battery at the Prison round the Companys bounds as far as the Cowkeys beyond Perrin's Gardens.[3] That each Inhabitants proportion towards the same shall be rated by the Jemindar. That the Space of Ground that will be covered by the Bank raised out of the Ditch shall not now or hereafter be Charged with Rent.

The natives wanted a cash advance of Rs 25,000 from the Company with which to begin the work, 'Bisnodaseat (Vishnudas Seth), Ramkissenseat (Ramakrishna Seth), Rassbeharryseat (Rasvihari Seth) and Omichund (Amirchand) engaging to repay the same in three months.' The Council allowed them to get on with the project and also lent them the money sought.[4] By early February 1744 the work had been completed 'as far as the Great Road that leads from the Fort Gate towards the Lake [modern-day Bowbazar] and is begun to be carried on as far as the Extent of the Companys Bounds at Govindpore'.[5]

The Court's views on the project were on expected lines for they once again focused on the need not to 'Offend the Countrey Government' and to control expenditure, especially in a case where defence works were needed to increase the sense of security among the inhabitants instead of adding to the 'Security of our own Estate'.[6] Indeed, in the eyes of the Court the defence preparedness of the settlement at this time was satisfactory both as regards the fortifications as well as the marine component. The Court, therefore, did not give its approval to the ditch project. Instead, it urged the Council not to increase expenditure 'than is necessary for your Safety'. However, since the English were not spending any money from their own coffers for the project, on 7 February 1745 the Court wrote to its Council that it approved of its 'Lending the Black Merchants a Sum of Money to Dig a Ditch round the Town at their own Expence.'[7]

As it happened, the scare subsided and the ditch was left incomplete in the south. Later, the Court had wanted the ditch to be completed in the south by taking it westward to Kidderpur, suggesting in its 3 March 1758 letter to the Bengal Council that 'by cutting the ditch from Dum-Dum to Perrin's Garden it would encircle Calcutta and render your settlement very strong'.[8] These suggestions were not implemented, which later led to complications regarding the limits of the Esplanade.[9] Reverend Long includes in his volume an entry from the Consultations of 29 September 1766, which tells us that there was a ditch all the way round the fort as distinct from the Maratha ditch, that is, on the northern, eastern and southern sides, the western side being marked by the river. The passage says that the Bengal Council ordered that 'the Ditch round the old Fort, which has lately been converted into a Custom House and Cotah, be filled up'. In a note, Long writes that on the eastern side of the fort, it was in this ditch that 'the bodies of those who died in the Black Hole were buried'.[10]

Plans for a ditch around the fort had in fact been drawn up nearly sixty years earlier. On 7 April 1708 the Court was writing to the Council[11] that Jonathan Winder—the third in Council in Bengal in 1702 who had also acted as chairman of the United Trade Council in 1706, returning to England in 1707[12]—had suggested that some defensive works be put up such as 'a Strong Wall' to the north of the fort separating Dihi Calcutta from Sutanati 'with one gate to go in and out' and with a 'redoubt or a Small ffortification near it to beat off an Enemy'. East of the wall would begin a ditch sixteen to eighteen feet broad and twelve feet or more deep, which would run along Chitpur Road 'but within the walk of trees planted by the broker' Janardan Sett. Winder felt that the ditch should also run 'within the Garden [the Laldighi garden] and so run down by the Burying Place [modern-day St John's churchyard] and here fall into the River'.[13] If the need arose, the ditch could be filled up with water with a sluice at the end of it where it connected with the river, use being made of the tide to keep the ditch clean on a daily basis. There would be just one drawbridge over it 'opposite to the ffort' with a redoubt built near it for defensive purposes just in case an enemy appeared on the scene.

According to Winder, the ditch would also serve as a drainage facility, perhaps the first such project envisaged for the settlement as a whole. As he saw it, in the words of the Court, the ditch

> ... would contain about 2,000 yards in the whole length and ... the Earth taken out of it would fill up the lower parts of the ground thereabouts that the Water should not ly and Stagnate there but might be made with a Shoot or a little Slope So as to carry the rain into the Ditch as our Ground in London Streets from which the Water runs into the Kennell with ease and is so conveyed to the Common Sewer That proper Drains might be made to run under ground Archt and built with Brick like our

> Common Sewers to carry away the Water from the ffort and Town into the Ditch which would discharge itself from thence into the River.

Winder had also proposed that since the ground was low-lying the ditch could be made easily 'and thereby the Neighbouring ground and the Town would be kept dry and free from the soking of the Rains which as the ground now is lyes so long upon it ... it is scarce well dry'd before the next rains come and thereby the Place is the more unhealthy'.[14] He had disclosed that the merchants of the settlement had offered to foot half the bill for the project, which means that the project had been mooted when Winder was still in Bengal. He also suggested that a wharf be made 'before the ffort on the Bank of the River and that all the boats who bring Goods out of the Country on Dusticks [permits] and all other Boats should be obliged to land there.'[15] Essentially, this was one of the earliest efforts to regulate trade for the suggestion also included the idea that all goods landed elsewhere would be treated as contraband and forfeited.

The arrangement proposed by Winder contained the seeds of the first customs facility of the English settlement, and that too at a spot very near to where the present Customs House in Calcutta is located. However, concrete shape was given to this arm of revenue governance only after the retaking of Calcutta in 1757, the Bengal Council intimating London that Richard Becher had been appointed the sea Customs Master as desired by the Court. A house and offices were required for Becher 'in some convenient place Where goods might be landed without risqué', the Council buying for that purpose Holwell's house 'contiguous to the Old Ditch'. In a manner of speaking, this house, therefore, can be said to have been the first Customs House of the settlement. By the end of the year, the Council was writing to the Court that it had ordered the ditch 'to be clear'd out for the reception of Boats' and had resolved that

> ... all goods brought by Water Carriage should first be enter'd at that Custom house and After the Boats were properly examin'd the Custom

> Master might permit the Goods to be landed at either of the three following Gauts as might be most convenient for the proprietors namely The Gaut commonly called Jacksons to the Nothward, The Gaut near the Old ffort in the Centre, and The Gaut called Mingha Bibby's to the Southward.[16]

The choice of house was not a good one: the experience of the next twelve months shows that the building could not withstand the impact of the rains. Since the cost of repairing it was considered to be 'more than the building deserved', another house was taken on hire which belonged to Hazarimal 'which Collonel Clive possessed'.[17]

Returning to the story of Winder's ditch around the fort, the Court was all for the proposals and told the Council that, if it felt the ideas were acceptable, it should go ahead with their implementation. Here again, two familiar points were emphasised by the Court: first, that the Council had to be as frugal as possible regarding expenses ('not a penny should be laid out but what is in your opinion really necessary for the Security of the Place'); and, secondly, that the construction of the ditch should be gone through as though it were primarily a drainage scheme and not a military project so as not to raise the hackles of the nawab.[18] Predictably, the Court wanted the inhabitants to foot as much of the bill as they could, and not merely just half the cost as suggested by Winder. It reminded the Bengal Council that the people of Madras had met the entire cost of building the black town wall, which could perhaps be emulated in Calcutta. The Court continued to plug this line, for writing to the Bengal Council fifty years later, on 3 March 1758,[19] on the subject of financing the completion of the southern section of the Maratha ditch, it was insistent that the inhabitants contribute their mite to the project. While discussing the security aspects of the town, which was just settling down following the nawab's successful assault and subsequent expulsion, it wrote:

> We are told there remains about a Mile to bring it to the River and the finishing this will be a sufficient Security, but as the Work will greatly strengthen

> Calcutta against an Indian Enemy, we will hope that the Inhabitants may be brought to bear a Share of the Expence; however if the whole burthen should fall upon us, and upon a Computation the Sum appears too heavy, in such Case transmit us the Estimates and forbear until you hear from Us.

The Council's response to the Court's letter of 7 April 1708 was proper but cool. It wrote on 18 February 1709[20] that there was no doubt that a ditch would make the place healthy but the 'very skillfull' French engineer indicated by the Court following Winder's suggestion[21] had died and that the Council would 'get one when they can and go about the Ditch and contrive it to Strengthen the place'. But, as regards contributions from the inhabitants, the Council made it clear that they would pay 'but a small part towards it', adding that Winder should have arranged for the contribution in his time. It also said that Winder should have added Sutanati and Gobindapur to the ditch project.

The Court struck back. It asked the Council[22] to lay its hands on 'the best man you can gett' to get on with making the ditch and the wharf and that it hoped to hear 'by your next [letter]' that 'you have made good progress' on the two projects. Also, it could see no reason 'why the Inhabitants should not contribute largely to the making the Ditch and the charge consequent thereupon since the thing is evidently for the health and cleanlyness and as well as Security of the Place.' It asked the Council to persuade the inhabitants not merely to foot the bill but also to finance the cost of keeping the ditch in repair. Faced with this tough stand, the Council had no choice but to fall into line with the Court's wishes. The tone of the Consultation of 9 February 1710[23] suggests that it was abject surrender on the part of the Council. In its previous communication to the Court, the Council had said it would build a 'convenient wharf'. On 9 February it went out of its way to reiterate that a wharf, as suggested by the Court, would 'be a great Security to the Banks and a strengthening thereto', and that orders had been issued 'to Sett about it and make it with brick and raise a Breast Work to

Plant cannon there'. Within ten months (on 16 October 1710) the Council was reporting that the wharf was 'near compleated'.[24] In the same letter, it told the Court that it would carry on work on the ditch 'and make it within the reach of the ffort Gunns which will compass ground enough to secure the Inhabitants ...' It also altered its previous view that Winder should have included Sutanati and Gobindapur within the ambit of his ditch: it now wrote it thought it 'needless to enclose Govinpore and Sootaloota'.[25] However, the dry dock suggested by the Court could not be built on a technical consideration: the river could not support ships drawing more than twelve feet. Even though the Court was insistent on the point,[26] the proposal could not be implemented.

By early 1712, however, the ditch project was getting enmeshed in problems threatening its implementation. While the Court wanted the funds required to be raised from among the people, the Council demurred. On 7 January the Council wrote to the Court[27] that it would be 'too chargeable to make a Ditch and bridges around the Town; the Inhabitants are chiefly poor the Merchants that come to them don't live always with them'. The point was also made that the ditch 'would fall in in the Rains as that by the Burying Ground did unless cased with Brick which will be an immense charge'. Later, the Council told the Court that if the ditch was made it would have passed 'through a large tank which proposed to lay the ships insecure'.[28] What this probably means is that the proposal on the ditch submitted by the Council had included the mooring of ships at its open end, which would have been rendered insecure because of the ditch having to pass through a tank. Was the offending tank the large one to the south of the Laldighi, beside the calicoe printers? If the ditch was to reach the burying ground from east of the Laldighi, the only 'large tank' it would have to pass, or encounter, on its way would have been the one just referred to.

The Court, however, continued to plug away at the prospect of the ditch being made. Early in 1713 it wrote to the Council[29] countering the point that the ditch would fall in unless its sides were paved with brick, a costly proposition. The Court argued that if the sides of the ditch were adequately 'sloped' this would 'hinder them from calving (sic) in in the rains, which their being almost upright makes them more lyable'. If this method did not work then the places where the banks caved in would have to be repaired, 'and if you did but turf them or plant some small Bushes or other Vegetables whose roots wou'd hold the earth together, We should think it wou'd contribute to the preserving the banks and sides of the Ditch'. The shopkeeper in the Court stood out once again, for it warned against the use of brick because of the higher cost involved. Even so, as was its wont, the final decision was left to those on the spot, the Court writing[30] 'If you don't think it adviseable to carry a Ditch round the Towns and make Bridges We acquiesce specially if the inhabitants are too poor to contribute largely towards the charge.' The Court resigned itself to waiting for a more opportune moment 'as We did for the Wall of the Black Town at Madrass which came at last when the People were afraid of a Siege and consequently of being plunder'd'.

The story of Winder's ditch ended on 11 December 1714[31] when the Council said that it did not now want it for drainage purposes because 'the ground (about the towns) is dry in a few hours after the heavyest rain'. No comment was made on its defence capability which was perhaps no longer of any importance to London. The *coup de grâce* was dealt using the cost argument, dear to the heart of the Court back in London, the Council arguing that since the soil was 'two or three foot clay then Sand and soon clay and sand', the ditch could not be made 'unless faced with brick and cemented with good Mortar'. Turfing and planting of trees, as suggested by the Court, would not do 'and it would cost 200,000 rupees'.

The subject of a ditch around the settlement figured once again in 1748 when the Court, writing to the Bengal Council on 17 June 1748,[32] floated the idea of two 'small Forts in the Nature of Field Forts' being set up above and below the town 'near the River Side'. The lower fort was to be built to the north 'of the Creek nearby

Govindpore'—probably meaning the shrivelled-up Adi Ganga which within a couple of decades would become the Hooghly opening of Tolly's Nullah—a 'broad Ditch and substantial Ramparts of Earth' being built along a line joining these two facilities and drawn 'round the Company's Bounds, or round so much of them as may be thought necessary'. Once again the point was emphasised that the entire project was to be financed by taxes imposed on 'the Principal Merchants and other Inhabitants'.[33] At the end of the century, the ditch once again figured in discussions on how to strengthen the defences of the town. In 1799 a suggestion was made to widen and deepen the channel with 'a wall on its far side' at a probable cost of Rs 1,20,000, a proposal which was argued against on the ground of being costly and 'oppressive to the inhabitants'.[34]

Notes

1 The fact that the natives went ahead with the project on their own financial steam points to not just their concern about the consequences of a Maratha assault, which they apprehended, but also their probable expectation that the Council would be loathe to take up the project if they did not contribute to its execution.

2 Wilson, *Old Fort William*, vol. 1, pp. 174–175.

3 This would mean that, to start with, the ditch was planned for just the northern part of the town and not entirely around it.

4 Ibid., vol. 1, pp. 175, 177. It took somewhat longer than three months for the repayment to be fully effected because it is only on 31 January 1746 that the Bengal Council wrote to the Court that the merchants had repaid the loan taken for digging the ditch. The Council informed the Court that the loan redeemed was Rs 9,980. Would this then mean that the cost of making the ditch had turned out to be far less than the earlier estimate, namely, Rs 25,000? (ibid., p. 186).

5 Bengal Council to Court, 3 February 1744 (ibid., p. 177).

6 Letter to Bengal Council, 14 October 1743 (ibid., p. 176). The Consultation of 29 March 1744 (ibid., p. 178) says the 'Merchants proposing to Defend the Ditch dug round the Town with their own People Provided we would allow them about Sixty European Soldiers to be Divided and Placed at the Several Bastions thereof in Order to Encourage their People, Ordered that the number of Soldiers they

require be allowed Them.'

7 Ibid., p. 180. For Orme's account of the genesis of the Maratha ditch, see ibid., p. 156. Also cf. ibid., vol. 2, pp. 21–22, for Orme's November 1754 views on the military and economic utility of the project. Among other things, he wrote that the incomplete ditch 'ought to be carried on down to the River and when the Advantage and Ease it will afford to all the Imposts on Goods brought out of the Country is likewise consider'd, I think there cannot be the least Hesitation about executing it immediately.' A detailed account of the defence plans considered for Calcutta following the 1742 Maratha scare is to be found in ibid., vol. 1, pp. 156–173.

8 Long, *Selections*, p. 172.

9 See Section Two chapters 'The Polhill Bungalow' and 'The Jagannath Sarkar Case'.

10 Long, *Selections*, p. 603; this Consultation is also to be found in Wilson, *Old Fort William*, vol. 2, p. 181.

11 Wilson, *Old Fort William*, vol. 1, pp. 69-71.

12 On Winder, see ibid., p. 69.

13 Winder felt a wall was better at this point because of the strong current of the river at the spot. A ditch being opened up there, falling into the river, 'might weaken the Bank and in Process of time overflow the Place especially during the rains' (ibid., p. 71).

14 Ibid., p. 70. Like other succeeding drainage solutions proposed for the early town, this one too, if implemented, was bound to be ineffective because the slope of the ground was towards the east and not the river.

15 Ibid., pp. 70–71.

16 Bengal Council to Court, 8 January and 29 December 1759 (ibid., vol. 2, pp. 146–147, 153–154). Wilson says the 'Old Ditch' mentioned in the Consultation was probably the creek which ran along the alignment of today's Hastings Street south of St John's Church. This is confirmed by Wells' map of 1753 which shows (see image 6 on pp. 90-91) that the two houses contiguous to the old creek were those marked as belonging to the Sett brothers and Holwell, there being another house owned by Holwell further to the north contiguous to today's Hare Street. See image 5 on pp. 88-89 for the situation in 1756–1757.

In a lecture on 'Calcutta during the Last Century' delivered in 1860 (reprinted in Alok Ray-edited *Calcutta Keepsake*, pp. 66–83), H. Blochmann held that the creek 'ran from Chandpal-Ghaut to

Ballia-Ghaut near the salt lakes', and that 'between Ballia-Ghaut and Calcutta there intervened a jungle two miles in extent, infested by tigers and other ferocious animals'. P. Thankappan Nair (*Calcutta in the Seventeenth Century,* p. 54) writes that before 1737 the creek was navigable and that it was 'the river route followed by merchants in the 17th Century from Dacca to Saptagram/Hooghly as the river below Tannah [Botanical Gardens] was infested with Portuguese pirates and their allies, [the] Mugs'. In the English records the waterway was known as the 'Ballegot passage through the woods'.

17 Wilson, *Old Fort William*, vol. 2, pp. 160–161. See also Ray Choudhury, *The Lord Sahib's House,* p. 22.

18 Wilson, *Old Fort William*, vol. 1, pp. 71–72.

19 Ibid., vol. 2, p. 140.

20 Ibid., vol. 1, pp. 76–77.

21 Ibid., p. 71. Wilson does not give the name of this Frenchman.

22 Letter dated 9 January 1710. Ibid., pp. 79–80.

23 Ibid., pp. 81–82.

24 The wharf remained a feature of the fort for many decades. In 1766 'the pier at the [old] fort' was surveyed with the intention of installing 'two Cranes … for the greater Convenience and dispatch of Shipping and landing of Merchandize', a decision being taken on 28 April 1766 to implement the project at a cost of Rs 15,000 (ibid., vol. 2, p. 178.) The cranes were installed following the move to convert the old fort, or whatever remained of it, into a Custom house.

25 Ibid., vol. 1, p. 83. Some interesting details on the ditch were provided in this communication such as that it would be forty feet broad and twelve feet deep, it would have three drawbridges, 'the tide to flow in one end, palisadoed the other with a gate, and to make a dock at the open end for ships to ly in'.

26 Letter to Bengal Council, 28 December 1711 (ibid., pp. 85–86). The Court referred to the June 1710 Samuel Blount proposal (*Early Annals*, vol. 1, p. 335) to build a dry dock, which had been accepted by the Council, commenting wryly, 'how to reconcile these two is not wee think very easy'. The Council replied on 10 December 1712 making it clear that Blount's design for the dock '[had been] laid aside' because it was 'not worth the Company's while to make' (Wilson, *Old Fort William*, vol. 1, p. 88).

27 Wilson, *Old Fort William*, vol. 1, p. 87.

28 10 December 1712. Ibid., p. 89. Wilson (ibid., vol. 1, p. 69, fn.2) says

that the ditch roughly followed 'the line of the palisades put up in 1747'. See Section Two chapter 'The Limits of Calcutta'.

29 Ibid., p. 90.
30 Ibid., p. 91.
31 Ibid., p. 95.
32 Ibid., p. 207.
33 Ibid., p. 209.
34 Robb, *Useful Friendship*, pp. 131–132, 262, Note 20.

6

An Influx of People

The scare of the 1740s which led to the digging of the Maratha ditch had one major consequence for the growing town, namely, the influx of people from the neighbouring areas, especially from across the river. There is some debate on the number of native people residing in the town with the Collector estimating in 1752 that the number was 'considerably over' 400,000 'without reckoning the multitudes that daily come in and return, but yet who add to the consumption of the place'.[1] Notwithstanding the veracity of figures, the fact is that even before the Maratha scare the town was growing rapidly in terms of numbers which, if anything, was a tribute—as perceived by the natives—to the quality of governance practised by the English as opposed to what existed all around the English settlement.[2] Busteed writes that business was flourishing with trade having exceeded a million sterling annually and that around fifty vessels or more were visiting the port annually.[3] The new entrants were settling down in the native town wherever they found a place to do so, crowding even more areas where there already was a press of people, clearing vegetation to stake out virgin land in inaccessible areas. Such indeed was the pressure that the English Government was already facing a problem in the mid-1730s in accommodating people who were contributing to its trading profits: the Bengal Council had begun deflecting pointed requests made by the Court in London to accommodate weavers in the town to supplement the cloth trade.[4] On 24 January 1735, for example, the Bengal Council wrote to the Court that, for the accommodation of weavers, it could buy some vacant land the filling up of which had entailed no cost. Frowning on the practice of people enclosing large tracts of land adjoining their houses to set up gardens, the Court had suggested that the 'ground made use of for Gardens' be converted into 'Habitations for Weavers and other such useful Inhabitants'.[5]

This appears to have been a recurring theme. Nineteen years later, on 18 January 1754, the Private Committee of Bengal was writing to the Court stating that it had taken cognizance of the Secret Committee's orders of the previous year 'to give all Encouragement for Weavers to come and Resort within our Precincts'.[6] This activity had nothing to do with military arrangements regarding which the Company was excessively secretive. But even here the effort to provide land for the weaving community was made quietly, again with the objective of not attracting attention. The Private Committee, which went about its task in a way 'to prevent all Suspicions of the design it was intended for', asked Holwell, the zamindar, whether there was 'anywhere within Our Bounds a Sufficient Vacant Space for the Number of Weavers in Calcutta and many others to be expected from different Parts of the Country to build Their Habitations on and proper to fix Rooms for the Manufacturing of many different kinds of Cloth.' Holwell wrote back to say that there were available only 321 bighas of untenanted ground belonging to the Company, which included the 'Fort Churches Gardens Cutcherry etc', and that this would not be adequate for the purpose mentioned. However, he added that

> ... to the Southward of and contiguous to our Bounds there is a large and commodious Space of Ground belonging to the Rajah Kissen Chund and the Zemindars Monore (Manohar) Roy, Joyram Roy, And Santose Roy Chowdry which would in all Respects be extremely proper for the Settlement you intend As it is high in a Clear open Air and in

> the neighbourhood of Good Water, and so Scituated within the Creek that runs from Surmans Bridge to Callygat, and under the Eye of the principal Guard to the Southward of the Town as to make it liable to no Molestation.

Holwell added that this ground would be available on a rent of a rupee per bigha 'provided the Use it is intended for is concealed until We gain Possession …' Since the ground was to the southward of the town but to the north of what later became Tolly's Nullah, it is safe to say that it was located at or near Gobindapur? The Committee asked Holwell to buy the ground mentioned and not take it on rent.[7]

The problem faced by weavers was but just one aspect of the consequence of 'over-crowding' of the town. Another was the increasing physical pressure of native clusters which were coming up very near to the houses of Europeans who tended to live in their own ghettoes so to speak in the best parts of the town. It is natural to expect that there would be a move to stave off this 'civic assault' from the native part of the population, which actually translated into an early effort to keep the white and black towns separate. Thus, the Consultation of 24 June 1745[8] tells us that

> … several black people having intermixed themselves among the English Houses, and by that means occasion Nuisances and disturbances to Several of the English Inhabitants Ordered that the Jemindar do make enquiry there and lay before us an Account of such Houses as are Inhabited by them in order for them to quit, and remove to Proper places in the Town …

This, clearly, was native encroachment in areas primarily populated by white people. There is no specific documentation whether the encroachers hailed from the wealthier section of native society or comprised primarily those doing menial chores in the English houses. In all probability it was the latter group because it can be presumed that the wealthy among the native population, like the wealthy among the white people, would hardly have created 'nuisances and disturbances' in the normal course unless there were festivities or traditional occurrences of some sort or the other. The effort at segregation of natives and Englishmen within fifty years of Charnock's arrival shows through clearly in the Council's resolve to remove the black people 'to Proper places in the Town'. Three years later, on 17 June 1748,[9] the Court wrote to Bengal asking it to make sure that houses 'belonging to our Servants or any English must not be sold to Moors or any Black Merchants whatsoever'.[10]

The influx of people from outside the settlement led to civic facilities being put under great pressure. On 21 October 1745, Bartholomew Plaisted, Surveyor of the Company's Works, was reporting to the authorities that 'many Inhabitants had fill'd up part of the Ditches which were drains to the Town and made Encroachments in the Roads and Streets'.[11] The Council responded by asking Plaisted, first, to make sure that no one held ground in excess of their respective pattas and, secondly, to conduct a survey of the encroachments and draw up an estimate of the expenditure likely on repairing them. He was also instructed generally 'to keep the Town Wholesome and free from the Offensive Smels and Ditches and Holes about the Town', the English zamindar of the time John Jackson being directed to take action 'to remove the Houses where any Incroachments were made and to order Ditches to be Open'd as Drains and Roads about Town which are now in hand'. Certain parts of the town were filled with vegetation, a leftover from earlier, pre-English times. The Council asked Plaisted to make a survey and report 'what Underwood was necessary to be cut down'.[12] The job of cutting down unwanted vegetation must have been quite extensive because seven years later, on 16 January 1752, we find the Court writing to the Bengal Council that

> … the great Number of Trees at the South and South East part of the Town contribute greatly to the Unhealthyness of the inhabitants in the rainy Seasons, by intercepting and stagnating the Air, which may, by

> thinning or cutting them entirely down, be in a great measure, if not altogether, remedied.

The situation must have turned critical because the Court gave the Council a carte blanche for 'the thinning or clearing away the said Trees, clean the Drains in and about the Town and do whatever else may be necessary for preserving the Healths of the numerous Inhabitants'. Here again the Court wanted to shift a part of the burden of funding the exercise on 'the Inhabitants, the Richer Sort at least' leaving it to the Council to work out the details.[13]

The disorganised state of land ownership was probably a direct result of the sudden influx of people in the early 1740s in view of the fact that in the years preceding the English Government had acted to clean up the mess in this sphere, which had marked the early years of the eighteenth century. We have seen Goldsborough's description of Sutanati in 1693 when people built houses wherever they felt like doing so and no account was kept of who sold or bought what. With time the confusion worsened and a point was reached where the authorities felt the need to regulate the property market not merely on account of revenue considerations but also to plan 'real estate' developments in such a way that the government's interests were not harmed. Among the first steps taken in this direction was the Bengal Council's move in 1704 to have 'a book ... prepared in which are to be entered [all] leases, bills of sale and agreements made by freemen inhabitants of Calcutta.'[14] By the end of 1716 the Council was able to write to the Court that all houses bought and sold by Europeans had been registered.[15]

The immediate provocation for the 1704 move was the letting out by James Johnson of his newly erected house outside the fort to Benjamin Whitley. However, no specific reason was cited for the introduction of the new regulation. A register keeping track of the sale of 'any brick house or any other house and compound' worth more than Rs 100 was already there 'to prevent Sham Sales and abuses'. This check was extended to mortgages on any house 'to prevent frauds and abuses too often practised in these cases in many parts of the world'. That the new regulation was being implemented with some rigour is suggested by the entry of 21 April 1707 which said that Josiah Jounsen was fined Rs 25 'for neglecting to register a house he had bought in the town'.[16] The system of leasing a house was not in vogue prior to 3 May 1703, for on that date we find an entry in the Consultations which states that 'Severall inhabitants who pay Ground Rent to the Right Honourable Company for the compounds they live in [want] leaces for the ground as customary in other places'.[17] Subsequently, the model followed by Fort St George was applied by the Bengal Council. Thirty-one year renewable leases were given to those who sought them on payment of a year's rent. The system was amended in due course: on 27 November 1716 the Bengal Council wrote to the Court that no 31-year leases had been issued, each house owner 'paying yearly ground rent and brick houses a year's ground rent when bought or sold and Lease receiv'd'. Cryptically, the thought was added that 'If the right to houses ends with the Lease' who would buy 'new ones of value'?[18] An entry in the Consultations of 6 September 1703 had said that a number of Englishmen were 'willing to take Leases for ground rent having laid out considerable sumes of money in handsome buildings', the inference being that leases provided them with long-term security for property as opposed to just payment of ground rent.[19]

It is not clear whether, at this point of time, approval had to be obtained procedurally from the Council regarding acquisition and sale of property by Company servants. There was, however, some form of control as indicated by the condition on which, in 1704, Benjamin Bowcher, the zamindar (or collector) of Calcutta, was allowed ground on the banks of the river, the stipulation being that he had to build 'two godowns of brick which he is to let out for the convenience of European shipping'.[20] Further proof that the authorities expected to be informed about any property developments is to be found in the Consultation dated 10 March 1707 where, on being informed that 'several of the inhabitants had built walls and digged tanks in their several compounds without leave from the Government at Fort William', the Council ordered that 'all such *irregular* proceedings' (emphasis added) were to be forbidden 'for the future'.[21] A 16 April 1704 entry suggests that the authorities were already keeping a close watch on whether appropriate imposts were being paid into the coffers by people who had property in the settlement. It says that Bowcher had been ordered to do a survey of the revenues of 'the three towns', his job being 'to measure everyone's compound, to see that they have not more than they pay for, to measure all waste ground, and to send into the Council a particular account of what each man pays'.[22]

The native part of the settlement was also on the Council's radar. On 27 April 1704 Bowcher was asked 'to call on all the black inhabitants, who have no writing for their tenements, and to give them writings, they paying the Company S*alami*, and he causing their ground to be measured'.[23] Further, all old pattas 'from former zamindars' were to be re-issued by the present Council. Did anything go wrong with this survey because on 16 July 1705[24] Bowcher was asked to undertake a fresh survey 'of every house under the Company's Government, and survey all the ground that is occupied either in tillage, gardens, or any other plantation'. The Consultation of 12 June 1707[25] carries the result of this survey which indicated that the Company was being 'cheated, many persons not paying for half the ground they possessed'. Furthermore, native rent collectors were found guilty of making 'false returns and farming out lands for their own advantage'. In an effort to plug the leak in revenue a new system was devised for Sutanati, Calcutta and Gobindapur. It was resolved that the zamindar would issue to the inhabitants 'a puta [patta] or ticket with a note affixed to it for the amount of rent he shall pay annually'. The tickets were to be produced when the monthly rent was paid and were to be renewed annually, the revenue officials keeping 'a book and duly [entering] each ticket'. Finally, the officials were to 'give in a yearly account of the increase or decrease of the inhabitants'.

Forty-six years later, in 1753, the settlement had grown to such an extent and so many houses were being bought and sold that the idea of imposing a regular tax on such transactions to beef up the finances of the Council was floated by J.Z. Holwell, the then zamindar. He suggested the imposition of a five per cent duty on every 'Europe house' sold, the conversion of the ground rent 'called *Cowrie mohull*' into sicca rupees, and 'raising the half rent to whole rent'.[26] Since the economic interest of Englishmen was involved, the Council left the decision to the Court but not without commenting that the houses, 'belonging to Europeans and others in the white Town, sell, from ten to twelve thousand Rupees each House, bearing upper rooms, and the Repairs thereof, are usually so large, as to afford little advantage to the Proprietors'. Finally, it adopted the status quo when it argued that 'We do not think proper to alter an Indulgence which has Subsisted from the Origin of the Settlement, for so trifling an Advantage', particularly as regards conversion of ground rent to sicca rupees and half rent into whole rent. More positively, it held that the proposed increase in the duty would be 'a Hardship upon the Proprietors of such Houses'.[27] The question arises whether the tax proposal was limited only to English householders. On 15 April 1706 the Bengal Council took the following decision:

> It formerly being a custom for all people who sold small houses or compounds to pay one-fourth part of the money they sell them for to the Company: and that the merchants or others that sold large houses or compounds paid but 2 per cent. Considering this is very hard upon the poor people , ordered that all people pay for the future 5 per cent, which we think to be reasonable and an encouragement to the poor tenants who paid in proportion a great deal more than the richer sort[28]

The implication here is that, on account of the 1706 decision and assuming that there was no subsequent change, there was already extant a property-sale tax of five per cent on 'merchants or others that sold large houses'. If in 1753 a tax of five per cent was being contemplated for the 'Europe houses' one interpretation could be that the earlier decision applied only to the native population. Secondly, it is interesting to note the redistributive logic involved in easing the tax for the poor and increasing it on the rich.

Both Sutanati and Calcutta were unhealthy places before the English arrived almost solely because of the stagnant water pools dotting the area. The high point was the river bank and as the ground stretched away to the east it sloped downward gradually towards the salt water lake which was the natural drainage reservoir. The gradient was uneven with the result that pockets of water collected all over the place, no doubt helped by unplanned housing which affected efficient drainage of the place. This was noticed early by the English, which was inevitable in view of the very high levels of mortality among them during the rains. The official records indicate a constant harping on the theme, an example of which was the Court's letter to the Bengal Council on 4 February 1709 which asked the local authorities 'to drain the grounds and fill up the Tanks' in view of the fact that

> ... the Standing Water thereabouts contributes to the unhealthyness of the Place and Subjects People to Agues ffeavers and ffluxes and no wonder for it has the same effect in England in our low Marish ground. therefore do all you can to take away the Cause that the Effect may cease.

Instructively, the Court said it was informed that

> ... the greatest part of the Standing Water thereabouts is occasion'd by the Peoples digging the Earth to make their Houses with and then the next rains the Holes are fill'd with Water which there Stagnates and corrupts That the natives rarely use any of that Water the River Supplys all their wants.[29]

In the same letter, Leadenhall Street asked the Council to 'do whatever you think proper to make the place healthy but with as little charge as may be'. By January 1712 the Bengal Council was claiming that the job of filling up the 'holes' had been completed.[30] But of course this could not have been the case because the problem of a surfeit of water bodies continued to plague the settlement as it grew into a town through the eighteenth century and also well into the nineteenth.

Yet another factor affecting adversely the health of people living in the growing town was, as the Bengal Council saw it in early 1711,[31] 'the thickness of the trees'. Among other things, this gives us an idea of what the villages of Sutanati, Calcutta and Gobindapur were like when Charnock arrived on the scene. Writing to the Court, the Council said that since this was 'injurious to the health of the place' it would 'thin them and keep them in rows and cut away all bamboos'. However, the expanding town had to wait till the 'troubles' of 1756 and the 'deliverance' in early 1757 for a decisive step to be taken to thin out the tree cover which had marked the area for centuries. The Consultation of 14 February 1757 tells us that

> This being a good Opportunity to open the Town by cutting down the Trees with which it is surrounded … Ordered that Permission be given to all Persons to cut down the Trees within our Bounds, Orange trees and other fruit Trees excepted, and that the Wood shall belong to those who pay the Labourers.[32]

It would appear that the eastern part of the settlement was relatively free of the dense vegetation and undergrowth which marked the southern and northern parts, which may explain why in the early years the Council settled on this part of the town to open up ground where genteel English society could take the morning and evening air. In February 1711 the Council said it had made 'a Walk 4 Mile long to the lake (the salt water lake to the east of the town), which will make the place healthy the ground levell'd and raised where necessary a ditch on each side to receive the water'.[33]

Notes

1 Busteed, *Echoes From Old Calcutta*, p. 6.

2 On 9 January 1719 the Court was writing to Bengal: 'We know no better way to People your Towns nor any better proof of it than the encrease of useful Inhabitants who to be sure will resort where they may best be secured from oppression or secret or open Squeezings and treated with humanity.The more such Inhabitants there are the more will our Revenues increase besides other benefits to the Place' (Wilson, *Old Fort William,* vol. 1, p. 106).

3 Busteed, *Echoes*, pp. 5–6.

4 See Wilson, *Early Annals,* vol. 1, p. 273 for the Council appointing a native overseer in 1706 to keep a watch on the work of weavers employed by the Company.

5 Wilson, *Old Fort William,* vol. 1, p. 141.

6 Ibid., vol. 2, pp. 1–2.

7 Ibid. At the end of 1775 some weavers placed a demand with the Government for land in Pargana Calcutta on which to build houses. Their petition read: 'We are Weavers in number 1,000 Families who reside in Pergunna Calcutta, and work for the Company. We have no spot on which to build houses for our abode, and, therefore, request you will grant some Land in Pergunnah Calcutta, whereon We may build houses, and continue to work for the Company.' The Calcutta Committee of Revenue promptly asked the *dewan* to find a 'competent spot' which could be given to them 'without Prejudice to the Public or Individuals' (Calcutta Committee of Revenue Proceedings, 11 December 1775, West Bengal State Archives).

8 Wilson, *Old Fort William,* vol. 1, p. 183.

9 Ibid., p. 205.

10 See Robb, *Sentiment and Self,* Chapter 2. See also Pradip Sinha, *Calcutta in Urban History* (Calcutta: Firma KLM Pvt Ltd, 1978), pp 8-9.

11 Wilson, *Old Fort William,* vol. 1, p. 186. Five years later, in the middle of 1750, much the same complaint was being made by the zamindar when he informed the Bengal Council that 'several of the Drains about the Town are stopped up and encroachments made in the high Roads by building Hutts and shops over those Drains' (Consultations, 23 July, ibid., p. 229).

12 Another instance where 'old trees and underwood in and about the town' were cut down figures in 1751, the primary objective this time being to provide fuel for the building of defence works being planned by Benjamin Robins (Wilson, *Old Fort William*, vol. 1, p. 233).
13 Ibid., p. 240. Another round of clearing the vegetation was effected in 1762 with the objective of improving the 'Healthiness of the Town, and of the Inhabitants' living within the Maratha ditch (ibid., vol. 2, p. 167).
14 Consultation of 27 March 1704 (Wilson, *Early Annals*, vol. 1, p. 247).
15 Wilson, *Old Fort William*, vol. 1, pp. 99–100.
16 Consultation of 8 July and 6 September 1703, ibid., pp. 55–57; Wilson, *Early Annals*, vol. 1, p. 282.
17 Wilson, *Old Fort William*, vol. 1, p. 55.
18 Ibid., pp. 99–100.
19 Ibid., p. 57.
20 Consultation of 27 March 1704 (Wilson, *Early Annals*, vol. 1, p. 247).
21 Ibid., p. 280.
22 Ibid., p. 249.
23 Ibid., p. 250.
24 Ibid., p. 266.
25 Ibid., p. 283.
26 Consultation of 23 and 26 July 1753 (Wilson, *Old Fort William,* vol. 1, p. 252).
27 Bengal Council to Court, 4 January 1754 (ibid., p. 255).
28 Wilson, *Early Annals*, vol. 1, pp. 271–272.
29 Wilson, *Old Fort William,* vol. 1, p. 75.
30 Consultation of 7 January 1712 (ibid., p. 87).
31 Ibid., p. 84.
32 Ibid., vol. 2, p. 105.
33 Ibid., vol. 1, p. 84. By the end of 1714 the Council was writing to the Court that 'the long walk made to the Lakes gives free passage for the Air so that now the place is as healthy as any in India'. The raised ground on which the walk was made would remain a feature of the topography of this part of the town in the years ahead. The building of the Beliaghata Main Road in the early years of the next century may have utilised this topographical advantage. A.K. Roy (*Short History*, p. 204) says that in 1757 Sealdah 'is mentioned as a "narrow causeway, raised several feet above the level of the country, with a ditch on either side, leading from the east"'.

7

The Early Roads

The correspondence between the Court and the Bengal Council in the early years of the eighteenth century indicates that improvement of the settlement's drainage had become an important task for the English Government run by the Company. Since a road was usually built on high ground and there were ditches on both sides to drain off water from the surface, it became a means to improving the drainage of the settlement. This was made clear in so many words by the Bengal Council when it told the Court in December 1720 that 'the reason for making the new roads was to drain Govindpore to bring Inhabitants thither this in time will increase the Revenues'.[1] There was a strategic reason for the works as well: the roads would enable the Council to 'see into the Neighbouring Jamidars Countrey who attack'd them two years since, and March better to support the Out guards if insulted by him, but he is very humble since'. Further, the settlement would become a healthier place because of 'the Winds free Passage to the town, the inhabitants at the charge of all.'

But what roads were these? Were they confined to Gobindapur itself, mainly to drain the place? This probably was not the case because the Council was writing that soldiers could be sent—obviously from the fort—along these roads to quell any disturbance created by the neighbouring zamindar. This would mean that the roads, or any one of them if there were more than one, led from

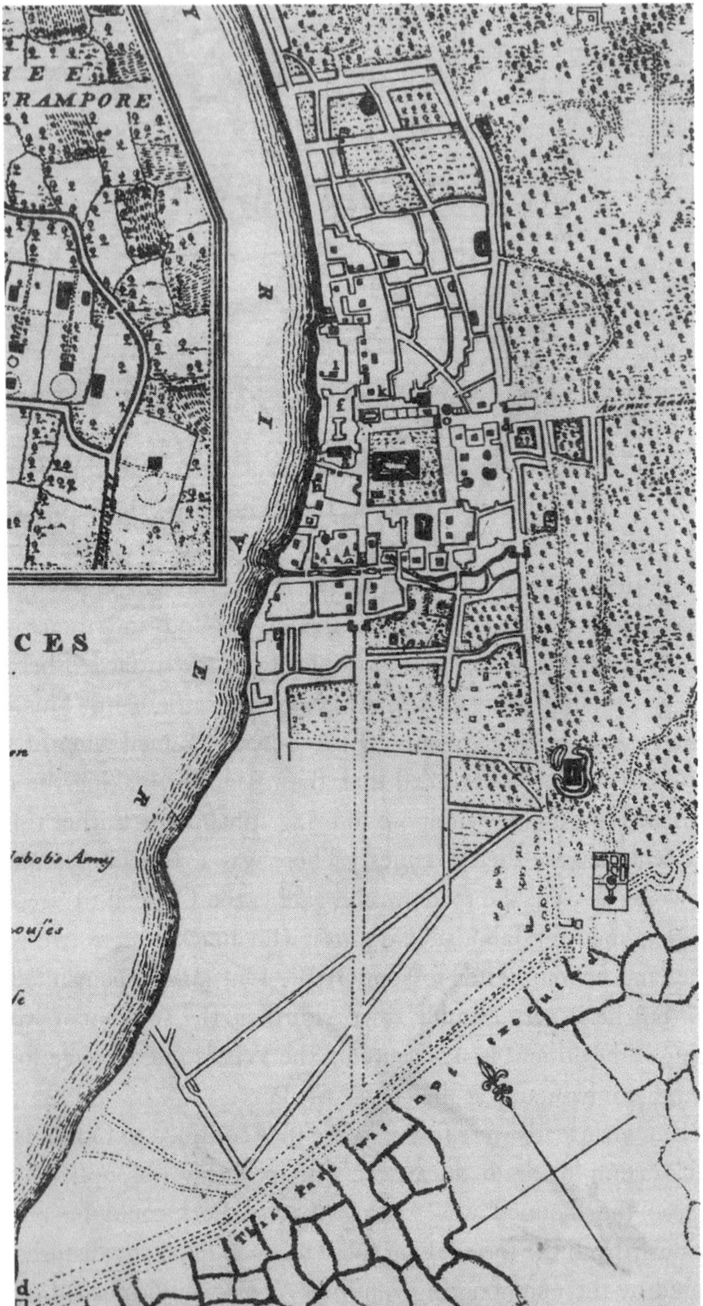
ERAMPORE
CES

the fort or its vicinity to Gobindapur.[2] If so, was the alignment of one of these roads roughly along the Course (the present-day maidan), which later shot into prominence in the social life of the town as the place for early morning and evening airings? Maps of Calcutta in the 1740s show a number of roads crisscrossing the region south of Calcutta a part of which was covered by Gobindapur. Among these roads there is one which traverses the Course, the latter being clearly marked out as such in Upjohn's

9 (facing page)
Plan of the territory of Calcutta in 1742, also showing the military operations at the time of the 1756 assault of Shiraj-ud-Daula

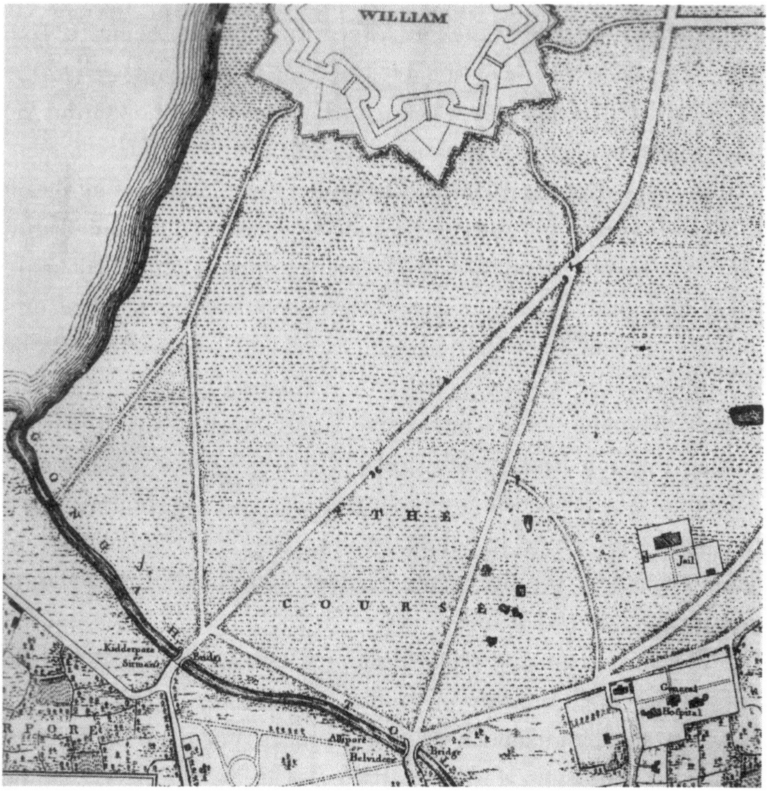

10 (below)
The roads in the maidan area of today in Upjohn's map, 1792–1793

map of 1792–1793.[3] As indicated by the Council's December 1720 letter, the inhabitants of Sutanati, Calcutta and Gobindapur were made to bear the cost of making the roads. Writing to the Bengal Council in February 1722, the Court provided some idea about the roads which had been made—'on the South-South-West and East to West Sides of your Towns'—when it commended the Council for the projects, especially the fact that the people had been made to foot the bill, which it described as 'a piece of good management'.[4]

The Consultation of 15 November 1749[5] provides a good idea of what the principal roads were like in the middle of the eighteenth century, the focus of the entry being on the cost of 'mending the high roads and repairing the publick streets and drains'. The first road which figures on the list—the outcome of a survey conducted by the English zamindar—is that 'from the dock-head to the stable and down to the side of the Park', the estimated cost being Rs 100. Maps of the time, including Upjohn's of a later vintage (1792–1793), show that this road was not a straight west-east one from the river to the park, following the alignment of today's Hare Street.[6] Wilson says that the Company's stables were located roughly on the spot occupied in his day—the closing decades of the nineteenth century—by the Standard Life Assurance offices, which still stand today though in a decrepit state directly opposite the ugly Calcutta Telephones building in BBD Bagh (see image 5 on pp. 88–89). The second road, the repair of which would also cost Rs 100, is probably today's Mangoe Lane connecting Tank Square with the road cutting through Kossaitallah (today's Bentinck Street) in the east. This road is described as 'going down to … Lascelles' house', which the maps show to be standing at the corner of Mangoe Lane and Tank Square, at the site of the heritage Currency Office building (see image 5 on pp. 88–89).

The next road, the repair cost of which was estimated at Rs 225, is described as running from Captain Lloyd's house 'to the New Buzar Chandpaul Buzar'. The latter part of the description is somewhat confusing. If it was restricted to just 'Chandpal Bazar' the road in question would correspond to the present-day alignment of Esplanade Row West (west of Raj Bhavan) running down to the river at Chandpal Ghat, Lloyd's house being located on today's Council House Street.[7] The next road, to be repaired at a

11 Detail of Upjohn's map (1792–1793) showing the stretch of Chitpur Road from Lalbazar to Bartala. Also Clive Street going up north by the river

cost of Rs 300, is that from the New Bazar to the 'Bartholla Buzar', which Wilson identifies as the stretch of Chitpur Road between Bartala Street and Lalbazar. The New Bazar 'is close by the Lal Bazar', but there is no clue as to where the Bartala Bazar is located although Bartala ('Bartollah' in Upjohn's map) itself is clearly marked out. The fifth road in the list is that from 'the Fort Gate to Mansing's Chowkey', the repair cost for which was estimated at Rs 500. This is the road which leads from the western end of Writers' Buildings to Sealdah in the east—the 'Road to the Lake' in the 1742 plan of Calcutta—the description telling us that, in his time, Man Singh had set up an outpost there. This is also the area where the Bread and Cheese Bungalow was located, the name suggesting that it catered to the hunting parties which visited the eastern part of the settlement's neighbourhood.[8] This road appears to have been a major passage in the settlement in the first half of the eighteenth century. Since there is little in the records to tell us when this road was made, one can surmise that it existed before Charnock's advent, being one of the ancient native roads which made its way from the interior of the country to the river.

The next road is that 'from Chourongeys Chowkey and Gasthulla Buzar'—repair cost estimated at Rs 600—an extraordinary feature of the description being the spelling used for modern-day 'Chowringhee' which gives the correct local pronunciation of the word. One early English variant of the name was 'Cheringee' which, as is apparent, was easier on the English tongue than the Indian pronunciation. But where was the chowkey, or guard outpost, located? Wilson suggests it was situated where the Asiatic Society now stands because that was the northernmost point of the area marked as 'Chouringhy' in Upjohn's map, the area south of it being called 'Dhee Birjee'.[9] As regards 'Gasthulla Buzar', Wilson's suggestion is that Gasthulla 'may be stand for Qasaitola'? It is difficult to accept the suggestion because while

12 (facing page) The map showing the seven batteries set up in 1742

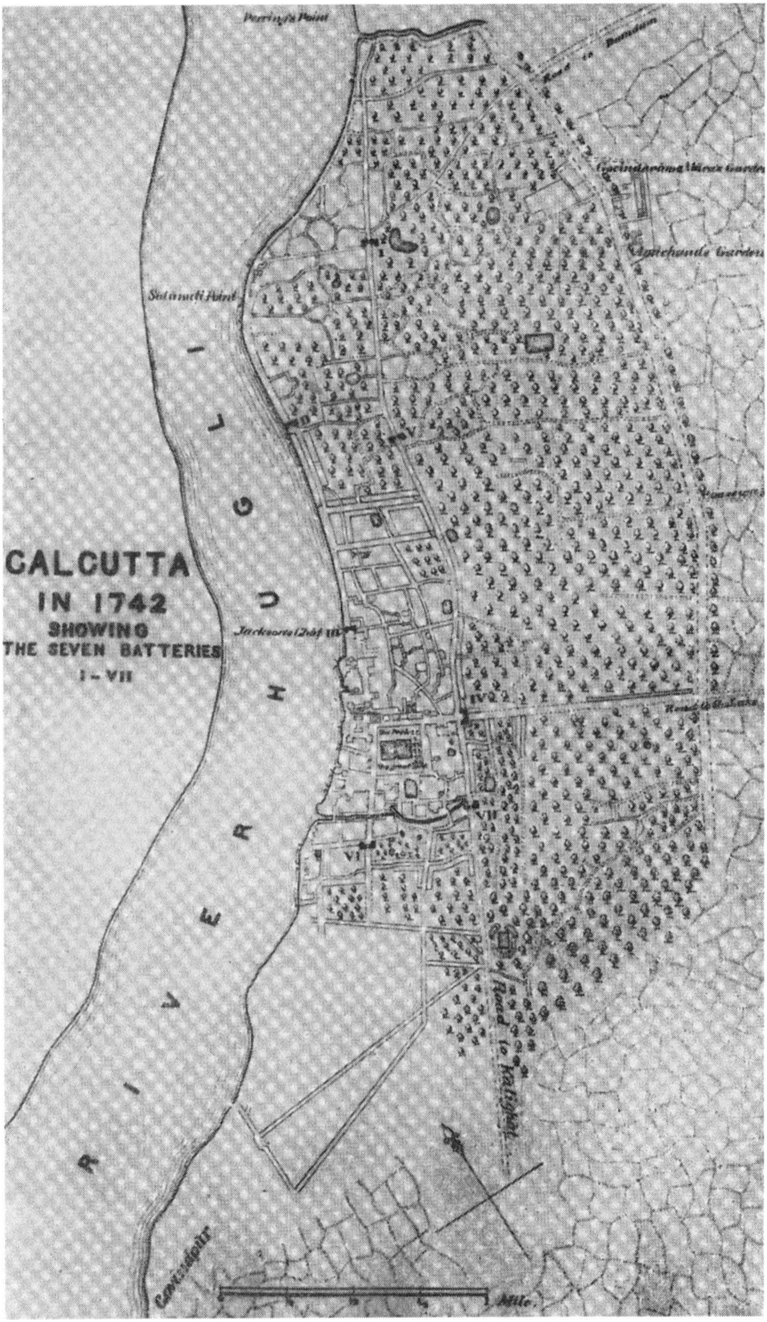

CALCUTTA
IN 1742
SHOWING
THE SEVEN BATTERIES
I – VII
RIVER HUGLI
Perring's Point
Road to Kalighat
Mile

Qasaitola, or Kashaitala (Cossitollah), relates to an *area* around modern-day Bentinck Street, Gasthulla Buzar is a *specific spot* on the map and, therefore, may not at all relate to the Bentinck Street neighbourhood. Further, the Consultation puts the length of the road to be repaired at 6,000 ft. Wilson calculates that this length would roughly give us the whole of the northern part of Chowringhee Road (from the presumed location of the chowkey) till the southern end of Bentinck Street. If this is correct it would perhaps be more reasonable to conclude that the bazar mentioned was located at the present-day Dharamtala crossing or thereabout. 'Gasthulla' may in fact be rendered as *Gachhtala*, or a spot under a tree, the inference being that there was a bazar at this spot held under the shade of a tree which, perhaps, subsequently grew into the Dharamtala Bazar.[10]

The seventh road mentioned is that from the house of Mr Margass 'down to the powder house'—a length of 5,000 ft—the latter being located roughly where St John's Church stands today at the north-west corner of Council House Street and Hastings Street (Kiran Shankar Roy Road; see image 7 on pp. 94-95).[11] Wilson writes that in 1742 the Margass house was located near the seventh battery (see image 12 on p. 135), that is, at a spot close to the meeting point of British Indian Street and Bentinck Street.[12] This, according to Wilson, would yield a distance of closer to 2,000 ft instead of 5,000 ft, which would also be consistent with the Rs 100 spent on the road's repairs.[13] The next road mentioned is that from the 'Purranna Gunge to Govindpore Chowkey' measured at 6,000 ft, the repair cost of which was Rs 250. Wilson has no clue to where the *purana* (old) *gunje* (market) was located[14] and, therefore, does not know which road is being talked about. First, the gunge referred to could have been located at Gobindapur itself: its description as 'old' is appropriate because we know it was an old market, in all probability harking back to the period before the arrival of Charnock at Sutanati. Secondly, the market was located near the river because we know that in an earlier time the river threatened it.[15] If there was a long road leading to it, as indicated by the Consultation, it would probably have had an east-west alignment instead of running along the river. It also stands to reason that there would have been, at some point on the road, a chowkey or outpost to collect taxes and perhaps also provide security to travellers. After all, in 1722 the Court was complimenting the Bengal Council for having made the 'roads' to Gobindapur because it would, among other things, facilitate 'the March of your Souldiers when necessary to support your outmost Outguards and prevent private Robberys in the night from Rogues abroad'.[16] The 1742 map of Calcutta (see image 9 on p. 130) shows a number of roads traversing the space between the settlement and Gobindapur; possibly, the Consultation refers to one of these roads.

The ninth road is that 'to the side of the Gaol down to Mr Frankland's Garden' the repair cost of which was estimated at Rs 200. This is an interesting road because it tells us of an important

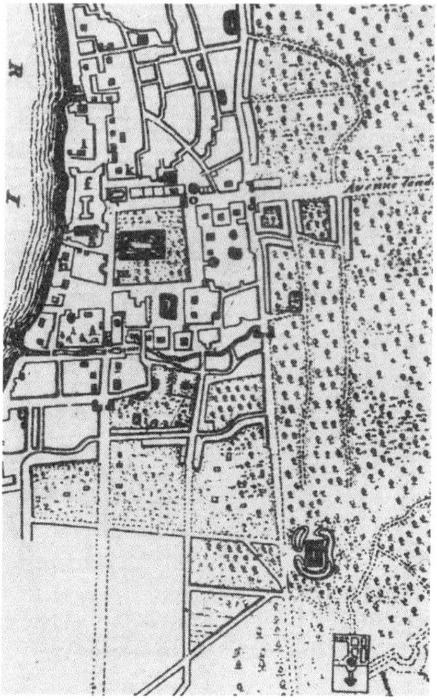

13 Detail of Orme's map showing the road (right) from the jail to Frankland's garden off today's Park Street. The garden is shown at the bottom right corner of the map

communication link in the native part of the settlement, which was probably in existence long before the English arrived on the scene. Wilson rules out the Bentinck Street-Chowringhee Road route to the Middleton Row area where the garden was located (a large part of this road is already covered by the Chowringhee chowkey-Gachhtala Bazar route discussed earlier).[17]

Although the repair estimate is rather too low for the length of the passage suggested, Wilson points to a road which is marked out 'in Orme's Map of Calcutta in 1756-57' but which he 'cannot trace so clearly in Upjohn's map'.[18] He describes the alignment of the road as running from the Harinbari Jail, north of Tiretta Bazar, 'along the line of the

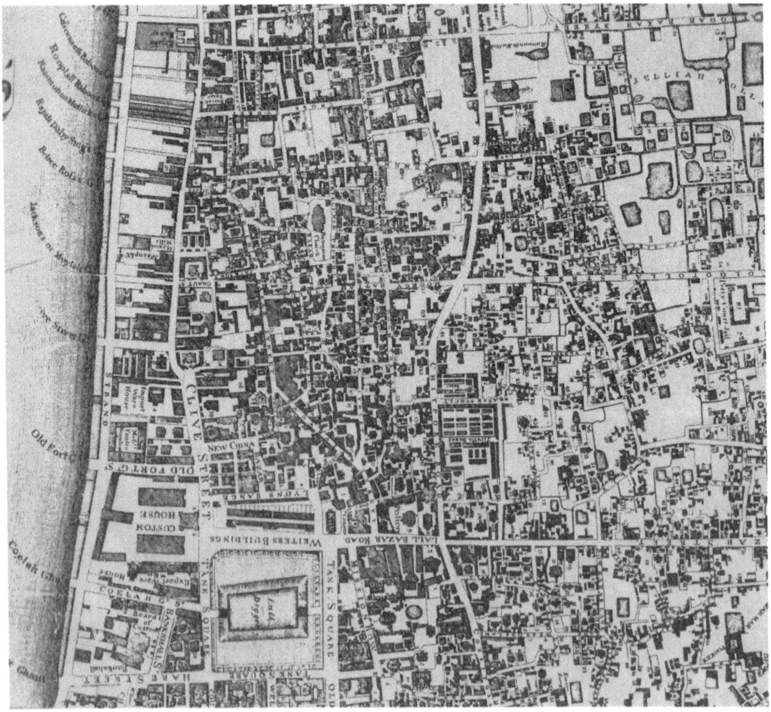

14 J.A. Schalch's map of 1824 showing the nineteenth century transformation of the ancient road from the centre of the town to Frankland's garden

present Kolootola Street, Phear's Lane, Bowbazar Lane, Khyroo's Lane, and straight on into Nilmoney Haldar's Lane[19] and Free School Street to Mr Frankland's garden at Middleton Row'. This road met that leading to the burying ground (modern Park Street) and possibly crossed it and continued into Middleton Row, towards Frankland's garden (today's Loreto Convent establishment), which is probably why the point is described as the 'crossroads' in course of a discussion on the protective ditch which Lt Col. Caroline Frederick Scott intended making around the settlement in 1755-1756.[20] Schalch's map of 1824 confirms that Orme's solitary road branching off eastwards from Chitpur Road (modern-day Rabindra Sarani) and then curving southwards is indeed the Chuman Gully (renamed Phear's Lane)[21] of later times. In Orme's map, this road intersects the 'Avenue Leading to the Eastward', or today's Bepin Behari Ganguly Road. South of this arterial east-west road Orme's road heads straight almost parallel to Chitpur Road (which is to its west) till it ends abruptly north-east of what is possibly the Jingeera tank between the Indian Museum and Kyd Street. It is possible that Orme simplified the alignment of the road which must have twisted and turned through fields and human habitation, as is suggested in Schalch's map of seventy-two years later.

The last (tenth) road indicated in the Consultation is that from Amirchand's house to Mirbahar Chowkey which, we can assume, was located at Mirbahar Ghat on the Hooghly, the repairs costing around Rs 150.[22] Wilson cites Wells' 1753 map (see image 6 on pp. 90-91)[23] to say that Amirchand's house was located in today's Lyons' Range,[24] and that the road mentioned was 'probably China Bazar and on to Mirbahr Ghat'. Orme's 1756 map (see image 13 on p. 137) clearly shows a road heading north from Lyons' Range and, after traversing some distance, turning west to meet the river. It needs to be ascertained whether the road shown in Orme's map goes anywhere near Mirbahar Ghat, because if it does the street in the Consultation could well be the one depicted in Orme's map.

There was a river 'waterside road' in the north in 1755, for we find the Bengal Council[25] stating that the zamindar had brought to its notice the poor condition of the passage 'from the Cotmahs Houses to Hautcola Gaut comprising a space of about 460 Yards which is now become impassable to any Carriage'. The Council ordered repairs and, importantly, asked the zamindar to find out the status of the ground near the road probably with the intention of taking over such ground in the future to widen the road. The entry is important because it is among the early ones to provide us with some idea about the road configuration by the riverside in the northern part of the town. Upjohn's map (see image 11 on p. 133) clearly shows that Clive Street, the road closest to the river, ran up north to the east-west road going to the Nabob's Ghat, there being another road beyond this point going north along the river right up to the Old Powder Mill Ghat. Hyde writes,[26]

> The Strand Road, as we now see it, did not exist in Bellamy's time; it has nearly all been reclaimed from the river. It was then, north of the Fort, a narrow roadway of very uneven line, bordered all along by the garden walls of bungalows and of a few upper-storied houses. Beyond the Fort it was broken by ship-building slips or small docks. There was a gated ghat at the foot of each of the principal streets.

Another old road is that which led south from the fort past the Governor's house, the hospital, the powder magazine till it came to the creek creeping eastward from the river to the salt lake. The Consultation of 1 May 1721[27] says that John Eyre, the then English zamindar or collector, 'brought in an account of the Charge of making a new Road and Bridges from the Factory towards Govinpoor; and of what Sums were collected from the Merchants etc toward the defraying that Charge.' Since the 'factory' at this time was located in the fort, the 'new road' here would denote today's Council House Street which, after 1756, came to be called the 'Road to the Monument', that is, the obelisk put up by Holwell to commemorate the spot where the bodies of those who died in the 'black hole' of Calcutta 'were promiscuously thrown into the ditch of the unfinished ravelin in front of the east gate' of the Fort.[28] The Consultation also makes it clear that the road was made with the help of funds provided by merchants although we are not told whether these were natives or Englishmen, or both. The road bore immediate results. On 31 January 1722[29] the Council was writing to the Court that revenues had increased over the past four months, one of the reasons for which was the completion of the 'new Road' and also 'draining the Grounds' which had led to wasteland being made inhabitable, attracting new inhabitants. In the same letter the Council wrote that it would take up the draining of Gobindapur because it would 'bring Inhabitants and make Calcutta healthyer'. What the Council probably meant by this was that people would shift to Gobindapur from Calcutta thus making it less crowded.[30]

As has already been pointed out, the 1742 map (see images 9 and 12 on p. 130 and p. 135) shows a number of roads criss-crossing the Maidan to the south of the settlement. Was one of these roads the early precursor of today's Kidderpur Road, that is, the road branching off westwards from Red Road towards Kidderpur? There is no clear indication of this but the Bengal Council Consultations relating to the early years of the eighteenth century do suggest that one of the roads in this area may have been made by John Surman, of Surman Embassy (1714-1717) fame, which however created a problem because it was made without the permission of the Council and the Court. Wilson writes[31] that Surman's garden was in Kidderpur 'beyond the Company's bounds, three miles and a half from the fort', which would place the garden on the other side of the Adi Ganga.[32] On 27 February 1727 the Court pointed out to the Bengal Council that Rs 3,668 had been spent on the road which Wilson, writing in the 1890s, says led to the garden 'over what is now Kidderpore bridge'. This is evidence that at least the rudiments of today's Kidderpur Road across the southern part of the Maidan were already there in 1727.

A point of interest is that the Court had pulled up Surman—who had died in August 1724—posthumously for having spent the Company's money on the road (it is not clear whether the money was spent to make the road or repair it because of 'damage by the heavy rains') without having informed London.[33] The Bengal Council had justified the expenditure, as also that on repairing the road to Perrin's garden, by arguing that it would benefit the town as well as the health of the inhabitants, which the Court promptly shot down by stating firmly that only Surman would have benefitted from the project and no one else ('to gratify his humour'). A point of principle was involved here, namely, the procedure adopted for expenditure on account of the Company, the Court's point being that the money on the road to Surman's garden had been spent without the Council ordering it. The Council had argued that the matter had in fact been discussed at a Consultation but that it had not been included in the proceedings. The Court issued a firm reprimand:

> We were surpriz'd to read in the Account you give in justification of Mr Surman, That our Money (For so we reckon all Fines to be) should be laid out by him without any Order of Council. We look on it as a fault that those Fines were not brought to Account of Revenues and accordingly paid into our Cash, to tell Us that it was laid out by Agreement of Council though no publick Entry made thereof is what we can never approve of, but do utterly dislike and forbid for the future.

This was a time when official procedure for a wide range of activity was being laid down, the Court decreeing,

> All Determinations at the Council board ought to be enter'd in Consultation, which should contain a true and full Account of all Transactions in our Affairs;, nd We expect they do so in all times coming, That We may judge of them, Whereas clandestine Proceedings

> are a plain indication they will not bear the light, It is not the first time We have complained of your Consultations not being so full with Relation to our Affairs as they ought to be, let it be so no more.

The Court added that had Surman been alive he would have had to return to the Company the money he had spent on the road to his garden.[34]

Notes

1 Wilson, *Old Fort William*, vol. 1, p. 111. The Bengal Council's letter to the Court of 18 January 1723 says that in March 1722 a 'high road' had been built between Calcutta and Gobindapur which led to 'the Low ground' between the two places being drained. This in turn had led to the ground becoming 'Tenantable' and the people had begun 'to build and enclose about it' (ibid., vol. 1, p. 113).

2 See later for Council House Street.

3 See later for Kidderpur Road.

4 Wilson, *Old Fort William*, vol. 1, pp. 112–113.

5 Ibid., pp. 222–224.

6 The process through which this part of the road network of the town was cleaned up had to wait till the early part of the nineteenth century.

7 Wilson (*Old Fort William*, vol. 1, p. 223) says that Lloyd's house was located 'near the Sixth Battery'. The 1742 map shows this battery to be located where the south-west gate of Raj Bhavan stands today. The location is confirmed by a French map dated 1742 (see image 7 on pp. 94-95) which names the battery as Batarie Cap Loid. Wilson himself (ibid., p. 159, fn. 2) gives the location of the sixth battery as the junction of Government Place with Esplanade Road West, at the corner of the Treasury Buildings.

8 Wilson (ibid., p. 180fn) says that the house was located 'at the junction of Bow Bazar with Circular Road'.

9 Ibid., p. 223, fn. 4.

10 See Section Two chapter 'The Dharamtala Bazar'.

11 This is a French map and the magazine is called *Magzin della Poudre*.

12 Wilson, *Old Fort William*, vol. 1, p. 159.

13 A map showing the environs of Fort William before 1756 (see image 5 on pp. 88-89) shows a house marked 'Mr Margas?' to the south of Chandpal

Ghat on what is today Esplanade Row West. Though there is some uncertainty about this house, it is closer to the powder house than is the 1742 location (in image 5 on pp. 88-89 the powder house is marked as 'magazine'). But it can be ruled out on the ground that, as far as the map shows, there is no street linking the two. A possible inference here is that Margass (or Margas) had two houses—one in the early 1740s and the other closer to 1756—the 1749 Consultation referring to the earlier house.

14 Wilson, *Old Fort William*, p. 223, fn. 6.

15 Ibid., pp. 116, 132–133. The 16 November 1724 Consultation in fact refers specifically to the 'Gunje at Govindpoor' which was under threat by the river. In December 1754 the Bengal Council was informing the Court that 'a part of the Market at Govindpoor' had been 'carried away by the encroachments of the River' (ibid., vol. 2, p. 20).

16 Ibid., vol. 1, p. 113.

17 Ibid., vol. 2, p. 160.

18 Ibid., vol. 1, p. 224, fn. 1.

19 At one point of time Nilmoni Haldar owned the Dharamtala Bazar. See chapter 'The Dharamtala Bazar'.

20 Consultations, 2 February 1756 (Wilson, *Old Fort William*, vol. 2, p. 40). Col. Scott died suddenly in 1754 with the result that his defensive projects were shelved (ibid., pp. 9, 42).

21 P.T. Nair, *A History of Calcutta's Streets* (Calcutta: Firma KLM, 1987), pp. 670–671.

22 'Mir Bahar' was the 'officer stationed at all important inland river ports' under Mughal rule. Though appointed by the emperor, he was 'subject to the command of the local Nawab or Viceroy' (Nair, *A History of Calcutta's Streets*, p. 584).

23 Wilson, *Old Fort William*, vol. 1, p. 224, fn. 2.

24 Commemorating Thomas Lyons to whom the Bengal Council 'leased in perpetuity' the ground on which Writers' Buildings stands today (Hyde, *The Parish of Bengal*, p. 23).

25 Consultation of 25 August 1755 (Wilson, *Old Fort William*, vol. 2, p. 27).

26 Hyde, *The Parish of Bengal*, p. 48.

27 Wilson, *Old Fort William*, vol. 1, p. 111.

28 Ibid., p. xxv.

29 Ibid., p. 112.

30 In a footnote (ibid.), Wilson draws attention to another abstract of the same letter which had stated cryptically, 'The Road on the South

side the Town finisht after some struggles with the Government'. The inference here is that there were problems with the nawab's people in the building of it.

31 Wilson, *Old Fort William*, vol. 1, pp. 120–121, note.

32 Tolly's Nullah of fifty years later.

33 Wilson, *Old Fort William*, vol. 1, p. 120.

34 In 1767 Surman's garden was sold by its then proprietor Edward Handle to the Company for Arcot Rs 10,000 (see Long, *Selections*, p. 634, Proceedings of 16 November). The Company bought the property because it felt that 'a spot so situated in regard to the fort and river should not fall into the hands of private persons'. A note by Reverend Long says that the gardens were located 'near the site of Cooley Bazar'. Wilson tells us that in March 1762 (*Old Fort William*, vol. 2, p. 167) the Surveyor had sent a report on the new rice *golahs* which were located 'nearest the new ffort'—following their shift from the spot where the new fort was coming up—stating that they were in bad shape and needed to be shifted yet again to a better site. The Council then said that Surman's garden 'and the ground adjacent' was a suitable spot, 'and the Garden being offer'd us by Mr Gray's Attorney for Arcot Rupees 3000', they agreed to buy it and remove to it the rice storage facilities. Possibly, the intention to buy was not implemented because if it was how could the Company have 'bought' Surman's garden once again in 1767?

8

An Infirm Hospital

Inevitably, another topographical fixture of the early years of the settlement was the hospital which, if Alexander Hamilton is to be believed, could not cope with either the rush of patients or the nature of the illnesses, or both. He wrote, 'The Company has a pretty good Hospital in Calcutta, where many go in to undergo the Penance of Physic, but few come out [to] give an account of its Operation.'[1] The genesis of the hospital set up in Calcutta lay in the pressing need to treat English soldiers who were arriving at the settlement, the Council resolving on 16 October 1707 that,

> Having an abundance of our soldiers and seamen yearly sick (this year more particularly our soldiers), and the doctors representing to us that for want of a hospital or convenient lodging for them, is mostly the occasion of their sickness, and such a place will be highly necessary as well for the garrison and sloops as the Company's Charter Party shipping to keep the men in health, it is therefore agreed that a convenient spot of ground near the Fort be pitched upon to build a hospital on, and that the cashiers pay out of the Company's cash for the said occasion towards perfecting it the sum of 2000 rupees, and what more may be gathered in by subscription from the Commanders of European and Country shipping and the inhabitants, which is to be forwarded and gathered in by Mr Ab. Adams, who is to look after the building of the same under the direction of the Council.[2]

With time the pressure on the doctors became so great that a second surgeon, William Hamilton, had to be appointed to the Company's service in addition to William James who was already serving as one.[3]

By early 1710 the hospital had turned partly into a barracks. The Consultation of 13 February[4] says,

> There being a great many English soldiers in garrison who, if they lodge about the town as usually, will create sickness and other inconveniences to themselves and others, therefore 'tis agreed the hospital be walled round and that barracks be made in it for the soldiers to lodge in, and that some of the officers do likewise lodge there, and see a good decorum kept amongst them.

Ordinarily, the soldiers should have been barracked in the fort itself but the entry suggests that there was no room for them there.[5] Within two decades the hospital had been reduced to an unsatisfactory condition, a 1730 survey done by Thomas Snow and John Oliffre reporting that 'all the Beams and most of the Window and Door frames [had turned] Rotten', so much so that there was a clear danger of the roof collapsing 'in next rains unless timely prevented by shoring all the Beams'.[6] At this point the hospital was a lower-roomed house, the need for 'a Couple of Upper Rooms' arising when it was felt that 'one of the Doctors (should) reside at the Hospital'. Along with this addition, a medicine shop was also built 'at one of the Ends of the Hospitall'.[7] By 1754 the condition of the hospital had once more deteriorated and a request was made to repair it. The report on the state of the building, prepared by the bakshi, Paul Richard Pearkes, reveals that the building had arches and had been struck by lightning, the south-west and western parts of the building being in such a bad condition that 'the Beams and the Burgers (had) gone', and that if new buttresses were not built that part of the house would collapse. The west wall had 'bellied out two feet' there being an urgent need to 'buttress them Immediately to keep the Wall standing'. The north-end of the hospital—this implies that the building had a north-south alignment—had 'cracked' in a number of places and needed reinforcing. The report concluded with the suggestion that the building needed to be 'speedily white-wash'd and Plaistered, as being entirely a *Cutch* building' and that should 'the Rains get into the Walls it will carry all the mud from between the Bricks and in Danger of the whole'.[8] The hospital must have been severely damaged in the fighting which took place in 1756. Consequently, it must have become an acute problem for the town authorities to look after the sick after Calcutta was retaken in January 1757.[9]

The quest to expand medical facilities was on, a result of which was the acquiring of George Gray's house for Current Rs 15,000 'for the reception of the sick'.[10] But even after this acquisition it would appear from the Consultations that hospital space was getting acutely scarce in the town. On 11 October 1762 the Council was noting that in view of 'the great Inconveniency for Want of Room in our Hospital and from not having the Benefit of a free and open Air, Agreed till such Time as the Hospitals can be built in the New Fort, that we build one near to Surman's with Fell Trees and cover'd with Straw'.[11] Meanwhile, the state of the old hospital building continued to worsen. On 3 March 1766 the Bengal Council read the civil architect John Fortnom's letter in which the precarious state of the building 'adjoining to the Head Surgeon's house' was recounted, the suggestion being made that it was in such 'ruinous a situation that it appears necessary to take it down to prevent its doing mischief'.[12] In September the same year the Council said that the only hospital functioning at the time was located in a temporary building in the old fort 'destitute of the needful accommodations'.[13] A decision was taken to build 'a commodious one', the civil architect being asked to draw up plans and find a suitable site for it as well as a new burial ground, the old one (in today's St John's churchyard which has Charnock's mausoleum in it) having been filled up. In his letter to the Council, Fortnom also said that the house 'lately occupied' by Gray 'is so much out of repair, that it will be necessary to rebuild the whole Virando and great part of the house', which implies that Gray's house bought in 1759 had not been used till then as a hospital. On 31 March 1766, the Council decided to sell 'the Company's Old Hospital, the small house for the Assistant Surgeon and the House lately occupied by Mr Gray'.[14] Six months later, in September, arrangements were made to provide accommodation for 'the Use of Surgeons' in rooms at the eastern end of the 'long row' in the old fort.[15]

Fortnom's first choice of a spot for a new burial ground was one 'lying near the river between the parallel lines now formed by Hastings Street and Hare Street'. This proposal, as we know from hindsight, was not implemented the burying ground being ultimately shifted to the eastern end of today's Park Street, at the time giving that road the appellation Burying Ground Road. As regards a new hospital, Fortnom did not think one could be set up 'on this side of the river', his choice finally being one of two places 'on the opposite side of the river ... one opposite Surman's Gardens, and the other opposite the Town, but recommending the former as the most eligible spot'. The Council accepted the suggestion and asked for estimates. Later, however, the project fell through. No reason was cited for this although it stands to reason that the logistical problems of ferrying the sick to the proposed hospital and its high cost estimate of five lakh rupees may have played a major role in the rejection.[16]

Linking the story of the old (first) hospital of the settlement to the subsequent Presidency General Hospital (today's SSKM Hospital), in April 1768 the Court was informed that John Zachariah Kiernander—who later set up the Mission Church on Mission Row—was the owner of a 'large strong new built garden house' which was bought from him 'and altered to form the Central block of the General Hospital, of which it constituted the oldest portion'. The note added that Kiernander 'speculated largely in building operations and it is certain that he was the contractor for and builder of the eastern and western blocks of the hospital'.[17]

Among other things, what this indicates is that as early as 1768, that is, just a decade after the sack of Calcutta and its retaking by the English, people were venturing out to the southern extremity of the settlement to build garden houses. This apart, since no buildings could be built on the esplanade of the new fort, the fact

15 The general hospital and the surgeon's house in 1800, by James Moffat

that Kiernander could build his garden house on this spot suggests that it fell outside the area covered by the esplanade.[18]

What is of special interest to the student of Calcutta's early topographical evolution is that there was hardly any comprehensive planning involved in the process. If blueprints were drawn up developments on the ground suggest that they were not implemented, perhaps because the time was not yet ripe for such an integrated effort. In January 1706, that is, within sixteen years of Charnock's arrival, we find the Court writing[19] that it was informed that the Council was busy building 'a new Calcutta' and 'making it more regular', which in the normal course of things was just the thing to be expected. After all, the English had become the new zamindars of the place and they could not but usher in improvements in their new domain especially in view of the fact that large parts of the acquisition had grown over the years without any centralised direction whatever and, perhaps more importantly, according to the mores of a culture which had little in common with that from which the new zamindar was extracted. There is, however, little indication in the official records that the Bengal Council was going about its work according to a well-thought-out plan of action.

An associated point of interest is whether the Court of Directors viewed the grant of the zamindary by the nawab as being equivalent to being given a 'kingdom' in the normal sense of the term? This perhaps partly explains the Company's keenness on having a strong fort at Sutanati, particularly after the transfer of the zamindary rights to the three villages. Certainly, the Court could not be unaware of the difference between a zamindary and absolute ownership of land, which would be tantamount to acquiring sovereignty. Yet, the tone of its letters to Bengal at the turn of the seventeenth century, in the first flush of acquiring of the zamindary rights, suggests that the Court treated the transfer as a shift in its basic status vis-a-vis the effective reigning powers in the eastern part of the subcontinent. While discussing revenue matters in its 20 December 1699 letter to the Bengal Council,[20] it focused on the issue of 'protection' for the people living within the Company's zamindary bounds, proclaiming that 'Protection [was] the true foundation on which all Pretences for raising Customs Subsidies and other Taxes are originally built, ffor this it is Tenants swear ffealty to their Lords, and All Subjects owe Allegiance to their Princes ...' A month earlier, on 21 November,[21] the Court had revealed even more clearly its own perception of its position in Bengal vis-a-vis the nawab when it asked its people at Sutanati to get on with strengthening the fortifications there 'without fear of giving Umbrage to the Moors, because they cant pretend to make an inquisition in a Place where they have nothing to do withal'. A year later, on 29 November 1700, the words 'Our ffortifications and Dominion in Bengall' are used by the Directors, which provides us with a clue to the mindset of the Court in distant London about the way events were unfolding in Bengal.[22]

It is perhaps to be expected that, at this very early stage, the Court's guidance to the Bengal Council on town development was geared first and last to the requirements of defence. On 18 January 1706 it asked the local authorities

> ... to order the Streets so as that the ffort Guns may be brought to bear on the Severall Streets to beat out an Enemy that should gett into them and that the Houses may be at such a Distance from the ffort as not to prejudice any part of it in Case by accident or design they should be sett on fire.[23]

Citing the example of the church, Wilson points out that this bit of advice was not acted on by the Council although it told the Court at the end of the year (1706)[24] that the streets had been made 'regular [so] that the Guns can bear on those near the ffort and the ffort Secured if the Town should be fired'. The Court had its informants in Calcutta and in April 1708 it wrote[25] that even though it had come to know that there were some English houses disrupting the fort's field of fire, it was not keen on having them demolished for the time being although in future they would have to be taken down if there was 'an inevitable necessity for it'. This suicidally expansive attitude as far as the fort's defence requirements were concerned became a fixture with the Court for, even as late as 1748, it was writing to Bengal that one of the reasons why the rules and guidelines for setting up fortifications in 'Our several settlements' could not be applied to Calcutta was 'the many Expensive Buildings which must be demolish'd to make Room for a regular Fortification and Esplanade of a proper Extent round it'.[26]

Most of these houses were owned by Europeans. Had they been owned by natives it is almost certain that they would have been demolished, the matter perhaps not going up to the Court at all. Writing from Falta on 13 July 1756, where the Bengal Council under Governor Drake had sought refuge after fleeing from Calcutta, Captain Alexander Grant, Adjutant-General, wrote,

> It may be justly asked why we did not propose, the only method that as I thought then, and now do, could give us the least chance of defending the place, in case of a vigorous attack, the demolition of all the houses adjacent to the Fort and surrounding it with a ditch and a glacee; But so little credit was then given, and even to the very last day, that the Nabob would venture to attack us, or offer to force our lines, that it occasioned a generall grumbling and discontent to leave any of the European houses without them. Nay, the generallity wanted even to include every brick house in the place, Portuguese and Armenian, and thought it hard that any inhabitant should be deprived of protection against such an enemy.

This apart, the time factor was also important. Grant wrote that even if a decision was taken to demolish the houses, there was not enough time to do so; 'nor would it be possible to destroy half the number in triple the time, especially as we had not powder sufficient to blow them up'.[27]

This then was the setting of the town on the eve of Shiraj-ud-Daula's assault on Fort William. In the words of Robert Orme written in October 1756:[28]

> The river Ganges forms a Crescent between two points, the one called Perring's Garden, the other Surman's Garden. The distance between these, measuring along the bank of the river, is about three miles and a half. In the deepest part of this crescent about the middle between the

two points is situated Fort William, a building which many an old house in the country exceeds in its defences. It is situated a few paces from the river side, on the bank of which runs a line of guns, the whole length of the fort from North to South, and this the only formidable part, as it is capable of annoying ships in the river. The ends of this line are joined to the two bastions of the fort nearest the river by a garden wall and a gate in each, which would resist one shot of a six pounder, but which would be forced by the second. Opposite to the two bastions mentioned are two others inland to the eastward, but within thirty yards to the North and forty yards to the South, the bastions are commanded by large houses. To the Eastward inland the top of the Church commands the whole of both the Northern and Eastern ramparts. Northward and Southward for the length of a mile and to the Eastward about a quarter of a mile, stand all the English houses, mostly separated from each other by large inclosures. Where the English habitations end to the Norward commence those of the principal black Merchants, which reach quite up to Perring's garden. To the southward down to Surman's garden the houses belonging to a lower class of the natives are conspicuous. Twelve years ago a ditch had been dug, beginning at Perring's and carried inland of the town in a crescent with an intent to end at Surman's, but only four miles of it are finished. At Perring's there was a drawbridge over this ditch and notwithstanding the southern part of the town lay open ...[29]

Notes

1 Alexander Hamilton, *A New Account of the East Indies*, vol. 2, p. 9.

2 Wilson, *Early Annals*, vol. 1, pp. 289–290. Abraham Adams was a member of the Council and bakshi. The patients, it appears, had to foot a part of the hospital charges, the Consultation of 6 December 1716 stating that the 'Dyet of Sick men, Candles and Oil' were to be paid by the patient to the steward, the charges not exceeding 'four anaes [annas] a day for each man' (ibid., vol. 2, p. 257).

3 Consultation of 27 December 1711 (ibid., p. 36). The entry of 20 August 1713 gives the regulations for the hospital as drawn up by the two doctors, William Hamilton and Richard Harvey (ibid., pp. 137–138).

4 Ibid., vol. 1, p. 327.

5 By March 1712 there were 140 'stout Europeans' as soldiers in the settlement (ibid., vol. 2, p. 44). The Consultations of 23 and 26 January 1710 state that a ship from England had brought thirty additional soldiers for Calcutta and a gunner to the fort (ibid., vol. 1, p. 326). The entry for 14 April 1709 (ibid., p. 314), says that a ship had brought out from England nine private soldiers sent by the Directors, these having survived the journey, the original complement being thirty. In November 1711, the ship *Derby* arrived from England carrying twenty-nine soldiers 'seventeen of them having died on board, and seven having deserted when the ship "put back to Remast"' (ibid., vol. 2, p. 34). By December 1713 the number of European soldiers in the settlement had increased to 242, excluding officers and others such as drummers, ensigns, rounders, etc., (ibid., pp. 149-150.) At times (1714) the problem of too many soldiers emerged which necessitated the dismissal of a part of the European, non-English soldiery (ibid., pp. 193, 197). On 26 September 1717 the Council decided to keep a standing garrison of 220 men because there was a frequent need 'to send small Parties to Convoy the Company's Goods from severall Places because Jaffer Caun Sooba [Murshid Quli Khan] of Bengall encourages the interrupting our Affaires and Stopping Our Goods' (ibid., p. 281).

6 Wilson, *Old Fort William,* vol. 1, p. 133.

7 The shop finally appears to have found a place on the upper floor along with the quarters for the doctor (Bengal Council to Court, 28 December 1735: ibid., p. 143).

8 Ibid., vol. 2, p. 10.

9 On 26 January 1762 the Surveyor reported that unless extensive repairs were undertaken he expected the hospital to collapse in the course of the year (ibid., p. 166).

10 Consultation of 6 September 1759 (ibid., p. 149). The house of Gray, surgeon to the Company, was not in good shape either and was in need of repairs before it could be put to use (ibid., p. 176).

The 'Current' rupee was the unit of currency minted by the English Government 'in which the Company's accounts were kept', 116 units being equivalent to 100 sicca rupees (Henry Yule and A.C. Burnell, *Hobson-Jobson* [Calcutta edition: Rupa, 1986], pp. 774–776).

11 Wilson, *Old Fort William,* vol. 2, p. 168. Long's *Selections* (pp. 377–378) refers to this place as 'Sumner's' and not 'Surman's' which

is clearly a misprint, its location being given in a note as being 'near Kidderpore'. Wilson doubts whether this hospital was ever set up because of a 1766 reference which states that the settlement's hospital was located in the old fort (see later).

12 Wilson, *Old Fort William,* vol. 2, p. 176.

13 Consultation of 29 September 1766 (ibid., pp. 180–181).

14 Wilson, *Old Fort William,* p. 177.

15 Ibid., p. 180. The old hospital remained on the Company's books till the beginning of 1769. On 2 February of that year the Council was writing to the Court that it was 'almost entirely destroy'd by a violent Storm, the remains of it [being] sold only for Current Rupees 414' (ibid., p. 182).

16 'Notes on the Origin of the old Presidency General Hospital, Calcutta', by D.M. Noir, *Bengal Past and Present*, vol. 6, July-September 1910, pp. 9–10 .

17 The Editor's Notebook, *Bengal Past and Present,* vol. 26, Part 1, July-September 1923, p. 108. See also *Bengal Past and Present*, vol. 6, July-September 1910, pp. 1–20.

18 See Section 2 for a controversy on the limits of the esplanade.

19 Wilson, *Old Fort William,* vol. 1, p. 61.

20 Ibid., p. 47.

21 Ibid., p. 44.

22 Ibid. p. 48.

23 Ibid., p. 61.

24 Ibid., p. 63.

25 Ibid., p. 73.

26 Ibid., p. 205.

27 Ibid., vol. 2, pp. 51–52.

28 Ibid. p. 74.

29 Some more detail about the eastern part of Calcutta is provided by Captain Robert Barker who was drawing up plans to build a new fort following the retaking of Calcutta. He wrote to the Bengal Council on 2 May 1757 (ibid., pp. 113–114) that he had examined the ground '... to the eastward of the present Fort, and am of opinion that, with a very little expense, a proper spot of ground might be cleared about 600 yards directly east of it sufficient for a Fort and Esplanade round it of seven or eight hundred yards, by pulling down six or seven of the principal or upper-roomed houses, as all the rest from the east of Lady Russell's House [located on today's Mission

Row directly to the east of Tank Square] to the Bread and Cheese Bungalow [at the eastern end of the Avenue to the Eastward] are houses of no consequence and black people's huts, and to the north and south huts with a few lower-roomed houses.'

SECTION TWO

The Town Spreads Itself

9

Esplanade Row takes Shape

Prior to June 1756, the town was nothing more than a haphazard collection of houses, the roads of the time—barring a couple of exceptions—emerging more out of the opportunities presented by the given position of houses rather than the other way round. The destruction of a large part of the English settlement, particularly around the fort, in course of the fighting of 1756 should therefore have presented the authorities with an opportunity to clean up the mess and to reconstruct that part of the town according to a well-thought-out plan keeping future expansion in mind. There is, however, little evidence to show that this was in fact the case even though the need for reform was pressing. On 3 March 1758, the Court had asked the Bengal Council to

> Encourage all Useful People to reside among you, and be not lavish of the Ground in Building and Gardening, allow only what may be convenient; and if such a Reform is judged right in the Town of Calcutta and a new Measurement necessary, make the Regulations immediately, for former Allowances, Encroachments or Indulgences must be no Rule now.[1]

Trawling through the published records of the time, one finds that the closest the Council came to laying down any *principle* of town planning was the public notice issued in early November 1759 which stated that all buildings 'that obstruct the streets or public roads' were to be pulled down.[2] It was during this period that an important alteration in a critical military facility provided by the town was made, namely, the establishment of docking facilities for His Majesty's ships 'at Surman's Gardens or thereabouts'. The reason given for not selecting a spot higher up the river was that the channel was shallow in the upper reaches 'and would for that reason endanger the loss or damage of the ships going up or coming down'.[3] The fort itself, or the part of it which was left standing after the fighting, was made into barracks owing to the French 'scare', this being among the very few occasions when it was cleared of export and import warehouses to make room for the troops.[4]

This was the time when plans for a new fort were being drawn up and new functions devised for the remains of the old one. Already, a part of the old fort had been set aside for use by the town as a makeshift chapel. Warehouses had disfigured its defence capability to such an extent that, apart from diehard optimists, no defence strategist had ever set great store by the fort as providing effective security for the town. On the riverside, the first major work taken up after the return of the English followed the decision to strengthen the Customs set-up, the Committee of Inspection proposing in April 1766 that the old fort complex be transformed 'into a Custom House'.[5] Subsequently, a couple of cranes was added to the old pier suitably repaired and strengthened, and gateways from the northwest and southwest bastions were proposed to be built 'to prevent Goods from being Clandestinely taken away before they have been passed by the Custom Master'. A 'Substantial Shed [was also proposed] to be run up the whole Length of the Curtain with Brick Pillars and a Slight Terras covering for the conveniency of securing the Goods in case of Rain.'[6] This proposed construction, the estimated cost of which was Rs 13,000, probably marked the first major alteration in the view of the town from the river since the completion of the old fort in the early years of the eighteenth century, a change which also enabled the Customs people to entrench themselves at a spot from where they have never been dislodged.

As the years rolled by, the southern maidan frontage of the town was also gradually taking shape. On 15 October 1764 the decision was taken to build a new Council House which was located to the west of the building known as Buckingham House,[7] both buildings being located within the compound of present-day Raj Bhavan. The location of the new Council House was selected keeping in mind the fact that the old one housed in Richard Court's premises was not merely 'exposed to the heat of the weather' but was also too close to the public offices, which was 'very ill-calculated for conducting the business of the Board with that privacy which is often requisite'.[8] The Council was in a hurry, for just ten days after the decision was taken to build a new Council House it decided to get on with the project 'as expeditiously as possible' according to the plan submitted by John Fortnom, the civil architect. However, when news about this reached London the response was not favourable. In its 24 December 1765 letter to the Bengal Council, which reached Calcutta some time in the middle of 1766, the Court shot down the proposal making the point that it thought it 'very singular' that the old Council House should be objected to for being 'contiguous to the publick offices', the Court holding that 'it should be in the Centre of the Offices that recourse may be had to the Papers more readily'.[9] The Court also felt that making a new Council House at the time would be tantamount to wasting resources 'as the New Buildings in the Fort, where all the Company's business is to be carried on, must soon be built'. Generally speaking, the Court was averse to the idea of the Council spending money to buy premises for the public purpose. In its letter the Court admonished the Council for doing so and specifically instructed it to 'buy no more houses for the Company as we suppose the Buildings in the New Fort will soon be ready'. Since the new Council House did finally come up on the spot selected for it by the Council, it would appear that by the time the

Court's letter reached Calcutta the building work had progressed too far for it to have been terminated.

This is reminiscent of the later case of Lord Wellesley's Government House, the only difference being that while Wellesley deliberately kept the news of the construction of his 'palace' away from London for as long as he could, so that it would become a *fait accompli* for the Court when it did come to know of the erection of the building, there was no such premeditation on the part of Vansittart's Council regarding the new Council House.[10]

Going back further in time, to the very early years of the eighteenth century, it appears from the records that, unwittingly or otherwise, the Court was also kept in the dark about the purpose of building the Governor's house within the old fort. In November 1705, the Bengal Council wrote to the Court informing it that it intended to 'build Chambers over the New House'.[11] While the entry gives us a precise idea of the status of construction of the Governor's house within the fort at this time, there is another piece of communication dated 18 January 1706[12] which tells us that the Court was not aware of the specific purpose of the new building being built within the fort, which is not a little surprising since it was no less than the chief of the settlement who was to live in it. However, unlike in Wellesley's case nearly a century later, the Bengal Council does not appear to have committed the official sacrilege of deliberately keeping its employers in the dark about the project before it was begun, but there was certainly no information about what was going on in Calcutta with regard to the project. This we know from the Court's letter of 28 December 1711[13] in which the fact was regretted that while the Directors had received the plan of the house there was 'no notice in the Generall Letter about it nor any account of its dimensions or figures of Reference to explain the Rooms or uses of it or give us any light therein …' On 19 December 1709 the Council had written to the Court that the 'new house in the Fort [was] finished' and that a 'new gateway' would be made to the west facing the river 'to face the New House and then shall have done with building'.[14]

Before Richard Court's house, the Council Chamber was located in the fort which was destroyed in course of the 'troubles' of 1756. As we have seen, in June 1758 the authorities in Calcutta felt the need for a separate Council Chamber, there being little indication of where they met during the previous two years since the recapture of the town. The Consultations[15] in fact contain a clue to another house, apart from that of Richard Court, which was used for the purpose of a 'Council Room and the Publick Offices', one which was initially bought for the nawab's use whenever he was in Calcutta. On 12 March 1764 the Court of Directors had frowned upon the Council buying the house offered by Warren Hastings for Arcot Rs 16,000, describing the purchase (on 24 December 1765) as 'an extraordinary Expence'. On 30 March 1767 the Bengal Council

16 Warren Hastings by Joshua Reynolds

explained that the need to buy 'another house for the Nabob' had arisen because *the one bought previously* 'had been appropriated to the use of Council room and the Publick Offices, *and the same is still occupied for that purpose*' (emphasis added).

Where was this second house used as a council room located? Was it somewhere to the north of today's Raj Bhavan? The house referred to as 'the old Council House' in a memorial to the Calcutta Committee of Revenue[16] was located to the east of the present-day Council House Street and south of the house marked as Captain Witherington's in image 5 on pp. 88-89. It is not known for certain when Buckingham House, the 'Government House' of the day, came up but there is a legal document extant which describes the edifice—which belonged to Warren Hastings at one point of time—as the 'new' house in 1765.[17] With these two buildings coming up on what came to be called Esplanade Row—extending from

17 A view of Esplanade Row showing the Council House, by Thomas Daniell, 1788

18 Another view of Esplanade Row, by W. Baillie, 1794

the river in the west to the Chowringhee-Dharamtala crossing in the east—it took but little time for the entire northern side of the row to be filled up, which means that the road was transformed into a construction site during the next few years.[18]

In March 1766, John Fortnom was writing about the 'Old Esplanade' stating that he had advanced 'near 5,000 Rupees' to build a railing 'round' it.[19] We know that at this point of time the new fort was coming up in the Gobindapur area, the esplanade of which was being formed by clearing away human habitation and vegetation. In other words, the maidan of today was taking shape. But what precisely is the 'old esplanade' that Fortnom is referring to? If he called it the 'old' esplanade, he must have done so to distinguish it from the 'new esplanade' appended to the new fort which was coming up at the time. Did the old esplanade then relate to the old fort? But did the old fort have an esplanade at all, even a truncated one? It did not and the need to build one arose only after the retaking of Calcutta

19 A. Bourne and Shepherd photograph of Esplanade Row taken in 1885, which shows its alignment as it must have been before Raj Bhavan was built in 1803

which led to the demolition of some houses to the east, north and south of the fort. Was the civil architect then referring to the open space created by the post-1756 demolition? If so, what was its extent? On the southern side, did it extend beyond the creek (roughly the old Hastings Street) to what became Esplanade Row in later years, which ran from the river eastward from Chandpal Ghat right up to today's Dharamtala-Chowringhee crossing, cutting across the grounds of Raj Bhavan to the south of the building? If Fortnom was referring to this area, he probably meant the setting up of a railing along this road, possibly to the south of it, marking the extent of the 'old esplanade'. Did this railing project extend to the northern and eastern parts of the old fort's post-1756 'esplanade' as well? The language used by Fortnom in his letter suggests that the railing in question would, when completed, run 'round' the old esplanade, the inference (as indicated by the substantial cost estimate) being that all three land-sides of the old fort would be included in the project. But no evidence has yet been unearthed regarding a railing to the north and the east of the old fort, which may in fact have never been taken up let alone completed. Old paintings—that by William Baillie of Esplanade Row (1794), for instance image 18 on p. 167—do indicate a railing on the southern side of the road but it cannot be stated with any degree of finality that this was indeed a part of the Fortnom railing project.

In the early days, the houses along Esplanade Row did not have the facade which one sees in later paintings. In particular, they did not have a fenced-in compound, the drainage ditch running along the road to the south being their natural boundary with the thoroughfare, the ground between the houses and the road being public property. An early suggestion by a resident to enclose a part of this adjacent ground and make it a part of his compound was that made by John White[20] who wrote to the Board of Revenue in February 1788:

> There is a small piece of ground situated immediately to the southward of my house which, in its present state, is a receptacle for vermin and filth of all kinds and in fact a nuisance. To obviate this inconvenience I request your permission either to purchase this ground, which is entirely distinct from the public road (being bounded by the great drain leading to Champaul Gaut (Gaut)); or if you are apprehensive of my impropriety in disposing of the ground so situated that you will allow me to enclose it, reserving to yourselves the power of reassuming it whenever the public service should require it.[21]

The Board sent the letter to the Acting Collector of Calcutta, J.H. Harrington, asking him whether there were any objections to White's proposal. Harrington said there could only be one objection, namely, that it would prevent 'a future enlargement of the publick road' in front of White's house, that is, Esplanade Row West of today. He referred the issue to the surveyor, Edward Tiretta, who felt there was no problem at all with White's plan: in particular, it would pose 'no kind of encroachment on the publick road or drain'. He added that White's plan to enclose the ground could 'never be of any detriment to the publick', even if the road was to be widened to the front of the houses, 'of which … I see no probability'. The surveyor also said that 'if the whole of the land [up] to the Council House Street were enclosed, it would be the means of removing many nuisances'. He added that if his proposal was accepted the ground in front of each house could be measured and disposed of by the Government 'at the ascertained value of the ground in similar situations which, if required, may be determined by arbitration'.[22]

Tiretta's report was sent to the Commissioners of Police who wrote back on 5 March 1788[23] that they had

> … no objection to the ground in question extending from Champaul Ghaut to the Cossitallah[24] being granted to the different proprietors but that, for the ornament and advantage of that part of the town, they recommend the several proprietors should in lieu of paying for the same in money be obliged to construct a proper pucka drain under the direction of the surveyor with a regular railing extending the whole length; that if this proposal meets the approbation of the Board of Revenue, the Commissioners will furnish them with a regular plan made by their surveyor of such intended railing, the conformity to which shall be the condition of the different proprietors obtaining a grant of such ground.

The Board of Revenue's response[25] shows that, at that point of time, it was not yet ready to accept proposals for a general sprucing up of the area even if the expense was to be borne by the community. It resolved that there was no need to adopt the 'general proposition' made by the surveyor and the police especially in view of the fact that no applications had been made to them 'by the proprietors of the several houses' apart from White. The upshot was that only the spot of ground fronting White's house was measured, the latter being given a patta for the ground 'at a value to be fixed by an equitable arbitration, and subject to the usual ground rent and chokedarry tax'.

But of course it was only a matter of time before the other residents of the area moved to occupy the ground in front of their houses. Thus, within two years the attorney, William Hickey, applied for the same privilege given to White, writing on 7 January 1790 to the then Collector of Calcutta, James Edward Colebrooke:

> Having taken the lease of a house lately built upon the Esplanade, belonging to Mr James Robertson, and he as well as myself being very desirous of obtaining the Hon'ble Company's permission to enclose a piece of ground between the present gateway and the ditch, in like manner as Mr White has done, I take the liberty of requesting you, as Collector of Calcutta, to lay such, my application, before the Board of Revenue, and as far as is consistent with the duties of your office to give your assistance in carrying it into effect.[26]

Citing the White case, the collector advised the Board of Revenue that it ought to have no objection to Hickey's proposal 'on the same terms' agreed to by White. On its part, the Board recommended to the Governor-General in Council that Hickey be allowed to go ahead with his proposal provided he followed the conditions laid down by the police, who were again asked for their views on this specific case.[27] Looking ahead, the Supreme Council agreed with the Board giving it the power 'to comply with all similar applications that may be made to you without any reference to us' thus laying down a general policy affecting the future development of the area.[28]

Notes

1 Wilson, *Old Fort William*, vol. 2, p. 140. In the normal course, demolition of houses near the fort for the purpose of defending it better would have been a sensible option for the Council to adopt. But this was not to be so in view of the strong opposition to the idea at

all levels, local as well as from the Court in London. However, what could not be attained before the nawab's assault in 1756 because of, among other things, the cost factor was accomplished following the retaking of the fort after six months. To cite examples, the houses of Edward Holden Cruttenden and Amirchand were demolished the Company paying compensation to both (ibid., vol. 2, pp. 129–130, 136). The reason behind the demolition—improving the defences of the old fort—was, however, shortlived because the old citadel was soon to be abandoned for a new fort at Gobindapur.

2 Wilson, *Old Fort William*, vol. 2, p. 153. The problem must have been deep-rooted because twenty-two years later, on 20 February 1781, we find the Governor-General in Council writing to the Committee of Revenue: 'Understanding from the Commissioners of Police for the Town of Calcutta that many of the Pottahs granted for Lands under the Denomination of [not decipherable] encroach upon the Public Streets and Roads, We have given directions to Mr [Edward] Tiretta to survey the same before the (said) Pottahs are in future granted by the Collector' (Committee of Revenue Proceedings, 22 February 1781).

3 Wilson, *Old Fort William*, vol. 2, pp. 141–142. Of some interest is the fact that around this time (June 1759) a proposal was made to build a dock facility in the Laldighi (the 'great tank') itself, a channel being dug 'between the Fort and the Master Attendant's House' from the river to facilitate the project (ibid., p. 148).

4 The Consultation of 3 July 1758 (ibid., pp. 143–144) says that the imperative of troops being quartered at one place was emphasised all the more by the need to increase the defence preparedness of the English settlement just in case the French chose to come to Bengal. In actual fact, they were scattered all over the place, 'dispersd att different houses', which underscored the 'impossibility of preventing their committing great disorders and destroying themselves with spirituous liquors'. It was, therefore, decided to clear the fort of the export and import warehouses to make room for barracks, the people responsible for the warehouses being asked to locate space in the settlement 'as they esteem most convenient and proper for carrying on the Business of their respective Offices and for keeping the Honourable Company's Cloths and Imports in'.

5 Writing to the Bengal Council on 16 March 1768 (ibid., p. 182), the Court rationalised the location of the Customs set-up in the old fort

by pointing out that the latter was 'in the centre of the Town and more convenient to the Merchants to land their Goods'. When he was in Calcutta in the first decade of the nineteenth century, Lord Valentia had written about the Customs establishment being located in the old fort, 'new buildings' being set up at the site in 1819 (ibid., pp. 184–189).

6 Consultation of 5 May 1766 (ibid., pp. 178-179, 180).

7 On Buckingham House, see Ray Choudhury, *The Lord Sahib's House.*

8 Wilson, *Old Fort William,* vol. 2, p. 173. In June 1758, Richard Court's house was bought by the Council to hold its meetings 'contiguous to the Secretarys and Accomptants Offices' (ibid., p. 143). There appears to be no agreement on where this house was located but we have a clue in the Consultation of 2 June 1766 (ibid., p. 180) which states that the 'Old Council House' was to be appropriated for the office of the military paymaster general *'where the office of his Employ is always to be kept in future'* (emphasis added). Basing ourselves on the fact that the military accounts operations were not shifted out of the area in the nineteenth and twentieth centuries, the point can be made that the military accounts offices on Babu Tarapada Mukherjee Sarani (formerly Koila Ghat Street) in Dalhousie Square, south-west of the GPO, probably occupied the spot where the early military paymaster general's office was located in the 1760s, the inference being that it was here that Richard Court's house—the old Council House—was located. See Ray Choudhury, *The Lord Sahib's House,* Chapter 4 for a fuller discussion on the subject. By 1762 the state of Court's house had deteriorated to such an extent that the 'north side' of the house had to be 'rebuilt ... as it appears absolutely necessary' (Wilson, *Old Fort William,* vol. 2, p. 167).

9 Ibid., p. 175. In the nineteenth century this specific issue became an important point with the authorities who wanted all government offices to be near to each other so as to facilitate official work and also reduce expenses.

10 Vansittart handed over charge to John Spencer in early December 1764 (F.C. Danvers, *Bengal, its Chiefs, Agents, and Governors*, 1888, p. 19). See Ray Choudhury, *The Lord Sahib's House*, for the Wellesley Government House case.

11 Wilson, *Old Fort William,* vol. 1, p. 60.

12 Ibid., p. 62.

13 Ibid., p. 85.

14 Ibid., p. 78.

15 Ibid., pp. 172, 175, 182.
16 Calcutta Committee of Revenue Proceedings, 29 August 1775.
17 See Ray Choudhury, *The Lord Sahib's House,* Chapter 4.
18 In 1784 William Hickey described the area as 'the best and most airy situation in Calcutta' (*Memoirs of William Hickey,* ed. Alfred Spencer, London, no date, vol. 3, p. 236).
19 Wilson, *Old Fort William*, vol. 2, p. 176.
20 A civilian, White was sub-secretary to the Governor-General in Council in 1790.
21 Board of Revenue Proceedings, 12 February 1788.
22 Ibid., 22 February 1788. Writing to the Board of Revenue on 10 March (ibid., 11 March 1788), Harrington said he had received the Board's instruction 'to submit the Surveyor's proposition enclosing the vacant spots of ground before the several houses fronting the Esplanade, from Mr White's to the Council House Street'. Two points of interest emerge from this statement: first, that White's house was probably located at the western end of the road, towards the river, and, secondly, that today's Council House Street had already got its name by 1788.
23 Board of Revenue Proceedings, 4 February 1790. This can be treated as an early effort to beautify this part of the town, a settled policy being suggested towards that end. Further, the recommendation provides an idea of the openness of the area, especially to the south, without which the plan could not have made much sense.
24 There was no Raj Bhavan (Government House) then to interrupt the progress of the road from the river to the Dharamtala-Chowringhee crossing.
25 Board of Revenue Proceedings, 11 March 1788.
26 Ibid., 14 January 1790.
27 In their response (ibid., 4 February 1790), the Commissioners of Police referred the Collector to their 5 March 1788 opinion on the White case.
28 Ibid., 15 February 1790.

10

Ground for Houses

In May 1795 Francis Gladwin, the Collector of Calcutta, wrote to the Board of Revenue[1] that he had received a letter from Alexander Colvin, an important member of the town's business community, applying 'for some *khamar* land lying contiguous to his premises', the land according to the Company's surveyor being 'clear of the public road' and comprising three kathas. Colvin had written that he had applied 'some time ago … for a piece of ground in front of my house which I wish to enclose [so] that it may not be a nuisance, which it at present sometimes is'. He said that following his application Edward Tiretta had surveyed the plot and had sent his report to the Collector. The land, Colvin said, 'can be of no use but to me, being directly in front of my house and must be crossed to get to the road'. Perhaps, in view of Colvin's social status, the Board took no time in recommending to the Governor-General in Council that the plot be given to him 'at the established rate paid for ground of this description subject to the usual ground rent'. However, the Supreme Council decided to take a close look at the issue and asked the Board to report the extent of the ground for which Colvin had applied, 'and describe more particularly the situation of it' so that the Council could judge for itself 'whether any public convenience will arise from the disposal of it'.[2]

For a year nothing much seems to have happened, and there is nothing in the records to tell us why this was so. Then, on 30 June

1796 Colvin sent another application to the Board of Revenue[3] in which he included a plan

> … of the road which passes … my property, near Cutchy Goody Gaut, and to solicit that you will be pleased to direct the Collector of Calcutta to grant me a pottah for the ground contained in the triangle form from Sir Robert Chambers' gate to the corner of my premises, leaving a sufficient passage for the entrance to the offices of Sir Robert Chambers as marked in the plan.

Colvin said the ground in question was in front of the house he had bought some time ago and which he had since pulled down because it had been 'rendered almost uninhabitable by a small suite of upper rooms built on Sir Robert Chambers' premises, directly to the south of this house'.[4] He had built godowns on the spot where the house stood and wished to obtain the ground in question 'to build necessary offices upon'. Colvin expressed the hope that since the ground 'belongs to the property [and] as there is no entrance to the godown but across it', the government would grant him a patta 'to be made out upon my paying the usual price of *comar* land which I understand this to be'. Following procedure, the Board of Revenue sent the application to the Collector 'with directions to ascertain from the police officers whether there are any objections to a compliance with Mr Colvin's application and report the result to the Board'.

The Justices of the Peace turned down Colvin's plea[5] on the ground that

> No part of the town is more frequented than Cutch Goody Ghaut, close to which the depth of the water being sufficient to admit of large ships, many vessels of that description are continually receiving and discharging cargoes; consequently, there requires a great space for hackeries, etc to stand without blocking the road. There are two places between this ghaut and Chaundpaul Ghaut which already narrow the

> road considerably and deface this part of the town, and any further encroachments thereon would, we conceive, particularly injure the commercial inhabitants as well as the public in general.

Basing itself on this view, the Board of Revenue turned down Colvin's proposal.

Not being prepared to take the decision lying down, Colvin wrote to the Board of Revenue[6] on 6 September 1796 restating his case for a patta to be given to him for a plot 'betwixt my house and the public road' by the river. Colvin's response to the view of the Commissioners of Police was that the latter had probably mistaken 'the ground I had applied for, which cannot without manifest injury to me become a stand for hackerys or anything else'. He wrote that the Justices of the Peace had referred to the 'accommodation of the public' while turning down his proposal. But, as he saw it, the ground in question had

> ... no kind of connexion with the Ghaut where there is plenty of room to land everything that comes to it for the markets in Calcutta; nor can the loading or unloading of large ships be in the smallest degree impeded by my possessing the ground I allude to which, as I have before said, is totally distinct and separate from the Ghaut, the great road and [the] great part of my premises being betwixt it and the Ghaut.

Giving details of the topography of the area, he said the ghat 'was bounded on the one side by the chokeydar's house or tannah, on the opposite side by the property of Mr Vrignon and is directly opposite to Hastings Street'.[7] The ground in question was 'to the left of my house at a distance of some hundred yards from the ghaut and is comprised within a line drawn from my gate to the corner of Sir Robert Chambers' premises, to the left of the road and without encroaching upon it in the smallest degree'. He added that he had occupied his house 'upwards of ten years' and the ground concerned 'has never been considered of any use to the public or to any individual but myself'. He said the ground had also never been used as a stand for hackeries 'for the purpose of receiving goods landed at Cutch Goody Ghaut, nor is it conveniently situated for that purpose, being at a very considerable distance from the ghaut'.

Colvin said that if the Board of Revenue took a close look at the plan of the ground's location, which he had sent with his 30 June application, it would become clear that the situation of the ground was such that

> ... it can only, with any kind of propriety, be granted to me, as were it to be granted to any other person, or were it to become a stand for hackeries, it would, very essentially, injure one of the most valuable properties in Calcutta besides obstructing the passage from my godowns to the road.

The Justices of the Peace had maintained that there was no similarity beween the Colvin ground and the ground 'situated between the houses upon the Esplanade and the Great Road [Esplanade Row]', which had been sold to the house owners concerned. Colvin said he had 'never considered it [the ground in question] as part of my property in the same manner that all the ground betwixt the houses on the esplanade and the great road has been considered belonging to them', and that he was applying for it so that he could enclose it 'to prevent its being a receptacle for filth and becoming a nuisance'. Additionally, and importantly, he argued that perhaps he could be treated differently in view of 'the improvements I have made in this part of the town, as well as from paying a very heavy tax to the police', perhaps, as he claimed, the highest tax paid by any individual in Calcutta.[8] Colvin's house was contiguous to the property of Sir Robert Chambers, Chief Justice of the Supreme Court of Judicature. As he said, care had been taken 'to do no injury to Sir Robert Chambers by a passage being left for his bearers and servants to the houses he has for them, which enter from the road instead of his own compound'.

So confident was Colvin of the reasonableness of his plea for a patta for the spot of ground in question that he told the Board of Revenue that in the event of his request not being granted he would take up the matter with the Governor-General in Council 'for his decision'.[9] The Board sent the letter to Gladwin, asking him to approach the Commissioners of Police for their views on it. The Justices of the Peace[10] wrote back to say that the issue had already been 'discussed and considered at a full meeting ... which our Superintendent and Deputy Superintendent of Roads also attended.' They said that, on further consideration, they did not see anything in Colvin's 6 September letter which would make them 'remove our objections'. They reiterated that the objections were 'well-founded' and, more importantly, they held that the ground in question 'is in no respect upon a similar footing with that situated between the houses upon the Esplanade and the Great Road'. Attention was then drawn to a point of principle, namely, that before anything was done 'to encroach, narrow, or in any way affect the streets, roads and thoroughfares of the town, an attention to the accommodation of the public supersedes all arguments drawn from what may or may not be convenient to this or to that individual'. In other words, the public good had to be given precedence over private gain and convenience. The Board of Revenue stuck to its earlier decision not to grant a patta to Colvin for the plot of ground in question, a stand which was approved by the Governor-General in Council.[11]

Another issue which may be described as belonging to the 'Esplanade Row fencing' category—much more than the Colvin case which related mainly to the need to keep the fledgling road by the riverside, later to become Strand Road, free of encumbrances—was that involving building on the north-south plot of ground between today's R.N. Mukherjee Road (Mission Row) and Hemanta Basu Sarani (Old Court House Street), running the entire length of BBD Bagh on the east with the east-west alignment of Mangoe Lane[12] forming its southern extremity. This was a time when the river could be seen from the houses on Mission Row 'across the Park' located

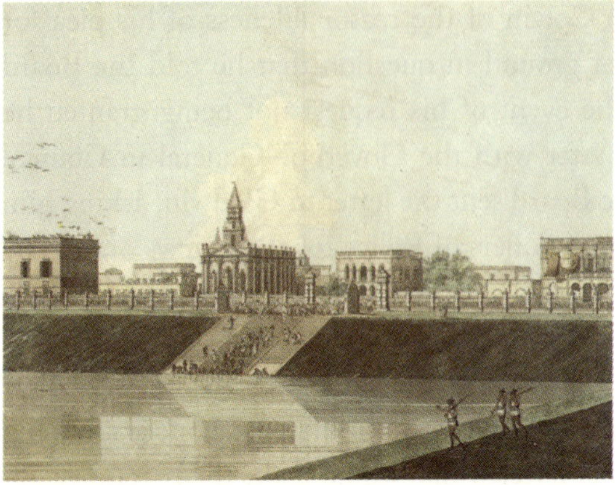

20 The east side of Tank Square, by Thomas Daniell, 1786, when there were no houses between Mission Row and the BBD Bagh Tank

21 The same area (east of BBD Bagh) after the houses were built between the Mission Church and the tank, by Frederick Fiebig, 1847

in what was then Tank Square, with the water body to its east and the old fort and the Governor's house to the west (see image 2 on p. 64). Wells' map of 1753 shows just three houses which include the Play House located at the corner of Mission Row and Lalbazar and the houses of Thomas Brown and Lady Russell.[13] In fact, in place of today's Mission Row there was the ropewalk[14] where severe fighting is said to have taken place during the assault on the town by Shiraj-ud-Daula.

As contemporary paintings show, there was open ground in front of the houses facing the tank and, in the absence of a firm official policy to keep it that way it was just a matter of time before an effort was made to acquire it. In August 1780 we find the

22 A portrait of Charles Weston

Governor-General in Council writing to the Calcutta Committee of Revenue[15] to grant a patta to Charles Weston,[16] 'the purchaser of the house in Calcutta inhabited by the late Commander-in-Chief', for the 'unoccupied ground lying direct to the westward of the said house, making it a condition of the grant that no house, wall or other erection of any kind whatsoever shall be built upon the ground excepting a palisade fence or railing'.[17] For about sixteen years Weston remained owner of the ground till it was noticed in 1796 that some changes were being made, which led to questions being asked. On being asked to find out what was happening, Gladwin, the then Collector of Calcutta, wrote to the Board of Revenue in February 1796 that it was a Mr Gowan 'who is enclosing the ground but that he has no intention of erecting buildings thereon'.[18]

This was not quite the correct position because on 16 March 1796 Gowan applied for a relaxation of the terms of the grant made to Weston, which would allow him to build on the plot in question.[19] Gowan argued that he had been induced to buy the land because 'several small huts' had been built on it and because 'of the probability of the place being filled with others of the same kind and lett to hucksters and other petty dealers in oil, ghee, etc, much to the annoyance of the families occupying the adjacent houses, and to mine in particular', the inference being that he already had a house close by. Secondly, he expected that the restrictive conditions would be relaxed or removed altogether because 'the cause ... of the prohibition [had been] entirely removed, and as buildings have been erected on the ground to the southward, which a few years ago was in a similar predicament'. The 'cause' of the prohibition was of course free ventilation and an unhindered view westward towards the Laldighi enjoyed by the house immediately to the east of the ground in question. Gowan assumed, perhaps naively, that the reason for not building on the plot in question was no longer applicable because Weston still owned the house directly to the east of the ground, and since it was Weston who had sold the ground to Gowan it could be assumed that the seller had implicitly agreed to a removal of the restriction included in the original patta.

The other part of his submission—namely, that since buildings had come up on ground similarly placed to the south of the Weston plot there was no reason why the earlier restriction on building on the ground he had just bought from Weston should be continued—appeared logical enough to back his expectation of a total lifting, or a relaxing, of the building restrictions imposed by the government. This part of Gowan's letter tells us that, to the south of his newly acquired plot (to the west of Mission Row), buildings had come up, which was not the case in the northern part of the area, that is, the area extending from Gowan's ground to Lalbazar. What this means is that the Mission Church still had an unhindered view of Laldighi and the park (see image 2 on p. 64), not to speak of the ships on the river, which was perhaps not the case with buildings to the south of the Gowan ground. Gowan also made the point that he had paid a much higher price for the ground (Sicca Rs 6,000) than would normally have been the case basing his purchase on the expectation that the building restriction—of which he was fully aware at the time of the transaction—would be discontinued given the general awareness of the need to prevent the area from being turned into an island of squalor amidst respectability.

Gowan asked Gladwin to communicate to the Board of Revenue his stand and also his expectation that it would 'have the goodness to grant me the same indulgence which others have had'. However, the Board was not impressed. It did not think it 'advisable to permit [Gowan] to infringe the conditions of the Pottah which was granted to Mr Weston', and that he would have to 'pull down the wall which he has built upon the ground'. Gowan was also warned that if he failed to abide by the Board's decision recourse would be had to legal measures 'to enforce the conditions of the deed'.[20] Gowan then wrote to George Dowdeswell, Secretary to the Revenue Board,[21] pleading with the Board 'to allow the indulgence' he had asked for and citing the same reasons which he had mentioned in his previous letter. To these he added a new point which focused on the need to spruce up the area. Gowan wrote that an additional reason for building a wall on his ground was that it would have been 'considered useful and ornamental to the part of the town, inasmuch as that the ground and drains would be kept in good order'. Despite the arguments, Gowan knew he was treading on infirm ground in view of the fact that he had not applied to the Board to remove the restriction imposed on the plot in question prior to his buying it from Weston. He even acknowledged this when he described the omission on his part as an 'inadventure' for which he hoped the Board would 'be pleased to receive my apology and that they will allow the present wall to remain'.

The Board of Revenue's subsequent letter to the Governor-General in Council is important because it makes it clear that it was only the condition attached to the Weston patta, a legal technicality, which was standing in the way of Gowan building on the ground bought by him. The Board wrote:[22]

> Considering it our duty to enforce the conditions of the pottah to direct 'that no house, wall, or other erection of any kind whatsoever be built upon the ground excepting a palisade, fence or railing', we in consequence of the communications made to us by the Collector of Calcutta informed Mr Gowan that we could not admit to his continuing the wall upon the ground contrary to the conditions of the tenure under which he held it.

At the same time, it added that it was 'not aware that there are any objections on any other grounds to a compliance with Mr Gowan's application'. Clearly, the message the Board of Revenue intended to convey is that, at this point of time, it was not keen on retaining the spot as open ground free of buildings and preserving the existing character of the eastern part of Tank Square. The restriction placed on Weston's patta related specifically to the ventilation and viewing advantage of the house to the east of it. The Board's note to the Governor-General in Council laid emphasis on the fact that the reasons cited above were not applicable to *all* the buildings on the eastern side of the ground, located between the row of houses to the east of it adjacent to the Mission Church and the street and Laldighi to the west of it. Perhaps this was due to the fact that no other applications had been made for plots on the ground immediately east of Tank Square. The point of interest to us is that, in the closing years of the eighteenth century, there was no comprehensive development plan for the area in question. This is clearly indicated by the Governor-General in Council choosing to overlook the technical obstruction placed before Gowan and opting not to insist 'on a rigorous adherence to the terms of the grant unless it should hereafter for public purposes appear necessary' to do so.[23]

The government had allowed Gowan to retain his wall, but there is nothing in the records indicating that he began building on the ground in question thus altering forever the visual character and topographical layout of the area. In fact, a decade had to pass before the change occurred. In 1806 Louis Barretto[24] informed the government that he had bought from Messrs Gowan and Horsley the Weston plot, asking it that the building restriction imposed on the land when it was 'originally granted' to Weston be 'removed' so that he could build on it as he wished. The old argument which Gowan had used was once again cited by Barretto when he specifically said that

> ... as the erection of any building whatsoever thereon could only be prejudicial to my own property by excluding the air from the western side and as the public road divides this ground from my dwelling house [that is, on Mission Row the inference being that Barretto had also bought the Weston house to the east of the plot], I am not apprehensive of any inconvenience whatever from the ground being built upon.

Barretto's plea was sent to the 'magistrates of the town', C.F. Martyn, W.C. Blaquiere[25] and Alexander Stewart, who advised that they were 'not aware of any inconvenience which can result to the public from the ground being built upon'.[26]

The researches of H.E.A. Cotton[27] have enabled us to trace the history of this specific plot of land till the first decade of the last century. Cotton wrote in 1909 that 'the premises No. 4 on the eastern side of Dalhousie Square, now in the occupation of Messrs W Newman & Co.' stood on the land once owned by Weston, 'the benefactor of the poor of Calcutta and friend of Holwell in his old age'. In 1795 Weston sold the land, presumably to Gowan, for Rs 6,000, the plot being passed on to the Barrettos in 1799. 'It remained waste for the next nine years', the restriction on building on it being

> … finally removed on the 8th May, 1806, by virtue of a certain 'letter bearing date, Council-Chamber the same day, under the signature of Thomas Brown, Secretary to the Government of Fort William in Bengal in the Public Department'. A house was thereupon built, and between 1830, when it was in the occupation of Messrs. Alport and Co., and 1833, it passed into the possession of the Bengal Club. It was sold for Rs 82,000 in 1836 by the assignees of the insolvent firm of Cruttenden Mackillop and Co., to James William Macleod: and retains its designation of the 'Club House' in a letter of August, 1841, in which a proposal of purchase for Rs 95,000 is made by Messrs Jenkins Law and Co., to Thomas DeSouza and Co. In 1882, the premises were purchased by the late Sir Walter DeSouza for Rs 1,80,000 and were sold by him a few years later for Rs 3,50,000 – a figure nearly sixty times as great as that which honest Charles Weston was glad to name in 1795.

Cotton added that W. Newman & Co. dated their possession of the house from 1882 and that in 1870 the tenants of the building called themselves 'Bodelio's Emporium of Fashion'.

Notes

1 Board of Revenue Proceedings, 29 May 1795.

2 Ibid., 16 June 1795. One way of interpreting the response on the part of the Governor-General in Council is that, at this point of time, the highest rung of the government did not always, and blindly, push the case of moneyed people. Alternatively, it may be argued that money-power, and the associated social status in the town, was not always successful in having its way with the government. Had it been so, Colvin's proposal, seconded by the Board of Revenue, would have sailed through smoothly.

3 Board of Revenue Proceedings, 8 July 1796.

4 One cannot be absolutely certain that this is the identical plot which figured in the May 1795 application made by Colvin to the Board of Revenue, but there is little doubt that the subject matter is the same, namely, Colvin wanted to buy property contiguous to what he already owned because it could not be of use to anybody else.

5 Board of Revenue Proceedings, 26 August 1796.

6 Ibid., 9 September 1796.

7 Hastings Street had, therefore, got its name by 1796, that is, just eleven years after the governor-general's departure from Calcutta.

8 The importance of Colvin is indicated by the fact that by 1817 Cutcha Goody Ghat had been renamed Colvin's Ghat (see *Atlas of the City of Calcutta and its Environs*, [Kolkata: National Atlas and Thematic Mapping Organisation, Third Edition, 2010, Plate 3]). At this time, he was also a member of the Lottery Committee for improvement of the town.

9 Board of Revenue Proceedings, 9 September 1796.

10 E. Jessup, C.F. Martyn, L. Ball, Matthew Louis, Thomas Boileau and Charles Rothman.

11 Revenue Index, 1796 (West Bengal State Archives): see under heading 'Calcutta'. Board of Revenue Proceedings, 23 September 1796.

12 Possibly, Mangoe Lane was the anglicised version of the native Mongoo Lane (in 1794). See *Bengal Past and Present*, January-March 1917, vol. 14, p. 192.

13 Brown was a senior civilian at the time. On Lady Russell, Cotton (*Calcutta Old and New*, p. 276) writes that she was the 'widow of Sir Francis Russell, sixth baronet of Chippenham in the county of Cambridge, who was a member of Council at Fort William in 1731 and succeeded to the title in 1738'. Cotton adds that after her husband's death 'she appears to have married a merchant of the name of Thomas Holmes in the following year: but to have retained her former style'. He says that she must have been among the refugees at Falta after the fall of Calcutta to the forces of the nawab, and that she 'must have died there, for her will, dated August 24th, 1756, was proved in the Mayor's Court in 1757'. Lady Russell's family 'was closely connected with Oliver Cromwell, whose favourite daughter Frances was the grandmother of Sir Francis Russell and mother of John Russell, Governor of Fort William from 1711 to 1713'.

14 The Company's rope-walk (a place long enough for hemp and fibres to be laid out for being twisted into cables, etc.,) came into existence very early in the life of the English presence in Bengal. The Consultation of 30 September 1704 (Wilson, *Old Fort William*, vol. 1, pp. 59–60) says that private parties were allowed to use the facilities set up by the authorities for a charge of Rs 2 for every cable made there.

The Consultation also tells us that the authorities had set up 'a Bank Sall to put the Hemp or Coyre in' and that its repair constituted 'some charge to the Company'. What this means is that the Calcutta bankshall (the dictionary defines 'bankshall' as 'a warehouse; the office of a harbour master, or port authority'), commemorated today by Bankshall Street to the west of Laldighi, first made its appearance at this time at a place which was to the east of today's BBD Bagh. H.E.A. Cotton (*Calcutta Old and New*, pp. 267–268), says that the word, which has been 'a puzzle to many ... first occurs as early as 1700, when the Court of Direcors ordered a *Bankshall* or marine yard to be built at Kedgeree, where ships of 400 tons burden and over could anchor, all vessels of less tonnage being directed to proceed up the river to Calcutta'. As a matter of fact, there is an earlier mention of the word, in the diary of Streynsham Master (*Diaries*, vol. 2, p. 236), when he writes on 9 September 1679 that 'we gott downe to the Bankesale (Bankesale) at the river's mouth by two or three a clock afternoone. The water being too low to goe over the Barr, we stopt there'. Again that on the same day, Chintaman Shah, one of the East India Company's chief merchants in Balasore, drove 'downe to the Bankesale in his Pallankeene' with a message from the Mughal Governor for the Company's agent. Further, on 11 September 1689 the Court wrote to Fort St George about the fort taken by Captain Heath at Balasore 'near the place where our Banksall was formerly' (Wilson, *Old Fort William*, vol. 1, p. 5). Cotton prefers the 'simpler' explanation that the word in Dutch meant Marine House, citing the fact that towards the close of the eighteenth century a Tackshall Street (probably present-day Babu Tarapada Mukherjee Sarani, formerly Koila Ghat Street) existed in Calcutta, the word *tackshall* in Dutch meaning Custom House 'which then stood at the south-west angle of the Fort on the river bank, to the east of the "New Wharf"'.

15 Calcutta Committee of Revenue Proceedings, 10 August 1780 (West Bengal State Archives).

16 Wilmot Corfield has the following note on Weston in his *Calcutta Faces and Places in Pre-Camera Days,* Part 1 (Thacker, Spink and Co., 1910), p. 7: 'Born in Tiretta bazaar, Calcutta, 1731. Apprenticed to J Z Holwell. Was absent at Chinsurah at the time of the siege. Clerk at St John's Chapel. Retired from business a wealthy man and became a noble benefactor of the parish. Died 1809. He suffered from rheumatism in the head and when at home always wore an ordinary

cotton handkerchief stiffly starched as a protection against cold. Weston's lane is called after him.'

A note on Weston in *The Bengal Obituary* (Calcutta: Holmes and Co., 1848, p. 94 [1991 edition]), says that, 'He was the founder of his own opulence; surely fortune never bestowed wealth better than on Charles Weston, a striking and existing example, that chaste and refined entiments are not confined to complexion or climate. This truly honourable man resided at Chinsurah *amid a group of necessitious people, soothed and supported by his bounty* (italics in original). Those who had seen better days and on whom fortune had ceased to smile, were comforted by Charles Weston. One hundred gold mohurs and upwards a month was regularly distributed to the indigent, from a box placed on his table; nor was there any Sircar to deduct or intervene; all came from his own venerable hand. He left a sum of about a lac of Rupees, the interest of which is still distributed monthly by the vestry of St John's, to a large number of the poor of Calcutta and Chinsurah.'

17 The patta was granted on 5 September 1780 and was signed by J. Evelyn, Collector (Board of Revenue Proceedings, 22 March 1796). A related point of interest is the location of Tremanundo's riding school which was set up in the vicinity a few years earlier (see chapter 13, 'Sprucing Up Chowringhee', note 30). There is no mention of the riding school in the official correspondence on the Weston application, but it was probably located just to the south of the ground for which Weston was seeking a patta. Was the timing of the application linked in any way to a possible expansion of Tremanundo's riding school, the apprehension being that an expansion northward would interfere with the westward view of Tank Square from his house?

18 Board of Revenue Proceedings, 8 March 1796.

19 Ibid., 22 March 1796.

20 Ibid.

21 Ibid., 1 April 1796.

22 Ibid.

23 Ibid., 26 April 1796.

24 Cotton (*Calcutta Old and New*, p. 529) writes that at this point of time the two 'opulent broethers', Joseph and Louis Barretto, were 'the heads of the Portuguese community in Calcutta and members of a family which has given two governors and a Patriarch to Portuguese India'. See also *Bengal Past and Present*, vol. 2 (1908), p. 266.

25 Neither Martyn nor Blaquiere was the epitome of honesty and efficiency. 'Martyn had long been notorious for his private life as well as the capriciousness and partiality of his legal judgements. Blaquiere was said to be the "corruptest man in the whole Settlement". At one count he held fourteen offices, but was still grasping for profit' (Robb, *Sentiment and Self*, p. 193). On Martyn being under suspicion of accepting bribes from scavengers for providing them with employment, see ibid., p. 134.

26 Judicial Criminal Proceedings, 17 April and 1 May 1806.

27 Cotton, *Calcutta Old and New*, pp. 271–272.

11

The Strand Road

Alexander Colvin's problems with his house by the river related to the spot on today's Strand Road very near to its junction with erstwhile Hastings Street. The official records of the time are silent on the state of the road. They only remind us that it was very much there and was much frequented by the town's commercial traffic on account of the location of the river ghats. One thing we do know from contemporary accounts is the ease with which those engaged in the goods insurance business could check the actual merchandise—which was either loaded on to the ships or stacked in the godowns waiting to be shifted into the holds of vessels moored in the river—which led to 'respondentia' contracts being struck on the bank of the river itself.[1] These commercial engagements were entered into on what was known as the Respondentia Walk, which was described as 'the whole of the space from the riverside which is bounded by the road leading to the Calcutta Fort gateway', shown clearly in an 1856 map. This is indicated in a letter written by the magistrates of the town to the Government in 1808[2] when discussing a demand made by genteel people that 'a riverside promenade' be developed which would add to the town's recreation facilities. The specific suggestion was 'to have the walk by the riverside, commonly called the Respondentia Walk, put into order for their accommodation'.[3] Before taking any steps, the magistrates wanted to know from the authorities whether the expenditure on the repairs 'of this part of the Esplanade' was their

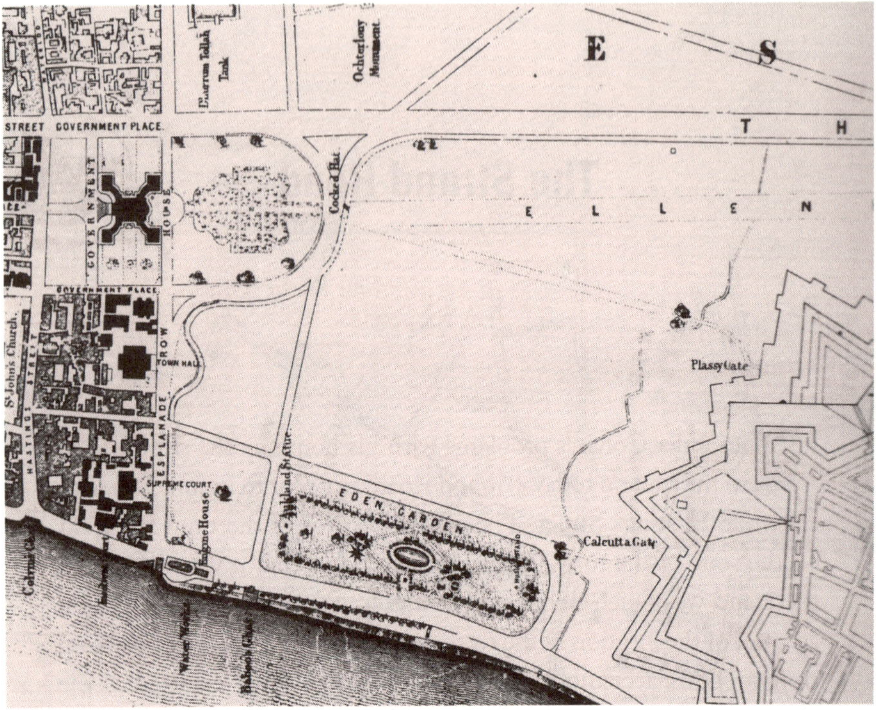

23 An 1856 map by W. Heysham showing the location of the Eden Gardens as it was formed originally by the Eden sisters. Also the ground which formed the Respondentia Walk earlier

responsibility or whether it fell under the jurisdiction of the engineer's department. The popular demand was that the entire space be 'closed in some manner against carriages and horsemen (with particular exceptions) and only palankeens and foot passengers be admitted therein'. The magistrates felt that if this was done those 'who resort thither for exercise of walking, and the numerous children that are sent in mornings and evenings to take the air, would then no longer be annoyed, and incur constant danger from horsemen riding furiously up and down, and carriages driving across in every direction'.[4] The Government responded by saying that though the walk in question fell under the jurisdiction of the engineer's department, it would consider the suggestion to 'enclose' it with a railing.[5]

The above makes it clear that the Respondentia Walk was not a road. However, Charles D'Oyly provides us with a different idea when he described it in 1823 as 'the row of buildings forming the southern edge of the city of Calcutta abutting on the esplanade, or the Maidan', that is, Esplanade Row. He wrote:[6]

> Great Respondentia, which in pristine ages
> Afforded petty merchants your assistance
> To calculate on gain – in all its stages,
> And settle policies; and ships' insurance;
> Now cleansed and beautified, you have th' assurance
> Boldly to rear your metamorphosed brow,
> Midst decorated piles, whose long endurance
> Thick walls and pucka roofs most amply shew
> As well's the reign of wealth and grandeur's ample flow!

However, in canto the fourth, stanza seventeen D'Oyly refers to the Respondentia as a walk along the riverside, which is not quite the same thing as 'the row of buildings' on Esplanade Row. He writes:

> The Respondentia – trotters, boldly stalk,
> For, with the bracing wind, they have a new
> Itinerant zest, and seek their favourite walk,
> Flank'd, on each side, by a poor avenue
> Of stunted trees – from cold not saving you;[7]

The Strand Road, as we know it today, was the work of the Lottery Committee in the early 1820s, some problems being faced by the layout of the road owing to the location of Fort William which it had to pass to the west. Twenty years after the road was built, the following description appeared in a book penned by a former member of the Bengal Engineers:[8]

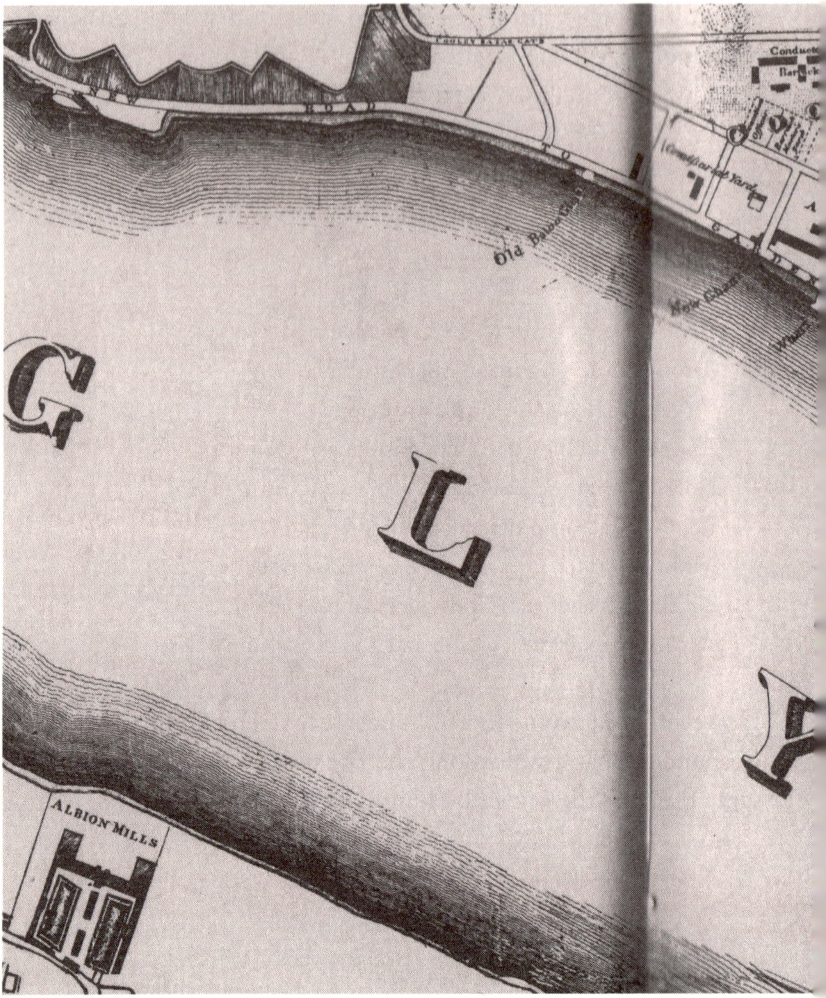

NEW ROAD
Old Barge
ALBION MILLS

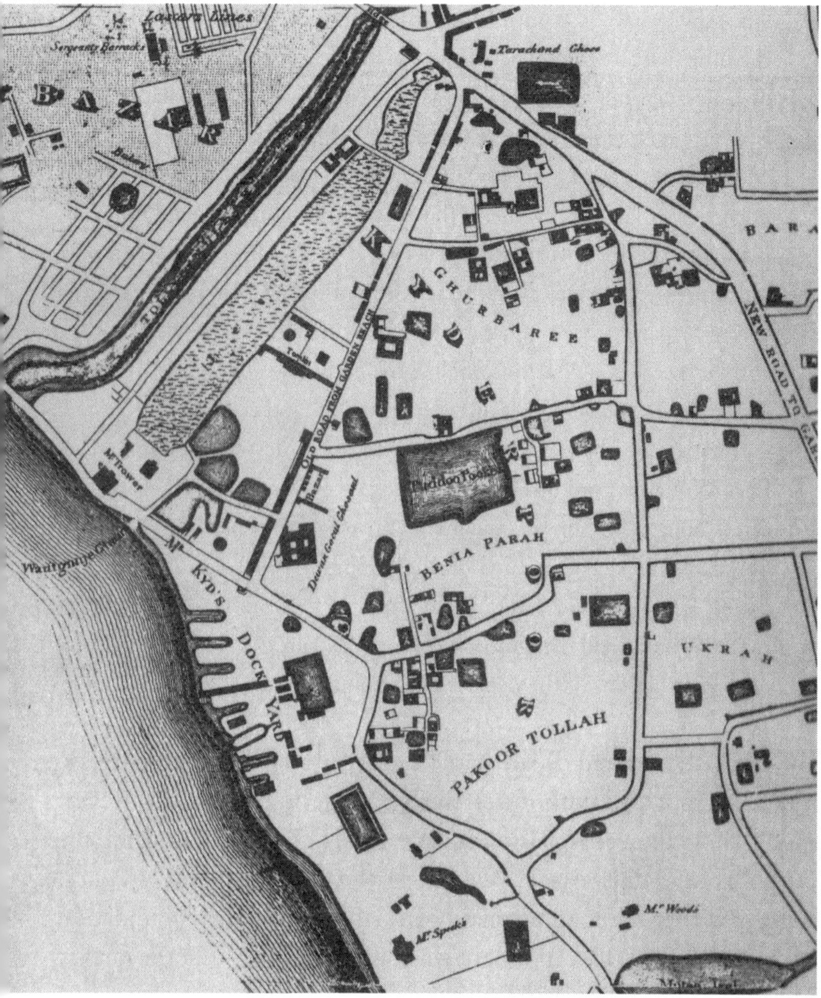

24 J.A. Schalch's map of 1824 showing the new road to Garden Reach along the river. It also shows the location of Cooley Bazar and the Ghoshal house on the old road from Garden Reach (Watgunje Street)

> The strand road … is one of the greatest improvements connected with the times past. It commences from the higher parts of the European city of Calcutta, and runs along the bank of the river, to the dockyards at Kidderpore, forming an extensive and beautiful walk or drive, mornings and evenings, and also greatly shortening the road to Garden Reach. But great as was the improvement, the then chief engineer would not allow it to pass the fort, without obstructing it to the utmost of his power. He expressed his fear that the terrific rattling of barouches, whether driven by pairs or four in hand – landaus, landaulettes, britzkas, with or without perches – phaetons of all sorts, high, low and pony – curricles, tandems, buggies, full, half or sweep-panelled, and champignys – would unquestionably, by their irresistible concussion, destroy the ramparts of Fort William! Lord William Bentinck, however, it must be allowed, often thought for himself, and merely answered the argument, by asking how many salutes were fired during a month? "Oh, a great many, my Lord!" "Ah! then we need not be afraid of the carriages!" The strand road was built, and the ramparts of Fort William still stand, as an insult to the predictions of the departed Sir Thomas Anbury, KCB.

By 1859 the Strand Road had become a busy thoroughfare, so much so that the authorities were considering using a different mode altogether of repairing it. Previously, *khoa* was used for the purpose but in that year, S. Wauchope, the Commissioner of Police, suggested that the road be relaid with stone 'over a new foundation of one brick flat'.[9] His argument was two-fold. First, that the quality of bricks then available, from which khoa would have to be made, had deteriorated greatly containing as they did 'a large proportion of sand', with the result that they were 'speedily pulverised'. Secondly, the traffic on the road had increased three-fold over the preceding decade and no brick road, 'even of the best materials, can possibly remain in a tolerable state for three years'. Wauchope wrote to the Government on the last day of the year that the road would have to be given a new foundation because 'the old foundation which was laid down many years ago by the lottery Committee is completely worn out', the cost of the project being computed at Company's Rupees 27,728-3-3.

As late as the 1790s, there was no free ground south of Sutanati which could be used for the building of a riverside road because the grounds of the houses on the east bank of the river went down to the water's edge. Direct evidence of this is provided by the official records when Mrs Frances 'Begum' Johnson applied to the Government for land measuring a bigha, thirteen kathas and two chittacks 'on the banks of the river adjoining to the foundations of the west side of her house and reaching to low water mark'.[10] The main reason why Mrs Johnson wanted the land was to protect her privacy. In her letter to the collector, Francis Gladwin, she wrote:

> Owing to the many inconveniences which I suffer from a number of the inhabitants of the town frequenting at improper times the side of the river under the west front of my house, I am very desirous of having this part of the bank of the river inclosed and request you will be pleased to represent my wish to the Board of Revenue informing them at the same time that in the event of my being permitted to occupy this spot of ground I am very willing to pay the usual rate of ground rent for the same.

The collector saw no objection to the land being given to Mrs Johnson 'there being many precedents on record of the proprietors of houses on the banks of the Ganges being allowed such indulgence'. The Governor-General in Council allowed her to have the land she wanted but on the condition, which was included in the patta, that the Government would 'have the option of cancelling the lease should any public inconvenience be hereafter found to result from the grant of it'. What is of interest here is that the Government took cognizance of 'public inconvenience' and held out the possibility of the lease in question being amended or terminated even when the applicant concerned was none other than a luminary of the Calcutta society of the time.[11]

25 Frances 'Begum' Johnson by Thomas Hickey, 1784

Not much changed over the next quarter of a century, but it was clear that the status quo could not last for very much longer because the town was growing rapidly both in terms of the people inhabiting it and its commerce. The need for a road along the river was bound to increase with the increasing demand for better access to the waterfront. The first stirrings in this direction were not the result of a public petition, which is what one would have ordinarily expected. After all, it was the general populace which was affected adversely by large swathes of the riverfront being closed to them. Instead, the first step was taken from within the Government, specifically the Custom House Committee of the time, comprising H. Shakespear, H. Mackenzie, Commodore J. Hayes, G.J. Gordon, and H.H. Wilson, which wanted to convert 'a portion of the bank of the river opposite the premises of the naval store keeper into a passage of communication with Coila Ghaut'.[12] The committee wanted 'a road or footpath [to] be left for public use between Coila Ghaut and the proposed Ghaut on the Police Ground'[13] which would entail the removal of 'the wall which forms the western boundary of the compound attached to the naval store keeper's dwelling house'. The committee added it would be happy if 'a road or footpath clear at high water would be left for the public between Coila Ghaut and the Police Office ground, with a sloping beach to the river, similar to that at the Custom House'. S. Swinton, who wrote on behalf of the committee, added, 'The Marine Store Keeper's wall must, the Committee imagine, be removed back a yard or two, but this could be done at a trifling expence, and the public advantages are evident'. What this means is that at this time there was no thorough passage for the public by the riverside southward from the Custom House which, as Upjohn's map (1793) tells us, was at the time located at the foot of Koila Ghat Street.

The proposal was promptly opposed by the Marine Board which held that the measure would be an 'encroachment' on the Naval Store Keeper's premises 'as well as on those of the Bankshall'. The Marine Board sought the views of the Master Attendant and the Naval Store Keeper, both of whom shot down the proposal. The Marine Board argued that 'the property lodged on their premises would be liable to depredation [and] their business interrupted, particularly in regard to the crane'. It approved of the Master Attendant's observation—described as 'just and pertinent'—'that any public access to the town, along the margin of the river independent of the public ghauts, must greatly tend to encourage and to facilitate smuggling'. The considered view of the Board was that it could not support the proposal of the Custom House Committee.[14]

In his submission, the Master Attendant, John Hayes, had written to the Marine Board that the proposed footpath 'could not be left for the public, between Coila Ghaut and the proposed ghaut on the Police Office ground, without great inconvenience to this department, and the naval store keeper's yard'. He referred to 'exposure to robbery of a great deal of the Hon'ble Company's property appertaining to those departments'. Hayes said that people would not be able to use the path while the crane was at work, 'which is almost continuously employed'.[15] In his reply to the Marine Board's query, the Naval Store Keeper, E.S. Ellis, felt his way forward cautiously. He wrote that he could have 'no objections to meet the wishes of the [Customs House] Committee … and am ready to comply with them as far as I am individually concerned' but how far it would be 'politic to make a public path so close to the naval store yard I leave to the Board to determine'. He, however, feared that the making of the path would be 'attended with great inconvenience at times owing to the Port of Calcutta being thrown open to ships of all classes and descriptions, and that it might endanger the Hon'ble Company's property if the seamen of foreign ships and free traders are allowed to pass and repass at all times'. He cited the situation of the naval storeyards in England which were 'kept free from access as [far as] possible'. Ellis said that with all the precautions already in place 'we have had instances of their being set on fire, and the Board are fully aware that almost all naval stores are of an inflammatory nature'. Ellis narrated a story to buttress his point regarding theft. He recounted:[16]

> On going down to the naval store yard about eight weeks ago, I found some Europeans in the yard at 9 pm. On asking them what they were doing in the naval storeyard so late in the evening, after some time they replied, 'we thought it was a public path'. They might have been smugglers for they evidently appeared to avoid the public ghaut.

These responses were passed on to the committee set up to report 'upon the best mode of appropriating the Government lands on the banks of the river', with directions to submit to the authorities concerned a report on 'the expediency of the measure of opening a communication along the bank of the river between Coila Ghaut and the new [Police] ghaut, about to be opened to the southward of the Master Attendant's premises, under directions of the Committee for the Improvement of Calcutta'.[17] On 5 August 1819 the Custom House Committee wrote to Holt Mackenzie, Secretary to the Government in the Territorial Department, that the 'proposed arrangement appears to us very desirable'. Of great significance for the future, the hope was also expressed that it 'be extended even somewhat beyond the scale contemplated by its original proposers', that is, to the southwards towards Chandpal Ghat.

The committee then went into the details of the project.[18] The first point it made was that, 'drawing a line along the front of the marine yard and master attendant's premises, in continuation of that already marked by the range of Custom House godowns which fronts the beach, the remaining space [could] be very advantageously appropriated for the accommodation of the public'. Secondly, the committee felt that

> ... the precise breadth [of the passageway] must depend on the quantity of rubbish that can be applied to the purpose of filling up the ground, but the buildings about to be destroyed in the vicinity are likely, we believe, to afford abundant materials for meeting a broad beach, and even a road for carriages, if such should be desired.[19]

Alternatively, the committee felt that the project would afford 'a convenient mode of disposing of a quantity of rubbish that would otherwise be expensive in its removal'. Reflecting the extent of holistic planning for the town's development which had already struck root, it was also suggested that the project be directed by the Lottery Committee, which 'will best be able to lay before Government all details connected with the arrangement of which his Lordship in Council may wish to be informed'.

The committee then took up the two principal objections to the project: first, 'that it would lay open to the public the premises of the Marine Department, expose the public property to risk, and facilitate smuggling'; secondly, 'that it would interfere with the Master Attendant's crane and wharf'. As regards the first point, it was argued that the premises in question were 'already as much exposed as they would be under the proposed arrangement, with the difference only that the access is inconvenient, a point not much considered by thieves or smugglers'. The committee suggested that the premises in question be walled in irrespective of 'whether the beach be rendered commodious and public or not'. Giving us an idea of what the precise configuration of the riverbank was like at the turn of the eighteenth century, the committee said that the Master Attendant's premises 'and a portion of the marine yard are left entirely open to the river'. It said that if the suggestion of a wall being built was accepted, access to the town would 'be limited to the two main streets, which can easily be guarded, while at the same time the openness and publicity of the beach will render the control over the boats plying to it comparatively easy'. As far as the 'jetty [the crane and wharf] attached to the Bankshall' was concerned, the committee said it would be necessary 'to throw it forward about 30 feet', which in any case was 'indispensable to its utility' and would not involve too much expenditure.

The Governor-General in Council agreed with the committee's suggestions and issued orders for the project to be implemented.[20] It can be argued that this 'passage' to Koila Ghat, which the Customs people wanted, eventually grew into the modern Strand Road under the auspices of the Lottery Committee.

Notes

1 'Respondentia' is a legal term denoting the hypothecation of the cargo or goods on board a ship as security for the repayment of a loan. The contract is called 'respondentia' because the money is lent on the personal responsibility of the borrower. The term is seldom used now, being replaced by 'bottomry' or 'bottomage'. See Yule and Burnell's *Hobson Jobson* (Calcutta: Rupa; 1986 reprint of 1902 edition; first published 1886), p. 761.

2 Judicial Criminal Proceedings, 21 October 1808.

3 Fourteen years earlier, in 1794, there were reports of a promenade being built on the river bank 'extending from Chandpaul Ghat to the new fort … which will add greatly to the beautiful appearance of the fort and the town, and be a source of health and amusement to the inhabitants' (*Calcutta Chronicle*, 6 January 1794). Did the 1808 suggestion relate to a sprucing up of this existing promenade?

4 To take an example of the regulations imposed, on 11 May 1813 the authorities decreed: 'No persons having dogs with them are allowed to

come upon the Respondentia walk or that part of the Esplanade: and the sentries have received orders accordingly' (*Bengal Past and Present*, vol. 26, Part 1, July-September 1923, pp. 75–76).

5 The step to enclose the ground was perhaps the kernel from which developed later the Auckland (Eden) Garden of the late 1830s on the initiative of the sisters of the then Governor-General, Lord Auckland. See image 23 on p. 192.

The article in *Bengal Past and Present* cited in the previous note says that the location of the walk was once marked 'by a row of fine trees which stood south of Baboo Ghat' (but see Charles D'Oyly's description of the row of trees), most of which were uprooted during the cylone of 1864. The walk 'filled up the intervening space between the Fort and the old Chandpal ghat', the latter being removed in 1923 'to make way for an embankment and the Port Commissioners' Railway, but [is] famous in history as the spot where India welcomed and bade farewell to her rulers'.

6 *Tom Raw, the Griffin*, by a civilian and an officer of the Bengal Establishment, London, 1828, Canto the Second, Stanza Five, p. 26. In this context, D'Oyly's note on Chandpal Ghat and the esplanade (ibid., p. 47) is of some interest. He writes: 'Chandpaul Ghaut is the principal landing place for passengers and luggage in Calcutta. It faces a long row of edifices forming the southern front of the city, called the Respondentia, in the very centre of which is the Government House. No buildings are allowed to be raised between this and Fort William, where there is an extensive grass plain divided in two by the main road leading from the city to Alipore and a cross road from the Fort to Chowringhee. An open space of two square miles, formed by the Respondentia on the North, Chowringhee on the East, by the river on the West, and on the South by Tolly's creek, is thus kept clear, and adds much to the comfort and salubrity of the city.'

7 Ibid., pp. 86, 109. Compounding the confusion, D'Oyly clarifies in a note that he is in fact referring to a road. He writes, 'There is a walk from Chandpaul Ghaut to the Fort by the river's side with an avenue of trees as described. Children and their attendants, and people fond of walking, are the usual pedestrians.'

8 C.J.C. Davidson, *Diary of Travels and Adventures in Upper India*, vol. 2 (London, 1843), pp. 208–209.

9 Judicial Proceedings, 27 January 1859 (West Bengal State Archives).

10 Board of Revenue Proceedings, 19 December 1794. Similar pleas had

been made earlier. On 20 July 1792 Thomas Barber had written to the Collector of Calcutta that the riverbank was 'contiguous to my house in Bazar Calcutta', and that he be granted a patta for ground '... down to the low water mark in order that I may be thereby empowered to take such measures as may appear best calculated for the preservation of my property by piling the ground as far as the limits of my premises extend, or taking other methods as may be deemed advisable for that purpose, and at the same time in no wise injurious to the navigation of the river.'

Edward Colebrook, the Collector, had written to the Board of Revenue in April the following year stating that he had examined the ground and that he saw no reason for the proposal to be rejected 'as you have granted the same indulgence to Messrs Hunter and Bazett' (Board of Revenue Proceedings, 25 June 1793). See Lottery Committee Proceedings, 4 May 1820 for details of Reverend William Johnson's claim to the land in this area which, at the time, was being considered for further development. This bit of land, including that given to Mrs Johnson, was later occupied by the import warehouse premises which are clearly marked in Schalch's map (*Atlas of the City of Calcutta*, p. 25).

11 H.E. Busteed—in *Echoes from Old Calcutta,* p. 203, note—writes that Mrs Johnson's house was located on the spot where the bonded warehouse stood on the river bank, north of today's Fairlie Place. She married four times, the last nuptial knot being tied to Reverend William Johnson in 1774. She was also the grandmother of a prime minister of England, Lord Liverpool, through her daughter by her third husband, William Watts. Known as Begum Johnson, she died in 1812, the 'oldest European in Bengal' at the time. See also Losty, *Calcutta City of Palaces*, p. 51.

12 Territorial Revenue Proceedings, 6 August 1819 (West Bengal State Archives). H.E.A. Cotton (*Calcutta Old and* New, p. 268) refers to the suggestion that Koila Ghat was the new name of the old *Killa* Ghat, or the Old Fort Ghat seen in old maps. Schalch's map of 1828, however, confirms that the two ghats were located at two different places, the Old Fort Ghat being to the north of the fort and Koila Ghat to its south. The map also shows Old Fort Ghat Street and Koila Ghat Street as different roads. Upjohn's map names the road south of the fort as Tankshall Street (according to Cotton, it should be *Tackshall* Street after the Dutch name for Custom house), one

interpretation being that the road came to be called Koila Ghat Street in view of the 'large traffic in coal [*koila*] in the early years of the 19th Century', the landing point on the river opposite the road being known as Koila Ghat. Upjohn's map of 1792–1793 does not show this ghat possibly because there was no substantial traffic in coal at this place at the time.

13 The Police Ghat was set up further south, at the foot of Hare Street.

14 Extract from Commercial Department Proceedings of 11 June 1819 quoted in Territorial Revenue Proceedings, 6 August 1819.

15 Ibid.

16 Ibid.

17 Territorial Revenue Proceedings, 6 August 1819.

18 Ibid.

19 Here one can detect the germination of the idea of the Strand Road of the future.

20 Territorial Revenue Proceedings, 6 August 1819.

12

Forming the Esplanade

Talking of the esplanade generally, a point of interest is whether all of the land that was subsequently turned into today's maidan was filled with unkempt vegetation or whether there was any human habitation in the area. This, however, does not include the Gobindapur area on which spot the new fort came up. Available evidence suggests that there were houses with grounds all of which were demolished to enable the new fort to have a clear field of fire. Inevitably, issues of compensation were involved. There was, for example, the case of W. Bonfield[1] the auctioneer after whom Bonfield Lane is named. Bonfield wrote to the Calcutta Committee of Revenue on 20 August 1779 that he had earlier approached it 'regarding a claim to a piece of ground in lieu of a piece I was entitled to which now appertains to the Esplanade' but had not yet received a reply. In his earlier letter, Bonfield had written that while going through the papers of his wife he had found some relating to 'the estate of Mr Richard Finley, deceased, her former husband' which mentioned a garden which, on enquiry, Bonfield found had been 'given up by Mr Peter Gallopine to Mr Vansittart [the then Governor] in order to make clear the Esplanade, to the northward of the New Fort'.[2] According to his wife, Vansittart had promised that she would be 'restored an equal quantity of Land, equally valuable, as also a surplus quantity, in consideration of the great expence Mrs Bonfield had been at in building a bungalow and digging a tank, planting sundry kinds of fruit trees, and walling the said ground round'.

Bonfield said that despite his best efforts he had not been able to find among the papers the patta which, given the length of time which had elapsed in the meantime, had probably 'been destroy'd or lost'. He, however, informed the committee that Finlay's *sircar*, 'who paid the purchase money', was 'still living, and resides in Calcutta' and could be approached by the authorities for 'truthful evidence' in the matter. He added that there were a number of 'credible' people residing in Calcutta at the time who could vouch for the fact that the 'garden was occupy'd by Mrs Bonfield for many years' and that the ground was 'a very valuable' plot. Imparting some colour to the transaction, Bonfield wrote that 'the ground being bought by Messrs Richard Finley and John Wood at the outcry of one Mr Hampton, and being too small for two gardens, Mr Wood gave his half up to Mr Finley'. On its part, the Calcutta Committee of Revenue asked the dewan to examine the records 'and ascertain whether any, and what quantity of ground situated in Govindpore stood in the name of Richard Finley, at the time of the appropriation, or at any time before, and whether he, his representatives or executors, have ever received any compensation thereof'.[3]

A second case related to a piece of ground belonging to Captain Thomas Fenwick[4] the claim being that no compensation had been paid after it was taken over for the making of the esplanade of the fort. This case is of more than ordinary interest because it provides us with details of the procedure adopted in those early days of compensating those whose property had been taken over by the authorities for a public purpose.

On 16 April 1778 Edward Fenwick, attorney to his mother Elizabeth Fenwick and himself a member of the Calcutta Committee of Revenue, wrote to the committee[5] that,

> In the Year 1165 B.S., answering to 1759 English Era, a pottah was granted to Mr Thomas Fenwick for 8 Begahs 14 Cottahs of ground

> in Dhee Govindpore. This spot he levelled and form'd into a garden, dug a large tank in it and otherwise expended to the amount of thirty or forty thousand rupees. He also erected two large bungaloes and some out-houses valued at about 10,000 Rupees.

Subsequently, the Company 'took and appropriated Dhee Govindpore for the purpose of erecting the new fort and, among many others, who on this occasion had their property taken from them, Mr Thomas Fenwick suffered in the loss of his'. Fenwick Junior, his son, said he had been informed that some of those who suffered like his father 'have had restitution made them, either by an allowance of an adequate quantity of the Hon'ble Company's *comar* land in the town of Calcutta, or an equivalent sum of money to the property they possessed paid them'. In the case of his father, no compensation had been paid although he had found 'from the Bengal Records of the Calcutta Committee of Revenue that the quantity of 8 Begahs 14 Cottahs of Ground appears inserted in the name of Mr Thomas Fenwick, and that it has never been transferred'.[6]

As the attorney of Mrs Elizabeth Fenwick, 'the sole executrix to the estate of Thomas Fenwick', Edward Fenwick laid claim to the compensation and informed the committee that the patta to the ground 'was lost among his other papers at the time of the troubles and capture of Calcutta, and therefore cannot be produced'.[7] The amount of compensation sought was Rs 10,000 'expended as before mentioned in erecting bungaloes, etc'.[8] Since there were no papers to back up his claim, Edward Fenwick was ready to produce before the committee 'four principal inhabitants of Calcutta natives to corroborate the above circumstances' and 'justify my claims'. These four natives were Gocul Gosaul, Monick Sircar, Bobhan Rassamghire and Rambudder Ghose. The attorney told the committee that if he failed to get justice from it he would have to take the case to the Governor-General in Council. As a matter of routine, the committee ordered the dewan to

> ... examine the records of the Bengal Year 1165 and ascertain whether the quantity of 8 Begahs 14 Cottahs of Ground situated in Dhee Govindpore then stood in the name of Mr Thomas Fenwick, and whether it was appropriated for the use of the new works; likewise that he do report whether any restitution has even been made to the heirs, executors or representatives of the said Thomas Fenwick for that quantity; also that he do call on Gocul Gosaul, Monick Sircar, Bauban Russengur and Rambudder Ghose for such informations as they can give him on these points and as to the value of two bungaloes, and some houses, at the time when it was so appropriated.[9]

The records indicate there was no movement on the issue for more than a year after Edward Fenwick first raised it in August 1778. This is a bit surprising because Fenwick was himself a member of the committee. The fact that he had to resort to the open threat of taking the case to the Governor-General in Council if he did not get 'justice' suggests that the ties between him and the other committee members were perhaps under some strain.[10]

On 10 August 1779 Edward Fenwick pressed his case once again, submitting an estimate of the 'land and appurtenances agreeably to the papers of Gocul Gosaul, who has been engaged in transactions of land in Calcutta, and Monick Sircar whose house is close to the spot'. The estimate ran as follows: 'Value of the ground 8 biggahs 14 cottahs @ 150 Rs per cottah – 26,100; Value of the appurtenances etc, namely, 1 bungaloe square with a thatched veranda round it, one tank with two pucka gauts to it, 1 garden with trees - 7,100. Total 33,200.' The substantive part of the reference was that 'the above gentleman had never received the price or value of the premises nor ever received an equivalent of land in exchange from the cutcherry of the ceded lands'. Fenwick further argued that his father

> ... was for some years in possession of the above quantity of ground previous to the registry made in the year 1165 [1759] which was made

> after the troubles when a new measurement of the lands took place: since which period no ground has been allotted him in lieu thereof or pottah issued, and that he paid rent to Ragoram Paul, the Hon'ble Company's *etmaumdar*, up to the year 1163 [1757], which can be proved from the accounts and papers of Ragoram Paul now in the possession of Indernarain Paul (Ragoram Paul's brother), the present *etmaumdar*, who, with Gocul Bose the *pottah neeveez*, can also give testimony that the Hon'ble Company took and appropriated Mr Fenwick's ground for the use of the new fort and esplanade.[11]

No doubt making use of his official position, Mrs Fenwick's attorney said that, 'with the assistance of the officers employed in the Accomptant General's office, [the] Public Department and in the Buxey Office', he had checked 'the general books for many years back as also the books and accounts of the old Board of New Works now deposited in the Buxey's Office' but had not found 'that the least restitution was ever made to Mr Fenwick'. However, he produced the following list of people who did get relief for claims made which were similar to that of his father:[12]

> *In the Year 1757*
> Paid account of gentoo houses thrown down – (Rs) 6,000.
> *In the Year 1758*
> Paid Mat: Collett[13] value of black inhabitants' houses – 3,480.
> *In the Year 1761*
> Paid the Collector for houses to be pulled down to form the Esplanade – 6,185-2-6.
> *In the Year 1762*
> Paid Peter Amyatt Esq.[14] for a house pulled down to form the Esplanade – 23,086-15-9-0.
> Paid Peter Amyatt Esq. for house and a piece of ground within the Esplanade – 3,515-6-3-0.
> Paid Peter Amyatt Esq. for houses and ground laying within the Esplanade – 2,612-12-6.

> Paid Peter Amyatt Esq. for houses pulled down to form the Esplanade – 9,865-5-0.
>
> *In the Year 1763*
>
> Paid Randolph Marriott for houses pulled down to clear the Esplanade – 3,692-6-6.

Spreading his canvas, Fenwick wrote that his enquiries had revealed that

> … restitution of an equivalent (quantity) of lands in Kidderpore and Simileah was also made to several natives who possessed ground in Dhee Govindpore and Dhee Calcutta and part of those who had ground allotted them in Kydderpore were afterwards transferred to the Seats' [Setts'] ground in Sutanooty in order to give Colonel Watson the lands at Kidderpore for the use of his Docks.[15]

The attorney also cited the action of the Calcutta Committee of Revenue

> … on 23 June last … restoring possession of some *comar* land to the Durrumtullah ryotts and a further quantity as an equivalent in some other place for the deficiency of the whole quantity they had been deprived of by the order of the Governor Vansittart for the use of making a road in Durrumtullah.[16]

In view of all this, Fenwick asked the committee that he be paid

> … the amount in cash of my claims and demand as established by the Duan's report; or grant me an equivalent of *comar* land in the town of Calcutta for 8 Biggahs 14 Cottahs, paying me in cash the sum of Rupees 7,100 as ascertained and established by the Duan's report for the bungaloe, outhouses etc.[17]

Clearly, Fenwick Junior had done his homework well and had presented the authorities with a strong case for compensation.

The committee ordered that Gocul Bose and Indernarain Paul be summoned to attend its meeting on 18 August 1779 with the relevant records, and also Manick Sircar, Rambudder Ghose and Bobund Russumghire. On the appointed day Bose laid before the committee[18] 'the original *teregey jummabundy* account', stating that

> ... after the English retook Calcutta, the old accounts which were in the hands of the different *mundles* were collected together and from them the *terege* was formed for one year [namely, 1164 Bengali year, or 1758]. No revenue was collected in the town of Calcutta[19] but afterwards, on the records being received from England and corresponding with this *tereje*, it was admitted as authentic, and the revenue was collected according to it.

Gocul Bose said that 'in this account Mr Fenwick's name is pointed out for 8 begahs 14 cottahs at the Rate of 21-12-9' and that the latter was 'dispossessed in Assin 1164 [1758] by Mr Bruire[20] and the ground taken for the Esplanade to the Fort'. He added that Fenwick had 'paid the *cazannah* in 1163 [1757] after which no revenue was collected [and] that no measurement took place' till 1171 (1765). On being asked whether there were any houses on the land in question, he said there 'was a garden, that he used to see it frequently in passing towards Govindpore, that he remembers there was a tank in it, with a pucka ghaut and a brick *chaundney* or Summer House'. In the course of his examination, Rambudder Ghose also said he remembered having seen Fenwick's garden 'before the capture of Calcutta about the years 1155, 1156, 1157 & 1158 [1749-1752] ... and that there were two octagonal bungaloes on it'.

The committee asked the remaining witnesses to appear before it at its next meeting on 20 August. Seetum Ram Paul, the *gomastah* of Indernarain Paul, said[21] that in 1164 B.S. (1758) Fenwick's ground was taken 'for the use of the esplanade', a fact indicated 'from the papers in his office which were formed in the year 1165, and state the particulars relative to the years 1163 & 1164'. Paul said that according to the records 8 bighas 16 kathas 'belonging to Mr Fenwick were added to the esplanade'. They did not, however, indicate whether any compensation had been paid to him, 'nor did he ever hear any was made'. Paul underscored the quality of his evidence by stating that he had been holding his present office of *etmandar* for twelve years. When the committee asked the dewan whether in the course of his enquiry it had 'come to his knowledge that Mr Fenwick, his executrix or their attorney had ever been made any compensation either in land or money for the piece of ground taken from him, and now forming part of the esplanade', he said that 'neither in the records of the Collector's Office, which he searched on purpose, nor by any other means has he learned that any compensation was made'. At this point, the committee put off consideration of the issue till its next meeting which was attended by Kishenpershaud, the younger brother of Indernarain Paul, the latter being absent on account of illness. Kishenpershaud came armed with the teregey accounts 'of the ground taken for the use of the fort' which, the committee said, indicated that 8 bighas and 14 kathas was 'the property of Mr Fenwick in the Bengal Year 1165 [1759]'.[22]

After concluding the hearing, the committee wrote to the Governor-General in Council on 23 August that the 'real state of the case' was that Thomas Fenwick

> ... held 8 bigas 14 cottahs of ground in Dhee Calcutta, that he paid the *cazanna* or land rent till 1163 [1757], that in 1164 [1758] it was taken to form part of the esplanade and that there had been a garden, tank, and some buildings upon it; but, whether Mr Fenwick at that time, or since received any compensation for his land we have not been able to ascertain.[23]

However, the committee did not suggest to the Council that Elizabeth Fenwick be paid the compensation due to her husband, which it could easily have done in the absence of any evidence that Thomas Fenwick was in fact compensated for his loss, which was strongly suggested by the depositions. On the contrary, the Council was told: 'We think it our duty to represent to you that we have reason to believe that there are other persons who have claims similar to that of Mr Fenwick's for ground included in the esplanade', which was nothing if not a nudge in the direction of the other outstanding cases being investigated before compensation was paid to Elizabeth Fenwick.[24]

In fairness to the Calcutta Committee of Revenue, it should be pointed out that a similar line was adopted in another case involving unrequited compensation, this time involving a native, which came up before it around the same time.[25] The story opens with the dewan reporting to the committee in September 1778 that on 17 November of the previous year (Bengali year 1184), he had been ordered 'to examine the Collector's records, and the witnesses Souberam Gose and Gocul Gosaul', regarding the complaint of Ramjoy Chowdhury that despite the collector's order that he be given 'an equal quantity of ground … at Entelly and Jagoolea' for the land he had been deprived of 'for the new fort' and that 'five years' rent was due to him', nothing had been done. The dewan had been asked to make an enquiry and to put Chowdhury 'in possession [of the ground] should it appear he was entitled to it'. The dewan wrote that from the 'records of the Collectory and the witnesses', it appeared that the land in the new fort 'has time out of mind belonged to the above Chowdry, and that the collector had decreed an equal quantity in the above villages in its stead, possession of which he has never received'. The dewan said that the rent 'of the land in [the] said villages is two rupees per bega per annum, in all 100 Rs per annum' and that Chowdhury wanted the revenues for twenty years, that is, from the beginning of 1164 to the end of 1184 'Bengal Stile'. As with the Fenwick case, here too the committee resolved to send the claim to the Governor-General in Council informing it at the same time that 'we have received several other petitions on claims of the like nature; requesting their instructions how far they ought to be attended to, and admitted'.

The records tell us about yet another claim to compensation, made two years later in 1781, relating to property in the same part of the esplanade, which would mean covering a broad swathe of ground stretching from the riverside south of Esplanade Row to Chowringhee Road. The complainant was Domingo Murzell who wrote to the Governor-General in Council in August 1781[26] that for

> ... some time past, he held a house and compound containing six cottahs of ground situated in the parish called Deeh Calcutta, within the districts and jurisdiction of the town of Calcutta, which have been abolished by order of the Hon'ble the President and Council for the use of the Publick Roads while your petitioner was absent on a long voyage.

Which 'roads' are being referred to here? Upjohn's map of 1792–1793 shows the road to the Calcutta Gate of the new fort and the old course as the only roads traversing the esplanade at this point of time. If Murzell's property was affected by the construction of 'public' roads in the area, it stands to reason that work on one of these two roads was responsible, possibly that on the road to the fort.

Murzell said that despite the fact that he held a patta for the property 'dated the Tenth day of July 1758, signed by Mathew Collit, then Zamindar or Collector of the Revenue of this town of Calcutta', he had not been compensated for the loss of his property requisitioned by the Government for a public purpose. The petitioner wanted 'either a piece of ground ... in lieu of his former property or a pecuniary satisfaction of value of his aforesaid house and compound'.

John Evelyn, Collector of the Calcutta Rents, inquired into the matter and reported to the Committee of Revenue[27] that Murzell did in fact have the ground claimed by him and that 'in the Bengal Year 1165 or English year 1768 this ground was taken with several other pieces to form the north esplanade of the new fort'. Evelyn

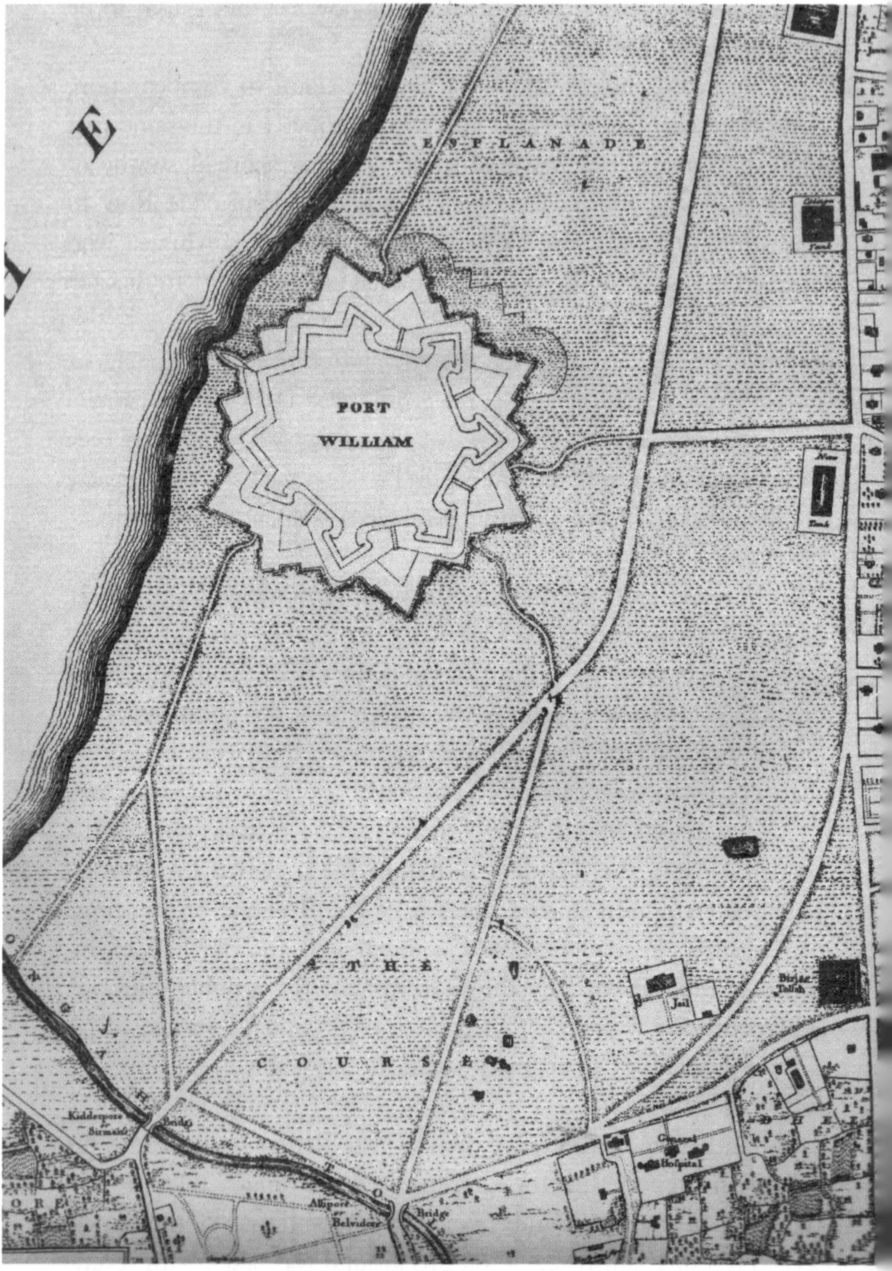
ESPLANADE
FORT
WILLIAM
THE
COURSE
Jail
General
Hospital
Bridge
Bridge

could not say whether any compensation had been paid to Murzell for the ground taken from him. Interestingly, in contrast to the cases of Fenwick and Ramjoy Chowdhury where the committee hesitated to take a decision and had recourse to intimating the Governor-General in Council that similar cases existed with regard to claims of non-payment of compensation, in the Murzell case it was prompt in directing the collector to 'enquire for a like quantity of Company's Comar Ground in Calcutta and give to Murzell as an equivalent, or in case he cannot find so much *comar* ground he do pay Murzell the medium price of ground at the time (he) had lost it, and the present time'.

Notes

1 Bonfield was one of the jurors 'who tried the indictment against J A Hickey for a libel on Hastings contained in the *Bengal Gazette* (No 9, March 24, 1781). A verdict of not guilty was returned on June 27, 1781' (*Bengal Past and Present,* vol. 25, January-June 1923, p. 148). See also Nair, *A Hiṣtory of Calcutta's Streets*, pp. 231–232.

2 That is, the garden was located somewhere in the area between present-day Fort William and Esplanade Row.

3 Calcutta Committee of Revenue Proceedings, 8 and 27 September 1779.

4 For Thomas Fenwick, see Wilson, *Old Fort William,* vol. 1, p. 196fn. Also, vol. 2, pp. 34–35.

5 Calcutta Committee of Revenue Proceedings, 20 April 1778.

6 Ibid.

7 That Thomas Fenwick was in fact the owner of the plot of ground referred to is indicated by the 31 January 1760 entry in the Bengal Public Consultations (*Old Fort William,* vol. 2, p. 156). The entry states that Captain Fenwick had written to the Bengal Council on 28 January requesting that he be compensated for 'a large Garden which has been taken and destroyed to make room for the New Works [that is, the new Fort William]'. The Council agreed 'unanimously

26 (facing page) Upjohn's map of 1792–1793 showing roads in the maidan area. It also indicates a possible old road going to the temple on the maidan, which was located roughly where the jail is shown to stand

that he be paid fifteen hundred Arcot Rupees as an Equivalent for the Buildings he had erected and the other Charges he had been at, and that another Spot of Ground be allowed him in some Other Place and that the Collector do put him in Possession there of'. In view of his son's application, the point to consider here is whether the instruction was at all carried out.

8 In a subsequent letter to the Calcutta Committee of Revenue dated 10 August 1779 (Proceedings, 13 August 1779), it was claimed that Thomas Fenwick had spent Rs 30,000 to 40,000 'in levelling the above ground, in digging a tank etc, and that about 19,000 rupees had been laid out in erecting bungaloes or thatched habitations and some out-houses'. However, as against this, the attorney had made a modest demand for just Rs 10,000 'because I cannot bring it to a satisfactory proof'.

9 In his 10 August 1779 letter to the Committee, Edward Fenwick had stated that the dewan had made his report but that it had, 'to this day', not been recorded in the Proceedings of Government. (It is instructive of the inner workings of the administration of the day that the dewan's report was made a part of the 13 August 1779 Proceedings only after this letter was sent by Fenwick.) Fenwick then quoted from the dewan's report as follows: 'I find upon a search into the *sheristah*, and from Gocul Bose Mohrir and other *amlah* of the town of Calcutta, that 8 Begahs and 14 Cottahs of Ground in 1165 (1759) were registered in the name of Mr Fenwick, and the said ground is situated in Dhee Calcutta to the south of Champaul Buzar and the house of Kelaram Sircar on the west side of the high road.'

Which 'high road' is this? Upjohn's map of 1792–1793 shows only the north-south road to the Calcutta Gate of the new fort in continuation of Old Post Office Street traversing the esplanade.

10 Wilson says in a note (*Old Fort William,* vol. 2, p. 174) that Edward Fenwick was appointed assistant at the Midnapore factory on 22 April 1765. He was dismissed from service in 1768 on the charge of breach of trust while working in the secretary's office in Calcutta and ordered to return to England. However, subsequently, in March 1769, he was allowed to remain in Bengal till the views of the Court were known (ibid., vol. 2, note, p. 180).

11 Calcutta Committee of Revenue Proceedings, 13 August 1779.

12 This list is important because it throws light on the extent of human habitation in the area subsequently converted into the esplanade of the new fort.

13 Matthew Collit was zamindar of Calcutta at the time.
14 Peter Amyatt was a member of the Bengal Council in Vansittart's time.
15 See chapter on 'The Jorabagan Dispute' for an overview of the proceedings.
16 Calcutta Committee of Revenue Proceedings, 23 June 1779.
17 Ibid., 13 August 1779.
18 Ibid., 18 August 1779.
19 This gives us some idea of the impact on revenue collection of the events of 1756–1757.
20 W. Bruere.
21 Calcutta Committee of Revenue Proceedings, 20 August 1779.
22 Ibid., 23 August 1779.
23 Ibid.
24 Ibid.
25 Ibid., 4 September 1778.
26 Committee of Revenue Proceedings, 17 August 1781 (West Bengal State Archives).
27 Ibid., 27 August 1781.

13

Sprucing up Chowringhee

While the new fort's esplanade was being cleared of buildings, the eastern part of it—that is, the area east of the old Pilgrims' Road, or the road to Russapuglah, today's Jawaharlal Nehru Road (Chowringhee)—was developing rapidly on the wave of private initiative. Enterprising builders were busy putting up houses with spacious grounds, encountering land problems on the way which were being settled with the help of the authorities. For a pictorial view of the state of affairs we have only to refer to the 1787 painting by Thomas Daniell which features a line of imposing edifices beside a broad road which is being used by natives as well as by at least one European carriage. What the painting tells us is that at the time Daniell took his notes for the canvas, the area had come to be settled in by the town's European elite. The canvas shows around nine or ten houses but there is no way of saying who owned them. A tank, or pond, can also be seen on the left although one cannot be sure which water body this is, whether it is the Colingah Tank (marked in Upjohn's map) opposite today's Nellie Sengupta Sarani (erstwhile Lindsay Street) or the one opposite the Park Street–Chowringhee crossing, with the Burial Ground Road branching off eastward. The records tell us that one of the busy builders in the area was Dr Andrew Williams,[1] who was something of a pioneer whose principal concern was to clear the area of native huts and open it up to the refreshing breeze from the south.

27 The houses along Chowringhee, by Thomas Daniell, 1787

On 11 November 1781 the doctor had written a letter to the Governor-General in Council[2] which kicked off with a panegyric to the Government for the good work it was doing to improve conditions in the town. Among other things, Williams wrote:

> Your exertion in promoting and encouraging improvements in which the public benefit is deeply interested are acts which attract public acknowledgement. Recent experience has evinced the utility of the improvement of the town, not only with respect to the convenience but also the healthfulness of it. Seriously considering your well disposed designs, I beg leave to offer to your consideration a request I have to make.

He then went on to say that he had built four houses 'at Cheringee' by virtue of which 'a large and extensive space of nauseous broken ground has been cleared and levelled'. The development had not only

> … caused a more agreeable aspect, but is also attended with many other advantages. By the huts being removed, the broken ground filled up, and the noxious jungle removed, it may even have been of some advantage to Calcutta, by the admission of a purer air, it being to the southward of the town.

There was the Calcutta militia sepoys' barracks in the area and Williams had discovered that, being 'too contiguous' and to the south of his house, they were a 'great impediment'. He felt the barracks were proving to be inconvenient not merely to his own house but also to all the houses in the neighbourhood. He wrote that if the barracks 'were removed and an elegant house built, which I would do on obtaining the ground they occupy, it would not only be an ornament to the row of buildings but of signal advantage to that part of the town'.

Williams' specific request to the Supreme Council was that the ground on which the barracks stood[3] be given to him 'on the usual and customary terms, and for the interest before mentioned'. He suggested that the barracks be shifted, and that

> … some ground near that on which the Governor-General's troop is cantoned might be suitable for that purpose, or a spot might be chosen between the jail and the hospital.[4] The sepoys being near the jail and hospital, an advantage results therefrom. The only reason that can be urged against either is their approaching nearer the fort than the present barracks: but even if that argument was used it must be on a calculation formed from conjecture, for I apprehend on examination the contrary would be ascertained. Besides, the sepoy barracks are temporary buildings, that on any occasion might in an instant be destroyed. Therefore, no harm could arise thereform.

Williams added that the 'principal' part of the ground behind the barracks was his, 'and also some on each side (of) the tank[5] where at present most of the families of the sepoys reside'. He wanted the families to be removed not only because it would be 'convenient to myself' but also because a new law had directed that 'all straw buildings within the precincts (of the town) are to be pulled down after the 1st of March next', the Riding House only excepted.[6] Williams offered to erect new barracks for the sepoys at his own expense 'in order to avoid being troublesome to Government'. There was also a personal element guiding the doctor's actions relating to his property move. As he put it,

> Added to the inconvenience I experience from the barracks, I likely in future may feel the weight of a still greater [discomfort] by the ground being disposed off to another person: uninfluenced by ill nature, yet partiality of opinion may direct his mind to build, much to the prejudice of my house.

Williams, in fact, had had his eye on this bit of land for quite some time. Six years earlier, in February 1775, he had written to the Calcutta Committee of Revenue[7] that, some time back, with the permission of P.M. Dacres, then president of the committee, an official had accompanied him and measured 'two Biggas eleven cottahs of ground to the southward of Mr Kiernander's house [Kiernander, therefore, had a house in the area] and northward of the great tank [in] Choringee', which he wanted to buy. Even at this early stage, Williams had written that if all the ground was built upon 'it would be productive of salutary effects to the Settlement, as in this case a large quantity of filth and stagnant water must be removed'. The interesting part of these early proceedings is that since the Calcutta Committee of Revenue found the Williams representation to be 'exactly similar to that of Mr Henry Guinand', it approached the Governor-General in Council for orders. The latter approved Williams' request,[8] the committee being told that it should fix the rent which Williams should pay for the land he wanted. Curiously, the Proceedings also indicate that the Governor-General in Council agreed with the committee 'disposing of the ground which Mr Guinand has requested after it shall have been properly valued and you fix its rent'. If the two purchase proposals were 'exactly similar', relating to the same plot of land (see below), how could the Governor-General in Council approve of both?

Henry Guinand's proposal to buy the ground 'on the eastern side of the great Tank near Chirringhy' was dated 17 October 1774, the ground being vacant and measuring three-and-a-half bighas 'entirely distinct and separate from the late Mr Weller's land and no ways interfering with the seapoys' access to the tank'. He added that the land was 'at present … useless to the Company being only encroached upon by daily building of hutts which pay no rent'. Guinand wanted the ground so that he could 'erect a bungelow, under such rent as to the gentlemen may seem meet'.[9] Giving us an idea of the evolving character of the land in the area and the use it was put to, the jarib amin, Mukun Chand, in his report to the committee,[10] said the land 'was formerly inhabited by divers ryotts who were removed in the Government of Mr Vansittart for the convenience of the seapoys quartered in the barracks built thereabouts in affording them a place for the residence of their wives and families'. The report said that these were the only inhabitants at present occupying the ground 'and that the Company have not since that time received any *malguzary* for it'. The committee's view was that since (as it appeared from Chand's survey) 'there is a very considerable spot over and above this which was dispeopled at the same time and for the same purpose, and the Seapoys now quartered at that station are but few in number', Guinand's request could be complied with 'without any detriment to the public service or injury to individuals'.

After Henry Guinand's death, the matter was taken up by his son J.H. Guinand who found among his father's papers evidence of rent being paid 'upon a grant of 12 begas of land situate at Chyringy made (over to) him by the president and Council so long ago as the year 1776 or 1777'. He further discovered that his father had 'applied by letter for a pottah and possession of this land in the year

1777 and verbally at several periods since; and was prevailed upon to suspend his claim to the latter while the lascars and corps of militia remained there'.[11] Importantly, in June 1783 John Scott, the then Collector of Calcutta, informed the committee that the plot sought by Guinand was 'the same spot for which Doctor Williams lately applied'.[12] Guinand Junior's plea to the authorities was that

> ... as the quit rent of my father's grant has been constantly levied and paid, I hope gentlemen that you will consider his estate entitled to a preference in any future [allocation] of that property and by way of compensation for the delay he submitted to from a [regard] to a publick convenience, that you will be pleased to put me in possession of the quantity above mentioned to the southward of and immediately contiguous to the spot upon which Mr Williams house stands now tenanted by Mr Bruere and on the same terms of purchase.[13]

The plea failed. On 19 August 1783 the Governor-General in Council wrote to the Committee of Revenue that it considered Guinand's 'claim to the ground at Cheringee as obsolete'. It added:

> At the time that we authorised the disposal of the ground the value of it was little or nothing whereas it is now become very considerable; and as Mr Guinand has suffered so long a period as nine years to elapse without taking up a pottah for the ground, we cannot allow him to possess it. Whatever sum therefore he can prove to have been paid on account of rent must be returned to him as it was received without authority.[14]

This then was the background to Dr Williams' renewed interest in the piece of land in question. The authorities did not act promptly on his 11 November 1781 letter. More than a year later, on 4 March 1783, the Governor-General in Council sent to the Committee of Revenue a second letter from Williams dated 27 February 1783 on the same subject.[15] Williams was provoked to write this letter, which was in the nature of a reminder to the Government, by the reports he had received that 'a large spot of ground between the new prison and large tank near the great road to the eastward[16] is … to be appropriated to the use of barracks and are ready for receiving them'.[17] Referring to his November 1781 letter, Williams asked the Government to expedite any move it was contemplating in this direction so that the removal of the sepoys to the new barracks could be completed 'before the commencement of the rains'.

Once more the doctor alluded to his contribution to the development of the town, in the process giving us an idea of what the area south of the Indian Museum was like nearly 230 years ago. He wrote:

> The pain which I have taken and the expence which I have incurred in the new buildings which I have raised at Cheringhee are not unknown to the members of your Hon'ble Board, and I believe it will be admitted for me that I have not been backward in contributing my full share to the improvements which have taken place during the Government of Mr Hastings in the aspect of the town. But my plan is not yet finished. What remains to be done is clearing the remaining ground to the southward of my new houses of the bungaloes now upon it, and to complete the row of buildings in that neighbourhood by erecting one or two elegant houses in their stead. And all this I pledge myself that I will do if the Board are pleased to comply with my request.

Williams added that he was prepared to purchase the ground in question from the Company 'on the same terms on which I bought that which my new houses stand on, or on any other that the Board may deem equitable and just'.

This time the Government acted with promptitude. It asked the Committee of Revenue[18] to make a valuation of the ground in question 'as also an accurate estimate of the expence that will attend the removing of the barracks [to] the place mentioned by Mr Williams as lying between the new jail and the hospital, reporting the same to us'. Within a month, the committee's jarib amin, Nimnarain Mitra, reported that the area between the new jail and the hospital measured twenty-nine bighas waste land and that the sepoy barracks at Chowringhee occupied nine bighas of waste land of which five bighas being 'next to the road' were priced at Rs 20 a katha, the remaining four bighas 'within' costing Rs 15 a katha. The total cost of the land would, therefore, come to Rs 3,200. The expense of removing the barracks would be Rs 500, 'but the building and adjustment of them on the same plan as they are at present will amount to 3,000 rupees'.[19] However, the Committee of Revenue was not happy with Mitra's pricing of the land. It thought it was 'too low' and asked the Collector of Calcutta, John Scott, 'to ascertain the real value of the ground and report thereon to the Committee'. Scott agreed with Mitra's estimate.[20]

It would appear that the pricing issue was not resolved and the transfer of the ground in question not effected, for two years later (on 6 April 1785) Captain Mark Wood, the Surveyor-General, was writing to the Governor-General in Council[21] for a plot of ground in Chowringhee which was in fact that on which the barracks were located. Wood wrote:[22]

> By the reduction of the Calcutta militia sepoys, the temporary sheds used for barracks having not only become useless but being a nuisance and retarding the improvement of that part of Calcutta, I am, from these considerations as well as the very considerable interest which I have in the adjoining buildings,[23] induced to submit to your Hon'ble Board proposals either for the purchase or exchange of this ground.

Wood offered to buy the plot 'on the same terms that I purchased the ground immediately adjoining and equally valuable from Mr Charles Short a few months ago'. He added that in future, if the ground in question was wanted 'for the cantonment and accommodation of a battalion of sepoys', he would 'exchange an equal quantity of ground a few hundred yards farther to the southward but equally well calculated for the purpose'. He would bear the expense of removing to the new plot 'the temporary shed that now stands on the ground at Cheringhy'. Routinely, the Governor-General in Council asked the committee to report on the sale of the ground involved and also whether there were any objections to the transaction. On its part, the committee sent the letter to the collector 'with directions to report upon the nature, property and value of the ground' applied for by Wood.[24] By the end of the year, in December, the Committee of Revenue was writing to the Governor-General in Council that it had enquired into the status of the ground sought by Wood and had not come across any objection to his request. It added: 'The spot which he wishes to purchase is unappropriated *comar* ground and contains 10 begahs 7 cottahs. The average price of ground in that quarter we understand to be from 40 to 50 rupees per cottah'.[25]

In the meantime, however, a new player, William Jackson,[26] had appeared on the scene. The Governor-General in Council informed the Committee of Revenue[27] in early January 1786 that it had been approached by Jackson with a plea to buy the ground 'occupied for the use of the late Sebundy Corps (the sepoys' militia) at Cheringhee'. Jackson had written that the 'barracks formerly occupied' by the militia had become useless on its abolition and that the accommodations 'are now inhabited by those strangers who took immediate possession of them'. He wrote that as it had become a practice with the Governor-General in Council 'to give grants of ground upon paying some consideration for the same' he offered to buy the plot mentioned. Like Williams, Jackson focused on the aspect of beautifying the town. He said that 'by destroying the remains of the present ruinous erections and building a handsome house or houses on the spot, it will rid the respectable neighbourhood of Chiringhee of a great nuisance and add to the ornament of Calcutta'.[28]

As with the application made by Captain Wood, the Committee of Revenue responded favourably to Jackson's request stating that there were no objections to the ground in question being disposed of. But it kept reminding the Governor-General in Council that Wood had applied for the same ground, once on 5 December 1785 and again on 5 January 1786. Faced with this situation, the Supreme Council opted for the auction route and ordered the Committee of Revenue to dispose of the ground 'by outcry upon a building lease'.[29] But this was not the end of the story for the plot on which the sepoy militia barracks once stood. While John Mackenzie, a member of the committee, proposed at its 30 March 1786 meeting that the orders for the auction 'be carried into execution', William Cowper, the committee president, did not agree with the order 'being executed at present having some time since received directions from the Hon'ble Board to delay the sale which he accordingly notified at the time to the Committee'.[30]

The delay in the sale was probably ordered by the Governor-General in Council after it received a representation from Wood who, like Jackson, was keeping a close watch on the proceedings. On 21 February 1786 Wood had written to the Governor-General in Council[31] that he had been informed by a Revenue Department official of the decision to hold an auction and that he was disappointed for a specific reason. He wrote:

> As my chief inducement for making proposals to your Hon'ble Board for either the purchase or exchange of this ground was to prevent its falling into the hands of people who might by either converting it into a bazar or erecting thereon inconsiderable buildings become a nuisance to the neighbourhood, and as I am apprehensive your resolution to dispose of it by public sale will by no means have this effect, I humbly assure myself that the considerable interest which I hold in the improvement of this quarter of the city of Calcutta will plead with you my excuse for once more troubling you on this subject.

Wood then injected into the picture a sentiment which was distinct from personal interest, which had not been mentioned earlier. He wrote:

> There is nothing more wanted in the city of Calcutta than a proper suite of rooms for public entertainments, assemblys, concerts, etc,

> but although this seems to be universally [agreed upon] yet I do not know that any steps have ever been taken to meet the wishes of the settlement.[32] The old Court House in which Government is obliged to give the public entertainments is [not] only ill adapted for the purpose, but at present there is great danger of its falling every time that it is used, and should this misfortune ever happen the lives of many of the most valuable citizens will be lost.

Wood said that some people had objected to the scheme on the ground that Chowringhee was 'too remote, but they ought previously to have recollected that in the more centrical parts of Calcutta no ground so proper is to be had'. He then looked into the crystal ball and proclaimed that 'it is probable in a few years this will be the most centrical situation of the European quarter of Calcutta, and that the extent of ground and (airy) situation gives it every advantage'.

Taking advantage of hindsight, it can be said that this was perhaps the earliest effort to make the area associated with Park Street what it became in later times, namely, the city's hub of entertainment and recreation. The details of Wood's proposal for 'a suite of rooms for public entertainment' were as follows:[33]

1. That for this purpose the ground at Cheringhy on which the Sebundy Corps was cantoned shall be given up, and that two gentlemen on the part of the Government and two on the part of the public shall be nominated to value it agreeably to what ground has been sold for in the neighbourhood within these last twelve months;
2. That Government be paid on account of the E I Company the value of this ground;
3. That Government be entitled to give all public dinners and entertainments in these rooms, and on such other occasions as the Hon'ble Governor General may judge proper;
4. That Government do allow the same monthly sum for the use of these rooms which they at present pay for the same purpose;
5. That a sum of money not exceeding one lack of rupees nor under

75,000 be raised for the purpose of defraying the expence of the ground and constructing thereon an elegant suite of rooms the plan of which to be submitted to the Hon'ble Governor General and Council previous to its being commenced;

6. That Lieut Charles Wyatt of the Engineers Corps,[34] who has been regularly educated as an architect, have the superintendence and direction of the building under the control of those by whom the money is subscribed.

Jackson does not figure in the records after this which could imply that he was no longer a candidate for the purchase of the ground in question. But Wood was soon to have a competitor in the shape of a group of people keen on setting up a riding school in the growing town. This group threw its hat into the ring with an application to the Governor-General in Council for the same spot of ground.[35] The application was made on 12 February 1786 for 'a free grant of … land at Cheringhee, the spot situated between the road leading the Burying Ground and Mr John Murray's [which probably was to the north of the road]'.[36] The land, the applicants[37] said, was being sought 'to erect a riding-school for the general use of the Settlement', adding that they would not have approached the Governor-General but for the fact that they could not find any ground in the town 'which would answer the end proposed'. The letter concluded with the urging: 'In this country where the horses are for the most part restive and vicious, the general utility of a riding school will be readily admitted.'[38]

Faced with two suitors for the same spot of ground, both enjoying a certain weight in Calcutta society, the matter had turned complicated. An effort was now made to explore the possibility of satisfying both parties. The Governor-General issued a Minute in which he said:[39]

In consequence of the two preceding letters [the one from the riding-school dated February 12, 1786 and Wood's submission of February 21, 1786], I propose that the Surveyor-General [Wood himself] be

> directed to make a survey of the ground at Cheringee now applied for, [and that for] the intended erection of a riding-school, and that he lay a plan thereof before this Board reporting also whether the ground be sufficiently extensive to admit both of the public rooms which he propose d to be built and of the riding-school mentioned in the address above recorded from the sundry inhabitants of Calcutta.

Wood carried out the survey, his finding being that the ground was sufficiently large both for the proposed public rooms and the riding school, 'but more particularly so should your Hon'ble Board be pleased to grant in addition three or four biggas of ground to the eastward ... by which means any inconveniencing that might be apprehended from the stables of the riding-school being so near the public rooms will be avoided'.[40]

The Governor-General in Council immediately ordered that, as indicated in Wood's scheme, a further four bighas be set aside 'for the erection of stables' so as to prevent it from becoming 'a nuisance to the other buildings in that vicinity'.[41] It was on the basis of Wood's survey that Benjamin Aplin, Secretary to the Government, wrote to the riding school people that, since a proposal had been received from Wood

> ... for building rooms for publick entertainments on the same spot of ground as that which you have solicited a grant of for erecting a riding school upon, (and) for both of which it appears from a survey that there is sufficient ground, they have been pleased to make a ground thereof for the abovementioned purposes, and of a further quantity of four biggas adjoining thereto for stables, information of which has been sent to the Committee of Revenue.[42]

Six months later, in August 1786, the riding school enthusiasts pursued their case with the authorities asking the Committee of Revenue for possession of the ground which was to house the school ('manege') and the stables.[43] W. Barton, John Bristow and John Hyde wrote that they wanted to be given possession

> … of one half of the ground, first mentioned, to the northward, reserving the other half, to the southward, for Major Mark Wood … and also that you will grant us the further favour of putting us in possession of the other four begahs of ground by issuing the usual sunnuds and pottahs.

The Board of Revenue asked the collector to prepare a patta for the ground concerned with the stipulation that it would be appropriated 'to the express and sole purposes for which it has been granted, namely, a public manege and stables'.[44] Importantly, since a token rent would still have to be paid, it was decided that a rupee per annum would be paid to the Government by the organisers of the school.

While the riding school project was making steady progress, perhaps because it was backed by the cream of Calcutta society and also because there was a felt need for it in view of a growing European population, Wood's proposal for public entertainment rooms was running into trouble. Cornwallis had assumed the Governor-Generalship in September 1786 and in February the following year the Governor-General in Council informed the Board of Revenue[45] that it had received a letter from Wood on 25 January 1787 in which the latter had said that he saw 'little probability of the plan for constructing of public rooms being carried into effect unless it should have the assistance of Government'. In view of this he thought it proper to resign 'the trust of the ground committed to my charge to whomsoever your Lordship may be pleased to appoint for this purpose'.[46] This was a blow not merely to Wood but also to the authorities who had set great store by the project because it promised to fulfil a pressing need being felt by the expanding town. One result of this was that the Board of Revenue was not agreeable to jettisoning the project so easily. It observed that the 'relinquishment of the ground granted for a house of public entertainment by Major Wood does not in their opinion invalidate the claim of the public to whom the ground was virtually granted'. It left the subject open for enquiry and asked Richard Johnson, the Advocate-General, 'to obtain the necessary information'.[47]

Those behind the riding school project were aware of the developments taking place. They took advantage of Wood's withdrawal from the scene, seizing on the opportunity to expand their own project. On 9 February, that is, just two weeks after Wood had written to the Governor-General in Council giving up his project to set up rooms for public entertainment, 'the committee of gentlemen formed for the purpose of establishing a riding-school' wrote to the Council[48] that, ever since it had made the original application a year earlier, 'a sum sufficient for building the riding-school had been subscribed and that, at a general meeting of the subscribers, we were elected a committee for the management of the business' (the letter was signed by William Barton, A. Kyde, John Hyde and John Bristow). The letter then amended the original application's stand on the land issue. It said that 'the half of the ground is not of sufficient extent for the purpose required, and as Major Wood has relinquished his claim we solicit your lordship will be pleased to favour us with a grant of the whole'. Possibly at the prodding of the Governor-General in Council (there is no official record of this), and despite the fact that the advocate-general had been asked to look into the issue, the Board of Revenue wasted no time and offered the land returned by Wood to the riding school 'with the resolution that the stables shall be built separately upon the 4 begahs to the eastward'.[49]

It was inevitable that claims to the ground in question would be made by other parties, which got the Government busy in probing their veracity before giving the plot to the riding school. In this particular case it was a native who became involved and it is instructive to note the extent to which the authorities went to examine his claim before taking a final decision on the issue. Specifically, even though Calcutta's European society was involved, the authorities did not hesitate to treat the rights of other people with sanctity, in this case the rights of a native answering to the description of a '*jemadar*'. The decision to hand over the ground to the riding school was taken only after the Government had satisfied itself that the claim could not be admitted.

In March 1787 we find Archibald Seton, the collector of Calcutta, writing to the Board of Revenue[50] that having been told earlier that Ahmed Sodial, the claimant, was 'a poor, old, infirm man', he thought it his duty 'to do everything in my power to endeavour to trace his right'. The Board of Revenue itself appears to have been sympathetic to the claim of Sodial—who claimed he had been granted land in the area north of today's Park Street 'in Mr Vansittart's time' (1764)—for it wrote to the Governor-General in Council that

> ... if in considering the circumstances of the (Sodial) claim it should be objected to as being weakened by having remained so long unasserted, it appears to us but just to remember that the timid character of the natives of this country might well have deterred Ahmed Sodiall from preferring his claim to Government (to whom alone it could be preferred) seeing that he was dispossessed with a view (to) accommodating their sepoys.[51]

The Governor-General in Council too exhibited a preference for adhering to the principle of protecting the rights of the individual irrespective of religion or social status when it wrote to the Board of Revenue:[52]

> We think the clear line for determining on the claim of Amod Sodiall is by ascertaining whether he has received any compensation from Government either at the time of his ground being first occupied by the sepoy barracks or since for being deprived of the possession. If he has, his present claim must be rejected. If not it must stand good in preference to the proposed grant for a riding-school.

While Sodial swore on the Koran that he had not received any compensation from the Government for the land taken over for the sepoy barracks, the collector felt that this was indeed the case, 'for if he had, it is probable that, notwithstanding the informality and inaccuracy with which these matters were formerly conducted, some mention of it would have been made in the records of the office, which, after the most diligent search, I do not find to be the case'.[53] In the end, both Sodial and the riding school committee were given pattas to the land in question, the denouement being wholly the handiwork of Archibald Seton who, in the closing years of Lord Minto's reign as Governor-General (1813), rose to become a member of the Supreme Council.[54]

The Proceedings dealing with the Ahmed Sodial case are also useful because they provide us with an idea of what the topography of the area was like at the time. Among other things, it would appear that the road, or at least a part of it, which used to be called Kyd Street (today's Dr M. Ishaque Road) was already there 225 years ago. In May 1786 Seton was writing to the Board of Revenue that

> … the angular piece of ground upon which the sepoy barracks formerly stood contains exactly 12 begas 8 cottahs after deducting a sufficient quantity *for a road to the back part of Cheringhy* [emphasis added] which, in consequence of a correspondence upon the subject with Mr Tiretta, the Public Surveyor, I find to be necessary for the convenience of the inhabitants in the neighbourhood.[55]

The collector also told the Board of Revenue that since the official records did not enable him to fix the precise spot of ground given to Sodial in 1764, and since the latter had claimed as his property the ground on which the sepoys' cantonment stood,

> … and as these were erected upon the spot contiguous to, and immediately to the southwards of Mr (Bernard) McCullum's house, now occupied by Mr (W) Farquharson, I considered the ground adjoining to Mr McCullum's as the property of Ahmed Sodiall, and accordingly measured off, in that place, the quantity specified in his pottah, namely, 8 begahs 6 cottah.

According to Seton, the plot was 'bounded' by McCullum's wall 'to the eastward and northward; and, on the west and south sides, by the road to Russapugly,[56] and that leading to the interior parts of Chowringhy'.

A year later, in May 1787, the collector wrote[57] that, given the length of time which had elapsed since the award of the patta to Sodial, 'a road leading to the back parts of Chouranghy has been suffered to be made through the ground to which, by this adjustment, he is entitled'. He said the road was considered to be 'an established and necessary road' by the police, which meant that it could not be closed at that point of time (1787). The implication of this for Sodial was that the area taken up by the road had to be deducted from 'the quantity specified in' his patta. The measurement of the road indicated that it covered an area of 12 kathas, which reduced Sodial's property by an equal amount, that is, from 8 bighas 6 kathas to 7 bighas 14 kathas. The impact of the road on Sodial did not end there. It was built in such a way that it passed through Sodial's property dividing it into two distinct parts. This led Seton to suggest that two pattas be made out in the name of Sodial for the two separate plots, one covering 7 bighas and the other 14 kathas in place of the single patta which he was given in 1764. The collector said that this method of allotting to Sodial his land left a spot of 3 bighas 13 kathas 4 ½ chittacks 'situated to the southward of Ahmed's property for a manege, and another situated to the northeast containing 2 begahs 15 cottahs 14 chittacks, which last will be appropriated to stabling agreeably to your directions of the 16th February last'. The dimensions of the latter plot were arrived at after deducting from it 'a sufficient quantity for the continuation of the .... road to the interior parts of Chourunghy'.

The part of Chowringhee extending to the southwards of Burial Ground Road was practically owned by a number of Europeans who had bought land during the time of Warren Hastings. Before Hastings' time (1772–1785), it would appear that the major English zamindar in this region was William Frankland, the Bengal Council Consultations of 5 January 1761[58] stating that the Council had thought it fit to buy for Governor Vansittart (1760–1764) as a country retreat Frankland's garden house to the south of Burial Ground Road. In its time, this house was located where the Loreto establishment in Middleton Row now stands. It is a different matter that the move was shot down by the Court of Directors which ultimately led Vansittart to buy the property with his own money.[59] Barring Belvedere and Clive's Dum Dum House, this is an early instance of the authorities venturing beyond the immediate confines of the old fort to choose a country retreat for the governor of the town.[60]

At the time of the Vansittart garden-house problem the South Park Street Cemetery was yet to be opened,[61] which means that the road turning eastward from the old Pilgrims' Road (modern-day Jawaharlal Nehru Road—Chowringhee Road) along the alignment of Park Street was hardly used at all, at least by the sahibs. It is not known whether it was used much by the natives either, or whether there was any road there worth the name at all. The area where Free School Street meets Park Street was probably far busier in terms of native traffic in view of the existence of a road from the Lalbazar locality to this place, as is indicated by Wilson and by early maps of the town.[62] Reverend James Long's description of the area being infested with 'dakaits' has already been cited.[63] That in such circumstances the Council should think it appropriate to locate the governor's country seat in this 'insecure' area tells us something about the way the minds of the authorities were working. Briefly, despite the memories of the sacking of Calcutta thirty years earlier, the political and administrative steps taken in the intervening years, not to speak of the decision to set up the new fort in the western neighbourhood, had had the effect of enhancing the sense of security to such an extent that residential forays by Europeans into 'virgin' areas were no longer considered to be risky ventures. The regular visits to the new burial ground had also made the sahibs familiar with the area in question. Not surprisingly, therefore, genteel folk began moving into this part of the growing town from the 1760s, a trickle which, as the records show, turned into a flood within a quarter of a century.

Another major English landowner in these parts was George Vansittart, the brother of the governor.[64] So was Charles Short who had extensive property all over the town and outside it. Henry Watson, who set up the docks at Kidderpur in the 1770s, was also in the same league. We are told[65] that in February 1784 Charles Short had sold to Joseph Bernard Smith of the Bengal civil service eight bighas in 'Dihi Birjee and Chowkerber [Chakrabere or Chakraberia]', which was bounded to the eastward by the garden belonging to John Dynely[66] 'lately occupied by Sir Elijah Impey (and) formerly the property of George Vansittart', that is, the country house and grounds of Governor Vansittart; to the southward by a road 'leading from the public road which bounds the Esplanade' (today's Chowringhee Road) to Dynely's garden, which suggests that the road followed the alignment of today's Middleton Street; to the westward 'by a road … running from north to south joining the road leading from the Chyringhy Bungalows[67] towards the Burying Ground (Park Street) and the road leading from the publick road which bounds the Esplanade to the house and garden aforementioned [Middleton Street]', that is, Russell Street (renamed Anandilal Poddar Sarani); and to the northward by ground belonging to Short. This would suggest that the eight bighas lay to the east of Russell Street, probably where the Royal Calcutta Turf Club offices and Meghalaya House are located today. The records say that the property was 'part of a piece of ground containing 819 bigas' in Birjee and Chakraberia 'near Calcutta' to the east of Chowringhee Road, 'lately purchased by the said Charles Short from Henry Watson of Fort William in the Province of Bengal, a Lieutenant-Colonel in the Service of the United Company of Merchants of England trading to the East Indies on the establishment of Bengal aforesaid, and Henry Halsey', the plot being formerly in the possession and occupation of George Vansittart 'of Bisham Abbey'.[68]

Notes

1 A medical practitioner, Williams was member of the Hospital Board (Board of Revenue Proceedings, 24 July 1787).

2 Committee of Revenue Proceedings, 6 March 1783. Williams was on a buying spree in the area because a few months earlier, he had applied for a patta '... for a tank near his house in Chowringhee called Teeklee Carras tank [possibly another name for the Jingeera-talao which one can see today to the south of the Indian Museum], it formerly together with the ground round it belonged to Gopaul Seit. In 1164 [1758] when Gobindapur was taken for the new fort this tank and ground was made *comar*, and *pottahs* have since been granted for part of the ground to others.'

The tank covered ten bighas and five kathas and there were fourteen kathas of waste land 'in the south and east side for the whole of which he [Williams] desires a *pottah* on condition that it shall remain open for all people to draw water from it as formerly'. The committee agreed to grant Williams a patta 'under the proposed conditions' (Committee of Revenue Proceedings, 16 July 1781).

3 Where, indeed, were the sepoys' barracks located? The records—along with Williams' specific request—seem to indicate that the ground concerned was to the north of Park Street, roughly on the spot where the Asiatic Society stands today and a bit to the north of it. But there is a reference which muddies the waters by hinting that the location could have been to the south of Park Street, that is, on the other side of the road. Property-transaction records pertaining to 5 November 1786 ('Materials for the History of Calcutta Streets & Houses 1780-1834, Part 1', *Bengal Past and Present,* vol. 14, January–March 1917, p. 48) tell us that, 'Pelegrine Treves sells to Bulleram Ghose for Sa. Rs 40,000 a new built dwelling-house and six bigas of land "at Cheringhee in or near Calcutta", "bounded to the northward by the Road leading from the Cheringhee Road to the European Burying Ground and by the Sepoy Cantonments of Cheringhee, to the westward by the Road leading from Cheringhee to Russah Pughlah, and to the southward and eastward by the ground and building of Captain Mark Wood which said house and premises are now in the occupation of Edward Fenwick, Esq".'

Is it possible that the barracks were located both to the north and south of Park Street, the road to the burial ground cutting through them on its eastward journey? The transaction quoted above also indicates that natives had begun to acquire property in the early years in localities which had hitherto been European preserves.

4 That is, the area between the Victoria Memorial Hall and the SSKM Hospital, formerly the Presidency General Hospital. As regards the jail, W.K. Firminger writes in *Bengal Past and Present* (vol. 14, January–March 1917, p. 63) that '... a letter of the Board to Court, dated 30th November 1778, shows that the "Birjee Jail" (i.e. the late Presidency Goal on the Maidan) had been erected in that year: but the new building was not used until 1781, when it was utilised for the accommodation of French prisoners of war.'

For details of the early hospital, see chapter 'An Infirm Hospital' in Section One.

5 The Jingeera-talao.

6 This by-law was one of the earliest steps taken by the English Government to alter radically the physical character of the town, making a sharp break with civic conditions which had their roots in the pre-English past.

7 Calcutta Committee of Revenue Proceedings, 3 February 1775.

8 Ibid., 16 March 1775.

9 Ibid., 21 October 1774.

10 Ibid., 10 November 1774.

11 Committee of Revenue Proceedings, 2 June 1783.

12 Ibid., 3 July 1783.

13 Ibid., 2 June 1783.

14 Ibid., 25 August 1783.

15 Ibid., 6 March 1783.

16 Probably the Birjee-talao, the remnants of which are to be found today squeezed in between St Paul's Cathedral, the Academy of Fine Arts and Rabindra Sadan.

17 Committee of Revenue Proceedings, 6 March 1783.

18 Ibid.

19 Ibid., 3 April 1783.

20 Ibid., 1 May 1783. Eight years earlier, the price for the land sought by Williams was put at Rs 50 a katha by a Calcutta Committee of Revenue amin, which was objected to by the doctor as being too high. He had then said that he bought the 'adjoining ground of private persons for 40 Rupees a Cottah; and the land purchased of the Company by Mr (Henry) Guinand contiguous thereto is only valued at the rate of 25 Rupees'. According to the committee, the amin had

put the difference in price down to Williams' ground being 'adjoining to the high road'. The Calcutta Committee of Revenue felt that the price of the Williams' land was estimated 'too highly' and had left the decision on price to be taken by the Governor-General in Council (Calcutta Committee of Revenue Proceedings, 14 April 1775).

21 John Macpherson had taken over the Governor-Generalship after the departure of Warren Hastings at the end of January that year.

22 Committee of Revenue Proceedings, 20 October 1785.

23 This makes it clear that Wood, like Williams, was already a property owner in this part of the town. Note the use of the word 'considerable'.

24 Committee of Revenue Proceedings, 20 October 1785.

25 Governor-General in Council Proceedings, 16 February 1786.

26 Jackson was attorney to the East India Company in 1790 (Board of Trade Proceedings, 18 January 1790).

27 Committee of Revenue Proceedings, 12 January 1786.

28 Chowringhee had, therefore, already become a 'respectable' neighbourhood within thirty years of the fall of Calcutta and its retaking by the English.

29 Governor-General in Council Proceedings, 16 February 1786.

30 Committee of Revenue Proceedings, 30 March 1786.

31 Governor-General in Council Proceedings, 30 March 1786.

32 Wood here describes Calcutta both as a 'city' and a 'settlement' in the same sentence. Was he distinguishing the 'European settlement' from the wider city which included the local people as well?

33 Governor-General in Council Proceedings, 30 March 1786.

34 The same Charles Wyatt who was chosen by Wellesley to build his Government House (Raj Bhavan) thirteen years later. Narrating a story about Wyatt which throws light not only on the man but also on the times he lived in, Dennis Kincaid writes in *British Social Life in India, 1608-1937* (Routledge & Kegan Paul, 1973), p. 37, that on one occasion Wyatt, returning to the barracks at dawn, 'thrashed a soldier for no imaginable offence, and then drawing his sword (ran) him through the body and finally, when he was dead, trampled on his face'. Wellesley, during whose time segregation between the natives and Europeans was encouraged, felt that 'the loss of his commission was perhaps sufficient punishment, for a gentleman would naturally feel this disgrace keenly'. Wyatt (1758–1819) joined the East India Company in 1780, was commissioned a Lieutenant in 1781, was captured on his

voyage out, and did not reach Calcutta until 1782. He was promoted to Captain in the Bengal Engineers in 1800, and also made Commissioner of Police, and in 1803 Superintendent of Public Works. He returned to England having made a fortune, and became a Tory MP (Robb, *Useful Friendship*, p. 260, note 8). James Wyatt, the English architect, was his uncle, but it is from Wood's description that we know that the nephew had had a 'regular education' in the same profession.

35 Seven years earlier, another riding school—perhaps the first in the town—had been set up by Antonio Angelo Tremanundo to the east of Tank Square on ground 'opposite the house known by the name of the General's House to the eastward, and also that of Mr Charles Child's and abutting in the road to the southward near the wall belonging to Mr Verelst'. The Government agreed to grant him the land for ninety-nine years 'on an annual quit rent of 20 rupees' on the condition that it be 'converted to the purpose of erecting a riding academy, and that no dwelling house be built upon it'. So successful was the venture that a year later Tremanundo asked for more ground so that he could expand his riding school, a plea which also was granted by the authorities. Specifically, the Governor-General in Council ordered '... that a space of eighty feet north of the northern range of Mr Angelo Tremanundo's stables, and running in a parallel line east and west commencing at the eastern ditch of the road leading to the Court House and ending at the ditch opposite to the house at present belonging to Mr Charles Weston, and formerly occupied by the Commander in Chief, be granted to Mr Tremanundo ... and under the same conditions and limitations as are specified in the grant of the ground lately allowed him' (Calcutta Committee of Revenue Proceedings, 13 January 1779 and 27 July 1780).

36 Board of Revenue Proceedings, 16 February 1787. The text of the original letter is to be found in the Governor-General in Council Proceedings of 30 March 1786. Both the Proceedings do not mention the quantity of ground sought, a gap being in place of the figure.

37 The list of applicants comprised a who's who of contemporary Calcutta society and included people like William Barton, John Collins, Robert Ireland, John Bristow, T.D. Pearse, John Evelyn, C. Burrows, W. McGuire, H. Scott, John Hyde, R. Goodlad, Shearman Bird, William Farquharson, W.P. Monik, J. Rider, Nathaniel Bateman, Thomas Legh, William Rook, E. Fenwick, John Bebb, John Hall, F. LeGros, A. Kyde, William Kirkpatrick, Christopher

Knudson, William Harding, George Bussell, William Scott, A. Malony, C. Benezet, C. Barber, E. Dandridge, N. Campbill, William Johnson, William Cowper and R. Johnson.

38 The move was inevitable given the growth of the town. As Peter Robb says (in private communication with the author), the Calcutta of the time was 'like European cities, very reliant on horses, despite the importance of palanquins and hand-drawn carts'.

39 Governor-General in Council Proceedings, 30 March 1786.

40 Ibid., 7 April 1786.

41 As ordered by the Board of Revenue, the then Collector of Calcutta, Archibald Seton, had done his own investigations on the ground and reported that the part of Wood's plan which had been marked for the purpose of erecting stables, containing three bighas five kathas, appeared to be 'very well-adapted to that purpose … as there are no houses situated to the northward of it' (Board of Revenue Proceedings, 7 June 1786). This gives us some idea of how the houses were distributed in the area. Of interest is the dissent note submitted by John Stables, a member of the Governor-General's Council, who held that 'the Company's property in land ought to be sold at public auction for the benefit of the Company', which is why he could not agree with the grant of land to Wood and the riding school (Governor-General in Council Proceedings, 7 April 1786).

42 Board of Revenue Proceedings, 16 February 1787.

43 Ibid., 29 August 1786. Incidentally, the letter makes it clear that the ground on which the school was to come up was occupied by the sepoy barracks, which were still standing at the time the letter was written. On 24 May 1786, Archibald Seton, the collector, had written to the Committee of Revenue that the sepoy barracks stood on an 'angular piece of ground', which in fact describes accurately the location of the Asiatic Society today at the western end of Park Street (ibid., 7 June 1786).

44 Board of Revenue Proceedings, 29 August 1786.

45 Ibid., 16 February 1787.

46 On 20 February 1787 Wood wrote to the Committee of Revenue again (ibid.): 'Many gentlemen in the course of conversation having joined me in regretting the want of rooms for public entertainment – and at the same time expressed a readiness to subscribe a sum of money equal to the construction of such a building in case the ground at Cheringhy could be obtained – I … addressed a letter to the

Governor-General and Council for the joint purposes of constructing thereon rooms for public entertainment and a riding school.'

Wood said that 'upward of twelve months' had passed since the grant of the ground 'and not a single person' had subscribed to the project 'or shown any inclination to forward the plan'. This had led him to return the land to the Government (Board of Revenue Proceedings, 20 February 1787).

Given the fact that public subscriptions were at the time 'a common way both of providing for public goods as well as private enterprises' (Peter Robb in private communication with the author), the mode of financing the project for setting up rooms for entertainment was not an extraordinary development. But it is intriguing why, after the propagation of the project at the highest levels of the Government, there was little follow-up action which, among other things, had the result of putting Mark Wood, its proposer, in an embarrassing situation. One simple explanation would be that since the two projects—the riding school and rooms for public entertainment—were vying with each other for the same plot of land and their respective proposers hailed from the same social strata, those backing the cause of horses were able to prevail on the 'rival' group to drop their proposal.

47 Board of Revenue Proceedings, 16 February 1787.

48 Ibid.

49 Ibid., 20 February 1787. Subsequently, this bit of ground passed to the Asiatic Society which built its rooms on the spot, where they still stand. On 6 July 1804, William Hunter, secretary of the Society, wrote to John Lumsden, chief secretary to the Government, that the Asiatic Society had resolved at its meeting on 29 September 1796, 'as a necessary means for securing the permanency of its institution, and for preserving such books and curiosities as may come into the Society's possession, that a house should be erected for their meetings, as well as for the purposes of a library and museum' (Judicial Criminal Proceedings, 9 August 1804). The secretary was asked to apply to the Government 'for the grant of a spot of ground proper for the site of such a building'. The request was made by the Society on 26 December 1797, but nothing came of it because, at that point of time, the Government did not have any ground in its possession to give to the Society. However, in July 1804, the Society 'having learnt that the spot of ground lately occupied

by the riding-school has reverted to Government', it wanted the Governor-General in Council to grant them the land for their projected building. Hunter wrote: 'The liberal encouragement which Government has always held forth to the investigation of Oriental literature, History, Manners and Customs, encourages the Society to hope that the assistance now requested towards facilitating the prosecution of their researches will be cheerfully accorded, if not inconsistent with the views of Government, respecting the appropriation of the aforesaid piece of land.'

Indicating the importance that integrated planning for the town's development was being given in these early years, a copy of the letter was sent to the Committee for Improving the Town of Calcutta on 4 August 1804 'for their consideration and report'.

50 Board of Revenue Proceedings, 13 March 1787.

51 Ibid.

52 Ibid., 27 March 1787.

53 Ibid., 8 June 1787.

54 Judicial Criminal Proceedings, 14 May 1813.

55 Board of Revenue Proceedings, 8 June 1787. Both Wood's map (published in October 1792) and Upjohn's of 1792–1793 (see image 28 on p. 250) clearly show the road 'leading to the interior parts of Chowringhy', Wood naming the road as 'Chouringhy Tank Street'. Both also show the 'angular piece' of ground at the north-western corner of Burial Ground Road (Park Street) referred to by Seton, marking out the area specifically as a 'manege'.

56 In the early years the official records, in more than one place, refer to Russapuglah as Russapugly. See later for an identical reference by one of the special committees set up by Wellesley's Committee for the Improvement of the Town of Calcutta in 1805. It is possible, though improbable, that, even though spread over a number of years, the 'gender-change' was not much more than just a slip of the pen. Even so, the point needs to be made that the antiquity of the name continues to remain clouded in a myriad possibilities.

57 Board of Revenue Proceedings, 8 June 1787.

58 Wilson, *Old Fort William*, vol. 2, pp. 160–161.

59 Ibid., pp. 165–166, 168.

60 On Belvedere see Ray Choudhury, *The Lord Sahib's House*, pp. 49–51. On Dum Dum House, the Bengal Council was writing to the Court on 24 March 1766: 'A place of retirement from business being

thought absolutely necessary for the President, we have purchased the house at Dum Dum for Current Rupees 23,000' (C.S. Srinivasachari ed., *Fort William-India House Correspondence*, vol. 4 [Delhi: The National Archives of India, 1962], p. 412).

61 It was opened in 1767, the last burials taking place in 1830 (*The South Park Street Cemetery*, 1978, brought out in association with the foundation of an Association for the Preservation of Historical Cemeteries in India, Calcutta, p. 3).

62 See chapter 'The Early Roads'. The Bengal Council Consultation of 15 November 1749 (Wilson, *Old Fort William*, vol. 1, p. 224) makes it clear that Frankland's garden was very much there in 1749. A 1742 map of Calcutta (see image 9 on p. 130) shows a house with grounds which is similar to the Frankland garden house. It does not, however, show the Burial Ground Road because the cemetery was not opened till 1767.

63 *Calcutta Review*, July–December 1852, p. 275. See chapter 'Around the Old Fort'.

64 See Ray Choudhury, *The Lord Sahib's House*, p. 42, note 70.

65 'Materials for the History of Calcutta Streets & Houses 1780-1834, Part 2', *Bengal Past and Present*, vol. 14, January–March 1917, p. 177.

66 John Dynely was Superintendent of the Office of the Bazee Zemin Dufter at the time. He had taken the 'roomy house and compound … lately occupied by Sir Elijah Impey' on a rent of Rs 800 a month and had converted it into his office on the plea that a large office was what he needed at the time given the expanding volume of his department's work (Committee of Revenue Proceedings, 9 August 1782). He was aware that the Government would not allow such a high rent to be paid, his suggestion being that he was ready '… to pay the required [surplus] myself until I can take a commodious house in town at a somewhat [lower] rent; such a one may perhaps be had in a little time, at the rent of 600 sicca Rs per month, and I shall not miss (with your permission) the opportunity of taking it.'

What we can infer here is that in February 1784 Dynely still had not shifted to the town proper from the Middleton Row premises, the initiative to move his office there being perhaps one of the earliest instances, if not the earliest, of a Government department being shifted out of the then limits of the town. Proof that Dynely did come to own the Vansittart garden house at some point of time is provided by the property-transaction records relating to 14–15 March 1788

('History of Calcutta Streets & Houses 1780-1834, Part 2', *Bengal Past and Present,* vol. 14, Part 1, January–March 1917, pp. 169–170).

67 Perhaps the sepoy barracks at the western end of Burial Ground Road.

68 Before George Vansittart a 'Mr Franklin' (probably the Franklin who was Collector-General in 1759—Calcutta Committee of Revenue Proceedings, 21 July 1778) was owner of the grounds (Committee of Revenue Proceedings, 3 April 1783). For details about the evolving ownership of the Vansittart garden, see Calcutta Committee of Revenue Proceedings, 31 October 1774, Committee of Revenue Proceedings, 13 January, 3 April and 2 June 1783. According to one writer ('The City of Calcutta and its Municipal Constitution', *The Calcutta Review*, vol. LXX, 1880, pp. 478–498), in terms of a plan published in the 1780s, there were just four houses in the area south of Park Street, of which the Vansittart garden house must have been one. Incidentally, he also says that, according to a plan of the town prepared in 1756, there were only seventy houses in the native town. This is difficult to accept but, if true, he must have been referring to pucca houses as opposed to huts made of straw and mud. He also writes without attributing any source that 'the site of the present fort was at that time a jungle, and the ground occupied by the fashionable and imposing line of buildings along Chowringhee Road was then covered with bamboo bush jungle, or paddy field swamps', which is what James Long had written about the area earlier.

14

The Dharamtala Bazar

While the sahibs emerged as the major landowners south of Park Street in the years between the retaking of Calcutta by Clive and Admiral Watson and the turn of the eighteenth century, further north along Chowringhee footprints still existed indicative of substantial native landholding in the area. An example of this is the spot on which the Dharamtala Bazar was situated, at the corner of Jawaharlal Nehru Road (Chowringhee) and what is today Lenin Sarani (old Dharamtala Street). Upjohn's map of 1792–1793 shows the spot as uninterrupted ground stretching from Dharamtala Street in the north to Jaun Bazar Road (S.N. Banerjee Road, formerly Corporation Street) in the south. In fact, the plot was indeed one unit till, at the turn of the eighteenth century, inability to meet the liabilities of a mortgage on the part of an owner led to its being broken up into lots. This resulted in the modern property profile of the area which, incidentally, is more than a century old.

Giving us a snapshot of what the area looked like more than two hundred years ago, the property is described thus at the fag end of 1802:[1]

> ... all that well-known extensive and much frequented Bazar, formerly the property of Messrs Smoult and Shakespear and then of him the Nilmunny Holdar, situate lying and being at the corner of the Dhurrumtollah and Chouringhee roads within the Town of Calcutta,

together with the piece or parcel of land containing about five bigas more or less thereunto belonging, on part of which land are erected a number of pucka-built shops and a new handsome and complete range of godowns or boutiques to the west with a verandah in front, and also all that small upper-roomed messuage, tenement, or dwelling-house then occupied by the Superintendent of, and adjoining to, the Bazar, together with the piece or parcel of land thereunto belonging and on part of which the said messuage, tenement or dwelling-house was erected standing and being, and also all that piece and parcel of land and divers godowns and other erections and buildings thereon containing one biga to the same more or less standing and being and lying in Calcutta to the southward of the Dhurrumtollah Bazar aforesaid and then known by the name of Smoult and Shakespear's Bazar, bounded on the east by a

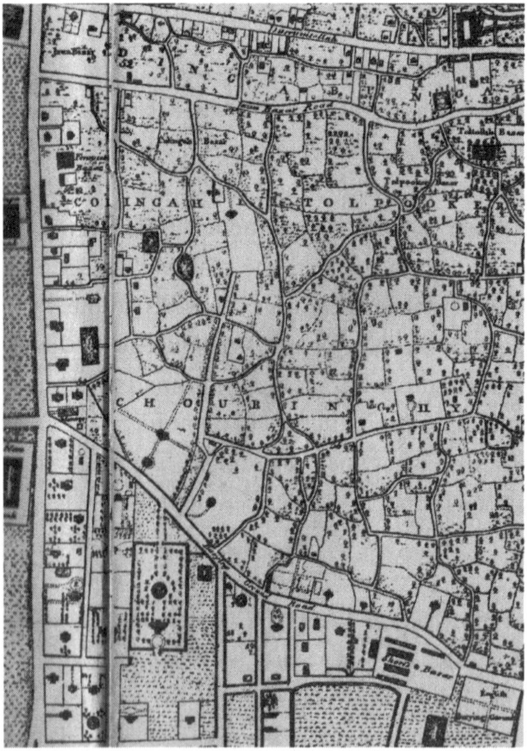

28 Upjohn's map of 1792–1793 showing the location of the Dharamtala and Fenwick's bazars and the angular plot at the south-west corner of Park Street, the scene of frequent road accidents at the turn of the eighteenth century

> piece or parcel of ground, the property of Moohur Khawn, on the west by the public road, on the north by the said Dhurrumtollah Bazar, and on the south by the Jaun Bazar.

The records say that in December 1801, Nilmoni Haldar mortaged the property to William Dring, George Urquhart Lawtie and Blisset William Gould for Sicca Rs 80,000, but Haldar having failed to meet his repayment liabilities the property was put up for auction on 29 December the following year.[2] Importantly, the property was broken up and the sale made in lots, 'the Bazar and Superintendent House, numbered as Lot No. 1', being sold to Rajanarain Ghose for Sicca Rs 53,500.[3]

An earlier transaction (April 1790) tells us that this same bit of ground was mortgaged as one block, extending from Dharamtala Road in the north to Jaun Bazar in the south. We are told:

> Ram Govind Mitter and Ram Chunder Mitter, being indebted to Fairfax Morseby, mortgage for the payment of Sa. Rs 24,377-5-3 a building and 8 bigas and 5 cottas of land at Durhumtollah, bounded on the east by a piece of ground of Monner Cawn and a house late the property of General Stibbert, and to the west Chowringhee Road, on the north the Durhamtollah Road, on the south a piece of ground of Monner Cawn and the Jaun Bazar Road, and also shops,etc and seventeen cottahs of land bounded on the south by the house of Oumurchund Seat.[4]

In February 1791 we find Ram Govind Mitter extending his property to the east of the Dharamtala Bazar, the relevant entry reading:

> William Smoult sells to Ram Govind Mitter for Current Rs 14,000 an unfinished upper-roomed house and ground (15 cottas) with a road 5 cubits in breadth leading to the high road to Chiringee, bounded on the east by the ground of Moncar Cawn, on the west partly by the said road to the said house, and partly by the ground commonly called

> the Dhurrumtollah Bazar, the property of Ram Govind Mitter, on the north by part of the ground belonging to the said Ram Govind Mitter and a house and ground belonging to General Stibbert, and on the south ground belonging to Moncar Cawn and by the high road called the Jaun Bazar.[5]

Earlier still, in 1781, the ground appears to have been a garden since it was known as Ananta Bagh.[6] The relevant entry reads:

> Tuckeram Oudassee[7] mortages to Henry Halsey for Sa. Rs 6,000 'all that piece or parcel of land containing nine bigas (little more or less) called or known by the name of Anunta Baug situate lying and being in that street known by the name of Dhurrumtollah'. On the west the property was bounded 'by the great road east of the Esplanade running south to Chauringee and on the north by the high road leading from the Esplanade aforesaid to Dingah Bungah'.[8]

Initially, William Smoult's effort to set up a bazar on the spot of ground in question was not received well by the authorities in view of objections lodged by Joseph Sherburne who had set up his bazar to the north-east along Dharamtala Road.[9] After a battle which lasted seven years, during which time Smoult had sold the property and re-purchased it, the Governor-General in Council allowed him to set up shop in 1793 on payment of a fixed annual sum, the basis of which had been worked out by Smoult himself.[10] Over the years, the Dharamtala Bazar flourished and became a landmark till such time when it could no longer keep up with the town's evolution into a city. The market's infrastructure had been set up in the 1790s and there was no improvement worth the name during the next six decades with the result that complaints began pouring in regarding its poor levels of hygiene and cleanliness. The most important of these was the 29 June 1863 petition[11] sent to the Lieutenant-Governor, Cecil Beadon, signed by nearly 700 people, which said that though the bazar

29 The Dharamtala Bazar in 1833, by William Wood

> ... is in a desirable and convenient locality for the daily supply of food to a very large number of the inhabitants of Calcutta, the state of the said bazar is filthy and unwholesome; that it is crowded with disgusting objects of deformity and contagious disease seeking charity to the manifest danger of all such articles of food as may be brought into contact with them; that a native village rife with sickness and [mortality] exists within the boundaries; and that, having been established thirty years ago[12] and never extended since, the said bazar is now utterly wanting in proper accommodation for the requirements of this rapidly increasing city.

The petitioners wanted a commission to be appointed to report on the 'condition' of the bazar 'and its requirements as regards space and accommodation, cleanliness, order and arrangement, drainage, and supply of water'. Pending the publication of the report, they wanted exclusion and expulsion from the bazar of 'all vagrants, beggars, and contagiously diseased persons'. The appointment of a Government Health Officer was also urged to ensure that the 'sanitary condition of the bazar be maintained, and that that officer have the power to compel the destruction of bad or unsound food'. Since extortion was also perceived to be a problem, the petitioners wanted officers to be posted at the bazar whose duties would be to 'take notes of actual prices paid by purchasers to vendors and of average prevailing rates'. These officers, whose job was also 'to facilitate the striking of such (an) average', were to file daily returns with the police, the Government making arrangements to publish the returns 'in the form of lists of prices current', which were to be printed both in English and Bengali, copies of them being put up in the bazar itself.

The Government acted promptly. As a first step, it asked the Commissioner of Police 'to prevent beggars and vagrants from loitering in the bazar'. On 27 July 1863 it followed this up by writing to the newly constituted Justices of the Peace for the town of Calcutta[13] that, since the matter was urgent, if they felt that the Government could directly act to improve the situation obtaining in the bazar they could ask it to do so in writing which would enable the authorities to take action. Ashley Eden, Secretary to the Government of Bengal and later (1877 to 1882) Lieutenant-Governor of Bengal, wrote:

> The Dhurumtollah market being private property the Government cannot interfere, as the Memorialists propose, with the space and accommodation provided by the owners of the market to persons resorting to it for the purpose of buying and selling. But the cleanliness, order, and drainage of the market are matters, the Lieutenant-Governor thinks, which can be easily regulated by the Justices in communication with the Commissioner of Police, who has already been instructed to take immediate measures for preventing beggars and vagrants from loitering in the market.

There was 'no doubt ... that the Dhrrumtollah market is in a most disgraceful condition, and it is certainly a discredit to a large town like Calcutta that a proper market place has not long since been provided'. Importantly, the Government then suggested to the municipal Justices whether they could not erect and maintain 'a market place suitable to the increasing requirements of the Town' or, if they were not disposed to do so, whether 'private capitalists' could not be encouraged 'to supply what all admit to be a great

30 The keranchee stand at Dharamtala, with the tank in the background, around 1865

want'. This clearly looks like an early suggestion being made to the authorities concerned to set up a municipal market, which in fact took practical shape in the establishment of the Sir Stuart Hogg Market, today's New Market, a few years later.[14]

While proper civic conditions were wanting within the Dharamtala market, the market itself, because of its location, had become a focal point of interest and activity for the people at large. Any bustling, centrally located market place always tends to be crowded and the Dharamtala bazar was no exception. A photograph taken in the 1860s shows the *keranchee*[15] stand at Dharamtala, opposite the bazar to the west of Chowringhee Road and to the south of the Dharamtala tank. Given the central location of the area as far as the growing city was concerned, the stand was more or less an unavoidable point of reference vis-a-vis the city's topography. The photograph shows the keranchee stand located off the road, but it was not so in earlier years. In the 1840s, if not earlier, it was located on the road itself before being subsequently moved to the position shown in the photograph. The reasons cited for the shift are similar to the arguments being put forward today to shift bus terminuses away from the city centre.

On 11 December 1851, the chief magistrate of Calcutta, W.H. Elliott, wrote to J.P. Grant, secretary to the Bengal government,[16] that as many accidents had 'lately occurred at the corner of Dhurumtola and Chowringhee Road' because of the 'great concourse of men and horses and vehicles of all sorts', some steps should be taken to improve the situation in this part of the city. Elliott listed five reasons for the congestion at that point: (i) a large number of people, coming 'on foot, on horseback and in carriages', gathered there, 'especially [in] the morning, who go to visit [the bazar] for their daily supplies'; (ii) the spot was 'a private rendezvous of loiterers of all classes who assemble from all parts of the town to hear the news of the day'; (iii) there was a watercart stand to the west of Chowringhee Road; (iv) a keranchee stand on the same side of the road; and (v) 'in the midst of all these, strings of horses pass, morning and afternoon, on their way to and from the great livery stables'. Elliott said that the first two points and the last could not be 'interfered with' because while (i) and (ii) were 'the least of the evils complained of' (v) was

> ... the worst, but that corner is the point which of all others is the one they most need to pass from the situation of the great livery stables and at which, if it were not from other causes so peculiarly crowded, they would not be more likely to cause accidents than in any other part of the town.

This left the watercart and keranchee stands, and Elliott felt that they could 'very advantageously be shifted from their present position, where they occupy alone one third of the road, to the inner or western side of the balustrade' (see image 30 on p. 255). The chief magistrate reasoned that such a step would not only clear the road and 'give the keranchees and watercarts a quieter stand' but would also enable the watercarts to get closer to the Dharamtala tank from where they drew their water. Elliott said his suggestion had been accepted by the commissioners for the improvement of the town who had had a survey done of the spot, had drawn up an estimate of the cost involved, and had then 'offered to undertake the work as a great public benefit at their own charge'. Elliott said the aqueduct to the west of Chowringhee Road[17] had to be 'arched over' to offer four passages, 'two for ingress and two for egress of the keranchees and carts', the construction cost of which would be Rs 173. The surveyor, I. Rowe, had also proposed the making of some railings—the utility of which was uncertain to the chief magistrate—which would cost Rs 192.

Elliott's principal concern was that, following their shifting, the proposed watercart and keranchee stands would now be located on 'a portion of the great plain, which must not be encroached upon without the sanction of Government'. He wanted this sanction, assuring the Government that the shifting of the two stands would in no way 'interfere with the amusements of the public who resort for air or exercise to the plain'. The proposal was accepted and the stands were shifted. It is tempting to suggest that this initial approval was perhaps the precedent for the iconic tram shelter that came to mark this corner of the esplanade in later years being built on ground reclaimed by filling up the Dharamtala tank which was excavated in 1790.[18]

Notes

1 'Materials for the History of Calcutta Streets and Houses 1780-1834, Part 2', *Bengal Past and Present,* vol. 14, January–March 1917, p. 196.

2 Haldar had bought the bazar for Sicca Rs 45,000 at an auction run by Tulloh and Company on April 18 1799. Contemporary reports suggest that the initial plan was to demolish the entire set-up (*The Calcutta Monthly Journal* for April 1799, p. 1226). The advertisement placed by the auctioneers described the property thus: the bazar then stood on 'nine bighas on which there were 207 pucka-built rooms, or shops, 143 arched, ditto, and 36 large cutcha godowns, yielding a gross monthly rent of sicca Rs 1,043'. It further stated that the bazar was 'bounded by General Stibbert's house on the east, by the Durrumtollah road to the north, by the Chowringhee road to the west, and by the Jaun Bazar to the south'. See W.H Carey, *The Good Old Days of Honourable John Company*, vol. 1 (Calcutta: R. Cambray and Co., 1906 reprint), p. 189. On Haldar, see Robb, *Useful Friendship*, pp. 160–177.

3 According to the records, 'The Superintendent's house, known by the name of Bibee Sophy's house, is ... bounded on the east by an upper-

roomed house formerly belonging to General Stibbert'. Giles Stibbert was officiating Commander-in-Chief of the Bengal Army in 1777 and 1783 (C.E. Buckland, *Dictionary of Indian Biography* [London: Swan Sonnenschein and Company, 1906], p. 405). The Committee of Revenue Proceedings of 2 April 1781 has an item which states that in the time of Henry Vansittart (1760–1764), when a road was being opened eastward from 'Dherum Tulla in the Town of Calcutta'—today's Lenin Sarani—a bigha and seventeen kathas out of the nine bighas and two kathas which Raja Hazarimal (the brother-in-law of Amirchand) owned in the area was appropriated by the authorities for the purpose. Of this ground eleven kathas were left over as it was not required for the road, but Hazarimal's claim to the ground could not be established later because there was no patta in his name for the ground in question. The dewan of the committee recommended that 'as so long a period has elapsed since the time of Mr Vansittart', the offer made by General Stibbert to buy it be accepted and that he be given 'a Pottah for the said ground upon his paying for it at the rate of 60 Rupees per cottah, the price at which it has been valued by the aumeen'. Possibly, the Stibbert house referred to here was built on this plot.

4 'Materials for the History of Calcutta Streets and Houses 1780-1834, Part 2', *Bengal Past and Present,* vol. 14, January–March 1917.

5 Ibid.

6 Board of Revenue Proceedings, 18 December 1786. There appears to have been a smelly fish market in the area if we are to go by a letter written to the 'Superintendent of Police' which appeared in Hickey's *Bengal Gazette or Calcutta General Advertiser* of 2-9 September 1780. The letter signed 'Sanitas' stated that owing to 'the erection of an extensive fish bazar, in the east front of the Esplanade', there was a continuous assault on the olfactory sense, borne by the southern breeze, which 'portend pestilential effects'. The correspondent urged immediate action on the part of the superintendent, 'especially as the interposition of Government will not be attended with any expence'.

7 On 24 May 1787, Archibald Seton, Collector of Calcutta, wrote to the Board of Revenue that 'the family of Huzzoory Mull [had] permitted Tickeram, a Hindoo religious [figure], to reside upon the spott without paying rent to them' (Board of Revenue Proceedings, 29 May 1787).

8 'History of Calcutta Streets and Houses 1780-1834, Part 1', *Bengal Past and Present,* vol. 14, January–March 1917, p. 7. Upjohn's

map indicates that Dingah Bhangah was the area between today's Lenin Sarani and S.N. Banerjee Road. A.K. Ray (*Short History*, p. 195) writes that, 'Dingabhanga, north of the Govindapur creek (Wellington Square and Creek Row), and Ooltadingi are both named from accidents to boats in the creeks that flowed through these localities in the old, old days, the one signifying "broken boats", the other "boats capsized", both, however, indicating the existence of a trade in fish at least, if not in any other article.'

It is clear from this that the name Dingabhanga refers to a locality. But see chapter 'Birth of a Canal' for an unambiguous contemporary assertion that the name in fact referred to the creek running from the river to the salt lake in the east.

9 Board of Revenue Proceedings, 18 December 1786. In January 1783 Joseph Sherburne was allowed to set up his bazar in Dharamtala on a spot 'commonly known by the name of Ishmail Sarang's Garden' (Committee of Revenue Proceedings, 4 November 1782). Smoult, who had bought the land in 1788, established his bazar at Dharamtala in May 1786 his claim being that he had merely re-established '… the Company's Old Dhurrumtollah Bazar [which] had always stood but which, from the pecuniary difficulties of the former proprietors – the seizure of it by the sheriff and from a rival bazar having been erected near it by Mr Joseph Sherburne – [had] been latterly neglected and reduced to a collection of four or five scattered shops not equal to the expenses of collecting' (Board of Revenue Proceedings, 8 October 1793).

10 Board of Revenue Proceedings, 8 October and 31 December 1793. Smoult had become sheriff in 1793 (Charles Moore, *The Sheriffs of Fort William from 1775 to 1926*, [Calcutta and Simla: Thacker, Spink & Co., 1926], p. 81).

11 Judicial Proceedings, July 1863.

12 The inference here would be that the bazar did not exist before 1833, which of course is not correct. *The Statesman An Anthology* (Calcutta and New Delhi: *The Statesman Ltd*, 1975, p. 202) draws attention to the association of the Seal family with the 'old Dhurrumtollah market'. In February 1848 the land at 'the corner of Dhurrumtollah Street and Chowringhee Road', measuring a bit more than six bighas, was recorded as being a part of Matilal Seal's property, the market remaining a part of the trust-property following Seal's death in May 1854 (Kissory Chaund Mitter, *Mutty Lall Seal* [Calcutta: 1993; first edition 1869], pp. 57, 79).

13 On 1 July 1863 a new Municipal Act had been passed 'creating a public corporate body, composed of all the Justices of the Peace for the town, as well as all other Justices of the Peace for Bengal, Behar and Orissa, who might be resident in Calcutta' ('The City of Calcutta and its Municipal Constitution', *The Calcutta Review*, vol. LXX, 1880, pp. 478–498).

14 H.E.A. Cotton (*Calcutta Old and* New, pp. 770–771) writes: 'The Calcutta Municipal market stands to the south of the Municipal Office. The establishment of the Market for the sale of all kinds of food for European consumption was for years under consideration: but it was not until 1866 that it was resolved to construct one on a large and complete scale, and the old bazar called Fenwick's bazar, with the filty lanes and bustee surrounding, was taken up for the purpose. The market was opened in 1874.'

15 In *Tom Raw, the Griffin*, op.cit., p. 50, the keranchee is defined as 'a kind of native hackney coach'. The note adds: 'The name here given them, and in general use among Europeans, is said to be derived from a general officer of that name breaking down on his way to Barrackpore to visit the Governor-General, and being obliged to make use of one of these vehicles to accomplish his journey, in which he drove up to the palace-door, to the great amusement of the great man and his suite.'

16 Judicial Judicial Proceedings, 14 January 1852 (West Bengal State Archives). John Peter Grant later (1859–1862) became the Lieutenant-Governor of Bengal.

17 This aqueduct, according to the plan enclosed in the Proceedings (ibid.), ran along Esplanade Row from west to east and then turned south into Chowringhee Road.

18 W.S. Seton-Karr, *Selections from Calcutta Gazettes*, vol. 2 (Calcutta: 1865), pp. 13–14.

15

The Polhill Bungalow

The esplanade being so large an expanse of ground, it stands to reason that despite the best efforts of the authorities encroachments were bound to be made, sometimes utilising the good offices of the Government itself. This was highlighted in 1853 in the course of a complaint made by two petitioners against the Chief Magistrate of Calcutta, W.H. Elliott, their grouse being that restrictions had been placed on them by the magistrate in putting up tents in a corner of the maidan.[1] In their petition to the Governor-General, Lord Dalhousie, Nilmoney Dey and Ramchund Mullick said they were 'dealers in tents' and that they had used 'the greens of the esplanade' to display their wares for the inspection of customers as distinguished as 'generals, colonels, captains, besides the railway company, also judges and magistrates at the upper stations'. Their contention was that although the chief magistrate had allowed them earlier to put up their model tents 'two or three times' he had issued orders putting a stop to 'your petitioners' trade'. A further allegation was made relating to the period allowed by Elliott in earlier times during which the model tents could be put up, namely, seven days. Referring to the request of 'the gentlemen of the railway company',[2] they urged the Governor-General to issue orders which would allow them to pitch their tents during the 'cold season', from October to either February 'or the 22nd of March every year'.

The petition opened a Pandora's box on the issue of encroachment. When Elliott was asked for his views he pointed to the existing practice of permission being given to certain people and institutions for specific periods which was utilised entirely for private gain. He cited three examples of this. The Chief Magistrate wrote:

> There is a small portion of the Calcutta plain, north-west of the Ochterlony Monument[3] on which it has been customary during the cold season to authorise under a pass from the Chief Magistrate the pitching of tents by persons desirous of availing themselves of that privilege. That custom has been, and is to this day, continued by me, and the two petitioners Neelmoney Dey and Ramchund Mullick, have during this very season profited by it to a very large extent – and might still do so without troubling His Lordship on the subject.[4]

Elliott's point was that this privilege had been misused by the two. He wrote:

> There is a call to moderation in all things. I found that these two men and another dealer, who has not joined their petition, were monopolising the use of that portion of the esplanade. They would at one time have 20, 30 or 40 tents pitched and servants and workmen living on the spot for weeks and months together, and should any other party wish to pitch a tent there, these people would expect the application to be made to them, as room could hardly be found.

The Chief Magistrate said he could not allow the petitioners to enjoy 'a right to the use of a given spot of ground for any indefinite time'. He was perfectly willing 'to let them pitch a few tents for a few days (eight days generally I allow) whenever they may show cause for so doing' and that he had 'merely opposed what they consider a right of occupying an indefinite quantity of ground for an indefinite period of time, and without reference to the convenience of other parties'.

Elliott said he had been forced to adopt this view 'by a sense of duty forced upon me by constant observation of the annoyance and loss which the state suffers from the great consideration shown in past times to individuals' suggesting that the dispensing of patronage and reliance on personal predilection were still in wide use in the discharge of official duty among senior officials of the Government.

He then cited the case of 'the very troublesome and dreadfully expensive encroachments on the Strand Bank' and the race course. Regarding the latter, he said that formerly it had 'a railing for a hundred yards, more or less, on either side of the Race Stand' but was now 'enclosed for about two-thirds or three quarters of its circumference to the great annoyance of all but the very few individuals connected with the races'. Further,

> … the plain between the Race Stand and the Nullah (Tolly's) has been given up to what are called 'rubbing down stables', supposed to remain only during the few weeks of the racing season, but which have of late years been more substantially built than they were wont to be, and one of which was, with the sanction of Government, converted into a riding school, and has been made a *puckah* building, and become the subject of litigation in the Supreme Court in the course of which it is not to be expected that the interests of Government will be thought of … But should the ground be hereafter required, the holder would not be dispossessed but at great expense from that which is indubitably Government land.

Elliott said that during his two-year tenure he had become unpopular by insisting on a written promise to dismantle 'rubbing down stables' before granting permission to set them up and also by 'remonstrating about the race course house'.

He also cited the case of the Calcutta Cricket Club ground, which he portrayed as a situation of encroachment by stealth. The chief magistrate wrote:

31 (left) The location of the cricket ground in Calcutta in 1847, by Frederick Fiebig

32 (below) A painting of a cricket match in progress in nineteenth-century Calcutta on the Cricket Club ground

At first the ground was rolled occasionally, then a tent was pitched on match days, then a few bamboos were put up to prevent equestrians interrupting the players, then the tents were kept pitched during the season, then a very large space of ground was enclosed by a permanent fence, then a great unsightly hut and a mat privy were erected in addition to the tents, and the whole appears to be considered a vested right; and the members of other clubs are much annoyed because I have refused them permission to make similar enclosures which would, in my opinion, ruin the freedom of the Plain and which are, I believe, altogether opposed to the wishes of Government, but to which I cannot deny that one club may have as good a claim as another.[5]

The Government chose not to interfere in the case addressed by the Dey-Mullick petition perhaps because the clientele for the tents included official personages. However, it took the general tenor of the chief magistrate's letter seriously. It asked him to

> ... intimate to the persons connected in the management of the race course and the cricket ground as well as to all other private persons who have been permitted to use any portions of the Maidan that they occupy only on sufferance and that all enclosures and buildings are liable to be removed at any moment at the pleasure of Government.[6]

Perhaps, it is because of these early corrective steps taken with exemplary firmness, and persisted with by the British Indian Government down to 1947, that the maidan of Calcutta today continues to remain an open expanse of ground in spite of the permanent tent-structures that dot the area and a clutch of isolated buildings which have come up on the fringes, on the western side near the river.

In 1854 the extent of the esplanade was marked by the Government of the day as being bounded on the north 'by the public road from Chandpaul Ghat along Esplanade Row West, the road south of the Government House compound, and Esplanade Row East, to its junction with the Chowringhee Road'; on the south 'by the Circular Road from Birji talao to Alipore bridge[7] and thence by Tolly's nullah to Hastings bridge'; on the east 'by Chowringhee Road from Esplanade Row East to Birji Talao'; and on the west 'by the Strand Road from Chandpaul Ghat to Hastings Bridge'.[8] Any map of the area will show that the Circular Road does not at any point touch Tolly's Nullah but runs alongside it to its north till the road reaches the Kidderpur Road. What this means is that the official limit of the esplanade at some point of time veered south from the Circular Road towards the Nullah where the Alipore Bridge crossed it.

It would seem that in the early days, when the ground was being cleared, the esplanade of the new fort did not extend as far south as it did at the end of the eighteenth century. According to initial plans, it stretched eastward to the old Pilgrims' Road, which had become Chowringhee by the end of the century. Northward, it went up to what had become Esplanade Row, the southern limit of the white town since the early days of the eighteenth century. To the west there was of course no esplanade because the fort was built on the east bank of the Hooghly, shipping on the river being easily accessible to the great guns of the fort. To the south the ground was cleared to a great extent but not till the Gobindapur creek, or the opening of Tolly's Nullah into the river. This is clear from the 21 November 1761 communication sent by the Bengal Council, comprising Henry Vansittart, Peter Amyatt, Culling Smith and Warren Hastings, to the Court stating that the engineer had 'represented the advantages of extending the Esplanade as far southwards as the Nulla or Creek near Surman's' (Surman's garden). The Council had discussed the issue in the light of an objection that the expense and loss which the clearing of the esplanade would entail would be too high to be justified, concluding that the 'advantages would be more than adequate to the expence'. The Council told the Court that, in its view, the loss of revenue estimated by the collector would not 'in reality be any loss as the inhabitants removed to another spot will pay the same rents'.[9]

In the 1780s, after the completion of the new fort, there was some confusion about the limits of the esplanade, light being thrown on the subject by two specific cases which cropped up during the decade, the first dealing with the status of a bungalow to the south of Circular Road and the second the location of the insane asylum south of the hospital premises.

On 11 October 1785 Lt Thomas Polhill, who looked after Warren Hastings' bodyguard, wrote to the Committee of Revenue:[10]

> Having erected a bungalow near the General Hospital, upon the spot of ground pointed out to me by the late Governor General [Warren Hastings] in order to attend to the duty of the corps lately under

> my command,[11] and having every reason to think my then situation permanent, was induced to lay out a considerable sum of money on those buildings (about 15,000 Sicca Rupees) which do not interfere with any other person, the ground being unappropriated. I am therefore led to hope that you gentlemen will indulge me, either by an indemnification of my expences or by a regular grant of the ground in question, and that as I consider the latter mode as the least oppressive to Government I request the favour of a pottah for the ground.

Since the plot lay within the jurisdiction of the Collector of Calcutta, the committee asked him whether there were any objections to complying with the application after which it would submit 'the propriety of the request' to the Governor-General in Council. The Collector, Archibald Seton, reported that the ground which Polhill wanted was located in Dihi Dollunda in Panchannagram, 'that it is Company's *comar* [waste] ground and contains 14 bighas 4 cottahs'.[12] He felt that the grant of a patta to Polhill would neither be an infringement 'upon private property, nor a diminution of the public revenue'. But Polhill was destined for a rough ride because of objections from another quarter and upon very different grounds.

Seton wrote that since the ground in question was in the 'vicinity' of Fort William he thought it proper to 'take the precaution of addressing the Chief Engineer on the subject'. Henry Watson put his foot down objecting to the plot being handed over to a private person 'because it would interfere with the space allotted to the Esplanade'. The Collector disagreed and pointed out that there had been no objection 'to erecting a hospital, which is constructed with much more solidity than the houses of individuals generally are, and is situated close to the ground in question; neither do the houses at Cheringhee appear to be more distant from Fort William than Lt Polhill's bungalo'. Seton added that it was not unusual to grant pattas applied for 'with certain restrictions respecting the nature of the buildings to be erected when the convenience of the public renders such a precaution necessary'.

The Collector sought the Chief Engineer's 'guidance' on two specific points: first, whether the ground in question 'was situated without the precincts of the esplanade' and, secondly, 'whether its becoming private property would be productive of any inconvenience from its vicinity to the new fort'. Watson replied three days later, on 20 October 1785, stating that the ground on which Polhill was allowed to erect his 'temporary bungalo' … 'has always been considered a part of the esplanade of Fort William although the new curvilinear road [Circular Road] is now frequently called the boundary'. Watson said he firmly believed 'that every part of the ground between the forementioned road and the nullah has always [been] deemed and ought to be continued as an appendage of Fort William'.[13] What probably rankled Seton in particular was the following outburst on the part of the Chief Engineer who said that 'no part of [the ground between the new road and the nullah] was ever within the jurisdiction of any Collector of Committee of Revenue since the first commencement of the works'. Watson added that he considered it his duty 'to oppose the Committee's present assumption or claim to the power of alienating any part of this land for which I am well persuaded neither motives of public consideration or private justice can be alleged by them or Lt Polhill'. On its part, the Committee of Revenue did not think it politic to get embroiled in the controversy at this stage and forwarded the correspondence to the Governor-General in Council.

The comparative distance between his bungalow and the fort clinched the issue in Polhill's favour. In January the following year the Supreme Council, presided over by John Macpherson, wrote to the Committee:[14] 'As the bungalow appertaining to Lieutenant Polhill stands at a greater distance from the Fort than the houses at Cheringhee, we do not perceive any material disadvantage which the fortifications can sustain by the ground on which it stands being confined in the present instance to the present occupant.' However, a condition was imposed for grant of a patta for fourteen bighas and four kathas 'in Dhee Bawhannypoor, Dhollundah,

Paunchwangong', namely, that Polhill 'could not erect any *pucca* dwelling or double storied house thereon, or any building whatever other than those already there'.

Archibald Seton was succeeded by J.H. Harrington as the Assistant Collector of Calcutta some time in July or August 1787. This was the time when a search was on for ground on which to locate the insane asylum, the Governor-General in Council suggesting that a plot be found 'in the neighbourhood of the hospital for the purpose of erecting a house for the reception of insane persons'.[15] The original request for the facility had come from the Hospital Board which had wanted seven bighas for the hospital and associated offices. Initially, the Board of Revenue had entrusted Seton with the job which now fell on Harrington. On 31 August Harrington sent his first report to the Board of Revenue[16] in which he declared that the seven bighas sought by the authorities near the hospital were not to be found. He wrote that as there was no such piece of land 'contiguous to the hospital', he had widened his search 'to every other quarter of the vicinity of Calcutta' but was sorry to inform the Board that, 'beyond the present boundaries of the esplanade, I cannot, after the most diligent search, find a single bega of untenanted ground', which provides us with an idea of what the land situation was like in the town at the time.

Not finding any vacant land, Harrington considered the exchange-of-land option for ground in the 24-Parganas as a way out. But here too he made no headway. 'The ryotts,' he wrote, 'are willing to dispose of such parts of their lands as they do not themselves reside on, for a compensation in money, but decline an equivalent in land elsewhere'. Thus, while the authorities were not keen on spending money to buy land for the insane hospital, the cultivators who had excess land were more interested in money than alternative property within the bounds of Calcutta. Could coercion then be used to get the land the Government wanted? Harrington[17] may have been an exception but his views on the matter do cast some light on the general attitude of some of the English officials working in India during the period immediately following the departure of Warren Hastings. He wrote: 'To compel them (the ryots) to this measure might be justified perhaps by precedent and by strict legal right, but I conceive you would be averse to enforce it except in cases of absolute necessity'.

The Collector suggested one of two methods to tide over the problem: that the Government buy the ground required or 'circumscribe the present boundaries of the esplanade'. If purchase was an option, he suggested that 'the twelve hundred rupees lately realised from the sale of two begahs to Mr Williams at Cheringhee will be more than sufficient to procure the seven beghas wanted near the hospital'. Important to us from the point of view of delineating the limits of the fort's esplanade was his reason for suggesting the second method. Harrington wrote that a 'local survey' of the present limits of the esplanade had revealed that they had been much 'extended from what it appears to have been the intention of Government to have fixed them about a few years ago'. He pointed out that on 27 May 1782 the secretary of the Governor-General in Council had written to the Committee of Revenue that the Governor-General had ordered the esplanade round the fort

> ... to be cleared and put in proper condition as far as a boundary line, to be drawn ... from the new jail to Surman's nulla [Tolly's nullah], and the ground situated between this line and the hospital, being 177 begahs 16 cottahs, was to be delivered up (after purchasing the private property included in it) to the Chief Engineer for the purpose of accommodating the Troops of Body Guard, Lt Polhill's Corps, the artillery lascars, etc.[18]

According to Harrington, in the intervening five years the limits of the esplanade had shifted south. The Collector wrote that the boundary line for the esplanade in 1787

> ... not only includes the above 177 begahs, but extends at least a quarter of a mile beyond the hospital in a southerly direction, to the bank of

> Colonel Tolly's Nulla and takes in both Lieutenant Polhill's bungalow and the fort burying ground, as well as a large vacant spot between these, part of which would serve exceedingly well for the house intended for lunaticks unless there should be a necessity for extending the limit of the esplanade thus far, though, as I have ascertained, … the houses at Cheringhee and the line of Calcutta buildings fronting the esplanade are both more than two hundred yards nearer the fort than even the new jail, which is considerably more contiguous than the spot alluded to.

Although it was not his specific brief to make such a suggestion, Harrington felt that the esplanade's boundary could be reduced 'without danger' to the military requirements of the fort. In doing so, however, the Collector was circumspect for he said that if there were any reasons for the southern limits of the esplanade to be greater than in the north and the east he was unaware of them. Nevertheless, he thought it incumbent upon himself 'to state such particulars as have fallen within my own knowledge [so] that Government may not be put to any expence to provide the ground required by them, if it can be obtained gratis without any inconvenience'.

The Board of Revenue sent Harrington's letter to the Governor-General in Council. On 10 October 1787 the latter got back to the Board asking it to instruct the collector

> … to fix on some spot sufficient for the building to be erected for the reception of insane persons between the ancient and the present boundary line of the Esplanade, and when he has done so to request the Chief Engineer to examine the spot which he may select for this purpose, and report whether there is any objection to the erection of a building on it similar to that which is proposed by Mr Dick.[19]

Harrington did as he was told and on 5 November he wrote to the Board of Revenue[20] that he had selected a spot of ground in the 'southward part of the Esplanade', which had been approved by Dick as well as the chief engineer, Colonel Thomas Call. The latter,

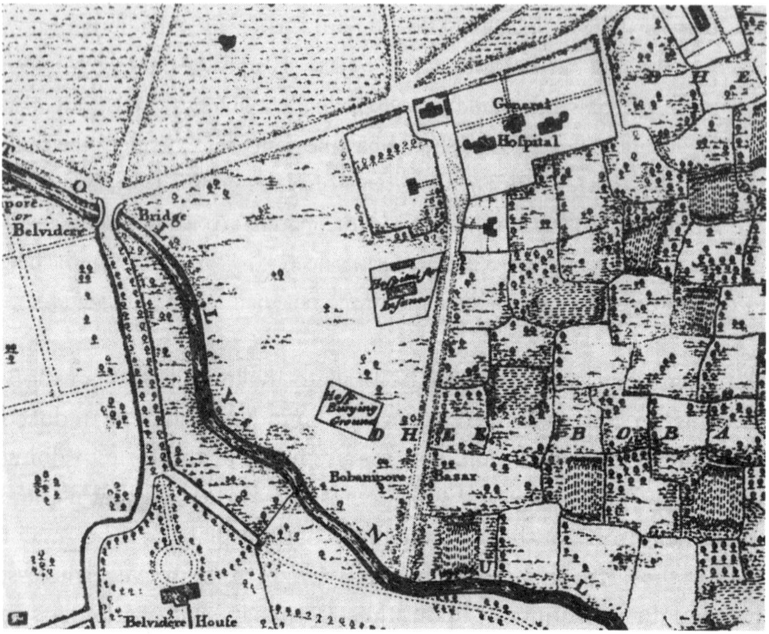

33 Lt Polhill's bungalow and the insane asylum to the south of it are clearly shown in Upjohn's map of 1792–1793

however, had applied a caveat, namely, that the ground selected should on no account 'become private property because it may so happen that future possessors, instead of using it for the purpose intended, may apply it to other uses very obnoxious to Government'. Call had written that he saw no objection to the spot of ground 'between the soldiers' burying ground [the Bhowanipore military cemetery] and Lt Polhill's bungalow (hitherto considered as part of the Esplanade)' being used for the purpose stated.[21] Three days later, on 8 November, the Government approved of the spot selected by Harrington and handed it over to Dick for the purpose of building a hospital for insane persons.[22]

That the limits of the esplanade were still not clear nearly a quarter of a century later is suggested by the official correspondence[23] on an issue which involved the removal of huts belonging to the staff of D. McLeod, the Barrack Master in Fort William, located near the general hospital. On 12 March 1810 McLeod had written to the commanding officer of the garrison complaining that the Acting Magistrate of the 24-Parganas, J.R. Barwell, had

> … threatened my people with immediate destruction to their huts if they did not forthwith remove from a situation near the hospital which was allotted to me by the Chief Engineer for the accommodation of the people of my establishment consequent to their having been removed by orders of Government from their former ground adjoining the sheds for the public cattle.

McLeod had in fact written to Barwell on the previous day that, as it appeared

> to be a disputed point whether the said ground near the hospital belongs to the esplanade or not, I have to request that you will let their removal lay over until the matter has been finally ascertained, more particularly as I presume from its having been hitherto unoccupied, that you have no immediate occasion for it, should it even prove to belong to the 24-Pergunnahs, and as it will occasion serious inconvenience in conducting the duties of my department there being no other ground for them.

Since the issue had been taken up by the Military Secretary, Major J. Johnston, the Government asked Barwell to 'furnish the necessary explanation of the points' raised in McLeod's letter.[24]

In his response, Barwell denied the allegation made by the Barrack Master, stating that 'the harsh measures' imputed to him by McLeod 'were [never] intended or executed and that I have been actuated in the measures I have adopted solely by a sense of publick duty'. He also wrote that, on being told that McLeod's people had been settled on the spot near the hospital by Captain

Wood, executive officer, he had written to the latter asking him on what authority he had done so. Since Barwell got the impression from Wood's answer that, in fact, the latter did not have any official sanction to take the step he did, the magistrate asked for the removal of the huts 'without however using force, nor has it ever been resorted to'. Barwell then gave Dowdeswell[25] the real reason why he felt that the barrack master's men should not be allowed to reside anywhere near the hospital. He wrote that

> … these people were removed from the place they formerly occupied in consequence of being too near the Company's bullock sheds. The same causes I presume which rendered their removal necessary make the situation they have taken up close to the general hospital, the public road, and near the sheds occupied by the convicts an improper one. These people ... (who) generally gain their livelihood by breeding swine will in the situation they occupy near the road side become a public nuisance.

The magistrate said the offending huts had not been removed, and that they would not be removed without proper orders.[26]

The views of the Presidency Superintending Surgeon, J.G. Henderson, sent to Barwell on 28 March 1810, were even more damaging to the cause of the Barrack Master and his principals. Henderson wrote that he had inspected the spot and had come to the conclusion that the huts in question and their inmates would be

> … much too near the hospital, and be a very great nuisance both to the patients and surgeons, for it is well known that these sweepers are of a class the most debauched, noisy and filthy of any people in India, and are the people who are generally employed by the soldiers to convey spirituous liquors to them clandestinely.

Giving us an idea of what the environs of the general hospital were like at the time, he added:

> There are now too many huts both to the eastward and southward of the hospital, and the huts now proposed to be erected so very near to the western wall of the hospital from which quarter the wind blows a great part of the year will convey from them and the inhabitants their hogs, etc most noisome effluvia to the patients.

Henderson, therefore, could not agree to the huts being allowed to be set up on the spot in question, his parting shot being that he could not 'divine any reason why they should be placed there particularly, as I understand there are plenty of vacant spots of Company ground much nearer to Fort William'.[27]

At the end of March, the Government ruled in favour of the magistrate stating that orders would be issued 'through the proper channel for the removal of the houses', that is, through the military department. However, it also took up the superintending surgeon's grouse against huts peppering the eastern and southern facades of the general hospital and asked Barwell to find out whether the ground on which the huts were located was public property, and if so 'by what authority they have been erected'. If the Government was not satisfied with the findings, it held out the threat that the huts would be removed. In his report[28] Barwell wrote that the ground to the east and south of the hospital did not belong to the Government. However, the ground situated to the west, 'extending to the nullah', was public property on which there were located 445 huts for the past quarter of a century. The magistrate had not been able to find out on what authority the huts had been allowed to be put up, his belief being that there was in fact none. He described the occupants of the land as being all of 'low caste', adding that since they were located 'some distance from the road and from the general hospital' he was 'not aware of any objection to their remaining there'. He said that if the Government allowed them to continue staying there 'in consideration of the length of time they have been established', they should be prevented from 'keeping swine and thereby becoming a nuisance to the publick, and in case of non-compliance to order them off the ground'. This temperate suggestion was not accepted by the Governor-General in Council,[29] the latter's stand being that even if the property belonged to the Government there was no reason 'for permitting the individuals ... to occupy it'. However, it was willing to compensate them for costs 'incident to the removal of their houses'. The magistrate was asked to clear the ground 'reporting the expence which should in your judgement be allowed for the purpose stated above'.

What all this implies is that the large tract of land between the hospital and Tolly's Nullah was none too clean and 'ordered' as the authorities would have wanted it to be. A cleaning up was urgently required given the 'development' pressures on the area. It was at this point that nature intervened and accomplished for the Government what the best administrator would have found it troublesome to implement. In 1813 the town was ravaged by fires which were so devastating that, to quote the magistrate of the 24-Parganas, John Eliot,[30] it led to natives in large numbers leaving the town for the suburbs. This in turn led to an increase in the incidence of fires breaking out in the suburbs themselves, 'particularly about Kidderpore, Bhowannypore and Russah, the suburb part [of] which the inhabitants from the town have in great numbers resorted [to]'. Eliot's main objective in writing to the Government on 22 March 1814 was to strengthen the official capability to fight the fires by having more fire engines and staff at his disposal, a plea which was sanctioned by the authorities.[31] The fires led to a large tract of land between the hospital and Tolly's nullah being cleared, which led to a radical alteration in the topography of that part of the suburbs lying contiguous to the Adi Ganga which had lain undisturbed for long years.

In a second letter to the Government,[32] written on the same day he despatched his first epistle (22 March), Eliot said that the fire which had broken out the previous day had burnt down 'a large portion of Kidderpore and Bhowannypore' and that, had it not been for the exertions of his staff, 'the whole of the convicts houses there would have been destroyed, and the conflagration would have in all probability extended even to Russapuglah'. Eliot continued:

> As the village of Bhowannypore between the convicts' houses, the nullah and insane hospital has been nearly destroyed by fire, and the ground is the property of the Government for which no revenue for years has been paid, I beg leave to recommend that any further erection of buildings on this spot be prohibited and that the ground be cleared and appropriated to the use of the livery stable people for the purpose of training horses, in order that these people may be removed from the Course, as they are in this situation a very great inconvenience to the public.[33]

The Government agreed to the suggestion and on 5 November the magistrate was writing to the Government[34] that he had cleared 'the whole of the ground situated beween Tolley's Nullah and the road lying between the general and insane hospitals and levelled the whole excepting where the convicts' houses are now situated'.[35]

34 The location of Kassiabagan and Sullan (Sultan) Mistry's bazar, from J.A. Schalch's map of 1824

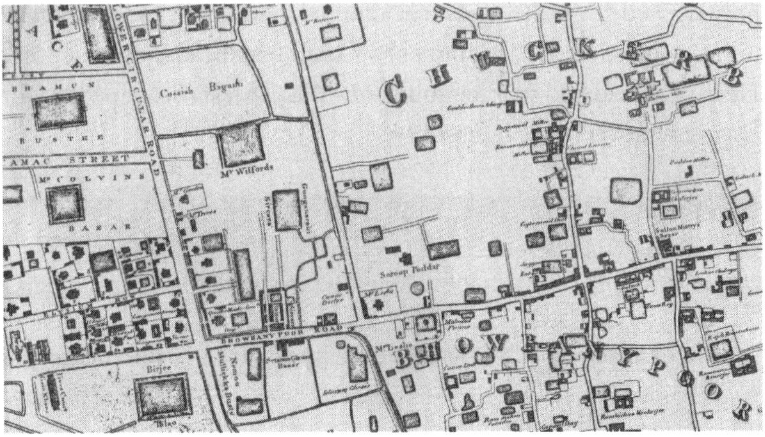

On the removal of those who were living about the hospital for insane persons, Eliot wrote that the effects were most beneficial as there could not have been 'a more filthy place' than this. It was populated by 'the lowest order of society, and the state in which they kept the place was beyond all conception and must have created a highly injurious atmosphere to the two hospitals'. He said the removal of the convicts' houses would complete the improvement of the area 'and free the course from all danger from training horses'. Giving an overview of the development work being done in that area, the magistrate wrote: 'It is with no small degree of satisfaction I have to report (that) I have succeeded in most completely draining all that part of Bhowanypore lying between the main road of the two hospitals and the Russapuglah Road, as far as Sullan [Sultan?] Mistry's Bazar', adding that he had

> … further opened large and spacious roads which has tended infinitely to the improvement of this place, and will no doubt conduce to render the atmosphere south of the General Hospital less liable to an infectious air, from the innumerable bogs which then existed in that part of the village of Bhowanypore.

As far as the native response to these measures was concerned, Eliot said that the people appeared to be 'fully sensible of the benefits now derived from the measures adopted, and as yet most cordially unite to promote the attainment of such beneficial consequences'. He said he had had to indemnify only 'the poorest sort of people' for having removed their houses.[36]

Notes

1 Judicial Judicial Proceedings, 17 February 1853.

2 In view of the fact that the railways had just begun their saga in India, this was a time when tents were in great demand by those who were out in the inhospitable regions of the interior doing prospecting work.

3 Probably the spot where Curzon Park is located today, to the south-east of Raj Bhavan.

4 Judicial Judicial Proceedings, 17 February 1853.
5 Ibid.
6 Ibid.
7 Upjohn's map clearly denotes what is known as the Zeerut Bridge today as the 'Allipore or Belvidere' bridge.
8 Judicial Judicial Proceedings, 20 April 1854. Cited in *Calcutta in the Nineteenth Century* (Bidisha Chakraborty and Sarmistha De [New Delhi: Niyogi Books, 2013], p. 201.)
9 *Fort William India House Correspondence*, R.R. Sethi ed., vol. 3 (Delhi: The National Archives of India, 1949) pp. 372–373.
10 Committee of Revenue Proceedings, 12 October 1785.
11 The following paragraph appears in a review of *Historical Records of the Governor-General's Bodyguard*, compiled by V.C.P Hodson, in *Bengal Past and Present*, vol. 6, p. 383: 'In 1782 Warren Hastings, as Governor-General, had also an infantry Body Guard, Captain Polhill's regiment of 750 men, taken over from the Nawab Vizir of Oudh. This corps was broken up in February 1785 (after the departure of Hastings), the men who composed it being either returned to the Nawab Vizier's service, or discharged.'
12 Committee of Revenue Proceedings, 24 October 1785.
13 Consequently, the location of the Bhowanipur military cemetery, located to the west of today's D.L. Khan Road (erstwhile Bhowanipur Road), was described by Watson in a letter dated 26 July 1784 as being '*near the corner of the Esplanade* [emphasis added] contiguous to the bridge leading to Mr Livius' gardens' ('Leaves from the Editor's Notebook', *Bengal Past and Present*, vol. 14, January–March 1917, p. 115). Providing an idea of its location, Walter Firminger, the then editor of *Bengal Past and Present*, says that the 'gardens' were marked by 'the present Magistrate's House and grounds at Alipore – once the property of Philip Francis and afterwards the early home of W M Thackeray'. The passage also confirms that there was at this point a bridge spanning Tolly's Nullah which, however, is not shown in Upjohn's map.
14 Committee of Revenue Proceedings, 19 January 1786. The patta is reproduced in the Governor-General in Council Proceedings of 31 August 1787.
15 Board of Revenue Proceedings, 24 July 1787.
16 Ibid., 31 August 1787.
17 John Herbert Harrington subsequently became an 'eminent Judge of the late Sudder Court' (W.S. Seton-Karr, *Selections from Calcutta*

Gazettes, vol. 1 [Calcutta, 1864] p. 232) and a member of the Supreme Council. Cotton (*Calcutta Old and New*, pp. 586-588) writes that 'As an authority upon the Indian system of jurisprudence of his day he stood without a rival'. Harrington Street (now Ho Chi Minh Sarani) was named after him.

18 Going by this stipulation, despite what Watson held in 1785, Polhill was clear in setting up his bungalow where he did.

19 Board of Revenue Proceedings, 23 October 1787. William Dick was a Company assistant-surgeon (Peter Robb, *Sex and Sensibility, Richard Blechynden's Calcutta Diaries, 1791-1822* [New Delhi: Oxford University Press, 2011], p. 72).

20 Board of Revenue Proceedings, 6 November 1787.

21 In his letter to Colonel Call dated 3 November 1787, Harrington had written that he had surveyed the '... southern part of the Esplanade, and find there is an extensive vacant spot between the burying ground of the new fort [the Bhowanipore military cemetery] and Lieut Polhill's bungalow, bounded to the eastward by a road running from the present hospital in a south direction to the Govindpore nullah [Tolly's Nullah; this road is today's D.L. Khan Road], part of which would be well adapted for the intended building for lunatics.'

The collector told Call that as seven bighas would be required, 'and as the highest ground will be most salutary, Mr Dick, who is to superintend the new hospital and who accompanied me on the survey, would prefer a strip of the above extent [seven bighas] immediately to the south of the southern limit of Lieut Polhill's garden'.

22 Board of Revenue Proceedings, 13 November 1787. Subsequently, the hospital for insane persons was moved across the road to a spot immediately to the south of the general hospital. On 21 June 1805 the surgeon of the 24-Parganas, C. Cornish, wrote to E. Thoroton, magistrate of the 24-Parganas, that the insane hospital had been completed and had opened on 1 June. The hospital was to house 'from 80 to 100 patients having 20 separate rooms with a deep verandah and a large compound' (Judicial Criminal Proceedings, 27 June 1805). The old insane hospital was in all probability not decommissioned because as late as 1814 present-day D.L. Khan Road is described as 'lying between the general hospital and insane hospitals'.

23 Judicial Criminal Proceedings, 16 March 1810.

24 The Judicial Criminal Proceedings of 30 March 1810 provide the background to the issue. On 9 March of that year, A. Greene,

secretary to the military board, had written to John Adam, secretary to Government, that '... the Military Board, understanding that the spot of ground mentioned by Major [Thomas Mathias] Weguelin on which the garrison sweepers might be conveniently hutted is in the 24-Parganas, request you will submit to His Excellency the Vice-President in Council that the necessary orders be immediately sent to the proper officer to deliver over the same for that purpose to Captain Wood, Executive Officer.'

Adam ordered that the ground in question be handed over to the executive officer 'provided it is not wanted for any other public purpose'.

25 Secretary to the Government in the Judicial Department.

26 Writing to McLeod on 14 March 1810, Barwell had made the bureaucratic point that 'the circumstance of the ground in question being within the limits of the esplanade does not, I conceive, authorise the Chief Engineer or indeed any one to erect buildings on it without the express sanction of Government'. He also made the point that the esplanade, 'according to the marks laid down, extends much beyond this spot of ground'. However, at the same time, it fell within the limits of the 24-Parganas, 'and being the property of Government I consider it my duty to prevent any one taking possession of it without (proper) authority'.

27 Judicial Criminal Proceedings, 30 March 1810.

28 Ibid., 26 May 1810.

29 Ibid.

30 Ibid., 26 March 1814.

31 Specifically, the magistrate wanted sanction for two fire engines to be stationed at each of these three places 'with the same establishment allowed to the fire engines of the town', the inference being that at this time there were no fire engines in the suburbs. The establishment attached to each fire engine comprised 'a naib, 20 bhistees, a tindal and 20 khalashies' which was to be retained 'until the commencement of the ensuing periodical rains', after which it was to be 'discharged'.

32 Judicial Criminal Proceedings, 26 March 1814.

33 This is probably how the stables came to be built on the eastern side of D.L. Khan Road, which were there even forty years ago but of which there are no signs today, real estate development having taken over the area. Eliot said that as long as the training of horses was allowed 'on this plain of general recreation, it is impossible to make the Course what it should be for public convenience or to free it of those clouds

of dust so truly unpleasant to all seeking the enjoyment of recreation in the open air'. He said that a curb on horse-training on the maidan was indispensable for any effort to improve 'the plain to the south of the town'.

34 Judicial Criminal Proceedings, 22 November 1814.

35 On the convicts' houses, the magistrate wrote that in view of the development work going on in the region and in the neighbourhood there would be 'a constant necessity for having five or six hundred convicts at Bhowanypore'. As such he proposed removal of all convict accommodation 'to the north-eastern extremity of the grounds cleared'. He added: 'As this place borders the village of Bhowanypore and (is) only separated by the main road, it will be necessary to have the convicts houses tiled', which would raise the cost of the accommodation 'somewhat considerably'. However, since the houses—three being required for the convicts as well as their guards—would be more firmly built, they would be less liable 'to excessive repairs or danger from casual fires that may occur in the village on the opposite side of the road'.

36 The Government approved the magistrate's plan to erect three new convict houses at Bhowanipore the cost estimate for which was Sicca Rs 2,966-4-0.

16

The Jagannath Sarkar Case

In 1787 the focus of attention shifted to the subject of the esplanade's limits following efforts by the military to clear the area of all unauthorised constructions. In the Board of Revenue Proceedings of 27 April 1787, we find a letter from Colonel Thomas D. Pearse,[1] Commandant of the Garrison, who wrote that 'in consequence of the orders of some months standing to clear the esplanade', he and Colonel Thomas Call, the Chief Engineer,

> … rode round it, and as the marks ascertaining the limits were fixed, I desired he would proceed to carry the orders into execution by causing to be removed all buildings within the limits of the esplanade except the stables and the bazar of the troops, a temple in a grove near the hospital, the huts of the servants of the hospital which are erected within defined limits, a bungalo built by Captain Polhill and a few huts of the servants of the burying ground.[2]

Pearse said all these structures were to be left standing 'but the rest were to be removed by the 20th April, and, if not then removed, I acquainted Colonel Call that a guard should be sent to enforce obedience'. Pearse emphasised that there was a need to put 'an effectual stop to encroachments [on the esplanade] and to the consequences of them' and suggested that the Committee of

Revenue 'examine the whole matter and ... ascertain by records and evidence the proper limits of the Esplanade'.

Once the schedule of demolition had been set the inevitable happened and Pearse received a number of applications 'for leave to stay ... which I refused to listen to'. However, Jagannath Sarkar of Kidderpur sent a petition which persuaded the commandant to launch an enquiry which was conducted by Call. Among other things, the latter was asked to make a list of 'all the other encroachments made or attempted to be made on the limits of the esplanade'. Pending the completion of the enquiry, the demolition plan was suspended because, as Pearse saw it, if Sarkar's 'buildings' were left standing when the rest was removed it could help to 'establish a right' in favour of Sarkar 'and might be attended with disagreeable consequences if his claim could be made good'.

In his petition to Pearse,[3] Sarkar had claimed that 'several' years ago he had bought sixteen bighas eight kathas of the Company's rent ground and three bighas of charity ground, 'all together (coming) to 21 bighas of ground situated, standing and being in the Dhee Fifty-Five villages, behind the soldiers' burying ground', that is, on the banks of Tolly's Nullah. Sarkar said he had enjoyed without interruption the ownership of the ground for which he had the patta and title deed till, in October 1786, Colonel Call 'forcibly put a pile upon the same ground'. When Sarkar objected showing him his property documents, the colonel said he would be given 'another piece of ground in lieu of the first, abovementioned ground, and that the same (would) be included or gathered to the new Fort William'. Sarkar told Call that when Colonels Campbell,[4] Watson, Silyman and Fortnom were engineers of the fort they had never made any application for his ground nor uttered any 'words to that effect'. Being the pugnacious man he was Sarkar told Call that if the authorities were really keen on taking over his property they should first 'take possession of the honourable Company's hospital, Captain Polhill's bungalow and the burying ground of the soldiers' and then turn their attention to his ground. He said that if the Company wanted to take over his land it 'ought to give your petitioner such a rent annually as your petitioner's said ground produces annually'.

After completing his probe, Call's conclusion[5] was that the patta produced by Jagannath Sarkar was for 'no part of the ground in question on the Esplanade and that his claim of 16 begahs 8 cottahs behind the soldiers' burying ground is not only ill-grounded but a palpable attempt to impose and defraud'. The chief engineer suggested that since the land in question was 'contiguous to the general hospital' (thus giving us an idea where the land was actually located) it would be 'improper' to give it to an individual like Sarkar. As he saw it, it 'ought to be kept as open and clear as possible for the benefit of the sick instead of which it is applied to the worst of purposes'. He accused Sarkar of digging 'immensely large pits' and making and burning bricks and of encouraging 'the most disorderly people to come and live there', not to speak of hogs being allowed 'to grab up the ground and a variety of irregularities (being) committed'.[6]

Pearse had asked Call to point out other encroachments on the esplanade. In his letter of 20 April 1787,[7] Call referred to the bungalow made by Polhill 'by indulgence of the Governor-General' which, since it was put up, had been embellished by 'a high bank with … bushes planted thereon and a trench dug round it'. Call said the bank should be levelled and the ditch filled up. Further, to the 'northward of, and near, the hospital' there was a '*tope*[8] … occupied by a fikkeer [*fakir*] who has a temple therein', referring to Lalgir Gossain (see below) without naming him. Call added that the fakir had been allowed to live there 'by indulgence' on the part of the authorities and that he had 'frequently abused that indulgence by encouraging many to build hutts in the *tope* and others to sell arrack there'. The chief engineer said that unless the fakir could commit himself to keeping the place 'free of such Intruders' he should be removed from the spot.

As regards the Chowringhee area, Call said that the inhabitants there had taken the liberty of 'erecting without their compound walls some sheds or hutts for the convenience of their servants or to put carriages therein';[9] further that 'some of them allow their servants to deposit rubbish on the sides of the road to the great annoyance of people passing that way'. He suggested that a brick drain be built 'close to the compound wall along the range of *new* [emphasis added] buildings erected at Cheringy; otherwise, in the rains, the water that falls between the compound walls and the public road, having no other channel, will overflow and destroy the road'. Call raised the issue of the expense involved in making the drain without, however, making any specific suggestion himself. He also pointed to the 'very great' encroachments made on the banks of Tolly's Nullah, stating that the grant to Colonel William Tolly did not 'allow buildings of any sort to be erected on the northern banks', the exception being limited to '20 feet for the purpose of tracking boats'. The chief engineer said that 'latterly, the holder of the grant[10] has not only claimed a right to build hutts and land goods at a very great distance from the banks of the nullah, but he lays claim to several bighas of land on the esplanade'. Call concluded his letter to Pearse by exhorting that it was high time that the 'limits and regulations respecting the Esplanade may be fixed and published'.

The Board of Revenue asked the collector of Calcutta to submit a report on the matter, which he did on 13 June.[11] Referring to the jurisdiction of the esplanade, as marked out by the chief engineer, Seton said he was taking it for granted because while Call and 'the Commandant of the Garrison' (Pearse) were well-equipped to do the job, his office had no records on 'either the quantity or the boundaries of the ground allotted to the erection of Fort William', which would have helped him to rectify any mistake the military officers may have made. As he saw it, his report was directed at answering three specific points, namely:

> What *malguzary* or *bermooter* lands situated within the *present* [emphasis in Proceedings] limits of the esplanade are now in the occupancy of individuals; whether the title deeds produced ... by the occupiers of

> these lands are respectively applicable to the spots to which they are said to relate [to] and whether they correspond with the public cutcherry records, in order that if their title deeds be good and yet their removal [is] necessary, Government may judge how far they are entitled to an indemnification; whether the lands held by the pottahs produced are one and the same with those pointed out by the Chief Engineer.

Seton's finding was that, excluding 'the soldiers' burying ground to which I conceive my enquiry is not meant to extend', the following plots were in the occupancy of individuals although these were 'within the posts lately set up by the Chief Engineer' (that is, they were in the area marked out as the fort's esplanade): twenty-three bighas one katha held by Jagannath Sarkar, fourteen bighas four kathas by Lt Polhill, and eight bighas four kathas by 'Loll Gheer Fuckeer'. As regards Sarkar, the collector said that the documents provided appeared to him to be 'satisfactory and such as are in general considered as sufficient to confirm the possession of property to individuals'. In his report, Colonel Call had not mentioned the three bighas which Jagannath Sarkar had said was charity land which he had acquired. Seton threw some light on this aspect of Sarkar's claimed holding when he wrote: 'A further 3 bighas was bought by Sarkar from Ghunsaum Pundit for which neither a *patta* nor a sunnud was produced, nor any other voucher than a bill of sale from Ghunsaum Pundit to Juggernaut'. A reference was made to the Dolanda *chittas* for the years 1765 and 1782 where it was found that two bighas thirteen kathas were registered as ryotty ground in Pandit's name. Seton then wrote that Nilmoni Thakur, the son and *vakil* of Ghanshyam (both father and son were alive at the time, according to Kirparam Lashkar, a deponent in the case), was called upon to 'produce his vouchers', and he said that he had none. He affirmed that the ground was *brohmottor* 'and had long been the property of his family although the sunnud was now lost'. Seton said that when he compared the chittas with the *jumabundee*, he found that while the ground figured in the former as ryotty land, it 'had never been registered in the latter as malguzary land, nor had [it] ever paid rent to Government'. Seton felt that this sort of discrepancy in the records was unique and that it tended to confirm the assertion of Nilmoni Thakur 'that the ground is *bermooter* and must have been registered as *ryotty* ground by mistake'. The collector said that testimony given by a couple of witnesses was in favour 'of Neelmony having been in possession of the ground previous to its being occupied by Jaggernaut'.[12]

However, to Seton the more important point was the issue of compensation to Nilmoni Thakur 'and the other old inhabitants to whom the property is traced'. Seton said it is 'probable' they were compensated 'although they were by indulgence suffered to continue in possession' of the land. He said it was not possible for him to ascertain whether any indemnification had been made 'as no records in my possession afford me any information upon the subject; and in cases like the present, where the inhabitants were neither obliged to remove nor their old pottahs demanded, it would be extremely difficult to prove it'. With regard to the Polhill ground, he said he had nothing to add to what he had already stated, 'which fully shows my authority for granting' the patta in question. As regards the Lalgir Gossain ground, Seton said his officers had informed him that 'about two or three years since, he [Lalgir] had received pecuniary indemnification from the Khalsa Treasury by order of the late Committee of Revenue in consideration of his surrendering it to Government'. Lalgir contested this and said that the indemnification in question related to the surrender of ground for the new jail and that 'the receipt which he gave upon that occasion would prove it'. The collector said the matter could be cleared up 'by a reference to the disbursements of the Khalsa Treasury'.

Basing itself on the collector's report, the Board of Revenue wrote to the Governor-General in Council[13] that it had been made abundantly clear that both Sarkar's and Polhill's titles to the land they held had been 'fully established' and that, 'if it be found expedient to remove them, they will have a just claim on Government for a reasonable indemnification'. It is noteworthy that no differentiation was made between Sarkar and Polhill based on the colour of their skin despite the fact that it would not have been difficult to have discriminated against Sarkar and created problems for him. On 31 August 1787 the ground was 'adjudged to be the property of Jagernaut by a formal decision passed by Government'.[14] As regards the Lalgir land, the Board asked for a 'further enquiry'.

For eight years Jagannath Sarkar enjoyed the fruits of ownership of the land concerned. Then, in late 1795, the issue flared up once again following an ejectment order served on him by the judge of the 24-Parganas on the ground that no individual property could be allowed to exist on the plot marked out as the esplanade of the fort.[15] Following the decree, Captain F.H. Pearson, captain of engineers at the presidency, complained to the Military Board in early November of that year that he was obstructed by Sarkar when he had gone to his ground 'to clear away the huts' there.[16] Pearson further said that Sarkar had not only prevented his men from carrying out their official work but had also told them that he would

> not permit any huts to be taken away without an order from the Governor-General or Mr Gladwin, the then Collector of Calcutta, alleging that the ground in question had been decreed in his favour in the year 1768 [this is clearly an error in the records and should be 1787] by the Governor-General in Council in consequence of a report made by Mr Seton, the Collector at that time.

Pearson said that in order to avoid 'unnecessary injury or trouble' he had applied to Gladwin to see the relevant Proceedings and Seton's report. Following in the footsteps of his predecessors, Seton and Harrington, Francis Gladwin was of no help to Pearson because, as the latter wrote, 'he is of opinion that the ground in question, although within the boundary of the esplanade, is the property of Jagernaut Sircar, having purchased the same from several natives who either swore to the fact themselves or brought others to do it'. As for Seton's report, Pearson charged the collector of Calcutta at the time (1787) with being ignorant about 'the exact course of the Tolly's Nullah at that particular place' and that he appeared to have 'mistaken entirely the principal evidence which, instead of confirming Jugernaut's claim, goes directly to destroy it'.

Further, according to Pearson, Seton felt it was 'absolutely necessary that a clear description of the boundaries of [the] ground should appear on the records, in order to confirm a good title'. But, the captain wrote, 'there is nothing of the kind to be found on the records to determine where this ground is; it may be there or it may be in the furthermost end of Bhowanipore'. Not only did the worthy captain run down the collector, he also pulled up the natives for their ingrained untrustworthiness. When it came to the quality of evidence given on oath, he wrote:

> It is true several people have sworn in favour of Jagernaut's claim, and the aumeens sent by Mr Seton to ascertain the fact have also given it decidedly in his favour. But it may be asked, do the natives ever, or do they often, take a false oath, or are the aumeens perfectly free from bribes?

Pearson ventured to suggest that if Seton had made a personal inspection of the ground he would have discovered that the witnesses 'except [for] one, had been guilty of perjury, and the aumeens had deceived him'. The captain then said that if it was found that Sarkar had had recourse to 'fraud and bribery' to strengthen his case with regard to the ground in question, 'as an example to deter others from attempting similar practices for the future, I beg leave to recommend that he be obliged to refund all that he had received from it, which I understand is sixteen thousand rupees'.

Pearson argued further that since the land on which the road existed and also the cut—from the hospital to the nullah—had been bought by the Government

> ... sometime before Jagernaut bought his ground, it is highly improbable that the boundary of the esplanade being formed by this cut,[17] and all the ground within it being purchased for the esplanade, that this small piece of twenty-three biggahs [held by Sarkar] should have been left unbought.

Pearson, however, referred to the fact that Colonel Watson had told the Board of Revenue that though all the ground was bought by the Government 'some of the people were permitted to remain on it', This, Pearson proclaimed, was the proverbial thin end of the wedge regarding subsequent claims being made for ownership of the ground, declaring that natives 'are [ever] ready to take advantage of such an indulgence by laying claim to every spot where they have been permitted to reside'. The inference here was that Sarkar may have done the same thing.

In fact, Pearson said that the twenty-three bighas which Sarkar officially claimed was only a small part of the ground actually held by him in the area. According to him,[18] Sarkar 'possesses three times more than the quantity of ground adjudged to him, viz. 23 biggahs, and has been permitted to make roads and pathways over all that part of the Esplanade'. The captain said he had taken the liberty of 'ordering these roads to be stopped up, also the huts and timber to be carried away'. On his part, Sarkar petitioned the Governor-General in Council on 16 February 1796[19] alleging that on 7 February, a Sunday, Pearson had 'sent a serjeant in company with a number of lascars and chaprasseys [who] broke down and destroyed about one thousand straw huts belonging to your petitioner's tenants, which are about three hundred, and took possession [of] the same'. Sarkar said the captain had then offered him 'such a sum of money as compensation for the ground which is not sufficient for one quarter part of the value thereof'.

Considering all these aspects, the Military Board was of the view that 'if, on a further investigation of the matter, Jagannath Sarkar should appear to have any legal claim to the property of the ground, a compensation should be made to him, and the ground appropriated for the purpose of the public service'.[20] On 12 February 1796, the Assistant Sub-Secretary to the Government, H. St. George Tucker, wrote to George Dowdeswell, Secretary to the Board of Revenue, that the Governor-General in Council wanted the Board to 'instruct the Collector of Calcutta to ascertain and report a fair valuation of the ground in question', which could only mean that Sarkar was to be dispossessed of the ground in question.[21]

The pricing issue took some months to be settled,[22] a point of interest being the increase in the price of land along Tolly's Nullah which ran up to the Sunderbans. Regarding Sarkar's land on the banks of the nullah, the collector wrote to the Governor-General in Council that,

> ... formerly, land in this quarter was not worth above 150 Rs per beegah, but since the communication with the Sunderbunds has been opened, the ground bordering Tolley's Nullah has become so valuable that no proprietor is desirous of selling, and I have not been able to obtain information of any other transfer since that period besides the 3 bighas 11 cottahs purchased for the general hospital in October 1794 at the rate of 540 Rs per beegah.[23]

On the main issue of compensation, the Governor-General in Council held that the claim preferred by Sarkar 'cannot be finally adjusted without more satisfactory information regarding the value of the ground of which he represents himself to have been dispossessed'. Further, since there were doubts about the actual ownership of the ground in question, it was resolved that 'Jagernaut be referred to the Courts of Justice for the trial of any claims which he may think proper to prefer with a view to obtain an indemnification for the property'.[24]

Shifting the focus to a broader canvas Pearson, in his 7 November 1795 letter to the Military Board,[25] had also written about the encroachments on public roads generally, which gives us an idea of the state of some of the principal roads of the town during this time. He wrote that

> ... many of the largest roads within the boundary of the town of Calcutta [have] been so much encroached upon ... that there is not room for two carriages to pass on roads that were originally made forty or fifty feet wide. There are houses built in the middle of some of the roads behind Chowringhee and the road which forms the boundary to the eastward and leads to Dum Dum and Chitpore [Circular Road].

Pearson said that natives had 'enclosed about one third of its breadth in some places, and have planted trees and made gardens upon it'. He feared that if the situation was to last 'a few years longer, they [the natives] will find no difficulty in producing *pottahs* and getting old men to swear for them'. The Governor-General in Council wanted details of the encroachments, specially instances where 'individuals have erected houses', so that 'the proper officers [can] be directed to survey the premises, and to take the necessary measures for removing the buildings and restoring the breadth of the roads'. What is surprising is that encroachments of so serious a nature had evaded the notice of the authorities till then, or if noticed that no action had been taken. Corruption among the public servants charged with the job of looking after the town's civic development was mainly responsible for the perceived official inertia in this sphere.[26]

Providing the details sought, Pearson mentioned

> ... the roads from Bowannypore towards the General Hospital, lying north and south, also other roads in the same place, lying east and west. They are now so confined with temporary huts on each side that there is not room for a common carriage to pass. They are therefore obliged to go over upon the Esplanade, which is cut up in all directions by them.[27]

On the state of Circular Road he said that the

> … great road which extends from the south end of Chowringhee to Chitpore, and forms the boundary of Calcutta, is so much encroached upon that in some places there is not room for two carriages to pass with safety, particularly at the cross road which leads to Dum Dum. In some places the natives have planted trees and made fences on the very middle of the road.

The road to Barrackpore was described as being 'the most public of any other',[28] Pearson writing that it had become 'so very narrow that a carriage meeting another cannot pass in many places, particularly at Chitpore and Barranagore; at the first place, a native has lately made a *pucka* drain above three feet upon the road'. Within Calcutta, the encroachments were 'innumerable in the different streets' so much so that 'many of them will not admit of two palanquins abreast; and as these places are become difficult of access, filth of all kinds remains unnoticed'. Pearson said this was particularly the case in the eastern part of Chowringhee and Colinga, or all that space (excepting the European houses in Chowringhee) between Jaunbazar Road and the Burying Ground Road as far back as Entally. The roads in these places, he wrote, were 'crowded with temporary huts and enclosures for the present, but when sanctioned by time, they will be made more substantial and claims made that perhaps cannot be controverted'.

Pearson suggested a method of getting the problem sorted out before it became too late for any remedy to be effectively implemented. He wrote:

> As it is I apprehended there will be now a good deal of difficulty in ascertaining the proper limits of the cross roads, to obtain which I would beg leave to recommend [the following]:, each person's ground to be accurately measured, and when compared with his *pottah* the fraud would then be discovered; however, that should be done in a regular, scientific manner, otherwise there would be no finding out the truth, …

> as the *pottahs* do not describe the particular situation and boundaries of the ground for which they are granted.

Pearson said the natives 'commonly produce *pottahs* [to answer their purpose] for any other piece of ground that may be in that district', which is how—he had been told by 'several natives'—Jagannath Sarkar had 'got the decree in his favour for the ground on the esplanade'. He said a map should be constructed having plots with their proprietors clearly marked out in different colours 'so that either the police or Collector, being furnished with a book of such maps, they could decide disputes with ease and accuracy without being imposed upon by their mercenary servants'. The captain felt that this procedure would be an effective way to prevent 'fraud and collusion between the native officers who are employed in measuring ground and making out *pottahs* and individuals'.[29]

The link between broad streets, general cleanliness and salutary health conditions was also emphasised by Pearson when he wrote that 'narrow confined streets in a large, populous city will readily generate putrid contagious disorders is well known, and perhaps the late mortality at the city of Moorshedabad had its rise from the cause'. Another observation relating to health was 'the extraordinary number of pits or small tanks scattered in every corner' most of which were to be found on 'what is called *besshey* ground, and [therefore] cannot be considered the property of anyone'. But Pearson felt that the pits and tanks could not be 'filled up or improved' ... 'whilst the streets remain so narrow'. On receiving Pearson's comments, the Governor-General in Council wanted measures to be taken 'for removing any recent encroachments on the publick roads in the environs of Calcutta not within the jurisdiction of the officers of the town police and for preventing the same in future'.[30]

Notes

1 T.D. Pearse was known as the 'father of the Bengal Artillery' and was Hastings' second in the duel with Philip Francis which took place

early on 7 August 1780. See *Bengal Past and Present*, July-September 1923, vol. 26, Part 1, p. 36.

2 It is of interest to note that the planned clearing activity was to leave unscathed the temple near the hospital.

3 Board of Revenue Proceedings, 27 April 1787.

4 Archibald Campbell was chief engineer at Calcutta from 1768 to 1772, returning to England in the latter year. He came back to India in 1786 as Governor of Fort St George but resigned his position in 1789 on account of ill health (*Bengal Past and Present*, January-March 1929, vol. 37, Part 1, p. 64).

5 The details, though instructive, have been omitted for reasons of space.

6 Jagannath Sarkar, who has a lane named after him at Kidderpur, was one of those colourful and 'explosive' personalities of native society of the late eighteenth century who did not fail to elicit extreme comment from their compatriots. He hurled the choicest of epithets, even officially, at people whom he perceived to be his enemies and obstacles in his path and did not have any qualms if he received them back with interest. In the case in question, he did not hesitate to describe two witnesses who had petitioned against him as being 'very low and bad natured people', their 'general profession (being) to interfere into every bad business and to give false evidence. In fact they are hired swearingmen'. The return-flak is instructive because of the light it casts on the reputation Sarkar had at the time in native society. One set of petitioners said that it was '... well-known to every inhabitant of the 24 Pergunnahs and of the town of Calcutta that he [Sarkar] is a very bad man, and his profession is to rob the poor people. He has no caste as his father was a *chandal* in caste, which is worse than a *mather*, or sweeper caste, and his situation was a *manjee* to a boat, and his mother was the wife of a *cuppoully*, or rope twister. His former name was Juggernaut Chundal, but since he made his money by robbing poor people he used the name of Juggarnauth Sircar' (Judicial Civil Proceedings, 11 March 1796).

7 Board of Revenue Proceedings, 27 April 1787.

8 C.R. Wilson defines *tope* as 'grove' (*Old Fort William*, vol. 1, p. 180fn).

9 What is being referred to here are, simply, garages for carriages. In the early years there were similar facilities for palanquins. The Bengal Public Consultations for 9 May 1726 refer to a 'pallenkeen house which was covered with thatch' (Wilson, *Old Fort William*, vol. 1, p. 119), the point at issue here being that since the cost of rebuilding it

after being burnt down so very often was so great it would be more sensible to build one of brick, a suggestion which was accepted by the Court of Directors (Court's letter to Bengal, 14 February 1728—ibid., pp. 124–125).

10 Anna Maria Tolly, the widow of Tolly who had died at sea in 1784.

11 Board of Revenue Proceedings, 19 June 1787.

12 There is a point of interest involved here relating to genealogy. If the Nilmoni Thakur mentioned here belonged to the Tagore family and was the grandfather of Dwarkanath Tagore, his father should have been Joyram who reportedly died in 1756 or thereabout which, however, is not the case according to the Proceedings. The records state unambiguously that Ghanashyam (not Joyram) was Nilmoni's father and that he was still alive in 1787. Further, we know that Nilmoni's father had property at Gobindapur (see, among others, Krishna Kripalani, *Dwarkanath Tagore: A Forgotten Pioneer* [New Delhi: National Book Trust, 1981], p. 20, fn. 4). The records (see chapter 'The Jorabagan Dispute') indicate that Nilmoni Thakur was given land at Jorabagan by the English authorities as compensation for property in Gobindapur following the construction of the new Fort William, which suggests that the Nilmoni Thakur who figures here did in fact belong to the (later illustrious) Tagore family. The point, therefore, is: are the Proceedings penned in 1787 wrong about Nilmoni's father, or does the explanation lie elsewhere?

13 Board of Revenue Proceedings, 19 June 1787.

14 Ibid., 26 February 1796. Extract from the Proceedings of the Governor-General in Council in the Military Department of 23 November 1795.

15 Board of Revenue Proceedings, 26 February 1796.

16 Ibid.

17 This point about the boundary of the esplanade is not to be found in Seton's 1787 report.

18 Board of Revenue Proceedings, 26 February 1796.

19 Judicial Civil Proceedings, 11 March 1796 (West Bengal State Archives).

20 Board of Revenue Proceedings, 26 February 1796.

21 Ibid.

22 The issue of a 'fair valuation' of Sarkar's ground (which is not included in the volume) provides an insight into the administrative procedures involved when a collector is pulled up by the Supreme Council for

an alleged lapse which the official concerned is initially hesistant to admit. The Governor-General at this time (1793–1798) was Sir John Shore, who was himself a Bengal civilian and who, therefore, was well-conversant with administrative issues involved at the grassroots level.

23 Judicial Civil Proceedings, 27 January 1797.

24 Ibid.

25 Board of Revenue Proceedings, 26 February, 1796.

26 On systemic corruption among officials native and European, see Robb, *Sentiment and Self*, pp. 132–133, 193–196.

27 Board of Revenue Proceedings, 26 February 1796.

28 This was the old road to Barrackpore, Wellesley's great avenue coming a few years later.

29 See chapter 'Temple on the Maidan', note 11 for the confession of a native official.

30 Board of Revenue Proceedings, 26 February 1796. The Judicial Civil Proceedings of 6 May 1796 has an extract from the Law Proceedings of the Governor-General in Council dated 25 April 1796 which gives the Council's response to the 'orders given by the Justices for removing the encroachments on the public roads within the boundaries of Calcutta', which were pointed out in a report drawn up by Edward Tirretta. The Governor-General in Council approved of the measures and asked the Justice Department to transmit the view of the Calcutta magistrates to those of the 24-Parganas and Krishnanagar. The Calcutta magistrates had written on 19 April 1796 that '… the roads from Bowannypore towards the General Hospital, lying north and south, and other roads in the same place lying east and west, as also the spot where a native has lately made a publick drain at Chitpore, together with the encroachments near Barnagore, alluded to in Captain Pearson's letter, are all beyond the boundary of Calcutta, and consequently without our jurisdiction.'

17

Temple on the Maidan

As we have seen in the preceding chapter, in 1787, along with Jagannath Sarkar, the authorities were also taken up with the compensation to be paid to Lalgir Gossain for land on the maidan. The subject is of more than ordinary interest because of the issues it throws up regarding the possible historical antecedents of the property he held at Gobindapur, going back to a time much before the English landed at Sutanati. In April of that year Colonel Call had referred to a 'fakir' who had built a temple in a grove 'northward of, and near, the hospital'. In his report of 13 June 1787[1] Archibald Seton, the Collector of Calcutta, had written that the ground in question measuring eight bighas four kathas was in 'the occupancy of Loll Gheer, a Gossayne, or Hindoo religious [figure], who has erected a temple there'. On being asked to produce his title deeds, Lalgir said that the land in question 'was the remainder of a large quantity of charity ground under the management of the late Jungle Gheer', an assertion which, according to Seton, was unsupported by any sunnud or other document. He then referred to the chittas of 1765 and 1782 and found eight bighas four kathas 'Sheo-Wutter-Ground registered in the name of Jungle Gheer, whose adopted son Loll Gheer declares himself to be'. The collector wrote that he could not say whether this was the very ground now in the occupancy of Lalgir, adding, however, that 'the present appropriation of it seems to correspond with the original purpose as it is devoted to the worship of Sheo, whose image is contained in the temple which is called the Mundir of Sheo Takoor'.

Such is the fragmentary written record of the 1780s regarding a temple on the maidan. Let us now have recourse to tradition as laid bare by Gaur Das Bysack—a scion of the ancient Basak family which, along with the Setts, put Gobindapur and Sutanati on the trade and commerce map—and try to see whether the topographical meeting point between the two is mere coincidence or something more than that. Writing in 1891[2] on the antecedents of the shrine at Kalighat, Bysack says there was reason to believe that 'the worship of the Kali of this place originated, in obscurity, sometime between the close of the fifteenth and the commencement of the sixteenth century'. The place is not mentioned in the *Ain-i-Akbari* which, according to Bysack, does not mean 'that the place did not exist in Akbar's time, though, no doubt, it is presumptive proof of its not having acquired any great celebrity'. In 1589–1590, Man Singh, Governor of Bengal and Behar under Akbar and a devotee of Kali, did not visit the shrine despite being 'not many miles from the holy spot'.

Bysack says that 'the celebrity of Kalighata could not have been very great even as late as the days of Aurangzebe, otherwise its shrine could not have escaped the iconoclastic fury of that fanatical monarch'. It was only

> ... in the days of the Sakta Maharaja Krishna Chandra of Nadiya, who was the Zamindar of 'Pargana Calcutta, etc' ... the current Kalighata legend had acquired maturity, and that, under some of the tolerant Nawabs of Bengal, but chiefly under British protection, even in the early days of the English period, Kalighata had reached the climax of its celebrity.

He attaches special importance to the view of Nawab Muhabbat Khan who wrote in his work, *A General History of India from the Time of the Ghaznivides to the Accession of Muhammad Akbar, at the close of the year 1806*, bearing the title *Akhbar-i-Muhabbat,* that

'Calcutta formerly was only a village, the revenue of which was assigned for the expenses of the temple of Kali Devi, which stands there'. Bysack says that, according to available historical records, Kalighat 'existed sometime during the fifteenth century, as a *Guhya-tirtha*, or not very well known sacred place of worship, but that it acquired celebrity at a very much later period'.

Bysack then moves on to the 'tradition' of how the shrine of Kali came to be located at Kalighat. He narrates the story thus:

> Once upon a time, it is said, a Sevayet Sannyasi, one of the *Dasanamis*, who had become a follower of the tenets of Yogi Chaurangi,[3] and Jangal Gir by name, was known devoutly to worship a certain symbol of the goddess Kali at some place on the eastern outskirts of the old site of Govindpur (now occupied by Fort William), where the Presidency Jail at present stands. The Kali image worshipped at Kalighata is made up of different members of the body, mechanically adjusted together; the real sacred object being, it is believed, the veritable stone emblem which the Sannyasi used to worship, and which is supposed to have fallen from heaven to mark the place where the toes of Sati had fallen in a former age. To account for Jangal Gir's selecting any particular spot in Govindpur for his worship, when it was thickly covered with jungle, a story runs that, when this wandering devotee was roaming there, he frequently saw herds of kine making a detour from their beaten-path towards a particular point, and, after a while, returning to their usual course. One day, he followed them, and found, to his surprise, that, on arriving at a certain place, they, one by one, stretched their legs over it, and allowed their milk to flow from their udders for a few minutes. He brought this to the notice of the cowherd, and, with his aid, having the ground excavated, discovered the symbol of which he had been previously apprised in a dream.[4]

Bysack says that the 'exact spot' where the symbol was for the first time set up is not known but 'there is no question' that there was a ghat

> … on the bank of the river, somewhere between the sites on which the Barabazar and Prinsep's Ghats stand, at which the pilgrims and people across the river, or from the neighbouring village, used to alight for the purpose of proceeding to her worship, and which soon, acquiring the name of Kalighata, gave, in turn, its own name to the present locality so called, and the title of the religious order of her first or earliest Sevayet, Chaurangi, soon became the eponym of the splendid Maidan that now graces our city.

Importantly, Bysack avers in a note that the ghat bearing the name Kalighat 'could not have been located on the banks of the Adi-Ganga, near the present temple, because the goddess was not removed to her present site till a much later period'.[5] While this may or may not be true, the existence of a ghat, or landing place on the river, on the Adi Ganga at a time when the shrine was located at Gobindapur can be rationalised on the ground that the distance between the Adi Ganga and the shrine would have been shorter than if a ghat servicing the shrine had been located between Barabazar and Prinsep's Ghat on the Hooghly. The poet Bipradas writing at the end of the fifteenth century says that on a river journey down to the sea his hero paid obeisance to the Goddess Kalika at Kalighat in the vicinity of Dolanda (the area where the SSKM Hospital is located today) *after* he had entered the Adi Ganga.[6] Was there then a 'Kalighat' on the Adi Ganga, or the later Tolly's nullah, serving the shrine when it was located at Gobindapur, the ghat's location perhaps being somewhere between today's Zeerut and Alipore bridges?[7] But where exactly was the shrine located at Gobindapur? Bysack quotes 'tradition' to suggest that it may have been set up roughly where the Victoria Memorial stands today. It is of some interest to note that old maps of the area (see image 26 on p. 216) show a road deviating to the west from the 'pilgrim path' at a point opposite Ho Chi Minh Sarani (Harrington Street), which could conceivably have taken worshippers to the shrine in earlier times.

Continuing his story about Jangal Gir's temple, Bysack says it

> ... was destined to be shifted from one locality to another. Her shrine,[8] if any, at Chaurangi ['a wretched hut is said to have served for her temple'], was demolished, when Govindpur was taken for the purpose of building the new Fort; she was removed to Kalighata, where she was similarly housed, if not on the very site, but in the vicinity, of her present temple, till, subsequently, in 1809, the Savarna Chaudhuris of Behala erected for her the present temple.

But why was the shrine shifted to present-day Kalighat on the banks of the Adi Ganga and not to any other place? Certainly, the existence of the Kali temple on the banks of the channel at 'Kalighata' could have been an important reason for the choice of location, but was it the only reason behind the choice?

What we have summarised above is Gaur Das Bysack's version of the story based on tradition of the early history of the Kali temple in Calcutta and its move to the present-day Kalighat. Let us now turn to the English records of the late eighteenth century and try to see whether they throw any light on the subject based on actual events. Among other things, the records provide us with some details about the fate of Lalgir Gossain's ground in the esplanade upon which, it is well-established, there stood a temple, or temples. On the issue of compensation given to Lalgir for giving up his land to the Government when the new fort came up, the Board of Revenue provided the Collector of Calcutta, Archibald Seton, with the details of the recompense made to Lalgir for ground he had surrendered (specifically in the area where the new jail had come up), asking him to find out whether the compensation also applied to the land presently under contention in Dolanda.[9] The Board said that in 1782 the Governor-General having ordered the esplanade to be cleared

> ... as far as a boundary line drawn on the north-east side from the new jail to Surman's nullah and having occasion to occupy the ground

> situated between that line and the hospital, a survey of this intermediate spot was made ... and found to ascertain, among other private property, 17 begahs (on which stood some *mutts*, or Hindoo temples) belonging to Loll-gheer.

The Board ordered that Lalgir be given for the entire property 'an equivalent ... in land or money', which led the Committee of Revenue to direct on 3 October 1782 that seventeen bighas be transferred to Lalgir 'in Monohurpoor'. Further, having ascertained the value of the temples, on 24 July the following year the Board of Revenue said that, in lieu of them, he should receive Rs 1,200 from the Khalsa treasury, 'which sum, however, ... appears to have been paid till September 1785, and then (in all appearance erroneously) charged as a consideration for brick walls and fruit trees standing on a spot of ground taken for the purpose of building the new jail'.

The Board told Seton that 'the precision of this charge' and the identity of the ground for which Lalgir received an equivalent could easily be confirmed by a reference to Nimnarayan Mitra, the jarib amin, who had conducted the 1782 survey. Seton was asked to find out from Mitra 'the exact situation of the 17 begahs then included in his survey as the property of Lollgheer, as well as the particular spot on which the Hindoo temples stood, and whether the sum of 1,200 Rs paid to him was not in consideration of these buildings'. The Board of Revenue said that from these findings 'an accurate judgement' could be formed whether the eight bighas 'now in the possession' of Lalgir constituted 'a part of the 17 before made good to him or otherwise'. It also asked the collector to find out if Lalgir 'was regularly put in possession of the 17 bigahs assigned to him in Monohurpoor'. Seton was told that, apart from the seventeen bighas in focus here, Lalgir had also 'established his title to 47 begahs appropriated to the new jail, for which an equivalent was first assigned in the Panchwangong [Panchannagram], but in consequence of a deficiency of comar ground, an equal portion was afterwards given him in the 24 Pergunnahs'.

Following up on his 13 June 1787 report, Seton wrote another letter[10] to the Board of Revenue on 30 June containing additional information on the ground 'in the occupancy of Laul Gheer Gosayne'. He referred to the earlier report and said that since he wrote it he had been informed by 'Nemoo Metre . . . the Jurib Aumeen of this Cutcherry' that in 1784 he (Mitra) had been asked by the Committee of Revenue 'to report upon the quantity of ground claimed by Laul Gheer, in the neighbourhood of the hospital as also upon the value of the trees, buildings, etc upon it'. Mitra found that the ground measured sixty-five bighas and 'the value of the trees, buildings (viz: two temples), etc to be Rs 1,200'. Mitra said the Committee decided that on Lalgir 'surrendering the *whole* [emphasis in Proceedings] he should receive in lieu thereof 48 begahs in the Calcutta Purgunnah and the remaining 17 begahs in Paunchaungong; as also that he should receive 1,200 rupees from the Khalsa Treasury as a compensation for the buildings, etc, etc'.[11]

Interestingly, despite being told by his own staff that this is what the Committee of Revenue had itself ordered, Seton said he was unable to vouch for the 'accuracy' of the information regarding the forty-eight bighas and the Rs 1,200. This, however, was not an insurmountable problem because the matter could be easily sorted out by a reference to the records of the Committee of Revenue. With respect to the seventeen bighas, the collector said that Lalgir was 'actually put in possession of that quantity in dhee Monnupoor (Monaharpur) in Paunchaungong agreeably to a Perwannah of the late Committee of Revenue dated on the 3rd October 1782'.[12] The collector added that the *perwana* in question did not state the reasons for the grant of land 'but the Monnupoor chittas specify that it is in lieu of *dewutter* ground surrendered to Government by him'. Seton said that Lalgir continued to persist 'in asserting that he only received these 17 begahs and the 1,200 Rs in lieu of the ground upon which the new jail is erected; but denies ever having received any compensation for that which he is now in possession of'. Seton's conclusion was that since Lalgir had been given forty-eight bighas in the Calcutta pargana and seventeen bighas in Panchannagram, apart from Rs 1,200 'in money', he could not 'justly claim the ground which he now occupies, near the hospital'. As far as the eight bighas four kathas on which the temples stood were concerned, Seton had earlier thought that Lalgir was entitled to the land. But now he felt that this ground too 'ought to be transferred and registered as the property of Government, if (as appears to be the case) he has been indemnified for the *whole* [emphasis in Proceedings] ground which was claimed by him in 1782'. As the Collector saw it, the entire problem had arisen 'from finding the 8 beghas 4 cottahs still registered in the name of Jungle Gheer' when in fact it should have been transferred to the Government 'at the time when the adjustment took place'.[13]

Where precisely was Lalgir Gossain given land as compensation at Monoharpur? Did it include the land on which stands today the Kalighat-Shib temple complex, including the Nakuleshwar temple? Did Lalgir shift his temples on the esplanade to this spot after being ordered to do so by the authorities? If this is in fact what happened, we then have a link between tradition and the official records on the Kali-Shib temple complex on the maidan and present-day Kalighat, the conclusion being that the idols were shifted to the new location in the late 1780s. Perhaps it was the Lalgir temple to Kali which was embellished by the Sabarna Chowdhuries in 1809 or thereabouts.

35 A pencil sketch of the temple at Kalighat, by Frans Balthazar Solvyns, around 1798

NOTES

1 Board of Revenue Proceedings, 19 June 1787.

2 'Kalighat and Calcutta', *Calcutta Review,* vol. XCII, January 1891, pp. 305–327.

3 Taking his cue from dates associated with Kabir (c. 1440–1518), Bysack writes without citing any source that Yogi Chaurangi 'must have lived in the early part of the fifteenth century, and Jangal Gir Chaurangi must have been one of his earliest followers'.

4 See Wilson, *Early Annals*, vol. 1, pp. 129–130, for a different account of Jangal Gir's experience. Of related interest is the article (signed by a contributor 'L' which appeared in the *Calcutta Christian Observer* of September 1833) on the temple at Kalighat which recounted the story of a cow which stood 'still on a spot which appeared to (a certain Brahmin of the name of Holdar) to have been illumined with a beam of resplendent light'. The temple was founded on that spot where the temple now stands, the time line being around 1633. The writer says that the 'descendants of Holdar are the proprietors of the temple. They have now increased to 25 or 30 families, who share all the offerings presented to the goddess'.

5 By the middle of the eighteenth century, the English were familiar with the name 'Kalighat'. In chapter 2, note 34 we have referred to a 1754 letter from Bengal to the Court of Directors which writes about 'the Creek [Adi Ganga] that runs from Surmans Bridge [located where the Kidderpur Bridge stands today, according to Wilson] to Callygat' (Wilson, *Old Fort William*, vol. 2, p. 2).

6 See map of the Hooghly to the sea in the sixteenth century 'according to De Barros and the Bengali poets', in Wilson, *Early Annals*, vol. 1, after p. 130.

7 Concurring with Gaur Das Bysack, Nair (*Calcutta in the 17th Century*, pp. 49–50), conjectures that such a ghat could perhaps have been located at, or near, the spot where Prinsep's Ghat stands today. The notion that the ghat catering to the shrine at Gobindapur was located in the early days on the Hooghly is tied to the view that the least inhospitable route for the pilgrims to take to visit the shrine was the Pilgrims' Road stretching from Chitpur in the north to Kalighat in the south. Bholanath Chunder, writing in the *Calcutta University Magazine* in January 1897, says: 'The pilgrims, who came from the other side of the river, landed at a ghat between the old Vanzan Creek and the Chandpal Ghat, as it was the nearest cut to the shrine by

the great highway that then came down *via* Chitpur from the seat of Patan government at Gour' (reprinted in Alok Ray ed., *Calcutta Keepsake,* p.6).

8 Was the shrine to Shib or Kali? As indicated earlier, the 13 June 1787 report of Seton had said that the temple on Lalgir's property was 'devoted to the worship of Sheo, whose image is contained in the temple which is called the Mundir of Sheo Takoor'.

9 Board of Revenue Proceedings, 19 June 1787.

10 Ibid., 13 July 1787.

11 There is little doubt that Mitra here was performing a job on which would be based action regarding compensation of the Government of the day. What were the chances of the jarib amin not providing a true picture to his bosses? Robb (*Sentiment and Self*, p. 133) says that the performance of such officials was not always above board and that it was in fact systemically tainted by corruption. Indeed, Mitra himself once had occasion to rationalise such behaviour. When Richard Blechynden, the surveyor (see note 13, chapter 28), had asked him whether he took bribes, the amin had replied: 'Sir – let the Company fill my belly and I will be honest – I have a wife and four children – my salary is 25 Rs per mensem and I pay 30 for my bearers'.

12 Lalgir took physical possession of the ground on 11 December 1783 (Board of Revenue Proceedings, 13 July 1787).

13 Lalgir Gossain had more land in the area because the Board of Revenue Proceedings of 5 December 1794 quotes a missive from the then Collector of Calcutta, Francis Gladwin, which tells us that he (Lalgir) had sold a plot 'adjoining to the General Hospital' measuring three bighas eleven kathas twelve chattaks to the Government for Sicca Rs 1900 and that the transfer 'has been registered in the books of this cutcherry with all the forms usual on such occasions'.

18

The Jorabagan Dispute

The problems faced by those evicted because of the setting up of Henry Watson's docks in Kidderpur in the late 1760s form an important part of the subject of compensation. The case was a special one in that the problems which arose were not merely confined to matters relating to the quantum and nature of compensation for people being moved from one place to another following the pressure of 'development' but also threw light on the failure of the authorities to anticipate the hurdles faced by those affected. The essence of the issue was that people had been moved to a spot which was claimed by other people, a knot which the authorities found so difficult to untie that they hesitated to give proper land-possession documents to the evictees for fear of attracting legal proceedings, which made life for the latter even more problematic than it already was.

The records tell us that on 31 May 1774 Radhamohan Sett, Pitambar Sett, Nemai Charan Sett, Ananda Charan Sett, Brajamohan Sett and others petitioned the authorities[1] stating that in 1767 Major Watson had received a grant of some ground in Kidderpur to set up his docks and that the people owning land there, who were affected, had been permitted 'to erect a gunge at Nimtoolah' on land on which the petitoners' forbears had built 'houses and buildings' at great cost and from which they received 'considerable rents from the occupiers thereof'. The new arrivals had driven away the tenants and demolished their buildings, all of which led to 'very considerable losses' being suffered by the landowners. A consequence of this was that the petitioners found themselves 'dispossessed of their property, which had belonged to them and their ancestors for many years back'. Further, a part of their land was 'rendered useless' and they did not ever receive any rent from the new settlers. The petitioners said they had made their grievance known to John Cartier (Governor from 1769 to 1772) and later his successor, Warren Hastings, who had asked Richard Barwell, the then Superintendent of the Khalsa, to look into the matter. Barwell had put them in possession of two bighas nineteen kathas of the ground, but had to interrupt his enquiries as he was sent away to Dacca on official business. The petitioners did not want the 'occupiers' of their land to be unsettled but merely sought redress by way of getting their rent as the land was 'really and truly' their property. They also wanted new pattas to be granted to them for the land that was unoccupied.[2] In terms of area, the Setts claimed that forty-seven bighas twelve kathas one chittack of their land was occupied by the evictees from Kidderpur from whom they demanded rent; 'repossession' was sought regarding fifty bighas seventeen kathas one chittack which was unoccupied.[3]

The Board took the most sensible stand that it could in the circumstances when it directed that the petitioners were entitled to regain possession of the land (fifty bighas sixteen kathas one chittack) 'which has not been appropriated by Government for the purpose of which it was originally attached, but remains unoccupied'. It asked the Calcutta Committee of Revenue to 'put the proprietors in possession of the unoccupied ground and grant them *pottahs* of their original right thereto'.[4] On its part, the Committee issued orders that the Setts be put in possession of the ground and be given pattas 'on their producing title-papers of their original right thereto'.[5] But this was the easy part of the business. With respect to the claim for rent from the land occupied by the new settlers from Kidderpur, the authorities let the matter rest 'for further consideration until they could satisfy themselves what compensation Major Watson has made to the Company for the ground of which the Kidderpore people were dispossessed in order to erect the docks'. Subsequently, orders were issued to maintain the status quo in the area with no further activities being allowed by the Kidderpur people, which, as the records indicate, were not complied with. In January 1775 Pitambar Sett, Radhamohan Sett, Birjumohan Sett and Ram Chand sent a plea to the Government stating that the latter's instructions directing that no one was to 'erect a house or land his goods upon the waste land of Neemtulla and Jourubaug without our knowledge' were not being followed. They urged that 'a peon may be stationed with us for a little time (to prevent such activity) and we will be answerable for his expences', which was acceded to by the Government.[6]

While the authorities were delaying taking a settled stand on the matter, those who had been given land at Jorabagh had begun to face the heat of legal action initiated by the Setts. To take one instance, Reginald Pires wrote to the Government[7] in early 1777 that 'in or about the year 1771', Stair Hawthorn Stewart, the late Surveyor of the Roads under the Collector-General,[8] had measured out to him one bigha fifteen kathas 'at Jorrabaug in the parish of Sootanutty, and [gave] it to your petitioner in lieu of his former ground situated in Keederpore Gunge'. The land had been with him ever since 'without the least dispute with any one'. But now Chand Sett and Radharaman Sett had staked their claim to the property alleging that he (Pires) had 'forcibly taken it from them', claiming also a rent for the entire period totalling Sicca Rs 4,200-0-0. Matters had gone so far that Pires had received a summons from the Supreme Court. Pires placed the ball in the court of the Government when he wrote:

> As your petitoner has the aforesaid piece of ground from the Hon'ble Company in lieu of his former property at Keederpore gunge, which was taken from him by the Hon'ble Company, therefore your petitioner humbly prays, you gentlemen will be so graciously pleased as to favour

> him with your protection, and clear him from the unjust complaint made against him by the aforesaid Chaund Seat and Radaramon Seat.

Following procedure, the Commitee asked the dewan to do the impossible, namely, report on 'the cause of his (Pires) not having been furnished with a pottah'.

The following is yet another example of a dispute over compensation problems. In November 1778, the Calcutta Committee of Revenue received a notice from George Foxcroft, attorney-at-law, on behalf of Huzzurimal, Jugal Addy and Ramkrishna Mallick regarding land in the possession of Kashinath Babu, which was originally registered in the name of Radhaballabh Sett, the land being obtained 'by the ryotts of Kidderpore' in exchange 'for the land taken up by the new fort'.[9] Foxcroft was arguing the case for pattas to be given to his three clients. Since the land in question, officially described as 'situate in Jewrah Baug dependant on Sootanuty', was included in the newly created taluk of Nabakrishna Deb, the Committee was presented with an escape route. It sent Foxcroft the message that 'as the ground he requests a *pottah* for his constituents is included in Sootanuty, and as that ground is granted by *sunnud* to Rajah Nobkissen by the Hon'ble Board ... we are not authorised to grant any *pottah* for the ground included therein'. Foxcroft went to court and had his way because in February 1779, Kashinath Babu's vakil told the Committee[10] that his client had been deprived of the two bighas two kathas he held at Jorabagh 'by a decree of the Supreme Court on a suit instituted by Huzzumul and others'. The East India Company was asked to bear the burden of Kashinath's defeat in the lawsuit, the vakil telling the Committee that, as compensation, he should get 'an equal quantity of *comar* ground either in Durrumtallah or to the southward of the Great Tank or near Champaul Gaut'. He also asked for reimbursement of costs in defending the lost suit and that the Company's attorney 'may be ordered to defend any other suit instituted on this account for rent or otherwise'. The

Committee's response to this[11] was that 'land at either Dharamtala or Chowringhee could not be granted without encroaching on the precincts of the new fort, or confining the great square to the unhealthiness of the town, and we know of no land at the last except the old burying ground'. It, therefore, offered him 'a pecuniary consideration on the same plan as the other petitioners'.

It is clear that till they were given proper titles to the land they were holding in Jorabagh the legal position of those who had been resettled in the area was weak. The Supreme Court was busy handing down judgments which went against the 'Kidderpore people' even though the resettlement was the result of Government policy. Even official documents had hinted at the impropriety of the entire business of land being taken away from owners holding pattas to the ground and not making use of it for the 'public purpose' for which the land had been acquired in the first place. Thus, on 29 August 1775,[12] the dewan made the following 'representation':

> There are 100 begahs 17½ cottahs of land in Jorabaug which are the real property of Bishnoo Doss Sait and Gopaul Seit, etc. However, agreeably to the orders of the Huzzoor the ryots and merchants have built houses and golahs upon it. Yet it has not been taken up by the Company, and at the same time it is out of the possession of the former proprietors. The *ryots* who now inhabit it pay revenue nowhere. There is due on this account from the beginning of 1177 BS [1770] to the end of 1181 BS [1774-1775] Rs 2,409-13-12. Should the ground be taken up by the Government the revenue will of course be collected from the present inhabitants. Should it be restored to the possession of the old proprietors they are ready to pay it.

A year later, in a statement on the 'rents of the Town of Calcutta with the Chokydaree'[13] the point was made that

> Jura Baug, formerly belonging to Luckycunt Seat and others, was kept these eight years to establish a Gunge, which has not been put in

> execution, nor has it been given back to him, and the rents have remained in the hands of the *riots*. This has repeatedly [been] represented, but no orders given upon it.

In these circumstances, it is only to be expected that those resettled would get together and take the initiative to petition the Government focusing on their plight, which they did in the closing weeks of 1778.[14] The petitioners wrote that they had

> ... some ground at Kiddorpore, where they had built golahs, houses, etc, and erected it in the form of a gunge, which they had long engaged: and afterwards, on or about the year 1769, it was given out that Major (now Colonel) Watson had been authorised by Government to satisfy your petitioners and take the aforesaid spot of ground for the construction of docks.

The merchants said that Watson had 'forcibly' taken possession of their land and had broken down the golahs and houses, an act which had 'illegally injured and oppressed' them and had left them 'without any remedy for some years'. What this implies is that no compensation was given to them by Watson and certainly not by the Government, the latter probably staying away from the proceedings for which Watson was responsible.[15] Subsequently, they 'were given to understand' that the Government had decided to compensate them 'for the loss of their ground at Kiddorpore by allotting them an equal quantity of ground at Sootanutty', which however had 'subjected them to many losses and inconveniencies by prosecutions in the Supreme Court, by the Saits, [Setts] etc who pretend to be proprietors of the ground allotted to them by Government'.

Specifically, the petitioners wanted compensation for the losses sustained by them when they were 'dispossessed of their ground by Colonel Watson' and payment of rent arrears 'from the period of their removal to this time for the part of ground which still remains due to them by Government, and for the other part, from the period of their removal to the time it was put in their possession'. They also wanted an order

> ... compleating their claims for the ground still due them, and to grant them *pottahs* for the ground allotted them in compensation, and also to indemnify them for the costs they have [borne] in defending the suits of the Saitts, etc, aforesaid, and at the same time to grant an order to the Hon'ble Company's Attorney at Law to defend these suits in future.

The sting was attached to the tail of the document, the petitioners stating that if the Government did not think that it would be able to comply with the 'requests', it would grant them 'immediate leave' ... 'to prosecute Colonel Watson for the damages they have sustained by his seizing of their lands'.

The stand adopted by the Government of Warren Hastings as far as this particular issue is concerned is suggestive of an approach sympathetic to the demands made by natives even when the matter concerned infrastructural development, and that too when the person concerned with the project had close links with the power-centre. As a matter of routine, the Governor-General in Council sent the petition to the Calcutta Committee of Revenue asking it to call upon the petitioners to produce their papers for the lands which they claimed they had been dispossessed of 'at Kiddorpore, and ascertain what portions of land have been given to them generally, in lieu thereof, at Sootanutty, and what further compensation is due to them'. The Committee was also asked to propose 'some means of satisfying the petitioners for the remainder', the specific recommendation being made that 'particular attention be given to this subject'.[16]

The Calcutta Committee of Revenue got down to work and, on 22 February 1779 asked the merchants' vakil, Paddolochun Sen,[17] to submit a general statement of the amount claimed by those affected 'on account of expences, loss and rent'. This statement was not forthcoming because, as Sen said, 'All my constituents are not in

Calcutta, and a general account may be made out when they shall be all assembled'. This may have been the case, but it does appear from a reading of the Proceedings that the persons affected were not inclined to cooperate with the authorities on this specific issue beyond a point. Thus, a week earlier, when the Committee wanted to know in writing from the merchants as to who had authorised them to 'severally [obtain] their ground at Sootanutty and what further compensation they required', they said they would 'not state this matter in writing'. The only point the petitioners were willing to concede to the authorities was that the ground given to them at Sutanati was measured 'by Mr Stair Hawthorn Stewart, and that they insist on [this] being confirmed to them by *pattas*'. Even earlier, on 30 December 1778, the 'principal petitioners for the land of Kidderpore' had attended the Committee's meeting—the first since the Governor-General in Council had asked it to get down to probing the matter—'but without any *pottahs* or other papers to establish their several claims'. At the 22 February meeting the Committee's dewan submitted the account of the land-holdings of the affected merchants and what they had been given at Jorabagh, drawn up as a result of arbitration, 'a copy of which was now in the *duftore*' (office).[18]

Earlier, on 16 January 1779 the dewan had laid before the committee the '*chuta* accounts of the ground measured out by Maukind Chund, under the orders of Mr Stewart, the Superintendent of Police and the President of this Committee, at Joora Baug in Sootanutty', stating that 'the petitioners have been put in possession of the ground but as no *pottahs* have yet been granted to them their names have not been adopted in the accounts of the district kept by Becho Mundel the *etmaumdar*'. He said that the '*curtcha wassil backey* and *jumma bundy* accounts of the district specify the names of the persons who held the land previous to the petitioners obtaining possession, and since that period there has been no receipts of revenue from them or the former holders'. The dewan added that the measurements made by Chund were begun in

1770 and completed in 1773, and that both Mr Stewart and Chund were dead.[19] The Proceedings of 10 February 1779 provide a yearly break-up of the land acquisition in Sutanati from 1770 to 1773, totalling fifty-three bighas one katha one chittack.

Regarding payment of revenue for the disputed land, in 1776 the Setts had petitioned the Government stating that ever since those evicted from Kidderpur had arrived at Jorabagh they had 'erected golahs, etc on this ground and we then ceased to receive rent from them'.[20] As regards the Setts paying their dues to the Government, on being asked by the Khalsa officials whether the rent for the entire land (that is, ninety-six bighas eight kathas fourteen chittacks) had been paid or only for the seven bighas eight kathas in their possession, the petitioners said that rent had been paid to the Company for the entire land till 1770–1771 but that since that time payment had been 'regularly tendered ... but the Company's officers would not accept rent for any part of the ground, not even for what is in [our] possession'.[21] In June 1782 the Kidderpur merchants said that they had 'continually paid the quit rent and tax for chowkeydarry of the ground allotted to them by Government'.[22] Two years later, the Collector of Calcutta, John Scott, wrote that the settlers at Jorabagh had

> ... remained unmolested on the ground till 1188 BS [1782], but the Seats having the *pottahs* and the others possession, and both wanting to pay the revenue, it was not collected from either from the year 1176 BS [1770], when the Kidderpore *riots* obtained possession, to 1188 BS [1782] when, in consequence of some of the balance of ground rent being received from the possessors, the Seats brought an action to a hearing in the Supreme Court which they had commenced in 1185 BS [1779] and obtained decrees against two people, one of whom was Dattaram Turrufdar. Action had been commenced in the Supreme Court in 1185 [1779] against several others but only these two ... were brought to a hearing, in consequence ... of which the collections were again stopped.[23]

In early 1786, Scott's successor, Archibald Seton, wrote that,

> For some years after [1777], the jummah was collected from the *ryotts* although the Seits always objected to it, considering such collections as a virtual annihilation of their rights. At last, in 1189 BS [1783] they complained to the Supreme Court in consequence of which the collections were then entirely put a stop to, since when they have never been received.[24]

Returning to the case, Sen, the merchants' vakil, once again appeared before the Committee on 5 March and, repeating his stand of 22 February, said that 'the absence of several of his constituents' had prevented him from getting ready the land-accounts he had been asked to work on at the previous meeting and that, what was more important, the work could not done 'under two months'. On being asked whether his clients were prepared to accept compensation other than 'the land at Jurabaug', he said he was instructed 'to demand *pottahs* in the names of his constituents for the ground they have already obtained possession of in Jurabaug, and a further portion of ground in the same place'. He asserted that his clients would not accept ground 'in any other place, nor any pecuniary compensation' and cited the case of Gobun [Gobin?] Turruffdar, the father of Dattaram Turruffdar, who had received possession of eighteen bighas in Jorabagh 'over and above the quantity entered in the Company's accounts'. The vakil said his clients wanted an extra ten bighas twelve kathas in the area, the total demand being for fifty-five bighas ten kathas of which forty-four bighas ten kathas had been received. The Committee then told the merchants' counsel that, without the orders of the Governor-General in Council, it could neither give them pattas for the ground given to them at Jorabagh nor additional ground in the same place 'as either would involve the Company in law suits, the Seats having already made a claim for the same ground'.[25]

Durgachurn Mitra was the only amin who responded to the Committee's summons to attend on 17 March 1779 (Sobharam

Basak and Bengally Naut were dead),[26] his dim recollection being that it was in the time of John Cartier that he and the others had been asked to draw up the account, a point corroborated by the Committee itself when it wrote to the Governor-General in Council that among the papers submitted by the Collector-General to the Committee's office with regard to the case 'there appears a letter from Mr Barber, the Secretary to the President and Counci, directing the Collector-General to appoint five persons to value the land at Kidderpore'. In his deposition, Mitra said that he 'and some of the other *aumeens* accordingly went and having called the officers of the cutcherry, the inhabitants and proprietors, they drew out an account of the value of the houses and ground and the loss which the proprietors suffered'. When the land account which the dewan had laid before the Committee was shown to him, he said he did not know 'if it is a copy of one drawn out by them or not, neither does he know in what manner it was formed, or what amount it stated', adding that he did not remember 'whether he and the other *aumeens* were appointed with the concurrence of the proprietors of the ground or not'.[27] If the setting up of the team of officials to draw up the account was a part of arbitration proceedings, it is probable that the concurrence of the landowners was not sought for the step taken.

The facts of the case suggest that the Kidderpur merchants could not be blamed for the stand they had taken because it was none other than the Government of the day which had drawn up and executed the entire procedure for 'giving' land at Sutanati as compensation for land surrendered at Kidderpur for Watson's dock project. The names of Stewart and Mukun Chund and their role in the issue had cropped up in Government documents and were not provided by the petitioners. The official involvement in the actual land distribution exercise had been strongly established though the logical completion of that exercise—mutating the names of the owners of ground involved—had not taken place, which was clearly the Government's headache and could not be laid at the door of the petitioners. Possibly, the authorities had come up against problems posed by the ground concerned having been already allotted to some other people, which was being given credence to by the Supreme Court. This, therefore, was a problem created by the authorities themselves for which those who had been given land by the Government could not be held responsible.

However, in its letter to the Governor-General in Council,[28] the Committee took a different line altogether. It wrote that as the petitioners

> ... have not shewn any right to the ground at Sutanooty – as it [does] not appear that they obtained possession of it by any regular authority from this Government, as no rent has been received from them during many years by the Company or their officers, and as the names of the former possessors still continue in the public records – we do not see any ground to consider that the petitioners are the rightful tenants of the lands, or that it is incumbent on the Company to support them in these claims in opposition to those of the former possessors.

To the Committee, the only issue that remained to be sorted out was that regarding compensation for the land the petitioners had given up at Kidderpur. It told the Supreme Council that in terms of the official land account drawn up by Durgachurn Mitra and others, the petitioners were deprived of fifty-four bighas three kathas which was valued at Rs 41,652-8. In addition to this was the 'expence of removing household effects Rs 4,522-8, expence of removing merchandize Rs 1,684, and the value of a brick house Rs 23,000', the point being made that 'no claim has ever been preferred to us for the three latter articles'. The inference here is inescapable, namely, that the Committee was doing the petitioners a favour by including the amount in the losses incurred by them without being asked to do so. In conclusion, the Committee argued that as far as compensation for the surrendered land at Kidderpur was concerned 'this valuation is the best rule that can now be adopted, and we beg leave to submit to your Hon'ble Board the propriety of tendering the value of each claimant's land together with interest at 10 per cent from the time when they were deprived of it'.

It would have been easy for the Governor-General in Council to have accepted the Committee's suggestion, especially in a situation where the legal case for the Kidderpur merchants was weak. But the Council under Hastings refused to be hustled into taking a decision which would have gone against the interests of the evictees from Kidderpur, in circumstances where the Government was clearly to blame for allotting ground to people without giving them proper ownership documents. So matters were allowed to rest where they were. Two years later, in July 1782, the Preparer of Reports informed the Calcutta Committee of Revenue that the Governor-General in Council was yet to take any action on the 29 March 1779 letter of the Committee.[29]

For three years nothing much seems to have happened except for the legal proceedings being played out quietly in the Supreme Court. The Setts had taken the initiative to go to court which ultimately resulted in the ejectment of some of the Kidderpur people in 1782, which in turn led to another petition being submitted to the authorities by the latter.[30] Compared to the earlier petition, there is nothing new in this one except for the revelation that those removed to Jorabagh were originally from Gobindapur from where they were moved by the Company ('for the conveniency of the new Fort'), the authorities demolishing 'the houses and buildings that they had built on the said spot of ground'. As compensation they were given 'a spot of ground at Bykuntpore' on which they set up hearth and home. The decision to move the market at Gobindapur to Baikunthapur was taken in October 1757. The Bengal Public Consultations of 17 October 1757[31] read:

> As the gunje must be removed from the place it stands in at present to build the citadel, and make an esplanade towards the river, and the spot near the nulla [subsequently Tolly's] on this side of Surman's Gardens

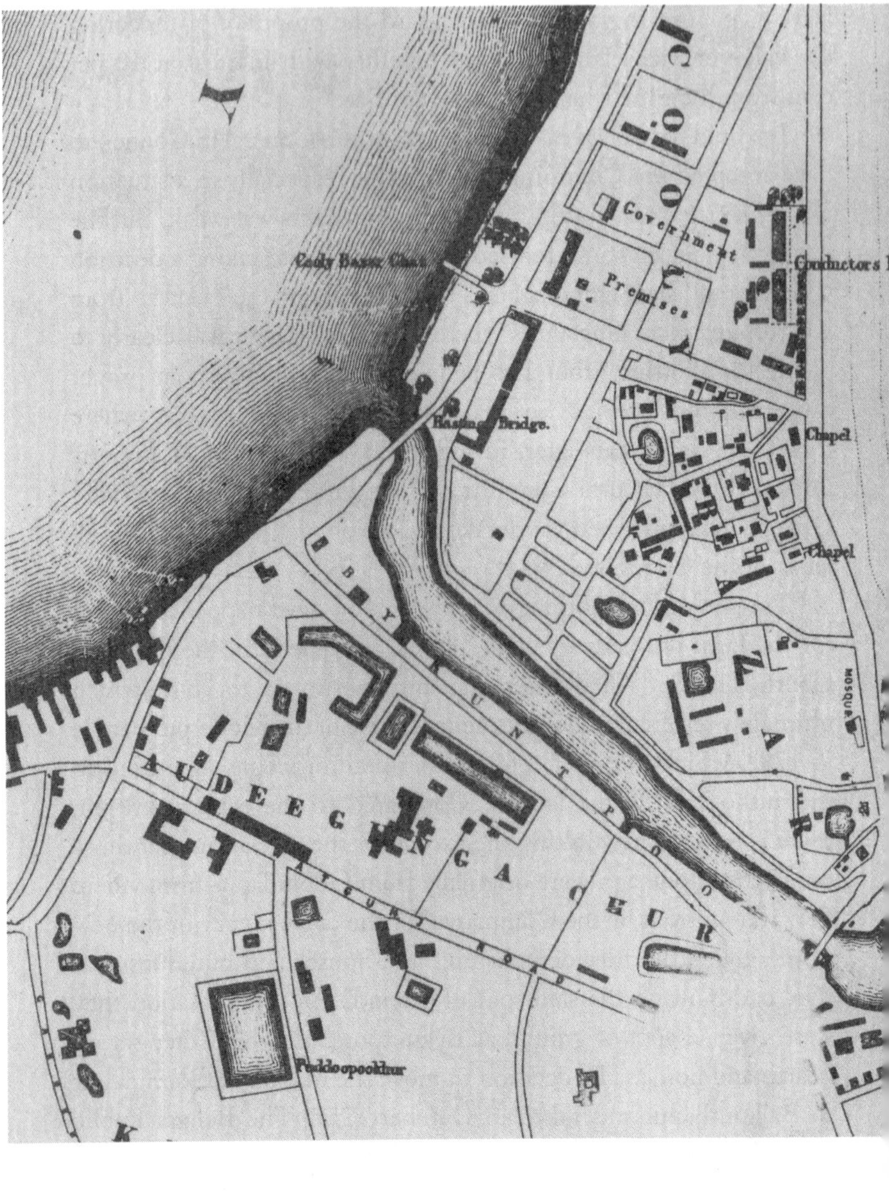

Government
Premises
Conductors
Hastings Bridge
Chapel
Chapel
MOSQUE

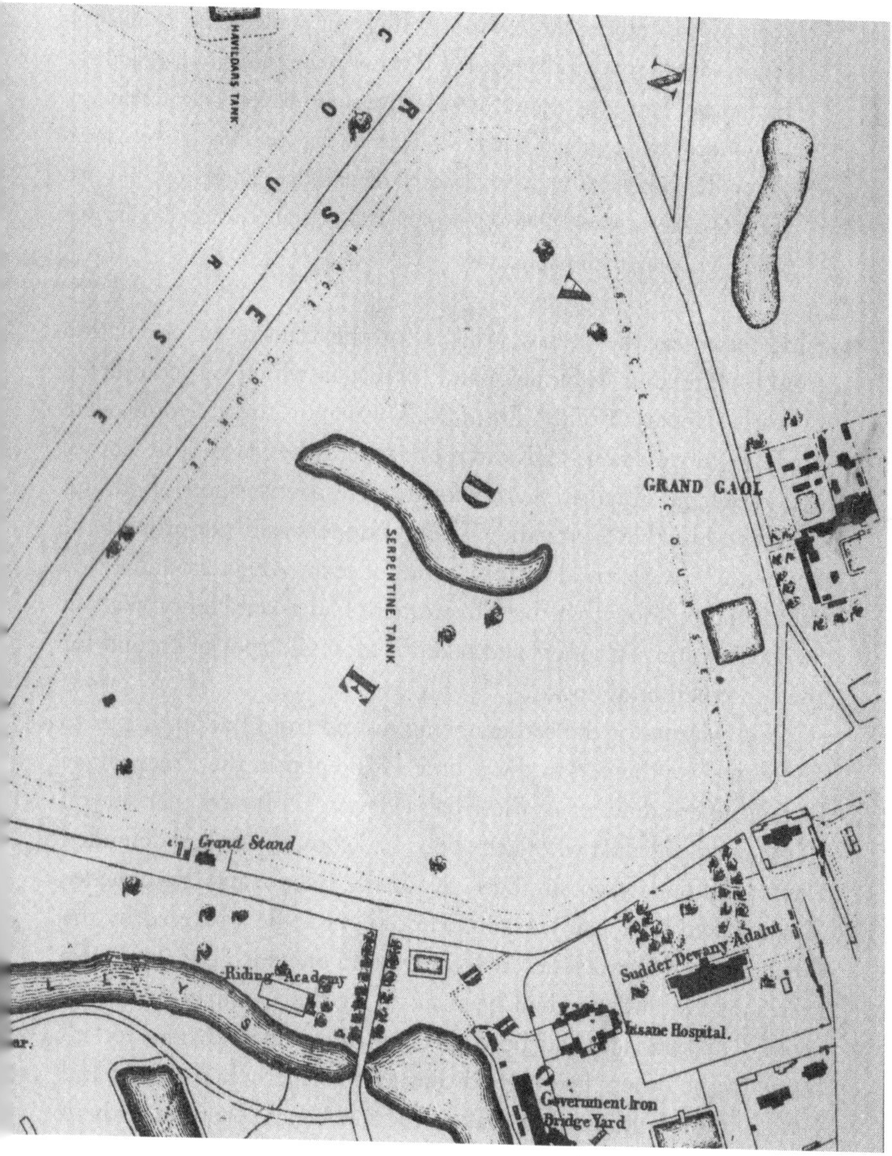

36 An 1856 map by W. Heysham showing the location of Baikunthapur at the mouth of Tolly's Nullah

> being a very proper and convenient situation, ordered the Zemidar to endeavour to procure that place, and remove the gunje thither, and as a number of houses belonging to the natives must be levell'd and removed for the abovemention'd purtpose, ordered the Zemidar to give them ground in Similea, and other places to rebuild their houses on, and that he make then a small allowance for the charge and expence of removing and rebuilding their habitations.

This then was the precise trigger for the transfer of population from Gobindapur to Simleah and Jorabagan which was completed by early January 1758.[32] From Baikunthapur these people were made to move again 'to Kidderpore where they also built houses and *golahs* and obtained *pottahs* for three respective spots of ground from the Hon'ble Company'. The petitioners said the property at Kidderpur was 'enjoyed ... for a series of years' when, around 1769, they came to know that the Government had asked Henry Watson 'to satisfy your petitioners and take the aforesaid spot of ground for the construction of docks'.

The reason for the settlers being moved from Baikunthapur to Kidderpur is provided in the 4 June 1776 entry in the Proceedings of the Superintendent of the Khalsa Records.[33] It says that several of the people against whom the Setts had complained had defended their positions. Two of these, Kasinath Baboo and Ramneedee Thakur, had held that the complaint ought to be answered by the Governor and Council because 'the ground on which they had their golahs at Gobindapur had been taken by the Company, and the ground in Jorabagh had been given to them in exchange for it'. Some of the others had argued that they formerly had golahs and gunges in Gobindapur but that on the fort being constructed there they were dispossessed and had been given ground

> ... in exchange in Bynulpoor [sic], upon which they built *golahs* and *gunjes*, but which after some time were thrown down to make room for the hospital,[34] and that Mr Vansittart gave them in exchange some

> ground in Kidderpore; that having filled up the holes and pits in this new ground they constructed *golahs* and *gunges* upon the same and carried on the business; but that in the Bengal year 1176 [1769-70] their *golahs* were again thrown down [on] the orders of the Governor-General[35] by Col. [Archibald] Campbell and Major Watson in order to make room for the construction of the docks.

The devastating impact of the Bengal famine had the region in its grip at the time, the evictees making the point (perhaps in the form of a protest) that their having to move their houses and business establishments at this juncture had rendered their condition 'exceedingly severe'. In this situation,

> ... Mr [Claude] Russell the Collector, confined them and informed them that it was the Council's orders that they should take some ground in Jurabaug in exchange for that in Kidderpoor and bring some grain into the town; that Mr Stewart, Mukund Chund, and Narrain Ghose, agreeable to the gentleman's orders, measured out and gave possession of land in Jurrabaug to each person in proportion to his *pottah*; that since that period they have continued to live there and bring grain into the town.

Jorabagh, therefore, was chosen by the authorities to settle the Kidderpur people in view of two attributes it sported at this point of time. The first was that grain had to be supplied to the town on an emergency basis in view of the prevailing famine conditions, and if the gunge at Kidderpur, an important grain-depot, was being disrupted because of Watson's dock project, there was no alternative but to find a place quickly to relocate it so that the supply of grain would remain unhindered. Secondly, not only was Jorabagh centrally located as far as the native town was concerned, it also had a lot of 'uninhabited'[36] ground—which in reality belonged to the Setts—which could be used to set up a gunge and grain market. What then had really happened was that, given the famine conditions, a hurried decision was taken to allot the ground available to the Kidderpur merchants, the Setts' ownership of the land being unwittingly pushed into the background. As much is hinted at by Archibald Seton, the then Collector of Calcutta, who later wrote to the Committee of Revenue[37] that after Watson had obtained possession of the ground 'upon which Kidderpore *gunje* is situated, and procured a *pottah* for it in his own name', the former inhabitants

> … complained to the Governor and Council who, in consequence, directed in 1175 BS [1769] that they should be [given] possession of an equal quantity of ground at a place called Jurah Baug, being a convenient spot for establishing a *gunje* in lieu of that which they had been deprived of.

Seton wrote further that 'the original proprietors of the land thus alienated in Jurah Baug should be indemnified by receiving an equal quantity in Baher Simleah'. The Collector said that,

> As the whole of Jurah Baug was the property of the family of the Seiths – *a circumstance that may not, perhaps, have been fully known at the time when the arrangement was framed* [emphasis added] – they naturally considered the order as an infringement of their rights, and petitioned against the adoption of the measure.

Warren Hastings left Calcutta in early 1785 and was succeeded *pro tempore* by John Macpherson whose term ended in September 1786 with the arrival of Lord Cornwallis. It may be suggested that it was because of Hastings' reluctance to take action against those who had been shifted from Kidderpur to Jorabagh by the Government itself without having been given pattas that the dispute with the Setts, the original owners of the land, had festered. The situation of course changed with the exit of the first Governor-General. Possibly, the authorities now found themselves less shackled in finding a solution to the problem, which perhaps explains the progress made on the dispute during the short time that Macpherson was acting Governor-General (February 1785 to September 1786).

The dispute had an impact on revenue collection. The two Collectors of Calcutta, John Scott and Archibald Seton, had pointed out that revenue shortfalls in the area under their jurisdiction—which could be held against them when their work was evaluated by their peers—was not the result of their inability to collect the imposts but was a direct consequence of the intractability in settling the Jorabagh issue, which had led to none of the parties (the original owners nor the new settlers) paying their land dues to the Company. Thus, Scott's letter to the authorities (December 1784) elicited the response that he was 'to suspend the demand for the rents of Joroo Baug until the Board's decision upon the abovementioned claims be passed'.[38] The situation was different in January 1786, that is, a full year after Hastings had left Calcutta. While submitting his accounts for Calcutta on 5 January of that year, Seton had proposed that the most 'eligible' form of collecting the revenue dues from Jorabagh was to send an official to the spot 'to ascertain the exact quantity of ground now in possession of the Seits and the *ryotts* respectively, agreeably to which the ... rent might be proportioned while the suit is pending in the Supreme Court'.[39] The letter was sent to the Governor-General in Council which, under Macpherson, stirred itself into action and, on July 19, asked the Preparer of Reports to make a full enquiry into the entire issue from the documents available with the Government. Focusing on the primacy of revenue considerations, the Governor-General in Council made the point that it 'could not admit [that] the right of Government to the revenue receivable from the ground in question to be in any respect prejudiced by the litigation of the claimants to, or actual possessor of it, either in the Supreme Court of Judicature or elsewhere'.[40]

Notes

1 Revenue Board Consisting of the Whole Council Proceedings, 31 May 1774 (West Bengal State Archives).

2 A table of those holding ground in the area was annexed to the petition among whom Gopal Sett topped the list with 40 bighas and 5 kathas for which there were regular pattas. He was followed by Bostomadass Sett 29-10-0, Radabullub Sett 13-18-0, Coonjoobehary Sett 5-0-(2), Collychurn Consary 1-6-0, Gopeenaut Shaw 0-8-0, Modone Cotmah 1-9-0, Sittaram Dass 0-4-0, Chandah Conkey 0-5-0, Ramram Sircar 1-8-0, Rasbehary Sett 2-17-0, Ataram Sett 2-19-0, Gocool Sean 1-12-0, Ozudearam Dutt 0-1-(4)?, Doyaram Mullick 0-1-0, Coogee Earmahamed 5-7-0 (land formerly in possession of the Setts for which no patta had been granted), Endgaw Fukeer 4-0-0 (same as previous). The area figuring in the list added up to 109 bighas 14 kathas 7 chittacks, of which 100-7-7 were supported by pattas with the Setts, the rest not being backed by any documents. From this total area was to be deducted 11 bighas 6 kathas comprising ground sold by the owners to other people, the area remaining being 98 bighas 8 kathas 7 chittacks.

3 There is some discrepancy in the land statistics provided in the same Proceedings (1774) as well as between official records separated by more than a decade. Most likely, this is the result of carelessness on the part of the writers involved in the transcription of the records because there is no official explanation for the difference, which for the most part is marginal. For our purpose here, in an effort to maintain uniformity, the land figures have been taken from the Committee of Revenue Proceedings of 29 December 1786. A reference to a difference in the figures has been made wherever felt necessary.

4 Revenue Board Consisting of the Whole Council Proceedings, 31 May 1774.

5 Ibid. According to the Superintendent of the Khalsa, this instruction on the part of the Committee 'does not however appear to have been ever put into execution, as the petitioners say they declined accepting any particular portion of the land they laid claim to being apprehensive that by so doing they might injure their claim to the remaining part of it' (Board of Revenue Proceedings, 29 December 1786).

6 Calcutta Committee of Revenue Proceedings, 16 January 1775.

7 Ibid., 11 April 1777.

8 Ibid., 29 March 1779.
9 Ibid., 27 November 1778.
10 Ibid., 5 March 1779.
11 Ibid., 29 March 1779.
12 Calcutta Committee of Revenue Proceedings of date.
13 Calcutta Committee of Revenue Proceedings, 28 October 1776.
14 Governor-General in Council Proceedings, 15 December 1778. The petition—'from some Merchants who formerly held a Gunje at Kiddorpore'—was signed by '… Cossinaut, Ramtonoo Dutt, Diaram Bose, Ramkissore Chuttopadea, Kissen Buxey, Dataram Turrupdar, Ramkissore Podar, Govindram Khan, Gocul Chaund Shaw, Ramanund Sumodar, Sentiram Khoond, Ramrooder Sircar, Ramkissore Sircar, Rammohun Doss, Molah Mahmud Aushab, Bhoobunnessore Terupdar, Rampersaud Chund, Fukirchaund Saha, Kissen Dutt, Kasubnundram Saha, Gorachund Sow, Kaunoynundee, & Saffuliram Nundee.'
15 That Watson did not act judiciously while acquiring land for his dockyard is indicated by a ruling of the Supreme Court which returned to Gokul Ghoshal of Kidderpur five bighas two kathas of ground which was wrongfully included within his (Watson's) premises (Calcutta Committee of Revenue Proceedings, 16 April 1779).
16 Governor-General in Council Proceedings, 15 December 1778.
17 Sen represented 'Ramanund Bishnuram, Ramkishno Podar, Dattaram Turruffdar, Mola Esha, Camdeb Podar, Kisno Dutt, Gonda Bancah, Govindram Cawer, Talley Conoy, and Sapulram Nundy'. The other vakil engaged by the merchants was Ramprasad, Kashinath Babu engaging a separate lawyer, Ajodhyaram, to argue his case (Calcutta Committee of Revenue Proceedings, 10 February and 5 March 1779).
18 Calcutta Committee of Revenue Proceedings, 30 December 1778, 15 and 22 February 1779; Appendix to February 1779 Proceedings. The following is the statement submitted by the dewan: 'Statement of the valuation of the ground of which different persons were deprived at Khidderpore from the account drawn out by Sobaram Bysaak, Bengaully Naut, Modun Mohun Dutt, Durgachurn Mitre and Ramsanker Dutt as Ameens, the quantity of ground which they have obtained in lieu of it at Jurabaug in Sootanooty, and the quantity and value of ground for which they have received no compensation.'

Name	Ground held at Khidderpore	Value of the ground	Ground received by claimant at Jurabaug in Sootanuty	Value of grou received at Sootanuty calculated at the rate of Khidderpore ground
Boobawn Tirreffdar	18.2.8	14,750	-	-
Ramkissen Dutt	1.9.8	737-8	1.9.8	737-8
Sark Ullah	0.3.0	75-0	0.3.0	75-0
Benod Ram Ghose	0.6.0	150-0	-	-
Callichurn Ghose	0.14.8	369-0	-	-
Bancheram Ghose	0.11.0	275-0	-	-
Mullah Isaac	0.16.8	412-8	0.16.8	412-8
Dyaram Bose	0.15.0	375-0	0.15.0	375-0
Callichurn Bose	1.9.0	725-0	1.9.0	725-0
Gorachawn Sahoo	0.12.0	300-0	0.12.0	300-0
Nimay Sircar	1.0.0	500-0	1.0.0	500-0
Neelmunny Takore	1.0.0	500-0	0.15.0	375-0
Ramkissorre & Rammanund Chaterjee	1.14.0	1,292-0	1.13.0	1,254-0
Birjoo Hazarrah	1.12.0	1,216-0	1.12.0	1,216-0
Ramnaut Gose	1.5.0	950-0	1.5.0	950-0
Gopynaut Gose	1.0.0	500-0	1.0.0	500-0
Safulyram Biswass zemany Gocul Sein	1.7.0	1,026-0	1.7.0	1,026-0
Dattaram Tirreffdar zemany Sitaram	1.6.0	988-0	1.7.0?	988-0
Conay Nundee & Safulyram Nundee	2.10.0	1,900-0	-	-
Ram Mohun Shaw	1.0.0	760-0	1.0.0	760-0

[..]uantity for [..]ich the [..]imants are [..]id to have [..]ceived no [..]mpensation	Value of the ground for which they have received no compensation	Expence which they were put to in removing their household effects, etc, etc	Expence which they were put to in removing their merchandise	Value of the brick houses
[..].2.8	14,750	1,820	-	23,000
	-	18-8	-	-
	-	9-0	-	-
[..]6.0	150-0	19-8	-	-
14.8	369-0	16-4	-	-
11.0	275-0	32-12	-	-
	-	100-8	-	-
	-	13-8	-	-
	-	211-8	-	-
	-	100-8	-	-
	-	27-8	-	-
[..]5.0	125-0	121-4	-	-
[..]1.0	38-0	285-0	258-0	-
	-	104-8	-	-
	-	116-0?	11-0	-
	-	24-0	28-0	-
	-	265-0(?)	-	-
	-	81-0	-	-
[..]10	1,900-0	45-8	-	-
	-	158-0	-	-

Rampersaud	1.4.0	912-0	1.0.0	760-0
Kissor Dutt	0.18.0	684-0	0.18.0	684-0
Fuckirchand Shaw	1.13.0	1,254-0	1.13.0	1,254-0
Kisore Nunderam	1.14.0	1,292-0	1.14.0	1,292-0
Mookteram Coondo	1.6.0	988-0	1.0.0	760-0
Ramanund Bisnoram	2.15.0	2,090-0	2.10.0	1,900-0
Ramkishen Podar	3.13.0	2,774-0	3.0.0	2,280-0
Tiradoo Cranny	1.15.0	1,825-0	1.15.0	1,825-0
Cunderji Gosaul	5.12.0	6,720-0	1.19.0	2,340-0
Pedroo Pareira	0.12.0	300-0	-	-
Sircar Batteer Cutcherry	1.15.0	2,400-0	-	-
Soburam Bysack	1.0.0	1,200-0	1.0.0	1,200-0
Ramchurn Roy	2.0.0	2,400-0	1.16.9	2,193-12
Ramkishore Sircar	1.11.0	1,860-0	1.11.0	1,860-0
Ramtonoo Dutt	3.7.0	4,020-0	3.7.0	4,020-0
Baboo Huzzerymull	2.10.0	1,250-0	2.10.0	1,250-0
Goberdun Haldar	2.10.0	1,250-0	2.10.0	1,250-0
Luckycunt Sett	1.3.0	575-0	-	-
Brindabund Sett	1.0.0	375-0	-	-
Baboo Cossinaut	1.0.0	500-0	1.0.0	500-0
Ramkisen Sein	1.0.0	500-0	-	-
Sircaree or Govt Godowns zameny Ramkishen Podar	1.3.0	575-0	-	-
Birjo Mohon Sircar	1.3.0	575-0	1.3.0	575-0
Ramchurn Sircar	0.14.0	350-0	0.14.0	350-0
Joydeeb Takore zemany Kissenchand Gosaul	0.8.0	200-0	-	-

4.0	152-0	178-8	-	-
	-	52-8	-	-
	-	151-4	-	-
	-	182-8	212-0	-
5.0	228-0	156-0	-	-
5.0	190-0	167-8	-	-
13.0	494-0	454-8	829-0	-
	-	55-4	-	-
13.0	1,380-0	2,025-0	7,022-8	-
12.0	300-0	-	-	-
15.0	2,400-0	27-8	-	-
	-	-	27-0	-
3.1	206-4	127-0	-	-
	-	191-8	128-0	-
	-	452-8	-	-
	-	173-0	85-0	-
	-	147-8	99-0	-
3.0	575-0	86-8	186-0	-
0.0	375-0	25-0	-	-
	-	33-8	178-0	-
0.0	500-0	11-8	-	-
3.0	575-0	39-0	-	-
	-	51-0	24-0	-
	-	32-12	-	-
8.0	200-0	26-0	42-0	-

Baboo Cossinaut	1.2.0	550-0	1.2.0	550-0
Moocan Chunder Baboo	0.5.0	125-0	-	-
Kissenchand Bose	0.6.0	150-0	-	-
Govindram Cawn Talley	0.14.0	350-0	0.14.0	350-0
Ramkishore Herry	0.10.0	250-0	-	-
Permissore Chattergee	0.1.0	25-0	-	-
Mr Handle	15.5.0	7,625-0	-	-
Kishno Buckshy	1.13.0	825-0	-	-
Ram Joy Takore	1.0.0	500-0	0.18.0	450-0
Ramkishore Doss	0.10.0	250-0	-	-
Mr Surman's Garden	-	-	-	-
TOTAL	100.8.0	75,220-0	48.18.9	37,337-12

19 Calcutta Committee of Revenue Proceedings, 16 January 1779.

20 Superintendent of the Khalsa Records Proceedings, 4 June 1776, quoted in Board of Revenue Proceedings, 29 December 1786.

21 Ibid.

22 Committee of Revenue Proceedings, 24 June 1782.

23 Ibid., 30 December 1784.

24 Governor-General in Council Proceedings, 1 January 1786; Committee of Revenue Proceedings, 26 January 1786.

25 Calcutta Committee of Revenue Proceedings, 5 March 1779.

26 Ibid.

27 Ibid., 17 and 29 March 1779.

28 Ibid., 29 March 1779. Among the signatories to the letter was John Shore, the architect of the Permanent Settlement under Lord Cornwallis and a future Governor-General himself.

29 Committee of Revenue Proceedings, 5 August 1782.

30 Ibid., 24 June 1782.

31 Wilson, *Old Fort William*, vol. 2, p. 132. See also Long, *Selections*, p. 151.

	-	42-0	-	-
.0	125-0	1-8	-	-
.0	150-0	32-0	-	-
	-	171-8	-	-
10.0	250-0	37-8	-	-
1.0	25-0	9-0	-	-
.5.0	7,625-0	-	-	-
13.0	825-0	-	-	-
2.0	50-0	-	-	-
10.0	250-0	-	-	-
	-	-	-	11,500-0
.18.7	37,882-4	8,308-0	9,091-8	34,550-0

32 Wilson, *Old Fort William*, vol. 2, p. 137.

33 Board of Revenue Proceedings, 29 December 1786.

34 'Bynulpoor' here should clearly be Baikunthapur because, in the early 1760s, there were plans for the settlement's hospital to be shifted to a place 'near to Surman's' (Wilson, *Old Fort William*, vol. 2, p. 168), the garden too being taken over for Watson's project. See chapter 'An Infirm Hospital'.

35 The position was created by Lord North's Regulating Act 1773.

36 This was how the Collector of Calcutta, John Scott, described the place (Committee of Revenue Proceedings, 30 December 1784).

37 Committee of Revenue Proceedings, 26 January 1786.

38 Ibid., 30 December 1784.

39 Ibid., 26 January 1786.

40 Board of Revenue Proceedings, 28 July 1786.

19

The 'Wyattgunje' Controversy

Though Jagannath Sarkar was embroiled in the 'esplanade limits' issue he had no hesitation to open another contentious front when he set up a bazar in Kidderpur. The crux of the issue here was the proximity of one bazar to another, which was an important regulatory element in the topographical layout of bazars in the growing town of the late eighteenth century.

In September 1789, Charles Wyatt—who was chosen by Lord Wellesley to design and build his Government House (today's Raj Bhavan) a decade later—petitioned the Government[1] that a couple of years earlier, around 1787, he had bought 'at a considerable expence an estate at Kidderpore, formerly the property of Mr Handel[2] but last in the tenure of Colonel Watson', on which stood 'an old dwelling house in which, at the time your petitioner made the purchase, he had an intention of residing but was afterwards deterred by the vicinity and the many tanks and stagnated waters'. Wyatt said he drew up an alternative plan, 'which met the concurrence of the natives in that district,' of establishing 'a *gunge* and *haut*, which it formerly had been'. The Government made the necessary enquiries on the usefulness of the gunge and haat to the neighbourhood at large and, the report being 'highly favourable', the projects were approved. As Wyatt wrote, 'the erection was authorised by *special* [emphasis added] direction of Government, paying a stipulated revenue to the Company'. In other words, a favour was bestowed on Wyatt for reasons which have not been put down on paper but which could conceivably be linked to the fact that Wyatt was already an influential personage with sizable property in Chowringhee.[3] Wyatt said that between the time he applied for the project and its approval by the authorities he had spent a 'considerable' amount of money 'in establishing and improving the premises', which amounted to Sicca Rs 40,000. Among other things, in gratitude 'for the encouragement of the Board', he built a 'large and commodious *pucka* gaut, or landing place, for the use and convenience of the natives', the ghat being 'entirely a public work and from which your petitioner does not, nor ever will, derive the smallest private advantage; nor has your petitioner hitherto received any benefit from the gunge and haut'.[4]

In view of this, he was apprehensive that he would be put to great 'hardships' if 'diverse unlicensed bazars and gunges should be permitted and suffered to exist within a few hundred yards of your petitioner's (which he has erected at so heavy an expence, and under the immediate patronage of Government) contrary to an express rule and regulation of the Board of Revenue'. Wyatt named the two offending bazars as those belonging to Jagannath Sarkar and to Ramnarain and Harinarain Gosaul, 'opposite to each other on the verge of the great Kidderpur Road near the Kidderpore Bridge'. Both the bazars were described as 'public nuisances', Sarkar's being described as 'not only unlicensed, paying no revenue to the Company, but is moreover a positive imposition as the name of Colonel Watson is introduced by Juggernaut Sircar as a fallacious pretext to mislead the Company'.[5]

In direct denial of what was later claimed by Sarkar, Wyatt alleged that 'the spot itself has not been more than nine months in the possession of the said Juggernaut since October last [1788], and that the same has been procured as waste ground by Juggernaut from the proprietors'. He cited Government rules for setting up a new bazar which stipulated that 'no bazar or gunge can be erected or opened in the vicinity of another', the point being made specifically that the bazars belonging to the Ghoshals and Sarkar were 'within 600 yards of the new licensed gunge of your petitioner, and of course the cause and subject of constant disputes'. Wyatt said that the 'standing orders' of the Government decreed that the minimum distance of separation between two bazars would have to be 'either 2 or 3 coss for reasons as palpable as salutary'. His plea to the authorities was that the collectors of Calcutta and the 24-Parganas (Sarkar's bazar fell within the jurisdiction of the former while that of the Ghoshals was included in that of the latter) should enquire about 'the right under which Juggernaut Sircar and the Gossals hold a bazar within 5 or 600 yards of that of your petitioner', and that if it was found that any rules were broken the bazars should be removed.

Responding to the Board of Revenue's orders to start a probe, Edward Colebrook, the then Collector of Calcutta, ably summed up the facts of the case and presented a clear picture for the Board of Revenue to deliberate upon.[6] He wrote:

> This petition objects to the continuance of two bazars in Kidderpore supposed by him [Wyatt] to be unauthorised. Of them the one held by Jaggernaut is, I believe, within my limits, and the other in the 24-Pergunnahs.
>
> The bazar in question is erected upon 25 cottahs of ground which were taken by Colonel Watson into the grant made to him by the Company for his docks. About 20 years ago, he, for the convenience of the workmen in his dock yard, placed a few *moodies* upon this spot. From the concourse of the neighbourhood, a gradual increase has taken place in the number of shops which now form a considerable bazar. The original proprietors of the ground , about two years ago, recovered judgements for it, against the administratix of Colonel Watson in the Supreme Court, and Juggernaut has lately bought it from them.
>
> Jaggernaut, whom I summoned to produce the authority under which he holds the bazar, acknowledges that he is not possessed of any express authority for the erection, or continuance of it, but pleads that the bazar having existed so long unmolested, he has a prescriptive right

for its continuing especially as Mr Wyatt knew of its existence at the time that he undertook his gunge and bazar. He also alleges the free grant to Colonel Watson as proof of a right in the Colonel to establish it originally, and he offers to pay a *jumma* for it to Government.

Mr Wyatt's vakeel, on the contrary, observes that whatever might have been Colonel Watson's right under the grant of the Company, Jaggernaut can derive no authority therefrom; that the decision of the Supreme Court, by proving the Colonel to have not obtained legal possession of this ground, invalidates the grant, so far as it relates to this ground, and restores the proprietors to the rights which they had prior to the grant, but gives them no rights conveyed by that grant; that Jaggernaut as purchaser of them could purchase no more rights than they were possessed of, and that therefore no original or prescriptive, no expressed or implied, authority in Colonel Watson to erect a bazar can rest in Jaggernaut; that there was no bazar on the ground when the Colonel took it and there ought consequently to be none now; that Jaggernaut's offer to pay a jumma proves his consciousness of the illegality of his bazar, and reduces him to the situation of a person petitioning for leave to erect a new bazar, against which Mr Wyatt, as the proprietor of an authorised bazar, objects; that Mr Wyatt's knowledge of its existence prior to his own grant is no argument, for Mr Wyatt equally knew it to be unauthorised and has been petitioning against it ever since he obtained his grant.

This statement of the allegations of both parties will, I believe, furnish you with sufficient evidence whereon to form your decision whether Juggernaut's bazar is an unauthorised one and therefore liable to removal as interfering with the interests of one erected under authority; or whether Juggernaut is possessed of sufficient authority for its continuance, upon a jumma, to be now assessed for it, nothwithstanding the injury thereby done to Mr Wyatt's bazar.

The distance between the two bazars is 800 yards.

On 2 November 1789 the Board of Revenue ordered the abolition of Sarkar's bazar on the ground that it was established 'without authority'. Sarkar was not prepared to let this go unchallenged. He unleashed a veritable flood of petitions, one to the Collector, two to the Board of Revenue and a fourth to the Governor-General in Council, between 10 and 16 November 1789.[7] The common thread running through all the petitions was the point that Sarkar was ignorant of the 1786 order which stated, among other things, that 'no new bazar should be established without permission from the Board, and that all bazars erected before that period were to pay the customary rent'. By admitting the oversight, Sarkar probably wanted the Government to take a lenient view of the lapse, a request difficult to concede because, normally, it would be expected of anyone prepared to make—in Sarkar's words—an 'immense' investment (to the tune of Sicca Rs 7,500) for a bazar to have done his homework on bazars, specifically the rules and regulations governing the establishment and running of bazars, before the money was invested. To the Board of Revenue, however, Sarkar's bazar was unauthorised, a point emphasised by it when it said that all the petitions taken together did not 'contain any matter by which Jaggernaut's right to the bazar in question is established'.[8]

In one of the two petitions to the Board of Revenue, Sarkar had raised the issue of the distance separating Wyatt's bazar from his own which the Board considered serious enough not to ignore. The Board argued that the decision to abolish the bazar had been taken on the ground that Wyatt's bazar 'was injured by the proximity of that belonging to Jaggernaut'. But since the point had been challenged by Sarkar, the Board felt that the very basis of the abolition decision had now been opened to question and, therefore, needed to be settled clearly.[9] On 14 December 1789 the Board asked Colebrook to suspend further execution of its orders on the abolition of the bazar till he received further orders.[10] It also asked the collector to probe the exact distance between the two bazars 'and at what distance from an established bazar a new bazar ought not to be erected agreeable to the custom of the country'.

Sarkar did not spare any effort to run down Charles Wyatt. While not a word on Wyatt was included in the petition to the Collector—understandably so because Wyatt had not petitioned Colebrook but the Board of Revenue—in that to the Board of Revenue, written on the same day (16 November), Sarkar expanded the canvas of the case considerably when he wrote:

> Your petitioner with astonishment finds that Lt Wyatt has lodged complaints to your Board of the injury he sustains by the bazars of your petitioner and others, which can be founded on no other basis but that of a malicious and selfish motive, as all the bazars about Kidderpore [were] established upwards of 14 years, before Lieutenant Wyatt established his; and in fact if any has a right to complain, it is the proprietors of the old established bazars against the injury they sustain by permitting Lieutenant Wyatt to establish one. But as they were confident that it was an increase to the Company's revenue, no hesitation was made about the admission of it.

Wyatt was then accused of misrepresentation when Sarkar alleged that he

> ... obtained a grant for establishing his bazar in the district of the 24-Pergunnahs and has settled a jumma or annual rent of Sicca Rs 271-3-6 whereas his bazar is situated at the inside of the dock yard, formerly belonging to Colonel Watson, in the jurisdiction of Calcutta and under the Collector of Calcutta.

Sarkar said he himself, as well as 'other inhabitants of Kidderpore' were prepared to vouch for the fact that the jumma to be paid by Wyatt should be Sicca Rs 3,000. The petition wanted the Board of Revenue 'to put a stop to Lieutenant Wyatt continuing a bazar in the district of Calcutta, so clandestinely carried on, when his grant is only for continuing one in the 24-Pergunnahs until a further investigation can take place'.

In the second, undated, petition to the Board of Revenue, Sarkar repeated the point about Wyatt locating his bazar in the district of Calcutta instead of in the 24-Parganas for which specific permission had been sought. Sarkar alleged that one result of this was that whenever the Collector of the 24-Parganas took steps to remove 'any of the arrack shops or other disorderly houses at Kidderpore, they [are] sure to find an asylum in Lt Wyatt's bazar, to the very great emolument of the owner'. Sarkar said one of the grounds mentioned by Wyatt for setting up his bazar was that there was no other bazar near it. Sarkar pointed out that there were, as a matter of fact, 'three bazars very near each other and without the owners of [them] having any objections one to the other before Mr Wyatt even purchased the ground upon which he is building his [bazar]'. The first of these bazars was 'on the south side of the great road (and is the only one of the three which is under the collection of the 24-Pergunnahs)'. This bazar, belonging to the Ghoshals, was set up 'above 30 years ago', that is, sometime in the 1750s. The second, 'on the north side of the great road and within the walls of the dock yard, and which is now the property of your petitioner ... was erected above 18 years ago by Colonel Watson with the permission of the Government of John Cartier, Esq,' that is, sometime in the early 1770s. The third bazar was located 'near the bridge' (Kidderpur bridge) and was set up 'about two years ago by Mrs Tolley [and?] Mr Wilkinson'.[11] Sarkar said that the Ghoshal bazar was about thirty ft from his own 'or the dock yard bazar', Mrs Tolly's was about 200 ft from the dockyard bazar. Wyatt's bazar was more than 3,000 ft from the dockyard bazar, the spot of ground being a garden before Wyatt's purchase. Sarkar wrote that if Wyatt openly wanted to set up an exclusive bazar he knew it would have been opposed by the bazars already there, which is why he chose the 'clandestine' route. Sarkar told the Board of Revenue that having in November 1788 purchased the ground 'with the bazar upon it', on 1 bigha and 14 ½ kathas, from Bancharam Ghose, Kalicharan Ghosh, Ramkrishna Dutt and Manik Adhikary, 'it would be utter ruin to your petitioner now to be interrupted'. The case of Wyatt was 'very different' because he had bought a garden house 'which he now wishes to make a bazar'.

Responding to the Board of Revenue's 14 December 1789 orders, the Collector of Calcutta referred to Sarkar's claim that the distance between the two bazars was 'upwards of 3,000 ft' and said that Sarkar was taking his measurements

> … from the spot on which his fish market was held to the spot where Mr Wyatt's fish market sits, which is at the western extremity of his [Wyatt's] ground. But as the bazar buildings commence at the eastern gate of Mr Wyatt's ground, at the very entrance of which his grain market is held, I still conceive that my first measurement from the western end of Juggernaut's ground to that eastern gate is the actual distance between the two bazars. This distance is exactly 2,460 feet.[12]

Colebrook said that, as far as the custom of the country was concerned, no new bazar could be set up 'within the distance where the sound of a drum beat in an established bazar can be heard', adding, however, that the custom 'has not on all occasions been observed within the town of Calcutta, the populousness of which requires less distance between the bazars'. As a result of the flexibility in the application of the custom, the Collector wrote that many bazars had been allowed to be set up 'sufficiently near to injure each other', the inference being that the 'general custom of the country' need not be made applicable to Jagannath Sarkar's bazar as a town bazar. Colebrook referred to the case of Fenwick's bazar, 'especially as it was in the most populous part of the European town[13] whereas Jagernaut's is on the very confines of the 24-Pergunnahs and, though situated in that part of Kidderpore which is considered a part of the town, is near three miles from any town buildings'. The abolition of Fenwick's bazar was demanded by Sherburne and Camac on the ground that its establishment 'would be injurious to their established bazars', the distance from Sherburne's ground to Fenwick's being 1,800 ft and that between Camac's and Fenwick's 5,000 ft.

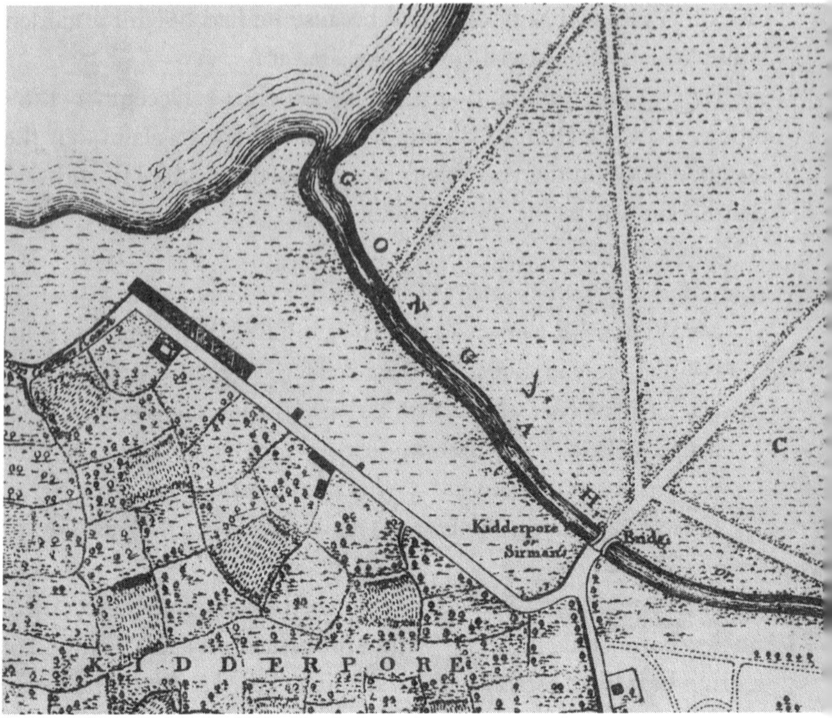

Getting to the heart of the matter, Colebrook wrote that since the Board of Revenue still felt that Sarkar had not established any right to the bazar set up by him, he was technically 'in the situation of a person petitioning for leave to erect a new bazar'. The Collector said that in the case of a notice being issued regarding the setting up of a new bazar,

> … objections would be brought by the Commissary of Military Bazars on behalf of the Fort Bazar, which is above half a mile from Jagernaut's, and by the proprietor of the Govindpore Nullah who has been permitted to make a bazar on the site of the old bridge at a distance of only 200 ft from Jagernaut's.

Sarkar, however, was determined to prove his point that since the bazars of the town were separated from each other by much smaller

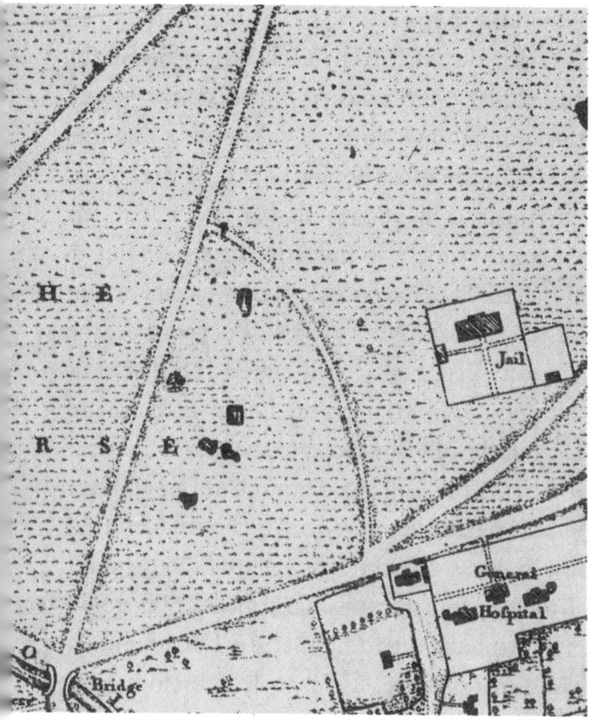

37 A section of Upjohn's map (1792–1793) showing the area in Kidderpur where Wyatt's bazar and those of Jagannath Sarkar and the Ghoshals were located

distances, Charles Wyatt had no business to object on the ground that his bazar was close to the competing bazars in Kidderpur. In an effort to buttress his point, Sarkar sent the Board of Revenue a sketch 'of the different bazars under the Collectorship of Calcutta, by which you will perceive the small distances of one bazar situated from each other, when compared to the distance of Lt Wyatt's from your petitioner's bazar'.[14] On 14 January 1790 Colebrook once again wrote to the Board of Revenue that Sarkar had sent him a sketch of the Calcutta bazars and their distances from each other, and that he felt the need to take up the issue 'lest you might think that in my report of the 28th December I omitted to state a circumstance apparently so much in favour of Jagernaut's claim'.[15]

The first point which Colebrook made was that he still felt that the distance separating the bazars of Sarkar and Wyatt was just 2,460 ft and not 3,342 ft, and that only two existing bazars within the town would be found at a smaller distance from each other. Secondly, even if Sarkar's measurements were correct, the distance would 'not be sufficient on the uninhabited skirts of the town compared with the distances of bazars in the most populous part of the town'. Thirdly, that in order to 'mislead his judges' Sarkar had stated 'the small distances between bazars which do not exist anywhere but in name, whereas the real distances between all existing bazars except two exceed the distance from his to Mr Wyatt's'. Focusing on the last point, the Collector said that Sarkar had stated the distances from Tiretta's to the Lalbazar as 600 ft, from the Lalbazar to the old Bowbazar as 900 ft, and from the old Bowbazar to the new Bowbazar as 1,500 ft. He said that 'neither the Loll bazar nor the old Bow Bazar are in existence; the nearest bazar therefore to Mr Tiretta's in that direction is the new Bow Bazar – 3,000 ft.' As regards the distance from Sherburne's bazar to the Dhurrumtolla bazar being 600 ft and to the Jaun bazar being 700 ft, he said that neither the Dhurrumtolla bazar nor Jaun bazar were in existence. Colebrook, therefore, said that the two nearest bazars to Sherburne's were Tiretta's (3,700 ft) and the Colimbah bazar (3,300 ft). On the distance from the Baitakhana bazar to the Company's new bazar being 300 ft, the Collector said that Sarkar himself knew 'that the new bazar was made in lieu of the old one which is now totally deserted'. As for the distance between Gopi Ghose's and Darpanarain Thakur's bazar being 1,200 ft, he said that both the bazars were small, 'the latter of which is rent free'. Further, 'their propinquities' were a source of daily dispute between the proprietors. Colebrook then proceeded to give the 'nearest distances between the existing bazars' as follows: from Tiretta's bazar to Bowbazar 3,000 ft; from Bowbazar to the new Baitakhana bazar 2,920 ft; from Baitakhana bazar to Gopi Ghose's bazar 2,700 ft; from Gopi Ghose's to Darpanarain Thakur's bazar 1,200 ft; from Darpanarain's to Short's bazar 3,500 ft; from Short's to Colimbah bazar 2,910 ft; from Colimbah to Sherburne's 3,300 ft; and from Sherburne's to Tiretta's bazar 3,700 ft.[16]

Sketch of Calcutta Bazars, by Jagannath Sarkar, Board of Revenue Proceedings, 18 January 1790 (No. 29)

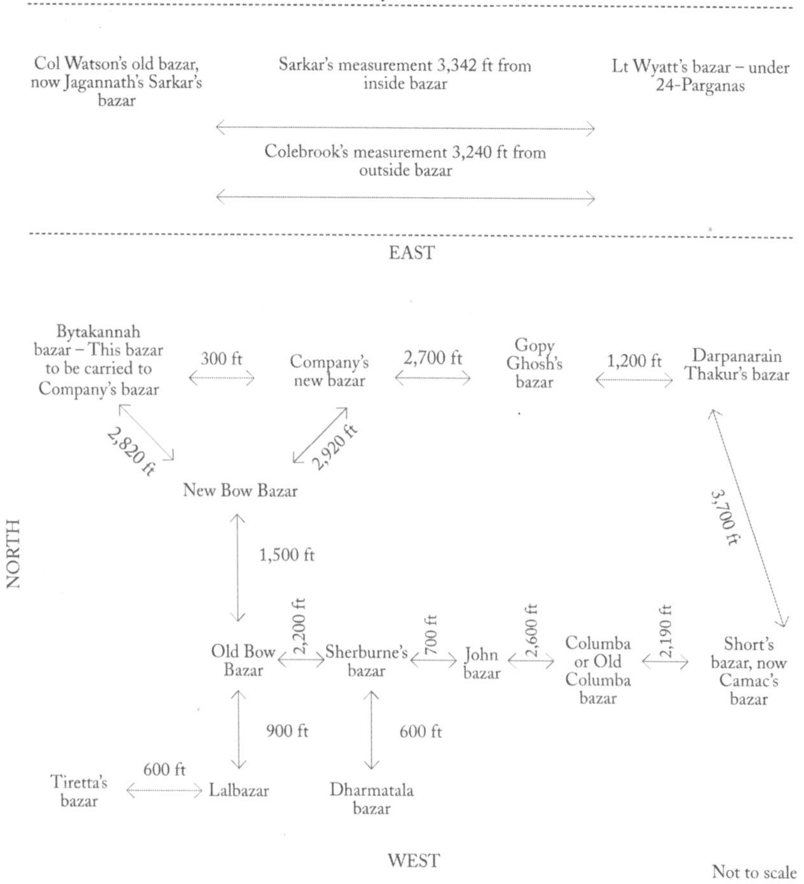

Faced with the Collector's version of the distances between the different bazars in the town, the Board of Revenue tersely ordered the immediate abolition of Sarkar's bazar at Kidderpur, also making the point that the bazar was set up 'without authority'. Sarkar was to be informed that if he wished to re-establish his bazar he had

38 Jagannath Sarkar's sketch sent to the Board of Revenue showing the distances between the bazars of Calcutta

to apply 'through you to this Board for permission so to do'.[17] Once more Sarkar sprang into action, petitioning the Governor-General in Council on 18 January[18]—despite the Board of Revenue's specific direction that an application would have to be made through the Collector—for re-establishment of his bazar, also sending it a sketch of the Calcutta markets similar to the one he had sent earlier to the Board and the Collector. The petition was duly transmitted to the Board of Revenue which informed the Governor-General in Council, in as brief a manner as possible, that it had received similar material from Sarkar sometime earlier and had taken a decision on the subject.

Having been slighted by Sarkar, the Board of Revenue was not too keen on taking any further initiative on the issue. But since Sarkar was not going to let that stand in the way of his campaign, he changed tack, fell into line and petitioned the Collector in early February[19] seeking permission to 're-establish his bazar at Kidderpore'.[20] In his note to the Board of Revenue, Colebrook said that 'a part' of the petitioner's prayer was that his request for re-establishing the bazar be granted 'without a previous public notification'. The Collector disallowed this because it would be a 'deviation from the usual form observed in [the case of] all such applications'. Sarkar wanted the bazar to be established first and then, if there were complaints by any other bazar owner that his revenues were being affected adversely, an official '*along with your petitioner*' (emphasis added) could be asked to enquire. Sarkar said that should any complaint prove to be justified, he would 'bind himself to pay such losses and deficiency to the Company'. His objection to having a prior notice being put up on the intended establishment of his bazar was that it would lead to 'false objections' being made by his 'enemies ... without any loss to them'. In his petition, he agreed to pay a yearly rent to the Company of Sicca Rs 600 'on a *mokorary* pottah being granted' to him. Sarkar's plea was rejected, the Board of Revenue asking the collector to make the necessary publications 'previous to our complying with Juggernaut's application'.[21]

Jagannath Sarkar's fears were proved right. The notice put up announcing the proposed establishment of his bazar drew unfavourable responses from a number of quarters, Wyatt and Mrs Tolly included, not to mention one by a native of the area, Darpanarain Chatterjee, who became the focus of Sarkar's ire for reasons probably linked to the politics of contemporary native society in Kidderpur.[22] The objection put in by Grahams, Moubray and Co., attorneys to Mrs Tolly, is of interest because of two specific points. First, it was alleged that Sarkar's bazar, being set up 'within a hundred yards from Surman's Bridge', would cause 'great inconvenience and loss' to their client, Mrs Tolly, being '*so close upon those established by the late Colonel Tolly by the authority of Government* [emphasis added], one of which is situated to the west of the said bridge and bounded by the ground upon which Jaggernaut proposes building his bazar, the other upon the site of the old bridge'. (Tolly, therefore, had established two bazars in the area when he had cut his canal.) Secondly, it was argued that it would be contrary 'to the laws and customs of this country *as well as it is to the laws of England* [emphasis added] to allow a new market to be erected in the vicinity of an old one whilst the latter is sufficient for the supply of the inhabitants'.[23] Darpanarain Chatterjee, the *naib* of Krishnaprasad Bidyalankar, 'the sebayet of Bookaylass in pergunnah Magra', submitted that he ran 'Surdekun and Callu bazars' in Kidderpur for which he paid the malguzari annually. Both these bazars were 'at the same place' where Sarkar intended to set up his bazar. Since the new bazar would be ten cubits from his bazars, Chatterjee's view was that 'wherever there exists a *jumayee* bazar it is forbidden by Government to make another within the distance of one corse'.[24]

Sarkar countered Tolly's complaint with the help of a technicality, arguing that the complainants had not fulfilled engagements made to the Company at the time of taking land to set up their bazar. Chatterjee's case is more interesting because here we see Sarkar in his elements once more, going on the offensive by proposing to the Government that the two bazars run by Chatterjee be closed down on the ground that 'they do not pay one anna rent to the Hon'ble Company, (neither) have they from the Collector of Calcutta or from the Collector of the 24-Pergunnahs any sunnud for the establishment of them'. Sarkar was vindictive enough to offer a 'security' of 400 rupees per annum, over and above the 600 rupees he had formerly offered for the establishment of his own bazar, for 'the total reduction of the bazars now held by the complainant'. Adding insult to injury, he wrote that he could produce proof for the charge that Chatterjee, 'zemindar of Kidderpore, under the former zemindar Mirja Naul Mahomed, gave a bribe and made out a jumma for (the) two bazars, which he now receives 100 rupees for, without any benefit to the Company, it never being entered in the jummabundy, or the zemindar's *doul*'. Sarkar made a special appeal to the collector of Calcutta 'for the sake of justice' that 'Kistnopersaud Biddalangour and Durpnarain Surmono should be compelled to produce before your Company by what authority they hold the bazar and what rent they pay to the Hon'ble Company'.[25]

There was no clearcut, unambiguous decision by the authorities. The Board of Revenue let Sarkar know that the Governor-General in Council had 'it in contemplation to take the bazar collections generally into the immediate charge of Government, but that, should not this measure be ultimately adopted, the Board will hereafter take his application into further consideration'. In other words, while the objections of Wyatt and Tolly could not be brushed aside, Sarkar's plea to set up a new bazar could not be dismissed out of hand either.

The records present a number of instances, involving both natives and Englishmen, where complaints were lodged with the authorities regarding the setting up of bazars close to existing ones, the plea always being to remove the newcomer because of an adverse impact on business. An extraordinary example of this, involving a clash between the executive and the judiciary, was the complaint[26] lodged by the owner of Sherburne's bazar at Dharamtala against one Petruce, an interpreter of the Supreme Court, who had set up a 'beetle and beetle-nut shop' opposite the bazar which was 'necessarily' injuring the business of the latter. The shop had lately been opened by Ramjoy Ghosh on ground 'belonging to Petruce between the road and the wall of the bazar'. When Edward Colebrook, the Collector of Calcutta, took the usual step of summoning Ghosh and telling him that, 'under the Committee of Revenue's orders of the 29th June 1782, his shop would be suppressed unless he should consent to pay the usual duties', both Petruce and Ghosh 'immediately lodged complaints before Mr Justice Hyde against my [the Collector's] dewan'. Colebrook said the latter was told by the judge

> … (after the latter had refused to listen to every explanation which the dewan attempted to give that it was a public transaction of the Collector under orders of the Government) that he [Justice Hyde] knew no man in a public capacity, that every person had a right to make what shop he chose on his own ground, and that unless a compensation were made to the complainants, an action should be brought.

The dewan told the Supreme Court Judge that he could not provide any compensation 'without receiving my [Colebrook's] orders'. When he was on his way back from the court, Petruce told him that the action would be begun the very next day. Since the Collector did not have the time to get instructions from the Government, he withdrew his peons posted at Ghosh's shop and put up a notice which said that the shop would be 'removed in 15 days … unless the proprietor consents to pay the established duties'.

Colebrook wrote to the Board of Revenue that if it chose not to press ahead with its case and establish its authority, 'all the public bazars will be annihilated'. He added for good measure:

> The notoriety of this interference of a Judge in favour of one of the Court interpreters against the public dewan has fixed all eyes upon the

> result; and should not the right of Government as declared in former orders be supported on this occasion, every person will, in hopes of protection and under such an avowed disbelief of these rights from the mouth of a Judge, erect shops on pottah lands for the sale of all *tehobazaree* articles, beetle and beetlenut (being) two of the principal among them.

The Collector appended to his letter an extract from the Proceedings of the Committee of Revenue of 29 June 1781 which read:

> The Hon'ble Governor General and (and) Council, having determined to assert and support the rights of Government within the town of Calcutta and to suppress the erections of bazars by private persons without the authority of Government, and having directed the Committee to support their rights, resolves as follows: That public notice be given that all bazars erected without the authority of Government shall be suppressed; that the Committee will however take into consideration all applications from private persons for the erection of bazars within their own grounds upon their consenting to the resolution on the 1st article of Mr [John] Evelyn's propositions in his letters of the 18th April [1781], and that their applications will be received for fifteen days after the date of the advertisement.

The Committee of Revenue then resolved that the Collector of the Rents of the Town of Calcutta 'do suppress all such shops, bazars and stalls where articles subject to duties are exposed to sale in Calcutta, upon the refusal of the parties to pay the established duties, or neglect to make the application set forth above after the expiration of the above date'.

The Board of Revenue took the stand expected of it, especially in a case where the authority of the Government was being challenged by a Supreme Court Judge before a huge native audience. It asked Colebrook to 'immediately enforce the regulations of the Governor General in Council of the 29th June 1781' and to inform the Board at once if any prosecution was brought against him or the dewan. It wrote to the Governor-General in Council that Justice Hyde was guilty of 'an interference ... in the execution of [Colebrook's] duty as Collector' and suggested that measures be taken 'to prevent in future a similar interference and interruption of the officers of Government in the execution of their duty'.

Notes

1 Board of Revenue Proceedings, 17 September 1789.

2 Edward Handel (Handell or Handle) succeeded Bartholomew Plaisted as surveyor in 1761. 'In 1758 he had purchased the town's arrack farm for Rs 4,000, but finding the distillery prejudicial to the military, the Board closed it, and compensated him Scavenger of Calcutta' (*Bengal Past and Present*, vol. 6, 1910, p. 108).

3 See 'History of Calcutta Streets and Houses 1780-1834, Part 2', *Bengal Past and Present,* vol. 14, Part 1, January–March 1917, p. 169. Also Notes to Part 2.

4 It is generally accepted that the name Watgunge is named after Henry Watson who had his dockyard in the area (see Cotton, *Calcutta Old and New*, p. 224). Arguably, if this was the case the name should have been Watsongunge, which it may have been at the beginning when the name began to be used, being shortened with time into the present Watgunge. However, it is not generally known that Charles Wyatt had built a gunge in the same area. In view of this, Watson may have had no role to play at all in the naming of the area as Watgunge. It is possible that the gunge built by Wyatt came to be called Wyattgunge to start with, which with time was metamorphosed into Watgunge, there being no difference of note between the native pronunciation of Wyattgunge and Watgunge.

5 Jagannath Sarkar does emerge from the records as someone who could be described as being a 'favourite' of Henry Watson. He was after all '*sarcar* to the Chief Engineer' and, on a number of occasions, Sarkar himself made no bones about the fact that it was Watson who had backed him to take up ground in the esplanade (Board of Revenue Proceedings, 27 April 1787).

6 Board of Revenue Proceedings, 2 November 1789.

7 Ibid., 14 December 1789.

8 Ibid., 2 November 1789.

9 It is of interest that the Board of Revenue gave a lower priority to the issue of Sarkar's bazar being unauthorised, which was pointed out by Wyatt and acknowledged by Sarkar himself. If the bazar itself was illegal, the issue of proximity ought to have become redundant.

10 As he wrote to the Board of Revenue on 16 November 1789, the Collector had already begun to take steps to carry out the Board's abolition order 'by placing peons to prevent the *tehobazaree* vendors from assembling' at Sarkar's bazar.

11 John Hooper Wilkinson. At the end of the first decade of the nineteenth century an advertisement appeared in the *Gazette* which said that a sheriff's sale had been announced 'of the remainder of a term of a certain lease from Anna Maria Tolley to John Hooper Wilkinson of a certain creek or nullah, commonly known by the name of Tolley's nullah or canal' (C.R. Wilson and W.H. Carey, *Glimpses of the Olden Times*, ed. Amarendranath Mookerjee [Calcutta: Eastlight Book House, 1968], p. 175).

12 Board of Revenue Proceedings, 18 January 1790.

13 Located to the east of Chowringhee Road, on the site of today's New Market. See image 28 on p. 250.

14 Board of Revenue Proceedings, 18 January 1790.

15 Ibid.

16 Ibid.

17 Ibid.

18 Board of Revenue Proceedings, 28 January 1790; Governor-General in Council Proceedings, 20 January 1790.

19 Board of Revenue Proceedings, 4 February 1790.

20 'Re-establishment' would mean that the bazar had closed down following the Board of Revenue's first abolition order issued on 2 November 1789. But had it, in fact, closed down at all? Writing in early December to the Board (Board of Revenue Proceedings, 8 February 1790), Wyatt said he was surprised to see the 'greatest part of the bazar still remaining, and a number of shops of various descriptions open and exhibiting every species of traffick in the same public manner as before'. The only part of the bazar which had seen any change was 'a few fish stalls and the removal of the … sheds erected in the centre of the bazar by Jaggernaut purposely to shelter the inhabitants from the late rains'. The rest of the bazar continued as before. Wyatt complained that 'crowds of people daily assemble

and [cause] the same injury to my property – and nuisance to the public, being on the verge of a high road – as heretofore'. Considering the confusion surrounding the closure order, which was followed by another on 14 January 1790, Wyatt felt that perhaps it was the ambiguity of the abolition orders issued to the Collector which was at the heart of the problem and not the neglect of the Government officers involved in carrying them out. Consequently, he suggested to the Board of Revenue that 'more complete instructions' be issued to the Collector as far as the abolition of Sarkar's bazar was concerned.

21 On 10 February the Governor-General in Council wrote to the Board of Revenue (the letter being signed by Cornwallis, Charles Stewart and Peter Speke) approving the course of action taken on Jagannath Sarkar's bazar (Board of Revenue Proceedings, 15 February 1790).

22 Board of Revenue Proceedings, 22 April 1790.

23 Ibid.

24 Ibid.

25 Ibid.

26 Ibid., 18 January 1790.

20

The Limits of Calcutta

Calcutta was never a walled city, but it did sport a fence or palisade on the northern, eastern and southern sides as is depicted in an 'anonymous plan of Calcutta showing the palisades' dated 1747.[1] But what did the fence mark off? The objective certainly was to mark out the extent of the English settlement, the fence being a sort of protective ring thrown around it separating it from the surrounding press of native habitation. H.B. Hyde, the senior chaplain in the Indian ecclesiastical establishment at the turn of the nineteenth century, describes the path taken by the fence thus:[2]

> The original town of Calcutta was at one time at least a 'fenced city', for a plan in the British Museum[3] shows it as enciented in some way by palisades which were continued even along the river face and the edge of the creek or "ditch" now reclaimed by the name of Hastings street. A point in this plan is thus marked: "The extensions of the palisades to the northward, from whence they go all round the town until they meet those at the southward." Every road issuing from the town was secured by a gate. It may be that these stockades were only erected around the boundaries in the Marhratta scare of 1742, when the native population almost surrounded the three towns by a moat, or they may have been much older – the question is as yet unexplored. The plan referred to is of about the date of the scare, but it contains no hint that the palisades were then recent. It traces none of the streets within the town but one of

the most insignificant and names none of the boundaries; nevertheless it is a clear guide to any one who desires still to beat the bounds of the two hundred and twenty acres comprising the original Christian Calcutta. Let him start from the tall building that stands out against the river blocking up the straight avenue of the Hastings street houses. Here was at the first a square earthwork sustaining a pair of bastions whence guns pointed down the river and up the creek.

The creek took a half turn round this battery and crept westwards beneath three gated bridges until the fences turned townwards from it at Fancy Lane. One of the bridges opened from the burying place, occupied, when the plan was made, by the mausoleum of Job Charnock, towers, pyramids and obelisks, and perhaps having even then the post office squeezed in at its corner. The second bridge opened from the spacious yard where sentries guarded the great bell-shaped magazine of masonry where the Company stored its gunpowder. But why should the town fences at the third bridge sharply swerve from the natural boundary of the creek? If *Fancy* be the native *Phansi*, the reason is revealed – they here avoided a gallows-tree.

39 Tombs in the old burying ground and the gunpowder magazine seen beyond the fence, around 1740

Fancy lane is the entrance to the bailey that ran round the whole town within the palisades. A short distance up this passage the enceinte turned again westwards parallel to the creek. It crossed the present Wellesley Place, and in doing so skirted Chaplain Bellamy's garden, thence it ran up Larkin's lane and its continuation, where some *Queen* among huckstresses so waged her trade that the place took on her name and fame.[4] Thence Barretto's lane, once called Cross street, opens on the left; this is the bailey beginning its long northward course and keeping, as it does so, at pretty even distance all along from the pilgrim road to Kalighat. The town was a settlement reserved exclusively for the three Christian nations, that is, the English, Portuguese and Armenians, with their immediate dependents, and was so laid out as to keep well clear of the busy heathen highway. Between the town and this road lay the hamlets of the butchers, the scavengers and the oilmongers: local nomenclature still remembers them.

From Barretto's lane and along a bit of Mangoe lane, the passage opens into Mission Row, where the memory of the old rope-walk has been supplanted by that of Kiernander's chapel and school.

Here the parish church lay open at many points in full view across the 'Park,' and the wide, sweet-water tank, and Fort William also with its handsome factory buildings gleaming white above its crimson walls. The Governor's house near the Bankshall, an ambitious edifice in its day, must also have been a prominent object from the rope-walk.

Thence the palisades ran up to the Lall bazar to a gate at the "cross roads" where the cutchery was, and where the police head-quarters still are, and where native offenders were judged and suffered; but the line of the bailey branched off at Radha's bazar.

A crooked alley, still the bailey, connects Radha's bazar with Ezra street. This was the straight back of the town, which is continued northward along Amratolla street – an orchard of 'sour-'khrote's' must have flourished hereabouts. Near by where the Greek church was built in later times, the bailey zig-zagged riverwards to Armenian street by a lane which the natives still call Hamam-gullee, though Turkish bathhouses have long ceased to exist in Calcutta. This lane passes near

> to the Portuguese church of "Our Lady of the Rosary." Here, when the old plan was made, the fences seem to have been recently thrown out at an angle, by extending the Armenian street line until they met the road running past the Portuguese church. The palisades turned round the burying place of the Armenians, within which stood their church of St Nazareth, much the same as now to look at, except that perhaps the nave had then not yet been extended to meet the steeple.
>
> Leaving this the bailey ran in and out down to the river by streets named after the sellers of reedmats and scouring-brushes, who traded at that end of the town, and the tail of the Old China Bazar.
>
> The northern-most limit of the town's river face was in the present Raja Woodmand street.[5]

There is no evidence of the fence existing at the time of the nawab's assault on Calcutta in mid-1756. Even if it did it would have been obliterated in the course of the fighting that took place at the time. In any case, the fence, as it was constructed, could hardly have had any military utility; in fact, it was never intended to have had one. It is, therefore, safe to suggest that with the making of the Maratha ditch, even if partially, it sank into oblivion. In its time the fence never marked the official limits of the settlement; the Maratha ditch was to play a much more important role in this regard, as will be seen later. But it was inevitable that a time would come when a conscious effort would be made to set the 'limits' of the town as accurately as possible, a task which would eventually turn out to be more complicated than initially envisaged.

One such moment came on 13 April 1787 when the Board of Revenue asked the Collector of Calcutta, Archibald Seton, to 'ascertain and report the ancient and present boundary of the town of Calcutta'. On the following 15 June[6] Seton wrote that with respect

> … to the ancient boundary [that is, previous to 1742 when the Mahratta Ditch was dug], the information which after much enquiry I have been able to obtain is by no means so satisfactory as I could wish. The records

> of the cutcherry afforded me no assistance whatever; neither could the oldest inhabitants of the place point out with accuracy the former limits. All that I have been able to ascertain is that the following divisions formed the component parts of the ancient Town of Calcutta: Baug-Bazar, Sootalooty, Bazar Calcutta, Dhee-Calcutta, Laul-Bazar and Govindpoor.

If, at the level of the collector, it was difficult to find leads throwing light on the boundaries of the early settlement, the inference clearly is that the subject had never before been gone into in any detail by the authorities. Seton wrote that since Bagbazar still formed the northern boundary of the town and Gobindapur, where the new fort was located, the southern limit, and as the western limit (the river) was 'invariable', it followed 'that the difference between the former and present extent of Calcutta consists of annexations to the eastward'. As he saw it, the additions comprised 'the following villages, namely, Chowringhy, Huggulcoory, Aurcooly, a kismut, or part of, Simla, a kismut ... Mirzapore, a kismut ... Molungha, a kismut ... Etally, a kismut ... Colimba'.

Seton wrote that with respect to the boundary of the town he had been more successful although there was a problem in the south where the Maratha ditch 'ceases'. In his words, 'The Town of Calcutta is entirely surrounded except on the western side by the district called Paunchwangong [Panchannagram], or the 55 villages, from which it is separated by the Marhatta Ditch, as far as that work is continued'. He said that so far as the ditch could be traced, he had considered it to be the boundary of the town. Thus, from its commencement at Chitpur to the place where it ceases altogether 'it constantly forms the exact and precise line of division' between the town of Calcutta and Panchannagram. Beyond that, he took 'the continuation of that line of division (as pointed out to me by the revenue officers and other natives) as the continuation of the boundary of Calcutta, from the place where the Marhatta Ditch is discontinued to Kidderpoor bridge, where the limits cease to be doubtful'. Typically of the conscientious administrator that he was, Seton wanted to know the mind of the natives on the issue. He directed the cutcherry officers and some of the old and best informed inhabitants of the place to lay before him a joint report 'specifying the boundary of Calcutta, as generally … understood by the natives, which they accordingly did'.

Seton then proceeded to

> … examine in person the boundary described in their report, accompanied by the persons who drew it up, and found that they too had considered the line of separation between Calcutta and Paunchwangong as the boundary of the town from the spot where the Marhatta Ditch ceases to the mouth of Tolley's Nullah.

Seton wrote that, on this principle, the limits of the town of Calcutta were as follows:

> On the west, the boundary is formed by that part of the Houghly River which is comprehended between the mouth of the Marhatta Ditch at the Baug-Bazar (or Chitpoor) Bridge, and that of Tolley's Nullah at Khidderpore.The north and north-eastern boundary is formed by the Marhatta Ditch from the Baug Bazar Bridge to that part of the Sham Bazar. On the eastside also the Marhatta Ditch forms the boundary. It can be traced from the Sham Bazar Bridge to the *chehar-rah* [*chowrasta*], or four roads of Etally, where it crosses the great road, leading from the Boyta-Khanna [Baitakkhana] to the burying ground;[7] whence taking a southwesterly direction it is carried, though with such interruption as hardly to be traced, to a spot well known amongst the natives by the name of Mrs Chapman's garden. There the Marhatta Ditch ceases entirely, and the only guide left to mark the boundary is, as I have observed, the limiting line between Calcutta and Paunchwangong which, as I was attended by the revenue officers of both the Calcutta and Paunchwangong cutcherrries, I have reason to think was pointed out to me with accuracy. [This line] is marked by a path which, from

> Mrs Chapman's garden, goes in a westerly direction till it meets the road immediately behind, or to the northward of, Mr Bellie's garden, between which and Captain Charles Rankin's garden house, now inhabited by Major Palmer, it proceeds till it joins the great road from Calcutta to the burying ground, then keeping along the northside of that road, in a westerly direction, it leads to the chehar-rah, or four roads of Chowringhee, where, in a southwesterly direction, passing between the road to the New Fort and that to Russapughly, it continues to Kidderpoor Bridge, separating Paunchwangong from Govindpoor, in the first of which divisions the general hospital and Jail are situated, and in the second Fort William.[8]

Seton then referred to the following passage in Orme's 'War in India' (first section, second volume):

> In the year 1742 the Indian inhabitants of the colony requested and obtained permission to dig a ditch at their own expence round the Company's bounds, from the northern part of Sootanooty to the southern part of Govindpoor. This work would extend 7 miles in six months. Three miles were finished when the inhabitants, seeing that no Marrattahs had ever been on the western side of the river, within sixty miles of Calcutta, discontinued the work; which, from the occasion, was called the Marhatta Ditch.

The Collector said that comparing this description with the 'present ideas of the inhabitants, as expressed in the enclosed report of the aumeens who attended me in making the survey, they will be found in general to correspond'.[9] The amins—Fakir Chand Das, Nimnarayan Mitra, Gokul Chand Bose and Ramanand Sircar—of the Calcutta cutcherry reported that,

> Agreeable to orders, we ascertained by a local enquiry and by consulting the etmaundars and others of the best informed inhabitants on the boundaries, both ancient and modern, of the town of Calcutta, and

find that Calcutta formerly consisted of the following villages, namely, Baug Bazar, Sootanooty, Bazar Calcutta, Dhee Calcutta, Laul Bazar and Govindpore.

The present limits of the town of Calcutta we find to be as follows:

On the west, the Ganges, from the Khidderpoor to the Baug Bazar (or Chitpoor) Bridge, (that is, from the mouth of Tolly's Nullah to the commencement of the Marhatta Ditch at Chitpoor).

On the north, the Marhatta Ditch from Baug Bazar Bridge to the eastside of Nund Ram Sayne's garden, otherwise called Talla Baug.

On the east, the Marhatta Ditch still forms the boundary continued from the east side of Nund Ram Sayne's garden to the Sham Bazar Bridge, and from thence passing through by Ameen Chand's garden and the Beyta Khanna to the chehar-rah, or four roads, of Etally.

On the southeast and south, the Marhatta Ditch continued from the chehar-rah of Etally to the south side of Mr Chapman's garden in Colimbah where the Marhatta Ditch ceases. From thence the boundary passes between Major Palmer's and Mr Belli's gardens, till it meets the road to the burying ground [this confirms that both the above gardens were located north of Park Street], along which it continues as far as the chehar-rah, or four roads, of Chowringhee, from whence it passes through the field [the maidan] (between the road to Russapughly [note the use of Russapughly in place of Russapuglah] and that to the New Fort) [today's Outram Road—that is, the boundary cuts across the maidan] to Khidderpoor Bridge.[10]

Seton then cited the Regulations for the Administration of Justice in the Courts of Dewanny-Adawlut according to which the limits of the town of Calcutta

> … are declared to be situate, and contained within, and bounded by, a line drawn by the bridge and nullah of Baug bazar, Shaumbazar, or Cow Cross, the Marhatta entrenchment, and the road adjoining the same [Circular Road],[11] continued to the westward of the Callighaut Road, Govindpoor Nullah, and the river.

The Collector said that the above description of the limits of Calcutta

> ... corresponds exactly with the results of my present enquiry from the Chitpoor Bridge to the chehar-rah of Etally, where the Marhatta Ditch crosses the great road from the Boyta-Khanna to the burying ground.[12] But then, instead of following the Ditch, the description which I have just quoted appears to carry the boundary in a southerly direction along the great road in question [Circular Road], about a quarter of a mile beyond the burying ground and then, in a westerly direction, joins Tolley's nulla behind the General Hospital.

He added that this boundary 'must be allowed to be just if the "Cally-Ghaut road" mentioned in the regulations be considered as the continuation of the great road from the Beyta-khanna; upon which point only the accuracy or inaccuracy of it depends'.

Seton sought the assistance of the police not merely because the town limits cropped up frequently in the course of the latter's work but also because amongst their numbers there were 'some of the oldest British inhabitants of this country'. The police referred Seton to Article 15 of the Bye Law which Seton found was 'literally the same with the 23rd article of the Adawlut Regulations which I have already quoted and which therefore threw no light on the subject'. The police also sent Edward Tiretta, the surveyor, to show him a plan of the south-east boundary of the town, 'as defined by the bye law'. According to this regulation,

> ... the limits are formed by extending the Great Road from the Beyta-Khanna, about 1/3 of a mile beyond, and to the southward of the Burying Ground; and then by a line carried in a westerly direction across the Collighhat Bridge,[13] as far as the general hospital, whence (enclosing the Hospital) it proceeds almost due south, till it meets Tolley's Nullah, nearly opposite to Mr Cowper's country house.[14] The remainder of the southern boundary is formed by the Govindpoor [or Tolly's] Nullah until it loses itself in the Ganges.

Seton wrote that

> ... as the bye law expressly specifies that from the 'road adjoining to the Marhatta encroachment' the boundary is to be continued to the westward of the Cally-Ghaut Road, it is evident that the Surveyor has considered that road as one and the same with the continuation of the great road leading southward from the Beyta-Khanna because from the place where the Marhatta ditch crosses that road and becomes no longer very distinguishable, he has carried the boundary along the road in question across the Cally-Ghaut Bridge, to the Govindpoor Nullah.

According to Seton, however, natives held a different view of the boundary of the town. He said he had made 'special enquires ... with respect to what they understood by the term Cally-Ghaut Road, and found that ... they all agreed with Mr Tiretta, although their ideas respecting the boundary of the town be different from what is laid down as such in the bye laws'.

The Collector submitted a plan of the limits of the town (which is not included in the Proceedings).[15] He wrote that

> ... according to the present state of the ground to the south-east of Calcutta, the limits certainly appear to be better marked and the extent of the town rendered more regular and compact in the plan prepared by the Surveyor in conformity to his conception of the Bye Law than they would be if the report of the aumeens were literally adhered to.

This was probably because of the passage of time. The 'roads, bridges, etc which now abound in that quarter did not exist in former times, and that, on the other hand, paths and roads which were formerly frequented are now entirely effaced'. For instance, Seton pointed out 'that part of the boundary which, according to the aumeens' report, is continued between the crossroads at Chowringhee and the Khidderpore Bridge is now no longer discernible from the rest of the lawn through which it is said to pass'.

Seven years after Seton presented his views to the Government on the limits of Calcutta the Governor-General in Council issued a proclamation fixing the limits of the town.[16] The river Hooghly was considered a part of the town, the northern boundary being marked by a line commencing on the west (that is, the Howrah side) 'at the north point of Colonel Robertson's garden called Jackapore, immediately opposite to the mouth of the brook called Chitpore Nullah or Baug Bazar Nullah' and continuing eastward across the river

> … to the south corner of the mouth of the said nullah unto the post No. 1 near the foot of the Chitpore Bridge; and from thence by a line drawn eastward and passing the south end of the said bridge to (post) No. 2; and from thence along the south side of the said nullah or brook to the post No. 3; and thence on to the post No. 4 passing the old Powder Mill Bazar until it reaches the foot of the bridge leading to Dum-Dum, where the post No. 5 is.

The eastern boundary was marked by a line commencing from post No. 5 and following the western, 'or inner', side of the Maratha ditch and the eastern side of 'the road adjoining thereunto' (Circular Road) till post No. 6 'at the northern angle next to the road of an enclosure called Halsee Bagan', which was included within the limits of the town. From there the line extended southward to another post also numbered No. 6 from where it travelled west 'along the northern side of the said ditch or trench' till post No. 7 where there was a thana. From this point the line went south along the western side of the Maratha ditch and the eastern side 'of the Boitaconnah Road as far as the remains of the said Mahratta entrenchment are visible' to post No. 8 'at the corner of Raja Ramlochun's Bazar, and of the road leading to Ballea Ghaut [Beliaghata] immediately opposite to Narain Chattoorjee's road'. From here the line continued south 'passing through Mirzapore … and leaving the Portuguese burying ground to the east until it reaches the Boitaconnah tree', where two

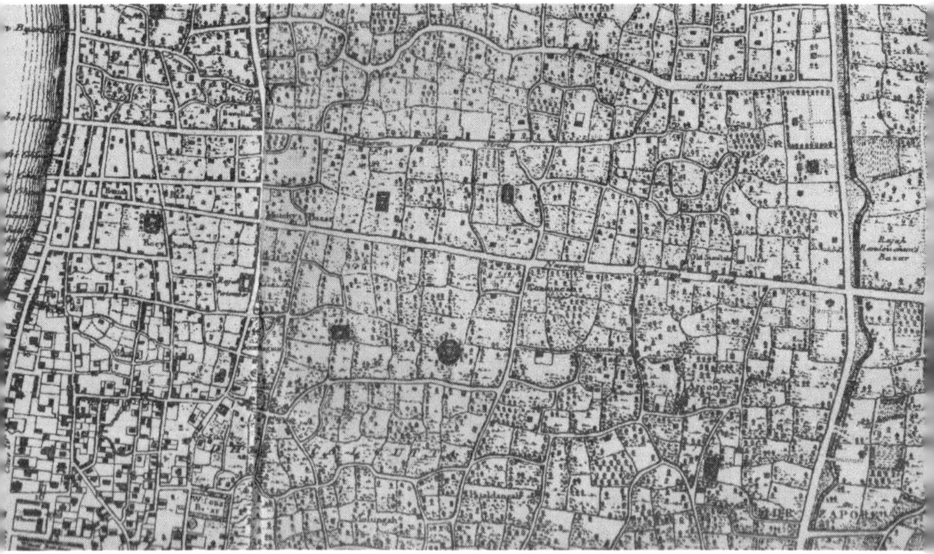

40 Upjohn's map (1792–1793) showing Narain Chatterjee Street and Raja Ramlochun's Bazar

posts Nos. 9 and 10 'are fixed on each side of the road opposite to the Bowbazar Road and Boitaconnah Bazar'. From post No. 10 the line continued south to post No. 11 opposite to Gopee Baboo bazar located between the Janbazar Road and Dharamtala Street;

> … and from thence in the same direction until the said line reaches the post No. 12 at the point of turning of the said road towards the west, leaving Dhee Serampore on the east, and thereby including within the limits of Calcutta the Protestant burying ground, Chowringhee, and the land thereunto belonging called Dhee Birjee.

The southern limit of the town was marked by the line commencing from post No. 12 and drawn westward

> … with a little inclination to the southward along the southern side of the public road excluding Dhee Chuckerbere, and including

> Bunneakpukah, otherwise called Arreapukah in Dhee Birjee, until the said line reaches the beginning of the Russapuglah Road immediately opposite to Chowringhee High Road where the post No. 13 is fixed.

From this post the line continued to run west to post No. 14 'fixed between the thana and the General Hospital', and then on to post No. 15 'at the foot of the Alipore Bridge', excluding the general hospital, the hospital for insane persons, and the hospital burying ground 'situated in Dhee Bowanipore'. From the south side of the Alipore Bridge the boundary is marked by a line drawn

> ... along the south side of the Nullah, commonly called Tolly's Nullah, at high watermark, to the post No. 16; and from thence passing the foot or south end of Surman's Bridge, commonly called Kidderpore Bridge, and extending to the mouth of the said nullah where it enters the River Hooghly, excluding Watson's Dock, and to the post No. 17.

The line then extended west across the river 'to the south-east point of Major Kyd's garden [the Botanical Gardens], and excluding the said garden and village of Sheebpore' where post No. 18 was fixed.

From this point began the western boundary of the town of Calcutta, the line being drawn along the low watermark of the river 'but excluding the ghauts of Ramkissenpore, Howrah and Sulkea' where posts Nos. 19, 20 and 21 were fixed. The line then extended northward to Colonel Robertson's garden where post No. 22 was planted, 'immediately opposite to the post No. 1 at Chitpore Bridge', thus completing the circuit.[17]

Notes

1 See Losty, *Calcutta City of Palaces*, p. 25.

2 *The Parish of Bengal*, pp. 43–48.

3 See note 1.

4 Raneemoody Gully, late British Indian Street, currently Abdul Hamid Street. See Nair, *A History of Calcutta's Streets*, pp. 121–122.

5 Woodmunt Street was named after Raja Uddanta Sinha, the nephew of Maharaja Debi Sinha, founder of the Nashipur Raj in Murshidabad district. See Nair, *A History of Calcutta's Streets*, pp. 727–728.

6 Board of Revenue Proceedings, 22 June 1787. Also reprinted in *List of Documents on Calcutta*, vol. 1, 1764-1800, The State Archives of West Bengal, Calcutta, 1990, pp. 123–127 .

7 This appears to be the stretch of the Circular Road from, roughly, the Moulali crossing to present-day Park Street, the burying ground being the South Park Street Cemetery.

8 The 'great road from Calcutta to the burying ground' appears to be present-day Park Street. From the Park Street-Chowringhee Road crossing, the boundary of the town appears to cut across the maidan towards the Victoria Memorial Hall but keeping to the north of it, with the result that while the jail (roughly on the site of the Hall) and the general hospital (where the SSKM Hospital stands today) fall within Panchannagram the fort is included within the town limits.

9 Board of Revenue Proceedings, 22 June 1787.

10 Ibid.

11 Constructed by Henry Watson (ibid., 27 April 1787).

12 This is an important point regarding the relative alignment of the Circular Road and the Maratha ditch. What it tells us is that the road was not throughout on the western side of the ditch, as is the general supposition.

13 There was of course no 'bridge' in the conventional sense at this point. Since every road of consequence had drains or ditches on both sides bridges over drains were a necessity, these being referred to as 'bridges' in the records. It is more than likely that the 'Kalighat bridge' here is probably one such bridge which was given that particular name because it was on the road leading to Kalighat and Russapuglah (today's Tollygunge). The alignment of the town's boundary indicated here is that of today's Circular Road (or A.J.C. Bose Road) passing the 'Exide crossing' (where the Calcutta Club is located) and going towards the SSKM hospital. This is probably what the regulation cited by Seton also meant, the 'Callighaut road' being the continuation southward of Chowringhee Road. If this is acceptable, what this means is that Kalighat at its present location had become well-known enough by the end of the 1780s for it to be used to describe a principal road of the town.

14 Probably William Cowper who later became president of the Board of Revenue and served on the Governor-General's Council.

15 The Original Consultations stored in the West Bengal State Archives could not be checked because of their 'inaccessibility'.

16 The Proclamation was issued on 10 September 1794; reprinted in Roy, *Short History*, pp. 116–119.

17 For the limits of Calcutta in 1884, see *Select Documents on Calcutta, 1800-1900*, compiled by Bidisha Chakraborty and Sarmistha De, Directorate of State Archives, West Bengal, 2011, pp. 62–63.

21

Assault on the Ditch

Even though not completed, the Maratha ditch was made to keep out an enemy from the town thus marking the territorial extent of the settlement. Since the ditch was there from the early 1740s it was inevitable that with the years it would come to be treated as the boundary of Calcutta. It was also inescapable that with time it would degenerate into the town's principal receptacle of filth. This is precisely what happened if one is to go by complaints to that effect stretching through the eighteenth century well into the nineteenth. Yet another complaint, particularly in the early years, was that the ditch was being encroached on by diverse interests for commercial purposes one of which was to use the earth from the ditch to make bricks, the demand for which was increasing exponentially in view of the rapidly increasing construction work in the town. Matters must have reached alarming proportions for the records indicate that senior members of the administration were taking note of the practice and asking for measures to put a stop to it. On 4 March 1778 John Champain, a member of the Calcutta Committee of Revenue, penned a minute[1] in which he charged that Raja Ramlochun and others had

> … cut and removed the earth forming the high banks of the Maharattah Ditch to the eastward of Calcutta, nearly I suppose, in extent, half a mile along the road leading from the Bytaconnah to Omychund's Gardens

> [that is, northward from Sealdah], for the purpose of making it into bricks and filling up tanks in their gardens contiguous thereto, and are actually at this instant burning bricks on the road which they have made with this earth.

Champain said that as this was

> ... an undoubted encroachment on the Company's property, which must tend to the prejudice of the roads and the inhabitants of Calcutta by creating a nauseous and unwholesome smell over the Settlement, I move that the Committee take such steps as will cause these persons to desist and oblige them to place [back] the earth they have cut and removed for the above purposes, as well as punish the offenders for such unwarrantable practices, as examples to others.

Champain also drew the committee's attention to another problem, namely, that

> ... some persons who have gardens on the eastward of this Ditch, have filled up that part adjoining to their premises to enlarge them, whereby the regular course of water is effectually obstructed, and large bodies must lie and stagnate for want of a free channel to the river which ebbs and flows therein.

He added that the 'nuisance' was 'equally prejudicial to the health of the Settlement'. An important inference here is that forty years after the ditch had been dug, it was still filled with water from the Hooghly, ebbing and flowing with the river's current, fulfilling a function originally envisaged for the ditch to act as moat in case of any assault on the town from the east. Taking note of Champain's complaint, the committee asked the president, John Holme, to find out who the defaulters were, what quantity of land they had 'cut and carried away, and the quantity of land which they have established and possessed themselves of by filling up the ditch'. Holme was also asked to place a guard 'with a written order to attach the bricks now on the spot and to prevent any more land being cut away'.

The records[2] suggest that nothing much was done in the weeks following to put a stop to the practice John Champain had complained of with the result that the latter placed a 'motion' before the committee stating that the people complained against were

> … still prosecuting these practices, the bricks not being attached, as I see them daily taking them away, and there is neither a *negabaun*, nor peons on the spot, as the Committee were pleased to direct, to compel these persons to desist, but more Bricks are moulding and burning on the Road as I before cited.

On the previous occasion, the president had been asked specifically by the committee to take measures to stop the practice complained of by Champain. This time the committee took action itself. It resolved that John Holme be requested to

> … give in the report of the defaulters as required by the Committee in their Proceedings of the 5th March last, and ordered that Sam-Churn *aumeen* be deputed to proceed to the premises, attach the bricks, prevent further encroachment on the Company's property, ascertain what quantity of land Raja Ramlochurn and others have taken for the use of making bricks, and filling up tanks in their gardens, as also to put a stop to the filling up of the public ditch.

The committee taking action on its own the second time around was nothing but an indictment of the president for his earlier inaction on a specific request made by the rest of the Committee which, among other things, throws light on the interpersonal relationships at work in the business of running the administration of the town.

While on the subject of brickmaking, the Calcutta Committee of Revenue Proceedings of 20 April 1778 tell us about another aspect of the activity which was literally leaving footprints on the ground to the detriment of the town's health and hygiene. On 8 April John Rosewell and James Ross of 'Intally Gardens' complained that 'the ryotts of Intally [were] burning bricks so very close to our dwelling houses that we are almost stifled with the smoke proceeding out from the kilns' and that 'so very near are they to Mr Ross's that the fire more than once has entered the chamber windows, and nigh fired that gentleman's cot and furniture in his room'. But the point of interest here is the physical consequence of brickmaking, a widespread activity, which must have been affecting other parts of the town as well. In their petition, Rosewell and Ross referred to the 'greater nuisance' of 'digging the ground full of holes' in the course of making bricks which, after they became too deep, were left as they were only to be filled up with water during the rains, turning them into 'so many nasty pools and … receptacles of the worst kind of virmin'. The petitioners wrote:

> How pernicious the air of course must be from vapours arising from such places we need not point out to you gentlemen. In short, from the brick-making business in general now carrying on, all along the skirts of the town of Calcutta, it will be well if the infectious air does not spread and become more and more detrimental to the health of the inhabitants thereof, by the daily increase of stagnated waters occasioned thereby, if not timely prevented.

Clearly, some amount of hyperbole was injected into the representation for effect, but the fact remains that extensive brick-making in the town and on its outskirts was affecting adversely living conditions in the town in the early years—a price the environment was paying for the imperative of development, a theme which has become even more familiar to us more than two centuries later.

While brickmaking was affecting the Maratha ditch adversely in the closing years of the eighteenth century, a hundred years later other issues with which we are more familiar in our time gained prominence. One such was the controversy over the sale of land by the Calcutta Corporation to the Watson Press Company (see later), which led to the setting up of the Marhattah Ditch Committee. In the course of its deliberations, the committee cast some light on the state of the ditch in the 1880s. The central issue before the committee was to consider

> ... whether the ditch should be transferred to the Calcutta Corporation for the purpose of its being connected with the Calcutta underground drains with power to levy a drainage tax on all holdings situate on the suburban side of the ditch, or will the Suburban Corporation take over the ditch from the Government for the improvement system of the suburbs.

The committee, comprising Gopal Chunder Mookerjee, Pran Nath Dutt and Kanti Chunder Banerjee, felt that 'it would be advisable for Suburban Commissioners to accept the offer of the Government of making over the ditch to them'.[3]

In the late eighteenth century, there were reports of encroachments being made on the ditch, instances of which were brought to the notice of the authorities. A century later, in the 1880s, the Marhattah Ditch Committee reported that 'large encroachments [had been] made on the ditch lands from various quarters, notably by the Calcutta Corporation and by the Eastern Bengal Railway Company, as also by private individuals'.[4] The committee said that the encroachments had 'not only brought it [the ditch] to its present filthy and undrainable state but have done great damage to the entire drainage system of those parts of the suburbs, which have and had drainage connection with the Marhattah ditch'. As the Chairman of Calcutta Corporation, Henry Harrison (after whom Harrison Road, now Mahatma Gandhi Road, is named) had pointed out to the Government, the ditch 'naturally belongs to the drainage system of the suburbs and does not subserve the drains of a single house in the town, excepting a minute area at the extreme north of it'. Harrison had argued that the ditch, 'being an integral portion of the drainage of the suburbs cannot be filled up without obstructing the drainage of most of the houses along the Suburban side of the Circular road'. The committee found that the ditch was connected with the drains of Ward I of the suburbs and also with several main drains in Wards II, III and IV. It felt that the only way for the suburban commissioners to have put in place 'proper drainage accommodation to those parts of the suburbs which lie on the Calcutta side of the Circular Canal' was to have used the ditch 'had that been allowed to stand in its entirety'.

In a note dated 29 July 1885, appended to the report,[5] Kanti Chunder Banerjee said that on the day the committee had inspected the actual route of the ditch it was raining, which was in fact a blessing because it filled out the drains and allowed the members to mark out clearly the course of the ditch. Providing posterity with as clear a picture as is possible of the state and course of the ditch nearly 130 years ago, he wrote:

> The commencement of the Ditch from the point where it originally joined the Hooghly River to a place called Jaliaparrah Bustee is entirely filled up and obliterated; the land seemed to be leased out. The present channel has its commencement at this place, where I noticed a sort of local hollow, full of stagnant water and jungle, giving shelter to the people to defecate promiscuously in and about the locality. This water seems to have an outlet provided for in the canal with a sluice opening at its tail. The Ditch runs through the bustee keeping close to the canal road, until it crosses the Tallah Bridge road (south), and then taking a sharp turn runs past Sham Bazar and crosses the Belgatchia road at the south-east corner of the bazar. The opening of the bridge under the road measures 15 feet clear, which shows that the drain which is only about 6 feet wide now, must have been of a width varying from 3 to 4 times its present dimension. This is an important fact as it shows the extent to which the Ditch has gradually been encroached upon ... [The water in the drain] is eventually drained into the canal by a branch drain leading to it from a point about 25 yards to the north of the Belgatchia

road bridge; the volume of water discharged through the branch drain is not very inconsiderable, as may be judged from the size of the drain itself ...

The Ditch continues its course southwards through the east of Sham Bazar eventually coming out and joining the Upper Circular road near the house of Babu Mohun Lall Mitter. It then flows past the suburban bustee of Nikareeparah which is entirely drained by the Ditch, the water being brought down by a large *nekassie* drain having low level. South of this is the bustee of Dhanniabagan, which has also a low level, the western part of which is drained by the Ditch. From this place we noticed a strip of land lying fallow, between the western edge of the Ditch and the Municipal line of tramway, of width varying for 15 to 20 feet; this land is evidently reclaimed by filling up a portion of the old channel. To the south of this is Jodoo Nath Mitter's lane, where apparently the summit of the drain is situated, that is to say, the portion to the north draining in that direction and eventually finding its outlet into the canal as described above, and the southern part to the south finding an outfall into the Circular road sewer, opposite Ooltadangah road.[6] Here the drainage is very imperfect, water in the Ditch (which measured 7 feet wide at this spot) standing nearly up to the level of the Goureebare road, which I was given to understand is submerged after a good rainfall. ...

It will be noticed that the Ditch here drains into the Circular road sewer and that the defect is owing to the state of the opening .... Further on, the drain is filled up and a *pucca* road constructed over the site by the Calcutta Municipality,pipes being laid under it to carry off the surface drainage. Beyond this and along the Halseebagan road, no trace of the Ditch exists, the branch sewer under this road being constructed on its site. Coming out at the Circular road we find the Ditch, running as in the north, to the east of the Municipal tramway down as far as the Mosque of Hazie Jackeriah, situated to the south of the famous Mahomedan burial ground at Manicktollah; at this point it again deviates from the Circular road, and making a short detour, crosses the Mannickollah road close by the former and resumes its position to the east of the line of tramway immediately to the south of the refuse platform, the drainage finding an outfall into the sewer. Further down its course the Ditch receives the drainage of Gurpar road and also of the western portions of Narkelbagan, Rajar bazar and the adjoining bustees, lying between Gurpar and the Narkeldanah roads, and empties itself again into the sewer under this latter road. Beyond this again is another refuse platform for the construction of which a portion of the Ditch was filled up .... ; continuing south along the line of [municipal] tramway the Ditch finally terminates in the compound of the railway station [at Sealdah]. The portion above described is the northern section of the Marhattah Ditch.

Below the Baliaghatta road, in front of the Medical Officer's quarter, the Court of Small Causes, the Campbell Hospital, and the diversion line of the Municipal tramway to Dhappa and even beyond to Mowlalli Durga, the Ditch is entirely filled up; and again to the south as far as the St James Church is greatly filled up for the construction of the Municipal tramway. In this section commences the series of suburban main drains (nine in number) which used to drain the Ditch leading its water to Dhappa, so that the remnants of it may easily be obliterated , and the drains, where needed, joined with these main drains. Towards Baniapooker and the new cemetery,[7] the state of the drain is very much the same as above, and it is not till we pass to the south of Kurryah road in Ward No IV Suburbs that a drain of some size is met with. Here are situated the heads of two fine main drains, No 5 and 6, so that the obliteration of the bits of the Ditch, which is so desirable, will be a matter of comparative ease. The Ditch follows the Circular road as far as the southern end of Chowringhee road, and then turning south by the Russapugla road crosses Porabazar and the Peepulputty road, and following this latter road for some distance, and passing through the north of Kansareeparrah, turns out at the side of the Bhowanipore road, and finally joins the Tolly's Nullah below Alipore bridge. The drain is of considerable size at Bhowanipore, the top width in places being as wide as 50 feet and the depth over 10 feet, and is the principal drainage outlet of the place including a number of large Government buildings

> to wit the General Hospital, both the European and Native Lunatic Asylums, the Garrison Hospital, the Mauritius Cooley Depot, and the Military Cemetery. The sluice at its end being defective it is liable to tidal inundations, the water in the spring tides running into the town as far back as the Circular road.

The report added that the ditch could be divided into two parts, the northern and the southern. The northern section, 'to the Sealdah Railway compound … in its present contracted and defective state [served] as an important outlet, carrying the drainage partially to the Circular Canal and partially to the sewer under the Circular road and its branches'. The report said the drain at the time was 'both insanitary and defective as a carrying channel' and stood in need of improvement. In the southern section, 'except the portion by the side of southern Circular road and in Bhowanipore, the greater part of the ditch is either filled up or stands as a disconnected open channel serving little or no useful purpose, the speedy obliteration of which is a matter of urgency'. Banerjee felt that

> … the drainage of the Government buildings described in the latter part of his note, and especially that of the large military cemetery, should be cut off from the ditch, and the drain adjoining it, and connected with the sewer under the Esplanade without delay, for the sewage running out of the *pucca* drains in these holdings, which are no longer under municipal jurisdiction, not only foul this huge open drain, but defile the water of the Tolly's Nullah, which is so extensively used for bathing and drinking purposes.

He suggested that 'a good sluice should be provided at the junction of the ditch with the nullah, to prevent the ingress of the tidal water'.

Banerjee's report focused on the state of the Maratha ditch in the mid-1880s and its precise path on the northern, eastern and southern fringes of the city. The ditch separated the area under the jurisdiction of the Calcutta Corporation and the Suburban

Municipality. But was it a no-man's land, or did it fall under the control of one of the two municipal bodies whose jurisdictions it separated? This was a contentious issue which was brought out into the open by reports that the municipality had sold a part of the ditch to a private party, the Watson Press Company Limited, around July 1883.[8] The then collector of the 24-Parganas, C.C. Stevens, drew the attention of the Commissioner of the Presidency Division, J. Monro, to the sale, in the process quoting from a letter written to him by the acting secretary to the Calcutta Corporation which claimed that the ditch

> ... was public and not Government property, and that since the [publication] of the Government notification of 10th September 1877 it had been in the [unquestioned] possession of the Corporation, who had recently sold a portion of the drain to Watson's Press Company, it being no longer required as an open drain.

Stevens differed and wrote to Harrison that the ditch 'was Government and not public property, and that it was [treated] in all plans of the Panchannogram estate as such, and that the Government [was in enjoyment] of rent of all silted up portions of it'. He then quoted chapter and verse to argue that the ditch fell within the jurisdiction of the Suburban Municipality. He said that

> ... under Section 3 of the Calcutta Municipal Act IV, 1876, the town included all places within the local limits of the ... Original Civil Jurisdiction of the High Court, and that under Section 11 of the Letters of Patent, dated 14th May 1862, these limits were those defined in the proclamation issued by the Governor-General in Council on 10th September 1794 (see above).

The Collector said that the posts and markers mentioned in the 1794 proclamation being no longer in existence, a reading of the proclamation would reveal that 'the boundary on the land side lay along the inner edge of the Mahratta ditch, which shows the ditch itself outside the limits of Calcutta'. He also referred to the expenditure for maintenance which was borne by the corporation, his point being that since no demand was made on this score to the Government no contribution was forthcoming, adding that if the corporation 'claims jurisdiction over the drain, it was its clear duty to maintain it'. Stevens further argued that even if the ditch was considered to be within the precincts of the town, 'it by no means follows that the land over which the drain runs becomes the property of the Municipal Commissioners as soon as it ceases to exist as an open drain'.

Finally, the Collector brought up the issue of heritage when he said that the sale of a part of the ditch to a private company would lead to 'the permanent obliteration and removal of a land mark of great historical importance'. He made one last point, namely, that if the drain in that portion of the ditch had ceased to exist, thus yielding land which was sold to the private company in question, 'it might have been amalgamated with the existing roadway leading to the river to the great advantage of the public. As it often happens in Calcutta, when an open drain has been altered into an underground sewer, the surface is converted into a road or pathway'.

Writing to the Bengal Government on 27 August 1883, Harrison said that since 1877 the corporation had acted under the belief that 'it was the intention of the Government to transfer the Mahratta ditch to the Calcutta Corporation', and that it was on this understanding that it had gone ahead and incurred 'heavy expenditure with reference to the ditch, entered into arrangements with the Port Commissioners and the Suburban Municipality on the faith of this supposed transfer, and [that] not one of its acts has ever been challenged until the Collector did so the other day'. According to its chairman, the corporation had nothing to do with the ditch 'except that portion which intervenes between Halsee Bagan and Circular Road', as the 'original civil jurisdiction of the High Court runs along the southern and western boundary of that ditch in all places except that specified'. Prior to 10 September 1877 the Suburban Municipality looked after the Circular Road and the Maratha ditch. When the notification was issued the vice-chairman of the Suburban Municipality asked the Calcutta Corporation (on 22 December 1877) 'to take charge of the drain [the Ditch] and keep it in proper order'.[9]

As regards the argument that even if the ditch was considered to be within the municipal limits of the town the Government's right to hold the land could not be interfered with, Harrison said:

> By Section 215 of the Municipal Act all public drains and all drains alongside the public streets, whether made at the cost of the Commissioners or otherwise, shall become vested in the Commissioners. The Mahratta ditch is a public ditch running alongside a public road, and that portion of it which subtends the northern part of Halsee Bagan is unquestionably municipal property. If the remainder of the ditch is transferred to the jurisdiction of the town, as a matter of course it is also vested in the Commissioners. On what other possible ground, it may be asked, should the Commissioners maintain or be called upon by the suburbs to maintain it?

On the antiquarian issue, Harrison had two points to make. First, the part of the ditch where the plot in question was sold to the private company had 'already been obliterated'[10] and, secondly, in an area where land had become so valuable, 'as the north corner of the town, it would be unreasonable on sentimental grounds to maintain the Ditch as a ditch'. However, the chairman said that if, along the rest of the course of the ditch, the Government 'considered on historical grounds it should be maintained as a ditch, the Commissioners would be open to any proposals which may be made with that object'.

The Advocate-General, G.C. Paul, ruled against Harrison. He said that the portion of the ditch in question 'was not vested in the Corporation of the town of Calcutta; that it lay out of Calcutta;

and that it was not their property, which they could sell'. Paul felt that before selling the plot to the private firm the corporation should have informed the Government. As for the future course of action, the advocate-general held that the Government could file a suit of ejectment for the recovery of the plot sold to Watson Press Company. However, he also advised that 'if no special object is to be attained by regaining possession, the Government might come to a reasonable arrangement with the parties with a view to confirm the sale'.[11] On 25 February 1884 the Government informed the corporation of the Lieutenant-Governor's view which was that a notification should be published in the Calcutta Gazette 'including the Ditch (which would be expressly declared to be Government property) within the municipal boundaries of Calcutta, and then lease it to the Commissioners on an annual pepper-corn rental'. This would enable the Lieutenant-Governor 'to confirm the sale of the part of the Ditch ... to Watson's Press Company on the same terms as that Company have arranged with the Corporation'.[12]

Notes

1 Calcutta Committee of Revenue Proceedings, 5 March 1778. The reference to 'high banks' suggests that the ditch was deep in some places, which gives us some idea of the nature of the town's defence arrangement planned and executed by the natives in the 1740s.

2 Calcutta Committee of Revenue Proceedings, 21 May 1778.

3 Municipal Municipal Proceedings, December 1886, File 14B 111-145 (West Bengal State Archives).

4 The encroachments had begun some years back as indicated by at least one case officially recorded (Calcutta Committee of Revenue Proceedings, 30 April 1779). The Proceedings contain a report by the jarib amin who said he had measured the ground of Mr M. Cossly by the side of the ditch and had found that it contained five kathas more than the seven bighas eleven kathas 'set down to him'. The report said that at the time of the 1774 measurement of the town 'an encrease was made of 1 begah 4 ½ cottahs upon the said 7 begahs 11 cottahs' regarding Cossly's ground which, the official explained, 'was made by annexing the Company's ditch adjoining to the premises'. However,

in course of time this extra land, barring five kathas, was 'inducted in the tallook of Rajah Nobkissen', and thereby hangs another tale. Ordinarily, one would have expected that *all* the land encroached upon would be returned by Cossly which was, however, not the case, the committee ordering that the surplus in terms of the 1774 measurement 'be deducted, and that a new pottah be made out for the amount *actually possessed,* being 7 begahs 16 cottahs'. Was this 'M Cossly' the Martin Costelly who was involved with the settlement's powder works in 1760? (Wilson, *Old Fort William*, vol. 2, pp. 155–156).

5 Municipal Municipal Proceedings, December 1886, File 14B 111-145.

6 The ditch, therefore, did not have a uniform slope throughout its course.

7 The Circular Road Cemetery.

8 Municipal Municipal Proceedings, December 1886, File 14B 111-145.

9 Ibid.

10 Writing to the Government on 10 January 1884, Harrison once again laid emphasis on the point that the aspect of historical interest could in no way be applied to that portion of the ditch where the sale had taken place. He wrote: 'The portion of the Mahratta ditch lying along the north of Calcutta has long since been obliterated in many places, and some years ago a portion of it was converted into a public footpath after being filled up, which remained in the possession of the Town Corporation. This portion of the ditch ceased to be used as a drain when the ditch to the east of Calcutta was provided with a separate outlet into the canal.'

11 Municipal Municipal Proceedings, December 1886, File 14B 111-145.

12 Bidisha Chakraborty and Sarmistha De, *Select Documents on Calcutta, 1800-1900*, p. 61.

SECTION THREE

A Time for Planning

22

The Stage is Set

On 29 January 1794, three months after taking over the reins of the Governor-Generalship, John Shore wrote to his wife who was on her way to join her husband in Calcutta:

> The cornice on one side of my bedroom, which is composed of solid masonry, fell down three days ago, and would have destroyed an elephant if it had been under it. About six weeks ago, I used to sit in that room, and very near to the spot where the rubbish fell.[1]

This was the state of Buckingham House built in the early 1760s, which was the residence of the Governors-General of India ever since Warren Hastings chose to stay in it after the Bengal Council leased it from its owner Mohammad Reza Khan, the nawab of Chitpur.[2] This was the house which was to host Shore's successor, Richard Colley Wellesley, the Earl of Mornington after his arrival in Calcutta in May 1798. However, the new Governor-General wasted no time. He took a look at the house and decided to build a palace for himself. What precisely led Wellesley to take the decision is not known but some years later Lord Valentia, writing about his travels to the East, lifted the veil on the subject when he wrote:[3]

> The sums expended on it [the new Government House] have been considered as extravagant by those who carry European ideas and

> European economy into Asia; but they ought to remember, that India is a country of splendour, of extravagance and of outward appearances: that the Head of a mighty Empire ought to conform himself to the prejudices of the country he rules over; and that the British, in particular, ought to emulate the splendid works of the Princes of the House of Timour, lest it should be supposed that we merit the reproach which our great rivals, the French, have ever cast upon us, of being alone influenced by a sordid, mercantile spirit. In short, I wish India to be ruled from a palace, not from a counting-house; with the ideas of a Prince, not with those of a retail-deaqler in muslins and indigo.

Wellesley built the new Government House—the present-day Raj Bhavan—on the spot where Buckingham House and the neighbouring Council House (to the west of it) stood, and in record time too, keeping the entire exercise away from the Court of Directors in London till it was too late for the latter to intervene and stop the building's construction.

41 Lord Wellesley

This is a fascinating story of a strong-willed Governor-General having his way with his employers which later led to charges being levelled against him of insubordination and wasting the East India Company's resources at a time when, according to the Court, funds were tight.[4] But what is of more interest to us is not so much why the new Governor-General wanted to have a splendid mansion built for himself and, to begin with, senior members of his Government, including their offices, but whether the initiative he had taken with regard to his own residence was merely the first step towards sweeping clean the 'mess' that was the town of Calcutta at the time he arrived and building one of a different sort. This is a thread difficult to follow through the huge mass of official correspondence, a cursory reading of the relevant records suggesting that while the Governor-General was bent on altering the situation, his chosen path was to take cover behind the idea that his Government was working on a plan to reduce 'the charges incurred by the Company for public buildings, which will be hereafter reported to you [London]'. This deliberate focus on economy on the part of Wellesley was the result of the Court's constant emphasis on the need for the Bengal Council to reduce expenses on buildings, military and civil.[5]

Wellesley's new Government House was completed by January 1803.[6] During this time he had had occasion to look around and see the 'un-English' state the town was in, not merely the areas inhabited by the natives but also those where the Europeans lived. He had already taken a handful of measures which had marked him out as someone who was more at ease with taking substantive steps to remedy a failing instead of tinkering about with a problem. Take the subject of ships carrying gunpowder up the river which on occasion had made things rather hot for the unsuspecting people of the town, which in turn led to the setting up of the 'powder mills'. On 20 August 1800 an American ship, the *Bedford*, while firing a salute to Fort William, sent one of its cannon balls hurtling into the town which, fortunately did not result in any fatality. Following the occurrence of a similar incident involving another American ship, the new Governor-General ordered a probe into the whole business of ships carrying gunpowder up the river with the result that a temporary 'powder depository' was set up at Achipur. Every vessel passing the spot had to 'put on shore at that place the whole of the gunpowder which they may have on board, as well as the powder in barrels, as also what may have been made up into ammunition above the quantity of fifty pounds'. Different regulations were drawn up for vessels going to Serampore, the Dutch enclave. These steps finally led to regulations being drawn up for the manufacture and possession of gunpowder within the limits of Calcutta. The permanent 'gunpowder magazine building' was built at Mayapur, 'almost a mile (below) Achipur', the original spot suggested being Budge Budge.[7]

The improvement of existing roads was another major area which Wellesley tackled, an example being Circular Road. The alignment of this road—known as Baitakhana Road during Wellesley's initial years and earlier—lay along the present-day Acharya Prafulla Chandra Road and Acharya Jagadish Chandra Road stretching from 'Brijoo *Talloa* [Birjee-talao] to Saum Bazar'.[8] The development of this road was among the major projects undertaken by Wellesley in the period immediately following his arrival in Calcutta in 1798 and before the committee for improvement of the town was set up in 1803. The total cost of the road's revamp—it was a 'revamp' because there is a mention of 'the old road' having had roughly the same alignment—executed between December 1799 and March 1802 was Sicca Rs 1,22,142-3-9. Of interest is the fact that this figure was much higher than it should have been ordinarily because of a concerted official attempt to transfer the exorbitantly high cost of the new Government House to the road.[9] A statement on the work done, submitted by Edward Tiretta and Richard Blechyden to the Government on 14 April 1802,[10] provides rich details of the topography of the area through which it passed. Basically, the road had been widened

> … very considerably in many places, so much so as to increase its median width from 70 ft to 86 ft 6 inches on its whole length of 27,600 ft, or 5 miles 1 furlong 180 yards, and have raised it on a mean from end to end 4 ft 6 inches above the level of the old road, to procure earth for which purpose we dug 20 tanks and excavated many ditches far to the east.

Of particular interest is the detail that the centre of the road extending to a width of thirty-two ft was pucca, the two sides being made of earth extending around twenty-four ft wide on each side. Two years earlier plans were drawn up to extend the Baitakhana Road northward from Bagbazar to Cossipore,[11] which confirms that it was Wellesley who gave Calcutta its arterial 'circular' thoroughfare extending from Barrackpore in the north to Kidderpur in the south. Such a road would no doubt benefit immensely the growing town, but the suggestion could also be made that the work was also geared to meeting the Governor-General's personal agenda. When Tiretta once met Wellesley to give him a status report on work on the Circular Road, the Governor-General 'had made no complaint but merely asked when he would be able to use the road to go to Barrackpore'.[12]

Another road re-developed in Wellesley's time before the era of integrated urban planning set in was that to Dum Dum and Barasat. This road was probably based on an ancient road to the river Hooghly and to the places of religious worship on its banks, coming down from Murshidabad in the north and touching Barasat and Dum Dum on the way. This was the road used by Shiraj-ud-Daula when he launched his assault on the old Fort William in 1756 and later by Clive to get to his garden house at Barasat. Given the growing importance of the road with the expansion of the English settlement on the banks of the river, it was only a matter of time before the sahibs got down to rebuilding it. The records tell us that this work was begun in February 1785 and completed by July the same year, a warning being issued about the need to keep the road in constant repair. Lieutenant W. Blundell, who oversaw the construction work, wrote to the Commander-in-Chief, Lt.-Gen. Sloper, on 8 March 1786:

> The road is now completely finished to Baraset, but such is the violence of the rainy season and so much is the road frequented that if it is not kept in constant repair, a few years will be sufficient to destroy all the good effects that may be produced from the labour and treasure that has been expended on it.[13]

In Wellesley's time the first shot was fired in October 1802 by the secretary to the Military Board who wrote to the Government that 'the public interest, both in civil and military points of view, will be considerably promoted by the construction of a good and permanent road to Dum Dum and Baraset'.[14] The Governor-General in Council agreed, describing the thoroughfare as being 'the principal and the most frequented road leading from the interior of the country to the town of Calcutta, and [also] that by which the chief part of the merchandise and the various supplies of necessary consumption, which are brought into Calcutta, are conveyed'. Richard Blechynden, the surveyor to the town's magistrates, found that the main problem with the road was that it was too low with the result that it was flooded 'at certain points every spring tide which soon ... [formed] large chasms ... and rendered the usual repair more difficult every succeeding year'.[15] Providing us with some idea of how quickly such repairs were carried out in the early days, especially when there was pressure from the military to move troops and equipment, Blechynden said that the repairs, to be carried out over roughly 21,760 ft of road, would take 'from 20 to 25 days', a schedule which he was able to stick to.[16] It was characteristic of Wellesley's style of functioning that he effected a major change in the superintendence and maintenance of the road by shifting the responsibility to the magistrates of the town from the Military Board, the reason cited being propriety ('deems it to be proper').[17]

A third existing road re-developed by the Governor-General into a brand new one was the arterial avenue from Calcutta to

Barrackpore where he was building for himself a new house for 'rest and recreation'. Incidentally, the house was never completed; on the contrary, Wellesley's grandiose plans for it were drastically pruned by his *pro tem* successor George Hilaro Barlow.[18] Begun in 1803 the new road was completed in the latter half of 1805, which means that this also was one of the projects which the Governor-General initiated on his own before issuing his Minute. As far as this road is concerned, Wellesley's initiative can be explained by the fact that, in his mind, the road was closely linked to the building of his retreat on the river bank, a project on which he had decided very early during his tenure.[19] Since, in a manner of speaking, this was Wellesley's personal project, it would have been understandable if he had bulldozed his way through obstacles like acquiring land and payment of compensation which were bound to litter the path of implementation. But this was not what actually happened. Admittedly, there were avoidable problems such as a delay in the payment of compensation which could be traced either to lethargic behaviour on the part of one collector of the 24-Parganas or to inter-personal problems between him and his predecessor. But far more important was the general approach adopted towards the issue of compensation which, as the records show, was marked by considerations of equity and fairness, with even future revenue remissions being allowed to cultivators to compensate them for the disruption they would have had to face in their farming operations.[20] It was inevitable that, despite the Governor-General being a man in a hurry, this would lead to a slower pace of implementation than expected. Within five years of its construction, however, the new road to Barrackpore had come under the scanner, adverse comments being made on it at the official level, even suggesting that it was too wide given the uses it could ever be put to.

On 20 December 1809 Richard Blechynden had informed the magistrates that he had surveyed the Barrackpore Road and had found 'the greatest part of it between Calcutta and the road to Tittaghur in a bad state'. Elucidating, he said:

> The *pucka* part of the road is in breadth 27 feet. Of these 12 to 16 feet of the centre part have been worn away by carriages constantly driving in the middle of the road. The ruts and hollows thus made by the wheels have formed receptacles for the water during the rains which, by softening the ground under the bricks, has occasioned many holes.

He suggested that, as the road had been particularly damaged 'from persons constantly using the centre of it', the magistrates should be

> … empowered to issue orders for all carriages to keep on their left of the road (which is their proper side). This will prevent accidents in the dark and wear the road more gradually so that the centre will always be the highest part, and aid the draining off of the rain.

Perhaps, the damage to the centre of the road was the doing of the Government itself. Four years earlier, in July 1805, the police office had specifically asked travellers to be careful when using the new road so that they did not 'injure the young trees planted on the side of the road'. Travellers, 'whether on horseback, foot, or in carriages', were required to keep to 'the central or brick part of the road, and not to pass through the side avenues'.[21]

The outbreak of fires was a scourge reflecting, among other things, the disorganised state of the town. They broke out with clockwork regularity especially in the native parts where straw huts abounded. Another severe problem was the flooding of large parts of the town during the rains and with the ebb and flow of the tide in the river. Given Wellesley's penchant for thinking big, he responded to these daily occurrences not by getting into a huddle with his officials and devising discrete ways of dousing the fires and easing the flooding but by contemplating remedies which were holistic and long-term in nature. These steps would have the effect of initiating a major break with the past as far as drainage, road building and a general cleaning up of the town was concerned. His June 1803 Minute on Calcutta's improvement, the first serious effort ever made to inject an element of planning for the town's development, should be seen in this perspective.

Wellesley wrote:[22]

> The increasing extent and population of Calcutta, the capital of the British Empire in India and the seat of the Supreme Authority, requires the serious attention of Government. It is now become absolutely necessary to provide permanent means of promoting the health, the comfort, and the convenience of the numerous inhabitants of this great town.
>
> The construction of the public drains and water courses of the town is extremely defective. The drains and water courses in their present state neither answer the purpose of cleansing the town, nor of discharging the annual inundations occasioned by the rise of the river, or by the excessive fall of rain during the south west monsoon. During the last week a great part of this town has remained under water, and the drains have been so offensive that unless early measures be adopted for the purpose of improving their construction, the health of the inhabitants of Calcutta, both European and native, must be seriously affected.
>
> The defects of the climate of Calcutta during the latter part of the rainy season may indeed be ascribed in a great measure to the state of the drains and water courses, and to the stagnate water remaining in the town and its vicinity.
>
> The health of the town would certainly be considerably improved by an improvement of the mode of draining and cleansing the streets, roads, and esplanade. An opinion is generally entertained that an original error has been committed in draining the town towards the river Hooghly. And it is believed that the level of the country inclines towards the Salt Water Lake and consequently that the principal channels of public drains and water courses ought to be conducted in that direction.
>
> Experience has manifested that during the rainy season, when the river has attained its utmost height, the present drains become useless; at that season the rain continues to stagnate for many weeks in every

part of the town, and the result necessarily endangers the lives of all Europeans residing in the Town and greatly affects our native subjects.

Other points connected with the preservation of the health of the inhabitants of this capital appear also to require immediate notice. No general regulations at present exist with respect to the situation of the public markets, or of the places appropriated to the slaughter of cattle, the exposure of meat, or the burial of the dead. Places destined to these purposes must necessarily increase in number with the increasing population of Calcutta. They must be nuisances wherever they may be situated and it becomes an important branch of the police to confine all such nuisances to the situations wherein they may prove least injurious, and least offensive. It must however have been generally remarked that places of burial have been established in situations wherein they must prove both injurious and offensive; and bazars, slaughter houses, and markets of meat now exist in the most frequented parts of the town.

In those quarters of the town occupied principally by the native inhabitants, the houses have been built without order or regularity, and the streets and lanes have been formed without attention to the health, convenience, or safety of the inhabitants. The frequency of fires (by which many valuable lives have been annually lost and property to a great extent has been destroyed) must be chiefly ascribed to this cause.

It is the primary duty of Government to provide for the health, safety, and convenience of the inhabitants of this great Town, by establishing a comprehensive system for the improvement of the Roads, Streets, Publick Drains, and water-courses, and by fixing permanent rules for the construction, and distribution of the Houses, and Publick Edifices, and for the regulation of nuisances of every description.

The appearance and beauty of the Town are inseparably connected with the health, safety, and convenience of the inhabitants; and every improvement which shall introduce a greater degree of order, symmetry, and magnificence in the Streets, Roads, Ghats, and Wharfs, Publick Edifices, and Private Habitations, will tend to ameliorate the climate, and to secure and promote every object of a just and salutary system of Police.

Being aware of the fact that the new focus on the need to improve living conditions in the town could be construed as criticism of the past work done by the town magistrates, whose job it was to look after the town generally, the Governor-General made it a point to refer specifically to the contribution made by these officials to town management. As noted earlier,[23] Blechynden's diary tells us that the magistrates were a particularly corrupt lot, their tentacles in the business of making illicit pecuniary gains spreading throughout the executive administrative system. Among other things, this had an adverse impact on the level of efficiency in the performance of their official duties which, it is safe to assume, was known to the higher echelons of Government not excluding the Governor-General. Even so, in the interests of maintaining bureaucratic propriety, Wellesley wrote that the observations he had made were 'entirely compatible with a due sense of the activity, diligence and ability of the present Magistrates of Calcutta, by whose exertions considerable improvements have been made in the general police of the town'. He pointed out that the Governor-General in Council had 'frequently expressed his approbation of the conduct and services of the present Magistrates of Calcutta, who have zealously and judiciously employed every effort within their power to mitigate the effects of the evils described in this minute'. But what was being projected for the future was something entirely different from what had been done till then by the officials in the normal course of their duties. It was a job which required indispensably 'the establishment of a more comprehensive system of permanent regulation … for the purpose of securing to the town the full benefit of the laudable services of the officers to whom the administration of the police has been entrusted by Government'.

Wellesley was aware the magistrates would not be comfortable with the new arrangement which would require the services of a different set of people, which may be one reason why he included them in the new team which he set up 'to consider and report to his Excellency in Council the means of improving the town of Calcutta'.

Along with the 'Justices of the Peace for the town of Calcutta' (the magistrates), namely, C.F. Martyn, W.C. Blaquiere, E. Thoroton and A. Macklew, as also Richard Blechynden, the surveyor who was in effect the executive arm of the town magistrates, the Governor-General appointed the following persons to the new committee: Major-General Fraser, Major General W.N. Cameron, Peter Speke, Thomas Graham, W.A. Brooke, John Taylor, R.C. Birch, Colonel James Pringle, Samuel Davis, George Dowdeswell (Superintendent of Police), Lt Col. Harcourt, Captain Merrick Shawe, Lt Col. John Garstin, Henry St George Tucker, William Fairlie, Alexander Colvin, David Ross, James Alexander, R.H. Colebrooke, Captain Charles Wyatt, Thomas Dashwood, Captain Thomas Anbury, Captain Thomas Preston, Captain James T. Blunt of Engineers and Captain B. Sydenham. Blunt was appointed secretary and Edward Tiretta was asked to attend the committee's meetings.[24]

Wellesley set a clear agenda for his team:[25]

> 1. To take the level of the town of Calcutta and the adjacent country and ascertain and report what alteration may be necessary in the direction of the public drains and water courses.
> 2. To examine the relative level of the river during the rainy season compared with the level of the drains and water courses.
> 3. To suggest what description of drains or water courses may be best calculated 1st to prevent the stagnation of rain water in Calcutta and the vicinity thereof, and 2ndly to cleanse the town.
> 4. To consider and report what establishment may be necessary for cleansing the drains and water courses and for keeping them in constant repair.
> 5. To take into consideration the present state of all places of interment in the vicinity of Calcutta, and to propose an arrangement for the future regulation of those places in such manner as shall appear to be best calculated for the preservation of the health of the inhabitants of Calcutta and its vicinity.
> 6. To examine the present state and condition of the bazars and markets for meat, and of the slaughter houses in Calcutta, and to propose such

> rules and orders as shall appear to the Committee to be proper for the regulation of those already established, for the removal of such as may have actually become nuisances, and for the establishment of new markets or slaughter houses hereafter.
> 7. To enquire into all existing nuisances in the town and vicinity of Calcutta and to propose the means of removing them.
> 8. To examine and report for the consideration of Government the situations best calculated for opening new streets and roads, leading from east to west, from the new circular road to Chowringhee, and to the river, and from north to south, in a direction nearly parallel with the new road.
> 9. To suggest such other plans and regulations as shall appear to the Committee to be calculated to promote the health, convenience and comfort of the inhabitants of Calcutta, and to improve the appearance of the town and its vicinity.
> 10. To form and submit to the Governor General in Council an estimate of the expense required to complete all such improvements as may be proposed by the Committee.

Wellesley knew that the availability of funds would pose a challenge, especially in view of the fact that the Court of Directors was already on the warpath regarding, among other things, the scale of expenditure incurred by him on aspects of governance not least of which was the expenditure on his two palaces, one already completed in Calcutta and the other at Barrackpore which he was about to build.[26] He, therefore, gave top priority to this aspect, stating that, 'The means for raising the necessary funds, for the purpose of defraying the expense, which must attend the execution of the important improvements suggested in this Minute, will claim the early, and deliberate, consideration of Government'. Since the Directors in London would no doubt read the Minute within a few months, he included the palliative that he had 'no doubt that those funds may be raised without subjecting the Honourable Company to any considerable expense, and without imposing a heavy tax on the inhabitants of Calcutta'. It would of course be 'the duty of Government to contribute, in a just proportion, to any expense which may be requisite for the purpose of completing the improvements of the town'.[27]

The Court's response[28] to the initiative was diplomatic but firm in its emphasis that the Company's resources had to be used judiciously. It said it was happy that 'our Government should take the lead in encouraging any measures tending to promote the health and convenience of the inhabitants of Calcutta, and therefore approve of the appointment of a Committee to consider of the best means of attaining this objective'. But it also added the hope that the Government would not find it difficult to raise the funds from 'the inhabitants of the town, which you represent to have greatly increased in population and opulence'.

In fact, the Court had already crossed swords with the Governor-General on the subject of watering the roads. In the same letter in which the Governor-General had intimated the Court of the appointment of the committee for improving the town,[29] he had sent it an expenditure estimate on watering the roads totalling Rs 12,182-13-11. In that despatch, Wellesley had focused on the indispensability of this activity given the menace of the swirling clouds of dust afflicting the denizens of the town. The letter said:

> Besides other inconveniences experienced by the inhabitants of the town of Calcutta, they are greatly incommoded by the dust during the dry season, and particularly from the commencement of the south-east monsoon until the beginning of the rains. This serious inconvenience, which necessarily increases with the increasing population and opulence of the town, is occasioned by the heated state of the atmosphere during those months and by the nature of the materials of which the public roads are constructed. It accordingly became extremely desirable with a view to the comfort and health of the inhabitants to obviate this inconvenience by watering the roads, the only remedy which it appeared to be practicable to apply.

Wellesley then let the Court know of the change he had affected in the superintendence of that activity. He said that the watering was originally conducted 'under the directions of an officer of the Corps of Engineers', that is, by the military department, but he 'subsequently judged it to be advisable to transfer the superintendence of that duty to the Justices of the Peace for the town of Calcutta'.[30]

The differences on the road-watering issue festered for the next five years. In 1808, in response to the Governor-General in Council's intimation that Rs 12,585 had been spent on such activity, the Court wrote:[31]

> We have already stated our opinion that the Company ought not to be exclusively charged with this expense; and although we are sensible that the majority of the natives may not be brought voluntarily to contribute towards it, and that no legal authority exists in the Governor-General in Council for raising funds to answer such a purpose, yet we are decidedly of opinion that all the European inhabitants of the town as well as the more substantial of the Asiatic inhabitants of every description ought to contribute by an agreed rate proportioned to their circumstances, or by voluntary subscription (as is not unusual in other large cities), to an expense by which the health and comfort of all the population of the place are promoted.

The Court then directed that in future the roads were not to be watered 'at the expense of the Company'.

The thrust of the Court's view was derived from its belief that it did not 'understand it to be the practice of any Government to incur the whole expense of public improvements'. Thus, when on 7 February 1807 the Governor-General in Council had informed the Court regarding an expenditure of Rs 7,200 on 'repairing the railing on the esplanade' and Rs 5,112 on 'building a wall round the Reservoir',[32] the Court in its reply chose to view both the activities as being 'essentially necessary to the health of the Community', and therefore agreed to the expenditure 'from the public treasury'.

However, it added that it was 'always desirous that legislative authority may be obtained for raising a local revenue applicable to the improvement of the town of Calcutta', meaning that taxes should be levied for the purpose.

The Court's mind on the subject of the Government footing the bill for roads and bridges is clearly revealed in its reply to the Governor-General in Council regarding the latter's intimation (in its 7 February 1807 letter) on 'several sums [being] authorised to be disbursed for the construction of roads and bridges'. The Court wrote:[33]

> The state of the public roads is no doubt an object entitled to the attention of Government and formerly, when the inhabitants of the territory we now possess were taxed without limitation, it would not have appeared unreasonable that the ruler should have been charged with all the expenses incurred for the internal convenience of the community as well as for the public service of the State. But now that the subjects of our possessions are taxed by fixed and known rules, and all beyond is the assured property of the people who thus enjoy the advantages that flow from being secured in the fruits of their industry, internal convenience and improvements ought to be at least in part defrayed by them.

The Court said it was not prepared to say that the time had come 'for general application of this principle'. But the time had certainly not yet come to admit that

> ... under the great change introduced by granting a perpetuity of land tenures at fixed assessments, the Government is forever to be subjected to all those local expenses before defrayed by it. And, indeed, this is so far from being an idea originating only in the practice of European States that Mr [James] Wintle, the 3rd Judge of the Calcutta Court of Circuit, in his report under date the 4th September, 1806, expressly states that even under the ancient constitution of Bengal the landholders were by their engagements bound to keep the public roads

> in repair, whence Mr Wintle has actually proposed the levying of a tax for this purpose.

The Court maintained that its Government had not adopted Wintle's suggestion 'perhaps conceiving that such an imposition might have been considered by the landholders as an addition to their jumma, and, therefore, a breach of the condition of the permanent settlement'. It, however, thought it reasonable for the Governor-General in Council to

> ... [direct its attention] to objects of this nature, particularly to the one in question, for as the benefits derived by the community, particularly in a commercial view from [the] facility of intercourse with distant points of the country, are not less than those afforded to the State, it is but fair that they should contribute a proportion of the expence.

By the middle of 1805 Wellesley's project to improve the town had been suspended. In a terse communication to the Court in October of that year the Governor-General in Council wrote: 'In consequence of the present pressure on the finances, the prosecution of the plan for improving the town of Calcutta and its vicinity has been suspended'.[34] Barlow had taken over the Governor-Generalship a week earlier following the death of Cornwallis at Ghazipur on 5 October 1805. Earlier, on 25 July, the Judicial Criminal Proceedings had quoted the Governor-General in Council's observation that circumstances had 'prevented the prosecution of the plan for the improvement of the town of Calcutta'. The sudden development falls into place when it is known that Lord Cornwallis was to take over the mantle of the Governor-Generalship of India for the second time five days later on 30 July. Consequently, Wellesley's 'improper' policies on town planning leading to substantial expenditure on the part of the Bengal Council were considered ripe enough to be sent into hibernation, at least for the time being.

Notes

1 *Memoir of the Life and Correspondence of John Lord Teignmouth*, vol. 1 (London: Hatchard and Son, 1843), p. 283.
2 Ray Choudhury, *The Lord Sahib's House*, p. 68.
3 Valentia, George Viscount, *Voyages and Travels to India, Ceylon, The Red Sea, Abyssinia, and Egypt, in the Years 1802, 1803, 1804, 1805, and 1806*, vol. 1 (London: William Miller), pp. 235–236.
4 Ray Choudhury, *The Lord Sahib's House*, pp. 121–122, 158–175.
5 Ibid., p. 158ff.
6 Ibid., p. 136.
7 Bengal Public Consultations, 16 July and 9 September 1801; India Office Records F/4/134 (British Library).
8 Judicial Criminal Proceedings, 29 April 1802.
9 Robb (*Useful Friendship*, p. 149) writes: 'Wyatt and his master [Wellesley] both knew that, to keep down costs at Government House, its building waste needed to be transferred at a good price to the circular road account … The opportunity for sharp practice and corruption existed partly because materials were scarce. Even with what was being produced at Government House, koa [khoa] ran out for the circular road … The real point, however, was that (as he had promised) Wyatt set a very high price for his materials … Blechynden reminded Tiretta that their estimate had been calculated using bazaar prices, and the amount Wyatt wanted to charge would make the road considerably more expensive.'
10 Judicial Criminal Proceedings, 29 April 1802.
11 Board of Revenue Proceedings, 10 June 1800. See Robb, *Useful Friendship*, pp. 151–156 for a conflict between formal and informal procedures involved in the acquisition of land regarding the extension of the Circular Road northward, specifically the role of Richard Blechynden and the Board of Revenue's 'interference'.
12 Robb, *Useful Friendship*, p. 150. Culling information from the voluminous diary of Blechynden, Robb portrays in fascinating detail the play of diverse human interest and temporal pressures behind the decision to make Circular Road pukka (ibid., pp. 134–141).
13 Governor-General in Council Proceedings, 7 April 1786.
14 Judicial Criminal Proceedings, 14 October 1802.
15 Ibid., 28 October 1802.
16 Ibid., 4 November 1802.
17 Ibid., 14 October 1802.

18 Ray Choudhury, *The Lord Sahib's House*, p. 183.

19 Ibid., pp. 179, 181. Board of Revenue Proceedings, 4 September 1804 and 1 February 1805.

20 Board of Revenue Proceedings, 28 June 1805. In fact, the problems affecting the payment of compensation form a separate field of enquiry throwing light on the principles involved and the methods and efficiency of implementation. Even so, it is instructive to note that despite the Government being a stickler for rules and a great believer in the practice of going by the book, there is at least one recorded instance where deference was shown to the indigo lobby (even in those early days) leading to a part of the old road to Barrackpore being retained (Board of Revenue Proceedings, 28 June and 9 July 1805).

21 Judicial Criminal Proceedings, 29 December 1809. See also Ray Choudhury, *The Lord Sahib's House*, p. 179.

22 Judicial Criminal Proceedings, 14 July 1803. The Minute is dated 16 June 1803. See also *The Asiatic Annual Register* for 1807 (London), Miscellany Section, pp. 10–109 for the text of the Minute.

23 See chapter 'The Jagannath Sarkar Case'.

24 Judicial Criminal Proceedings, 14 July 1803. By July 1805 the committee's membership had undergone a drastic change with some thirteen members dropping out within a year. The total number of members (excluding Tiretta) too had fallen to twenty-five from thirty a year earlier, the new secretary being M.G. Prendergast in place of Blunt.

Tiretta's inclusion as an invitee is somewhat surprising in view of the fact that he was seventy-six years old at the time (Robb, *Sex and Sensibility*, p. 4; Tiretta's date of birth is put at 1726). Perhaps it was because of his experience at the grassroots level in tackling problems associated with the town's infrastructure since the late 1770s that he was asked to proffer advice on practical issues which were bound to crop up in course of the committee's deliberations. It could also have been the result of an appeal for assistance made by Tiretta to the Governor-General two years earlier. On 31 August 1802 he had written to the Governor-General (Judicial Criminal Proceedings, 23 September 1802): 'My Lord, permit me with the greatest submission to trouble your Lordship and to submit to your generous consideration my present situation. It is now 38 years that I constantly reside in Calcutta under the happy protection of the English Government, and … [for] 21 years I have endeavoured to honorably fulfill the laborious duty of my station as Superintendent of the

Roads … etc with the best of capacity. But my age being now so far advanced (very near to 71) I find myself wanting that vigour, strength and activity requisite to support the hard nature of business which oblige me daily to run in the sun. Therefore, though most cordially wishing to retire, I am [at a] loss what step I should take having no fortune, and being a widower with a daughter of six years of age, and a young sister-in-law an orphan now in education in London, which all depend on me. This circumstance induces me to throw myself into your Lordship's generous hands, and if your Lordship is of opinion that my steady services for upwards [of] 21 years deserve a moment of your kind attention, I most humbly request that your Lordship will be so gracious as to take my humble representation into your consideration; and in the meantime I am in the greatest hope that your Lordship's humanity will be propitious to me on this occasion by granting me such relief, as your Lordship's justice and liberality shall think proper, which the utmost gratefulness will make me very happy the remainder of my life, which in all probability shall not extend to a very long period.'

Writing to the Court on 28 February 1803, the Governor-General in Council referred to this appeal, pointing out that in the capacity of being the civil architect he drew a salary of Rs 232 a month 'immediately from Government' and that as 'surveyor of the roads to the Justices of the Peace' he got Rs 700 a month, yielding a total of Rs 932. To this was to be added the salary of Rs 300 a month given to R. Blechynden 'as assistant to the civil architect', making an aggregate of Rs 1,232, which was taken from the fund 'appropriated by Act of Parliament to the cleansing and watching the streets of Calcutta'. The Government wrote that as Blechynden had succeeded to the position of surveyor of the roads on the resignation of Tiretta on a pay of Rs 700 a month and the post of assistant to the civil architect having been abolished, the remaining Rs 532 a month 'out of the abovementioned funds' had been set aside as a monthly pension for Tiretta 'for his life in consideration of his advanced age, which exceeds seventy years, and of the length of time during which he has been employed in the public service' (General Letters to the Court of Directors, 28 February 1803—West Bengal State Archives).

The Court expressed its displeasure at the step taken 'without previous reference to us, being directly contrary to our orders in the Public Department of the 15th April 1795, which direct that all pensions granted by you shall be on the express condition of their being revocable by us should we see cause to disapprove of the same'. However, it chose to make an exception in the case of Tiretta—on the ground that he 'is now far advanced in years, and had been for a long time employed by you as civil architect'—and confirmed the pension (General Letters from the Court of Directors, 20 June 1804—West Bengal State Archives). On Tiretta's retirement and pension, see also Robb, *Sex and Sensibility*, pp. 5, 223 notes 22 and 23.

25 Judicial Criminal Proceedings, 14 July 1803.

26 Ray Choudhury, *The Lord Sahib's House*, p. 176ff.

27 Judicial Criminal Proceedings, 14 July 1803.

28 General Letters from the Court of Directors. Letter to the Governor-General in Council, 28 February 1805 and 25 April 1806.

29 Letter to the Court of Directors, Judicial Series, 30 September 1803 (West Bengal State Archives). Regarding the funding of his town-improvement project, the Governor-General had written that he was 'not at present prepared to state in what manner the funds which may be required for the improvement of the town of Calcutta can be raised'. However, keeping in mind the Court's strong preference to cut down on expenditure, he hastened to add that the measures which would ultimately be taken toward this end would not interfere 'with the other branches of the public expenditure'.

30 Initially, the Justices of the Peace had estimated that the job would entail an expenditure of Sicca Rs 17,888-12, the actual spending, however, coming down to Sicca Rs 12,182-13-11.

31 Letter from the Court of Directors, Judicial Series, 14 September 1808 (West Bengal State Archives).

32 Today's BBD Bagh.

33 Letter from the Court of Directors, Judicial Series, 14 September 1808.

34 Letter to the Court of Directors, Judicial Series, 17 October 1805.

23

A Fire-Fighting Exercise

The Committee for the Improvement of the Town of Calcutta got off to a flying start. It had been formed on 2 July 1804 'to consider and report to Government the means best calculated for improving the town of Calcutta, and particularly for preventing the occurrence of accidents by fire'.[1] Two days later, on 4 July, it provided J. Lumsden, secretary to the Government, with a concrete plan of action.[2] It wrote:

> With the view of carrying into effect the intentions of your Excellency, we judged it to be advisable to select special committees to consider, in the first instance, the different objects of improvement under the following designations: a special committee for surveying those quarters of the town which have been recently burnt down, and preparing a plan for rebuilding the houses in a manner more consistent with the safety, convenience and health of the inhabitants; a special committee for the purpose of considering the most eligible situations for opening new roads, with a view to facilitate the communication between the various parts of the town of Calcutta, and to promote the general intercourse and convenience of the inhabitants; a special committee to consider the most effectual means of draining the town of Calcutta; a special committee for considering the nuisances which exist throughout the town and proposing the best means of removing them; a special committee to consider and report upon such

> improvements in the vicinity of the town as may tend to contribute to the convenience of the inhabitants of the town and neighbourhood of Calcutta; a special committee for the purpose of considering the easiest and most effectual means of raising the funds necessary for carrying the intended improvements into effect.

Six special committees were, therefore, appointed to assist the general committee with the work entrusted to it by the Governor-General. Their reports were submitted by the end of the month (30 July 1804).[3]

Sensing that the Governor-General in Council's immediate interest was to investigate the reason behind the recurrent fires in the town and how the phenomenon could be effectively curbed, the general, or apex, committee was quick to communicate the findings of the special committee set up for the specific purpose to the Government.[4] The first point made was that apart from the climate, which led to 'the easy combustion of such materials as those with which the generality of the native habitations in and about Calcutta are composed', a variety of other causes were responsible for the 'dreadful and destructive conflagrations' that had taken place lately. Drawing a picture of the way natives lived at the time, the special committee said that the most important causes of fire breaking out were 'the contiguity and junction of the houses, the careless and ill-managed use of fire amongst the lower class of natives both in cooking and their favourite habit of smoking'. To this the committee added the 'apathy, disinclination from prejudice, and a superstitious adherence to the doctrine of Destiny' which prevented the people from 'making any exertion or indeed any attempt to arrest the fire in its progress'. On the last point, the special committee said that it had been observed

> ... that when, with the least attempt, a fire might have been subdued by putting down a few of the adjacent huts, they would rather allow it to continue its consuming course than assist even in removing a single

> contiguous *chopper* though it would have preserved that under which they and their whole family were sheltered.

Another reason for the rapid spread of fires were 'the flakes and large portions of lighted straw or grass which are carried to distant parts by the high winds which invariably prevail at that season when fires are most frequent, and where most probably fire would not have occurred but from this cause'.

According to the special committee, the behaviour of the natives was itself another major cause of conflagrations having the impact they did. It wrote that it did not 'appear to be doubted that many of the late fires have proceeded from incendiaries', but whether this was the result of 'private malice with a view to plunder or to cause an increased demand, and consequently an enhanced price, for straw, grass, bamboos, matts and other building materials in the bazar is not perhaps exactly ascertained'. The committee said that people had been apprehended 'on suspicion if not actually detected in the very act' of setting houses on fire. It wrote, 'It is also known that one if not more of the recent fires have commenced in huts where fire had not been in use for many days previous; in such a case a very fair presumption lays that it must have originated from a wilful cause,' the conclusion being that 'where straw huts exist fire must frequently happen'. This, clearly, was a weak reason cited by the special committee because for the fires to have attracted the notice of the highest authorities they must have occurred on a large enough scale; and for people to have set fire to houses on this scale deliberately would be improbable unless anti-social behaviour had become endemic in the town, generally or for specific reasons, of which the records do not contain any evidence. In its letter to the Government, the general committee did not elaborate on the human element but focused instead on suggestions of how best 'to improve the construction of the several quarters of the town which have been lately burnt, and to prevent the destructive effects of fire in those places in future'.[5]

But how could fires resulting from the 'attempts of wilful and malevolent incendiaries' be prevented as also those breaking out from 'accidental causes'? The special committee felt that the first step was to change the materials of which most of the huts were made and that those who had lost their shelter in the recent fires should be asked to rebuild accordingly. But then the committee was aware that implementation would not be smooth. As it said, this was 'regulation that appears not easy, if at all possible, to be enforced as a law, throughout the town, and that the experiment can only be tried in such places where recent fires have destroyed the straw huts originally erected'. The committee laid down the following method of rebuilding: 'walls of mats plaistered with mud, walls of gramstick plaistered with mud, walls of bamboos, split, wattled, plaistered with mud. Mud walls, cutcha brick walls or cutcha pucka walls, and all roofed with tiles'.

There were, however, two points which would make acceptance of the recommendation difficult, namely, the difference in construction cost and the 'loss of comfort' involved when the two systems were compared. While there was little doubt that in hot and humid Calcutta a straw hut was always much cooler than a tiled one, on the cost front it was clear that frequent fires would lead to frequent rebuilding of straw huts which in the end would cost 'considerably more than one originally built of less combustible articles'. As for tiled comfort, the special committee suggested that 'putting matts under the tiles' could render the huts cooler. To add weight to its arguments, the committee said it had been 'proved by existing instances that houses constructed of the materials before mentioned have completely resisted the flames without any appearance of injury'. If, however, it was found impossible to implement the changes suggested in rebuilding the gutted huts, the special committee hinted at the use of force. It said it would then be the responsibility of 'the Government or the police to carry into effect such regulations in rebuilding the houses lately destroyed as may be deemed in some degree useful towards the prevention of fire in future and improvement of the [affected] quarter of the town'.

The special committee felt that 'a most favourable opportunity' had now presented itself for

> ... the opening of two or three principal streets and intersecting them as nearly as possible at right angles by others of a breadth not less than will easily admit of the largest sized fire engine and the people necessary to work it, with room to turn and move it in all directions.

The report said that these streets would

> ... form divisions or cantons easily superintended by a *jemedar* or such other of their officers as the police may think requisite. To each of these an engine may be attached, to be kept in a pucka building at the tanna or guard with a proper proportion of fire hooks, firebills, buckets, and such other implements as are found requisite to stop the progress of fire, with an adequate establishment of firemen or lascars a party of whom should be always on duty at the spot where the engine is kept. From this party, patrols should be furnished and kept moving in all directions throughout the division to report what is going on, and to give the earliest information of fire, [so that] the engine may be run to the spot with the least possible delay, and alarm given to the adjoining division to be prepared by every means to stop its progress in that direction. By these means the fire would in all probability be prevented from extending beyond the division in which it commenced.

In order to render the fire engines properly workable, the report suggested that

> ... in each of these divisions, and as near as may be possible to the road, as many wells as may be found necessary should be dug, of a depth sufficient to afford water during the dry season, or a tank to every two [divisions], so situated as to be equally serviceable to both.

A guard from the engine establishment could be posted 'to prevent the soiling of these tanks and to superintend the use of the water'.

As regards financing of the scheme, the special committee was aware that the cost would be considerable 'and probably beyond what the present assessment is equal to defray'. In view of the projected imbalance, and since the objective of the scheme was 'for the immediate protection and accommodation of the native inhabitants of that part of the town', a higher tax on the houses built in those divisions 'of straw, grass or matts, or a duty on straw, grass and matts sold there, might be levied equal to discharging the additional expence of the establishment proposed'. The general committee ordered 'the substance of this paragraph' to be referred to the special committee dealing with finance.

Despite the fact that the natives were tradition-bound, the special committee felt that those living in the area affected would be persuaded to use the new materials suggested to rebuild their huts. It wrote: 'Traversing that part of the town where the fires have been, it does not appear that any particular aversion exists to tiled buildings, for even in the very course of the fires there are several which still remain unhurt. The cost seems to be the principal obstacle'. As a financial inducement to build the right sort of huts, the committee felt that the grant of 'a remission of assessment, or even an advance of cash of the value of one year or more assessment' could be tried out. The report said that despite the fact that it was 'but a very small proportion indeed of the inhabitants of the quarter bounded by the Durrumtolah, Chowringhee road, the Burying ground road, and the Circular road that have been burnt out', it was nevertheless desirable that 'those who wish to inhabit that quarter again may be induced to conform to the mode of building least likely to cause a return to the calamities that have just happened'.

As regards the plan suggested for the new streets, the special committee felt that it was the

> … least likely of any that could have been pointed out to incur a very heavy expence in purchase of buildings necessary to be pulled down to form the streets, and will facilitate the communication with Chowringhee and Circular roads nearly centrical between the Durromtolah and Burying Ground roads. An intersecting road, also embracing like advantages, has been traversed from nearly opposite the late Mr Bristow's garden [south of Park Street], by the Free School crossing the Jaun Bazar and opening into the Durromtolah nearly opposite the Reverend Brown's.

The line of another street had also been traced

> … still more to the eastward, apparently not likely to incur any very considerable expence in the purchase of property to form it of the breadth required, intersecting the principal road also, and thereby forming nine distinct divisions and throwing that quarter of the town completely open. These divisions also may be subdivided as Government or the police may think requisite.

The area under the special committee's scanner was, therefore, bounded on the east by Circular Road, on the south by Park Street, on the west by Free School Street and on the north by Dharamtala Street. The special committee asked Richard Blechynden, the surveyor, to 'survey and mark the directions in which they conceive the new roads ought to lead', a work which the committee felt would take a fortnight. In the meantime, Blechynden had been asked to forward to the Collector of Calcutta a list 'of the owners of such property as will fall within the lines of the intended roads'.

Along with the views of the special committee on fires and roads, the general committee submitted its own views on the subjects.[6] The document on tackling conflagrations contained much that had already been discussed in the special committee's report. Among the new points made by the general committee was one which suggested that the houses

> ... be constructed in straight lines or as nearly straight as may be practicable, leading from east to west, with streets or passages running in the same direction so as to admit only a double range of houses between each passage, and with other streets and passages running north and south at the distance of 150 or 200 feet from each other.

Secondly, complementing what the special committee had already said about water sources, it suggested that wells and tanks be dug strategically 'in the different wards of the town', and that a fire engine 'be established in the principal wards, or at such other places as shall appear to be most convenient for affording assistance in case of fire'. The apex committee was convinced that these steps would mitigate the impact of fires and that 'the primary object of securing the persons of the inhabitants from injury ... would be completely attained by those means and that the town in general would become more healthy'. That the fires breaking out in the town affected the local people the most and that steps to curb them would help this section of the population greatly was emphasised when the general committee wrote that although fires would still break out even after the preventive steps were put into effect, 'their effects would by no means be so destructive, as at present, to the property of the natives'. This apart, the healthiness of the town would also be improved because of the larger number of tanks, not to speak of the advantage flowing from levelling the ground in some areas with the earth dug out to make the tanks, which would result in better natural drainage.

The general committee recommended a selective approach in implementing the proposals. It said that since the area south of Dharamtala had been affected by the fires, which had led to the destruction of huts and other habitation in the area, the projected improvements be, 'in the first instance, carried into effect in that quarter'. It suggested that the Government buy the land required for opening up streets or passages 'through the different wards in that quarter of the town' and also for digging the wells and tanks, the point being made that the plan could be extended to the entire town later if it met with success in the targeted area. However, the apex committee did not agree with the special committee's view that official encouragement could be extended for huts to be rebuilt with tiled roofs, etc., through the tax-remission route. It argued that the assessment on straw huts was low—'not exceeding in some cases two annas per quarter'—and that, therefore, a remission 'could not operate as any encouragement to the natives to build or occupy houses with tiled instead of thatched roofs, the expense of the former being double that of the latter'. On the other hand, if the tax on houses with thatched roofs was increased compared to houses with tiled roofs, it was felt that people would opt for the latter instead of the former. However, this alternative was not pressed by the general committee perhaps because it did not want those living in houses with thatched roofs to face even greater financial hardship. As far as a 'land tax' was concerned, the general committee felt that the leverage-capacity of such an instrument was limited by the fact (according to the collector of Calcutta) that the amount of the tax on ground 'occupied by all the tiled and straw houses throughout Calcutta is only Sicca Rs 7,346-13-4 per annum'.

As for the opening up of new streets with a view to facilitating 'communication between the different parts of the town, of affording a more free circulation of air in the populous quarters, and finally of improving the drainage of Calcutta', the general committee said that such roads should be made 'from Chowringhee to the new Circular road, and again from the Burying Ground road to the Dhurrumtollah'. It was aware that such openings could not be made without considerable expense to the Government, and that this expense 'would be greatly enhanced in the more populous and wealthy parts of the town'. But it argued that if the measures were considered suitable later the associated expense would be 'heavier' because of 'the increasing wealth and population of Calcutta'. In view of this, it recommended that the ground required for the roads be purchased by the Government and that the roads be opened 'as soon as the necessary compensations shall have been paid to the proprietors of the ground and buildings'. Priority was attached to this project because roads would determine 'the site and arrangement of the wards of the town'. Drainage received a lower priority as also 'laying the roads [probably existing roads] with bricks', both of which could be put off till funds were made available for the projected improvements and if 'those funds shall not be required for objects of more immediate urgency'.

What emerges is that the building of new roads appeared to be the centrepiece of the planned improvements contemplated by those whom Wellesley had appointed to find ways of making Calcutta a better place to live in. Concluding its 4 July 1804 letter to the chief secretary, the Committee for the Improvement of the Town of Calcutta wove in this aspect of town improvement with the official focus on fighting fires by stating that, with the building of new roads, 'there will always be a passage for fire engines to the different wards in that quarter, and this measure will considerably facilitate the other arrangements which we have proposed for extinguishing fires'. Some experimentation would of course be involved here in view of the fact that what was being attempted by way of town-planning had never before been tried out in Company-ruled India. Sensibly, the committee was unsure of the end result. It wrote to the Government that the experience gained in the course of implementing the project would enable it 'to form a more perfect judgement how far that plan of improvement can be extended generally throughout Calcutta'. If no serious problems were encountered in implementation, 'such other roads as it may appear to us advisable [could be opened] in the central and northern parts of the town'.[7]

Notes

1 On the face of it, there is a seeming problem here with the dates. Wellesley had appointed his committee 'to consider and report to his Excellency in Council the means of improving the town of Calcutta' on 16 June 1803 (see previous chapter). The Judicial Criminal

Proceedings of 14 July 1803 tell us that J. Lumsden, secretary to the Government, had informed the committee members of their appointment on 16 June the same year. If this is correct, how could the committee members write to the Government that the latter had appointed them on 2 July 1804 'to constitute … a Committee to consider and report to Government the means best calculated for improving the town of Calcutta, and particularly for preventing the occurrence of accidents by fire', unless of course the first committee had been disbanded and replaced by a new one. If a new committee had in fact been formed, which is probably what occurred, the available records in the West Bengal State Archives are silent on the development. The records do not carry any substantive report on the work done by the 16 June 1803 committee. On the other hand, the 2 July 1804 committee did a lot of work, in the shape of drawing up the reports of the special committees which figure in the present chapter. The membership of the two committees was also different (Judicial Criminal Proceedings, 14 July 1803 and 26 July 1804).

2 Judicial Criminal Proceedings, 26 July 1804.

3 Ibid., 25 July 1805.

4 Ibid. The members of the special committee were Major-General W.N. Cameron, Rev. D. Brown, Capt. T. Anbury, W.C. Blaquiere, J.J.B. Proby and R. Blechynden. The committee had met at General Cameron's quarters in Fort William on 11 June.

5 Judicial Criminal Proceedings, 26 July 1804.

6 Ibid.

7 Ibid. The letter was signed by W.N. Cameron, C. Green, H. Colebrook, G. Dowdeswell, R.H. Colebrook, Thomas Anbury, Thomas Preston, Alexander Russell, Charles Martyn, Edward Thoroton, W.C. Blaquiere, Richard Blechynden and M.G. Prendergast.

24

Private Property on a Pedestal

That Wellesley had a mind of his own and was not willing to rubber-stamp all that was being suggested by the 'experts' is indicated by his Government's response three weeks later (on 24 July 1804) to the general committee's suggestions.[1] The committee, as we have seen in the last chapter, had focused on the area south of Dharamtala, the Government describing as 'judicious' the 'lines which you have proposed for the direction of the new streets intended to lead from the Chowringhee to the Circular Road and from Durrumtollah to the Burying Ground Road'. The authorities felt that the streets be opened up as quickly as possible and that they should be made of 'pucka brick with sufficient drains on each sides'. But before the Committee for the Improvement of the Town of Calcutta went ahead with the implementation the Government pointed to two problems which had to be tackled first, both being of strategic importance.

The first was that relating to the town's overall drainage. It was clear that if the drains to be made on each side of the proposed streets were to be useful they would have to be part of a larger scheme of things. J. Lumsden, the Chief Secretary to the Government, wrote that before the drains for the proposed streets were laid the Governor-General in Council wanted the principle on the best means of draining the town as a whole to be settled. The members of the special committee appointed to go into this subject were, therefore, asked to get on with 'their enquiries ... with all convenient expedition and that their report, with the observations of the general committee, [be placed] for his consideration and orders as soon as may be practicable'. Since Wellesley was a man in a hurry—the Governor-General knew he did not have much time left in India—he suggested that the drainage issue need not hold up the actual laying of the new streets 'as the work to be performed before the drains can be constructed will certainly require a considerable period of time'.

The second strategic point was the protection of private property rights. In the emerging pattern involving the principal streets that were to be constructed according to the plan suggested by the general committee, there were 'quadrangular spaces' where it was proposed that tanks could be dug and small roads made 'in a direction parallel to the great roads at the distance of 150 or 200 feet'. The Government had no problems with the scheme as it appeared on paper. Its main point of concern, however, was that in the course of all this work the property rights of the people of the town should not be tampered with. This aspect of town development was taken so very seriously that the authorities even went to the extent of dubbing the committee's plan to improve the town as 'impracticable', Lumsden writing:

> The ground is the property of different individuals who cannot be compelled to allot their estates for building according to any prescribed plan; and the purchase of the whole, with the houses now standing thereon, would require the expenditure of a sum of money too considerable to admit of any attempt for that purpose.

The Government, therefore, wanted the plan for 'small avenues' dropped, arguing that the most that could be accomplished at the time was the building of the 'proposed great roads from north to south and from east to west, with the digging of tanks and wells in convenient situations in the intermediate spaces between their intersections, and the construction of avenues for the passage of fire engines from the tanks and wells to the great roads'.

Even here the authorities laid stress on the issue of compensation to be given to those private individuals affected by the measure. They maintained without any ambiguity that since the ground for the main roads and the tanks was to be bought by the Government, 'the disposition of the roads and passages which are private property, the allotment of the ground for houses, and the size and situation of the houses must be determined by the convenience, or by the choice, of the proprietors'. After the main roads had been built and the new tanks dug, the chief secretary said that plans for 'further improvement of the intermediate spaces' could be circulated among the 'proprietors of the ground' with the object of putting in place a 'system [which] with the concurrence of the proprietors might greatly improve the health and convenience of the town without injury to the private property or offence [to] the prejudices of the natives'.[2]

Water bodies were to play a big role in the improvement of the town, which explains why the digging of tanks was accorded so high a priority in the scheme of things. There was good reason for this. Lumsden wrote to the committee that 'great advantage' would undoubtedly be derived 'from a sufficient number of tanks [being dug] in proper situations'. One of the advantages would be the availability of adequate water with which to fight the numerous fires that inevitably broke out in localities populated by straw huts. Secondly, there was a surfeit of stagnant pools in the town, a leftover from earlier times when there was no drainage system whatever for the land on which the town stood. On how the 'surfeit of stagnant pools' came to be formed, as noticed earlier (see chapter 6), the Court of Directors had written to the Bengal Council on 4 February 1709:[3] 'We are inform'd the greatest part of the Standing Water thereabouts is occassion'd by the Peoples digging the Earth to make their Houses with and then the next rains the Holes are fill'd with Water which there Stagnates and corrupts'. The digging of tanks was expected to facilitate the filling up of such pools with the earth taken out to make the tanks. The water in the tanks could be used by the people for their daily use, a great part of the sickness prevailing in the town being the result of the population having to rely on water that was anything but clean. The Government felt that the creation of a large number of tanks would increase the responsibility of the police in keeping them clean, which would lead to an improvement in the general public health. While the advantages flowing from the digging of new tanks were apparent, Lumsden wrote that the Governor-General in Council had doubts whether there was in fact a need 'for so many tanks as proposed by [the] committee'. The Government was merely being circumspect when it told the committee that 'the determination of this question as well as the situation and size of the tanks may be postponed until you shall have made further enquiries on the subject and until an estimate of the projected improvement shall have been received'.

The subject of fires breaking out in the town with great frequency had been discussed by the general committee in its 4 July 1804 letter to the Government. In its 24 July response the latter attached great importance to the subject, the point being made that the police would be responsible for operating and maintaining the fire engines 'in each ward'. However, the point was also made that it would be jumping the gun if issues like the number of fire engines required, the size of the staff to be attached to each of them, and their location were to be finalised before the tanks and wells were dug, especially when the subject of tanks would take some time to be given final shape. Without the tanks being functional the fire engines would be useless given 'the impossibility of procuring water [in] the season when fires are most prevalent'.

The general committee had proposed that all the houses destroyed in a recent fire be rebuilt with 'mud or pucka walls with tiled roofs', which would reduce their combustibility. While the technical justification of the scheme was easily acceptable the Governor-

General in Council felt that in all probability 'no encouragement which could be offered to the native inhabitants to adopt this plan of building would suffice to render the plan general'. The further point was made that, even if persuasion was successful, there was no certainty that 'the great majority of them could obtain the means of erecting such houses in the first instance, however economical they might ultimately prove'. There was also the practical side to be considered given the various moods of the Calcutta weather. Lumsden wrote that the straw huts used by natives

> … afford at all seasons of the year more comfortable accommodation than houses having tiled roofs, and it may thence be inferred that the use of the latter would not become general even if the tax on houses and the ground rent were remitted to all who should construct tiled buildings for their residence.

In its infinite wisdom, the Government left it to the natives to rebuild as they felt appropriate the houses destroyed in the recent fires. However, the magistrates of the town were at liberty to recommend 'such an arrangement of the new houses and streets as may be best calculated to ensure the easy extinction of accidental fires, and at the same time may be compatible with their pecuniary circumstances'.[4]

However, as far as the Wellesley Government was concerned, the most important issue was how quickly the projects could be implemented. On 24 July Lumsden asked the Board of Revenue to get in touch with the general committee 'with respect to the quantity of ground which may be required for the purposes [mentioned]' and also take steps for completing

> … as soon as circumstances shall admit of it the purchase of such grounds as may be absolutely necessary for the construction of the proposed streets and avenues, and for the tanks and wells to be dug in that part of the town which is situated to the southward of the Durrumtollah.

The Board was asked to draw up an estimate of the cost to be incurred for purchase of the land required. The task entrusted to the Board of Revenue was not only heavy but unprecedented as well, which led to teething problems at the level of implementation. The task in hand was stupendous and dedicated hands were needed to handle it. The Board wrote to the Government[5] that since it had no assistant who could take on the work relating to the purchase of ground for the new roads planned, 'we should consider the Collector of the 24-Pergunnahs to be the proper officer for carrying into effect your Lordship's orders'. But as the Collector was burdened with a number of other responsibilities, the Board felt he 'might not be employed on the duty in question, if any other officer can be selected'. One must remember that this was the time when the onerous business of paying compensation for ground acquired for the new road to Barrackpore had commenced, an operation which was marred by avoidable delays on the part of the Collector of the 24-Parganas, J.J. Proby, which led to administrative problems later.

Six months passed before the Board of Revenue could respond with a report on 'the estimates of the expense necessary to be incurred for the purpose of improving the town of Calcutta', particularly regarding the purchase of ground required 'for opening new roads from north to south and from east to west'.[6] Around Sicca Rs 1,09,507-8-8 would be needed and most of the landowners concerned had agreed to accept the price set by the authorities. On the land-pricing issue, which was at the heart of the compensation process, Richmond Thackeray,[7] the Board's sub-secretary who had been entrusted with the job, explained that every effort had been made to get at the 'real value of the ground and buildings in general' and that the owners of the ground in question appeared 'satisfied with the compensation offered them although in some instances demands have been made which it was impossible to comply with'. He said that the ground had been valued per katha 'according to its local situation, and every circumstance has been considered which would tend either to increase or depreciate its value'. Focusing on the modus operandi of the valuation process, Thackeray wrote that the buildings standing on these plots had been 'minutely surveyed by able mistries, and appear to be valued with the greatest accuracy'. Where there were differences with the proprietors on the valuation, 'the whole has been resurveyed by other mistries'. Thackeray noted that in some cases, 'with a view to improve their estates', the owners had bought 'small pieces of ground adjacent to their dwellings' at a high price which had not been taken into account. Only the 'real value' had been considered, which was lower than the amount paid for the plots in question. Thackeray suggested that, in the event of the actual purchase of the ground being made, it would 'be necessary to allow them such further remuneration as they may prove themselves entitled to'.

The Board said that where there was disagreement a 'further enquiry' into the issue would be held but that it would be better if the probe was 'postponed until we shall be furnished with the sums requisite to enable us to complete the purchase'. Given the Government's stand on protecting the interests of private property, the Board said that in cases where the landowners expected 'more than what is considered to be the actual value of the land, on the ground of their having actually paid a larger sum for the land, in consequence of it having been of more value to them from contiguity of it to the other lands belonging to them', such proprietors, on their providing proper proof of the associated transactions, were entitled 'to a further indemnification than is proposed in the accompanying estimate'. The procedure of the extra payment was also outlined by the Board, which said that if any landowner disagreed with the official price estimate 'a jury of the inhabitants [would be] summoned for the purpose of assessing the value of ground, and of any buildings situated on it'. In the same 22 January 1805 letter the Board of Revenue suggested to the Government that 'the ground ... on which the public roads at present stand may, we conceive, be disposed of to individuals if not required for any public purpose'. The letter also contained Thackeray's report dated 16 January 1805 on 'the probable expense to be incurred on the purchase of ground for the intended new roads intersecting Chowringhee'.

Notes

1 Board of Revenue Proceedings, 27 July 1804. See also the Lottery Committee Reports which are presently lodged at the Victoria Memorial Hall, Calcutta.
2 Ibid.
3 Wilson, *Old Fort William*, vol. 1, p. 75.
4 Board of Revenue Proceedings, 27 July 1804.
5 Ibid.
6 Board of Revenue, 22 January 1805.
7 The father of William Makepeace Thackeray (C.E. Buckland, *Dictionary of Indian Biography* [London: Swan Sonnenschein and Co., Lim., 1906], p. 419).

25

Funds and Other Projects

The work of the Committee for the Improvement of the Town of Calcutta was suspended at the end of July 1805, but it is due to the foresight of Lord Wellesley that the good work already done was not wasted. The records indicate that following the suspension of the plans to improve the town, the Governor-General in Council thought 'it proper to record the following documents for future reference, if necessary'. These documents comprised the reports of the special committees, and the remarks of the general committee, on funds, the environs of the town, and 'existing nuisances'.[1] Needless to say, the reports are of great value because, among other things, they provide us two centuries down the line with the fullest idea possible of what the growing town of Calcutta was like at the turn of the eighteenth century.

On the subject of funds, the special committee tackling it suggested that the assessment within the town be raised on all houses 'the rent or computed value of which shall exceed one rupee per mensem, from 5 to 7 ½ per cent', which would fetch an extra Rs 50,000. The surplus revenue from Tolly's Nullah could add another Rs 30,000. Around Rs 10,000 could be got from the 'fees of office' collected by the town magistrates, and another Rs 6,000 and Rs 10,000 from the surplus revenue 'arising from the markets within the town of Calcutta and Fort William', and the Court of Requests, respectively. The committee also said that an annual lottery could be established 'for the same purpose under proper management and controls', which would garner Rs 60,000. The total income from the six measures would, according to the committee, be around Sicca Rs 1,65,000.

The general committee's remarks on the suggestions are important because they convey the impression that the scale of the resources computed would be inadequate to finance the scheme. In fact this constraint had prevented it from submitting 'so comprehensive a plan as we could have wished for the purpose, effectually, for the discharge of the expense of the improvements ... we consider to be so essential to the convenience and health of the inhabitants of this populous city'. The committee said that what had specifically prevented it from suggesting additional steps to raise resources was the 'lack of flexibility' in the existing arrangements, mainly the restrictions 'existing by law on raising taxes within the town of Calcutta' for the specific purpose in hand. For example, on the suggested increase in house assessment, the general committee said that under the relevant Act of Parliament (passed in the thirty-third year of George III's reign) there did not appear to be any objection to raising the assessment. The problem, however, lay elsewhere, namely, the uses to which such funds could be put to. It was pointed out that, in the language of the Act, such funds 'must be exclusively applied to the cleansing, watching and repairing of the streets' and that they could not be diverted 'to any other objects of improvement'. Thus, could 'drainage' be included in the activities included in the 'cleansing' of the roads? The committee argued that the Act's precise stipulation ought not to be taken as an impediment to raising funds through the higher-assessment route in view of the fact that 'considerable funds' would be required 'for purposes falling strictly within the intent and meaning of the Act of Parliament, particularly that of improving the present very defective plan of draining the town'.

The special committee had proposed that Rs 60,000 could be gathered from an annual lottery. The general committee's response was that it was aware of the arguments 'universally raised against raising supplies in that way'. However, focusing on the specific applicability of lottery funds in India, it held that, whatever the force of the arguments elsewhere, 'it does not appear to us that any ill consequences are likely to result from the establishment of a lottery in India'. The committee argued that

> ... the habits and confined means of the lower order of the natives effectually exclude them from any participation in a lottery conducted on a large scale. Even in England the evil does not arise so much from the purchase of tickets as from the offices which are opened for ensuring them, which would of course be entirely prevented in this country.

The point was also made that the existing situation was bad enough and could not get any worse. If lotteries were indeed 'necessarily injurious to the morals of the people, the evil is at present experienced in Bengal in as great a degree as it could be if the plans now proposed by us were to be adopted, as lottery tickets are regularly sent around for sale from Madras'. The significance of these comments lay in the fact that the use of lotteries to raise funds for development in a very general sense, as opposed to specific projects, was to become the vogue in Calcutta a few years hence, a resource-garnering route that was to facilitate development work till the mid-1830s, laying in the process the foundations of modern Calcutta.

As for the other measures to raise funds suggested by the special committee, the apex committee said they did not constitute 'new resources' but that they would 'now or shortly ... form part of the general revenue of the State'. Its considered view was that if a project as crucial as the town's overall development was to be implemented, a dedicated resource-centre was necessary for the purpose, such as the navigation proceeds from Tolly's Nullah. The committee suggested that, considering

> ... the extensive nature of those improvements, it appears to us that it will be necessary for the Government either to set apart further funds

> for the purpose in question, or to advance a considerable sum during the next two or three years, to be gradually liquidated from the different supplies now proposed in the plan which we have the honour to submit.

In other words, a facilitating loan was sought so that critical town development work could be taken up, the loan being repaid with the implementation of revenue-raising measures over time.

The report of the special committee on funding the plan to improve the town was the most important of all the reports drawn up because without resources nothing would move. This was all the more so given the East India Company's tight leash on expenditure. However, this particular report did not throw any light on the state of affairs prevailing in Calcutta topographically at the turn of the eighteenth century. Such details were provided in abundance by two other special committee reports, one on 'improvements in the vicinity of the town as may tend to contribute to the convenience of the inhabitants of the town and neighbourhood of Calcutta', and the other on tackling 'nuisances' within the town.

To take one example, the suggestions to improve conditions in the neighbourhood of Calcutta tell us what access to Garden Reach—on the southern bank of the river along which a line of handsome garden houses had been built since the 1780s—was like in the early years of the nineteenth century. The report said that the road leading from the house and grounds of a certain Mr Logan[2]

> ... along Garden Reach and Watson's wall (marking out the dock premises) to Surman's bridge be widened,[3] that the ditches be cleared, and that such drains and bridges be constructed as shall, on a survey, appear to be necessary for keeping the road free from water at all seasons of the year.

For want of such facilities, a part of the road was frequently flooded during the rains the stagnant water 'lying on the side of the road [being] offensive to passengers and ... injurious to the health of persons residing in that neighbourhood'. Further, since 'the narrowness of the road and the abrupt turning near the premises belonging to Colly Sunker Goshaul' (see image 24 on p. 195) made that part of the road dangerous to its users, the special committee recommended that the house be 'at all events … taken down', not least because 'so far as a judgement can be formed without an actual survey, it would appear to be in an insecure and dangerous state'.

The records indicate that the road to Garden Reach had been beset with problems even earlier. In August 1782, the Committee of Revenue[4] was writing to Samuel Touchet, the assistant in the 24-Parganas, that complaints had been lodged 'that the publick road leading from Surman's Bridge to the end of Colonel Watson's wall is almost wholly occupied by a bazar to the great inconvenience of passengers and carriages' and that he was to take action to 'order a proper breadth of road to be marked off and to remove every stall from such limits, and to inform the proprietor of the bazar [that] if … any future interruptions shall happen from stalls being advanced upon the road, the bazar will be wholly removed'. Three months later, in November,[5] Touchet was again told that 'the great road leading from Surman's Bridge onwards to the line of the garden houses is greatly encroached upon by houses and bazars' and that he was to give directions 'for the whole road to be marked at the same breadth as was lately done at Surman's bridge [the August measure] and that no houses or bazars be suffered to be erected upon it or any encroachment made'. In July the following year[6] Samuel Charters, a member of the Committee of Revenue, wrote about

> … the inconvenience to which the gentlemen who are proprietors of the garden houses are exposed owing to the great road leading from Surman's Bridge being occupied by bazars, stalls … shops and a variety of other nuisances which have not only encroached upon the publick roads to such a degree that two carriages in many places cannot pass, but have also rendered it impracticable for the gentlemen to keep the road in any degree of repair.

The committee agreed to the proposal and authorised Charters 'to adopt such measures as will have effect in removing the nuisances which he has stated, and for establishing the public road as far as the garden houses extend, in such manner as will remove the inconveniences at present felt by the proprietors'. More than two centuries later, the road still remains crowded though it has been widened substantially throughout.

Wellesley had already built the new road to Garden Reach the alignment of which is today followed to a large extent by Karl Marx Sarani (the erstwhile Circular Garden Reach Road), which left a broad swathe of ground between it and the old road to the garden houses by the river (see image 24 on p. 195). The special committee wanted a survey done of 'the ground and villages lying between the old and new roads' and also of the area between the new road and Alipore (that is, across today's Diamond Harbour Road) 'with a view of determining what improvements can be made in those suburbs'. Garden Reach had in fact been chosen initially as the site for Fort William College,[7] the institution being moved later to some of the houses comprising today's Writers' Buildings. Wellesley justified the choice with the argument that

> … the ordinary residence of the Students should be so near that of the Governor-General, as that he may have the constant means of superintending the whole system and discipline of the institution. The distance of fifteen or sixteen miles, in this climate [possibly with Barrackpore in mind], would often embarrass the communication.

Writers' Buildings had been ruled out specifically by Wellesley 'on account of their being placed in the centre of the town; nor could it have been practicable in that situation (even if the property could have been purchased on reasonable terms) to have obtained an area of ground sufficiently spacious for the new building'.[8] Had the Governor-General settled on Writers' Buildings—put up by Thomas Lyons—as the location for the college, it is just possible that Calcutta may have had to look elsewhere to house its principal Government offices.

The special committee then shifted its focus to the southern bank of Tolly's Nullah, stipulating that 'the exact limits of the road leading from Surman's bridge round Allypore, to the Allypore bridge, be ascertained, and that all encroachments be removed, and that posts or other marks be fixed to define the limits in future'. This is confirmation that the road which today skirts the zoo on the north has been there for more than two centuries.[9] Moving further south, the committee suggested that the cantonments of the native militia be removed because they were considered to be a 'nuisance by every person riding or walking round the Allypore road', the road

42 An 1817 map of Calcutta showing Alipur Road and the Khalashi militia and the Calcutta militia lines along it

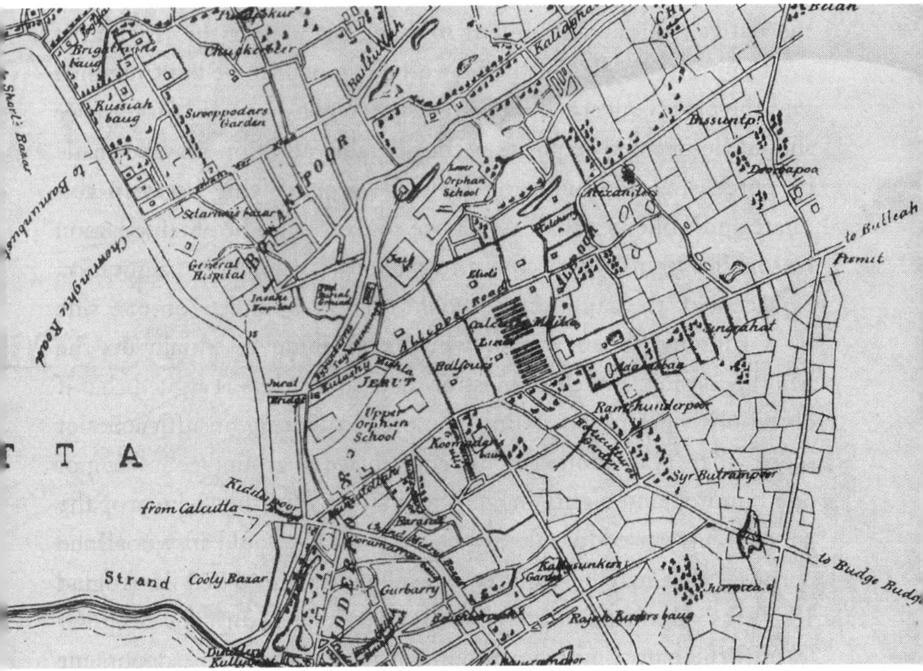

being 'otherwise calculated as much, or perhaps more than any other, to become the general resort of persons taking the air during the mornings and evenings'.[10] The general committee backed the proposal on the ground that the house and grounds forming the cantonment could be 'immediately appropriated to some public purpose, as for instance, a *cutchery* or one of the public offices, which would completely indemnify Government for the expenses of removing the above-mentioned corps to some more convenient situation'. One of the places suggested to the apex committee where the native militia cantonment could be moved was 'the vicinity of the jail of the 24-Parganas' at Russapuglah. It noted that disturbances had occasionally broken out in the jail: on one occasion, when the prisoners exceeded nine hundred, 'the military guard stationed for their protection and the security of the jail was so inconsiderable that the most serious consequences might have arisen had the prisoners acted with concert and unanimity'.

The apex committee was so taken up with the idea of moving the native militia cantonment to some place near the jail that it even submitted a plan of the new establishment to be built there. It said the place concerned measured sixty bighas, 'and if a large space should be deemed requisite a considerable addition may be made by purchasing and annexing to it the ground lying between this estate and Tolley's nullah, which we conceive may be obtained upon reasonable terms'. The committee felt that should its suggestion be accepted, the cantonment would then be bounded 'on one side by a running stream which would contribute essentially to the health, comfort and cleanliness of that Corps'. It was argued that if objections were raised against the proposal citing 'insufficiency of space', there was 'another house and a piece of ground consisting of one hundred and eighty biggahs and situated in the vicinity of the jail once advertised for sale, which we conceive would answer all the purposes that may be required'. A memorandum dated 21 August 1804 was submitted to the general committee against the proposal to shift the native militia cantonment from Alipore, the document being sent from the 'Militia Lines, Allypore' suggesting that it was an 'inside' job. The date also tells us when the special committee on the improvement of the town's environment had submitted its report to the general committee. The memorandum[11] is important because it gives us an idea of the topography of the area comprising modern-day Tollygunge at the turn of the eighteenth century. Incidentally, some light is also thrown on the duties of the native militia and the nature of the jobs it was entrusted with.

The memorandum argued that the cost of moving the cantonment's physical infrastructure to the new location would be around Rs 30,000. Added to this would be the price of the ground selected by the general committee which would 'amount to probably not less than 20,000 Rs'. This apart, as far as the ground was concerned, it was pointed out that there was hardly any spot which could be 'less adapted to the reception of the troops'. There was 'no good water at any season and the tanks are nearly, if not wholly, dry for several months of the year'. The ground was

> not adequate to the accommodation of the Militia Corps by at least 100 begahs, and the mansion house, which is very large and very low, stands nearly in the centre, and would effectually prevent on either side the construction of the lines or the exercise of the battalion, and consequently the discipline of the Corps would be ruined.

Further, there were no 'offices' and the mansion house was in such a 'ruinous and uninhabitable condition (the venetians falling out and the roof apparently falling in) that it is even dangerous to enter it'. Since between Rs 15,000 and Rs 20,000 would be required to repair the house, it would be 'a very expensive concern to the Government'. The grounds—'nearly a square of 60 or 70 bigahs'—were bounded by public roads on three sides, which would have to be shut down if, as the general committee had proposed, additional ground was to be purchased. Moreover, all the contiguous ground was said to be 'too low and swampy' and was, at the time, covered with paddy, all of which indicated that the final cost would be prohibitive for a military cantonment.[12]

The point was also reiterated that the location of the native militia should be a function of the services it provided. If this were so, the shift from Alipore to Russapuglah would be nothing short of a disaster. The memorandum said that when the militia was instituted in the mid-1790s,

> ... certain duties in and about the town of Calcutta, and the garrison of Fort William, were particularly assigned to the corps, the performance of which duties must be greatly retarded, if not indeed, defeated, by the removal of the corps to Russapuglah or to anywhere at so great a distance from Fort William ... Hardly a day passes that calls are not made for men, many of which are to be complied with at (a) moment's notice, and occasionally orders are received at the dead of night to have parties ready by gunfire in the morning to go on board of ships. The calls from the treasury are constant, and sometimes on account of the intervention of holidays, to be immediately attended to while, on the other hand, it now and then happens that the cash on the boats to carry not being ready when the escort arrives, the sub-treasurer is under the necessity of ordering the men back to the [camp] until further orders.

Such being the nature of the public duties of the militia, the document pointed out that it would be 'extremely harassing' for the troops to commute 'between Russapugly and town, independent of the delay and interruption that under such circumstances would necessarily attend' the prosecution of their duties.

This was not all. Applications were 'constantly received from the export warehouse to and from which about 50 or 60 sepoys are perpetually going and coming, during the regular season, more particularly of loading the Indiamen'. This apart, 'on every exigency in the town, sepoys from this corps are required whether it be to attend our own festivals or those of the natives, to search for deserted seamen, to hunt perhaps for Frenchmen, or to catch dacoits'. All these requirements had to be met by the native militia 'whether they come at a day's, or an hour's, notice'. Giving an example of the sort of work the corps had to cope with, the memorandum said that 'very lately, the Mint Master wrote to the Commanding Officer a pressing note in the afternoon requesting an additional guard in consequence of a great sudden influx of bullion, etc with which he did not consider himself safe'. The contingency was of course met immediately which, the memorandum argued, would not have been the case had the cantonment been located at Russapuglah. A second instance of rapid deployment cited was 'the late predicament of the militia which, in common with the other corps at the presidency, was in orders to turn out at a moment's notice for several days together to proceed to town to receive the Hon'ble Major-General Wellesley [the future Duke of Wellington]'. This service was provided 'without any inconvenience either to the officers or men, but it would have been otherwise if the corps had been stationed at Russapugly'. Given the political strength of the forces ranged against them, the authors of the memorandum were perhaps aware that they were fighting a losing battle for at the very end of their argument they took recourse to the plight of sick sepoys (six to eight of them on a daily basis, especially during the rains) who had to 'find their way to the hospital'. Describing this as the most important reason against the move of the cantonment to Russapuglah, the memorandum pointed to the logistical problems involved if the 'poor fellows' had to walk all the way to the hospital from Russapuglah.

Apart from a projected move of the native militia cantonment, the special committee had also recommended that the ground on both sides of the road, 'near to the house occupied by Mr Brookes, down to Allypore bridge', be bought by the Government and that 'the houses be removed'. The house being referred to here is probably Belvedere, the expanded and rebuilt version of which today houses the National Library. But if this were so why was it not mentioned specifically in view of the fact that, at the time, it was widely known as 'Belvidere House'? The association between

Brooke and Belvedere is based on the fact that the former stayed for many years at the house as a tenant of Mrs Tolly, the widow of Colonel Tolly who had bought it and its grounds from Warren Hastings in 1785. One possibility is that he may still have been living there in 1805 although the house had been sold by Mrs Tolly three years earlier. In fact, the house had begun to be used as the Calcutta Court of Appeal in the 1790s and Brooke, who had been appointed a member of the Committee for the Improvement of Calcutta by Wellesley in 1803, had become one of the three judges of that court in the mid-1790s. Is it possible that the house was being used as a court as well as the residence of an individual at one and the same time? There is, however, no mention in the records of this dual use at the time the house was selected as the venue for the Court of Appeal.[13] In the early years of the nineteenth century not many Europeans were living in the area, and if Brooke was one of them it is only to be expected that his house would be treated as a topographical point of reference.

The general committee backed the proposal as it already had information that the Government 'has long has had it in contemplation to purchase the ground in question'. Further, it was also pointed out that 'in the last and former years, considerable inconvenience was experienced during the season of the rains, from the pools of stagnant water on the ground to which these remarks allude'. The committee felt that by purchasing the ground 'and putting it in order by the labour of convicts, and with the excavations which must at all events be made from the Nullah [Tolly's], and afterwards by the disposing of the property under restrictions, or applying it to some public purpose', the ultimate cost to the Government of developing the area would be 'very inconsiderable'. A visit to the area today shows that a large part of it north of Judges Court Road, and even to the south of it, is Government property. Perhaps, this is a result of the process of land acquisition in the area which the authorities were contemplating in the early years of the nineteenth century.

Moving to the east, the special committee throws some light on the area to the south of the general hospital extending to Tolly's Nullah. It proposed that the ground lying to the south of the general hospital 'be levelled and the holes filled up with earth to be excavated from the nullah'. In fact, such was the state of the area that it had been more than once the 'subject of representations to Government as being injurious to the invalids and convalescents in the hospital'. Further steps would be needed to improve the situation than those suggested, two measures proposed 'formerly' being a 'cut' to be made from Tolly's Nullah, 'not far from the Allypore bridge, through the ground lying at the back of the hospital', and the digging of one or more large tanks in the neighbourhood. The general committee was not enthusiastic about the extension from the nullah or the digging of the tanks because 'the present is not the season [of] the year for carrying into effect works of that nature'.[14] However, it backed the proposal to level the ground and fill up the holes 'as far as may be practicable in the manner above suggested'. The committee's attention to detail is underscored by the following remark:

> With respect to the execution of that work, we conceive that the earth should be excavated during the time of the ebb and carried away to the proper places by labourers and carts during the flood tides, when the men cannot be employed in excavating the earth. It appears that a considerable body of convicts might conveniently be employed in the execution of this work.

The next point suggested by the special committee was farsighted in view of the fact that it ultimately resulted in the making of two roads which are still with us. It suggested the construction of a road 'from near the hospital to unite with Russapugly road, about a mile above the bridge near the Brijoo *talow* in a direction nearly west and east'. Another road was suggested 'from near the hospital' going 'to Colly Ghaut', which would 'intersect' the road just proposed, both the roads being of 'material convenience to the natives'.[15] It is difficult to say with any degree of confidence whether the present-day roads in the area would correspond precisely with the 1804 proposal, but in later times two major roads, namely, the arterial Harish Mukherjee road and Sambhu Nath Pandit street, fulfilled the special committee's objectives.

The special committee then considered the road to Russapuglah which had already become an important passage to the suburbs. 'Russapugly, in the Pergunnah of Khaspoor',[16] was some distance from the

43 An 1817 map of the town showing the road to Russapuglah and the location of the jail at Etalgutta

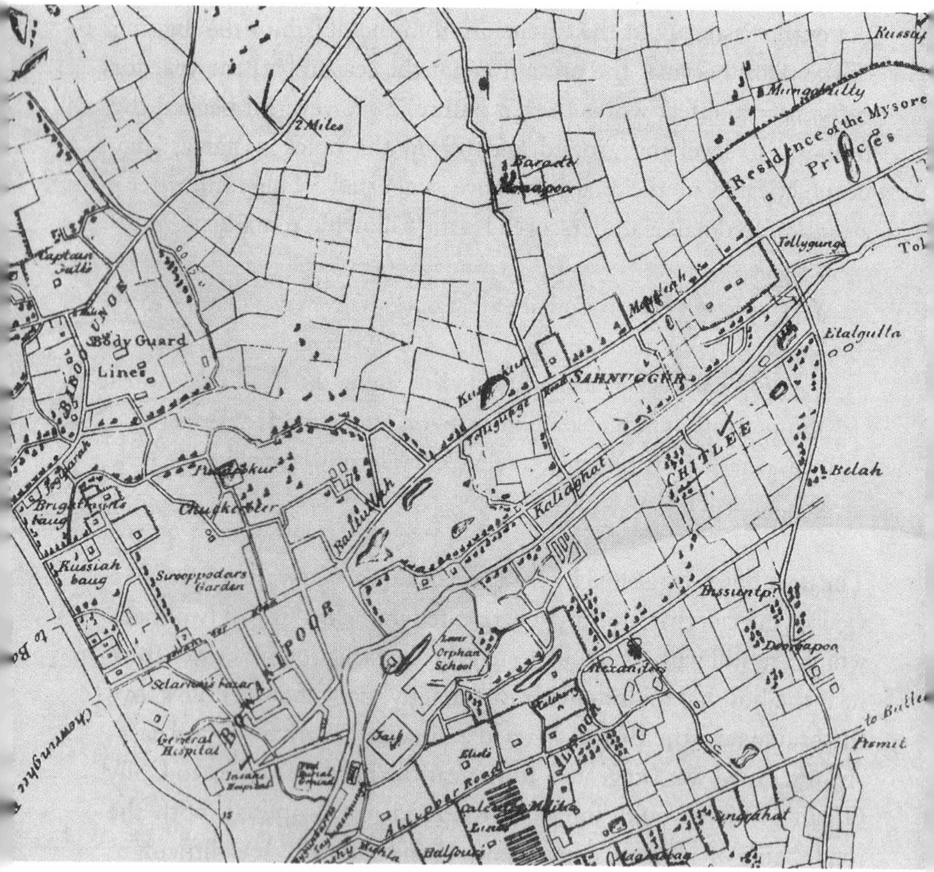

town and it was normal to expect that the sahibs would take time to move out and 'colonise' it. There is little evidence in the records of any movement in that direction before 1756. In the 1770s large tracts of land were bought by Europeans to set up garden houses in the area. That the road was gaining in importance is indicated by the growing awareness of its poor condition and the consequent requests being made to repair it. But the Government was not always forthcoming when faced with such demands. The following letter, written on 29 January 1787 by Jeremiah Church 'and other inhabitants of Rossapuglah' to the Governor-General in Council,[17] gives us an indication of the evolving state of affairs:

> We ... proprietors of houses and lands either in or contiguous to Russapuglah, in which some of us constantly, and others frequently, reside, beg leave to represent to your Lordship that prior to the time the above mentioned property became possessed by Europeans, the road leading from Calcutta to Russapuglah was seldom or ever used as a carriageway except by country carts for the transport of goods, and was in many parts exceedingly narrow and ill adapted for a carriage road, and rendered still more so by the frequent encroachments made by the inhabitants residing on each side of it; that notwithstanding large sums of money have from time to time been expended, as well by us as [also] the former owners of our lands, in the repair and improvement of the road, yet the original evils still exist with the additional inconvenience of numerous large tanks and deep holes in many parts and on each side of the same. [These] evils, notwithstanding all our vigilance, [have been] daily increasing and becoming more and more dangerous and alarming to ourselves and to others using and passing the road; that it has long been and still is one of the greatest channels or highways for various articles and commodities both of consumption and commerce from different parts of the country to Calcutta, and may therefore be considered a high and public road; that having now for several years past supported the road at our private expense and finding all our efforts to keep it in a sufficient state of safety and repair frustrated by the

> perpetual encroachments of the natives on each side of it, we are driven to solicit your Lordship to permit the road to be classed with the other high roads of the Presidency and delivered over to the Chief Engineer whose official situation can alone overcome the difficulties we have so long but in vain encountered.

This is a good example of an existing road increasing in importance following the impact of 'progress'. However, not much importance was attached to the plea, the Government setting aside the matter to 'lie for consideration'. Seven years later, the Governor-General in Council turned down another specific suggestion to get the road repaired, a request which had been backed by the Collector of the 24-Parganas as well as by the Board of Revenue.[18] In course of the representation, Richard Goodlad, of Rangpur-uprising infame who was then the Salt Agent of the 24-Parganas based at Baruipur, argued the case for the road's repair by stating that it was 'not only the high road to the centre of the 24 Parganas but [also] a great part of the trade from Tolley's nullah is conveyed by it to Calcutta. It is a road as useful to the town as the road to Ballia Ghut'.[19] By this time also the jail for the 24-Parganas was coming up at 'Maugrah pargana, Ittalghauttah mouza' (see image 43 on p. 440), which increased the pressure of traffic on the road even further.[20] Later, in 1810, in response to the reported difficulties being faced by the Mysore princes who lived on the road at its southern extremity (see image 43 on p. 440), the Government agreed to sanction funds (Rs 5,802) for a makeshift repair of the road, which is said to have had 600 holes in it. The request for repair had been made by Lt-Col. J. Hawkins, Superintendent, Affairs (of the) Mysore Princes, who wrote that the road had become 'almost impassable' causing 'very great inconvenience [to] the families of the Mysore Princes, as they receive all their supplies from Calcutta'.[21]

The special committee wanted 'the Russapugly road from Girrya Haut to Birjoo *talow* to [be] repaired, the exact limits of the road ascertained, all encroachments removed, and, where necessary, additional ground ... purchased for widening the road'. 'Almost impassable' at the time, the state of the road had led to a depreciation in the value of 'several considerable houses at Russapugly', no doubt owned by Europeans. It had also led to disruption of normal life in view of the fact that it was 'one of the principal avenues for the importation of articles for the daily consumption of the town' which came from the interior of the country through Tolly's Nullah. In an attempt to shorten the distance for ferrying goods brought from the interior of the country using the Tolly's Nullah into the town, the special committee suggested that a road be made from 'Russapugly through Baloogunge to unite with the great Circular or Boitaconnah road near the European burying ground'. The committee argued that the suggested route would enable 'wood and other articles brought from Russapugly [to] enter the populous part of the town without passing over the esplanade or the principal parts of the town occupied by European gentlemen, as is the case at present'.

In the same breath, a widening of the 'Bally Ghaut' (Beliaghata) road was proposed, the road being at the time 'too narrow for the number of people, hackeries and bullocks which are continually passing along it'. This road was made in the early 1790s, providing evidence of growing activity in the eastern part of the town. The process, however, had begun much earlier as reflected by property transactions in the area involving Europeans, Christopher Keating for example, in 1773.[22] Inevitably, problems arose during the making of the road. In the resolution of one of the problems—the making of bricks—further evidence is provided of sympathetic treatment of the interests of natives by the English authorities. In December 1789 the Collector of Calcutta, Edward Colebrook, wrote that he had, according to directions, fixed upon 'several places' as fit for the brick-making work. All of these were patta lands but he had 'failed to persuade the proprietors concerned to voluntarily part with their land on a temporary basis'. Instead of settling the issue forcibly which could have been done easily, the Governor-General in Council wrote back in January the following year asking Colebrook to look for 'any other spot than that now chosen which the proprietors can most conveniently spare for the purpose of making bricks for the road from Balliagaut'. Even so, the penchant to crack the whip was always an attractive proposition to the sahibs, which led the Governor-General in Council to state that the proprietors 'should be told that the amount of the compensation on this account may be arbitrated, but if they decline this mode of settlement the Collector will report what in his judgement the compensation should be'. The Collector was also told to point out to the landowners

> … the advantage they will generally derive from a new road, and the expectations of Government that the public convenience should be assisted by their [agreeing] to part [with] the ground required for making bricks to execute the work, particularly as requisition goes only to a temporary appropriation of the ground, and the quarter-master general has been instructed to fill in such of [ditches] as might be detrimental to the future [usefulness] of the land whenever the road is completed.[23]

The general committee found the proposal on the road from Russapuglah through Ballygunje attractive when it considered 'the large daily supplies brought into the town from [Russapuglah] and the great advantage which would be gained by conveying those articles of consumption into the populous parts of the town by the easiest possible routes'. However, it felt that the special committee's other suggestion to have a road made from near the hospital connecting with that linking Birjee talao and Russapuglah was probably a better candidate for quicker implementation rather than the road 'from' Russapuglah itself, which was located further to the south. The apex committee argued that this shorter road could be continued 'through Balloogunge to unite with the great Circular road opposite to the burying ground' stating that a road in this direction 'would be productive of several advantages and would answer many of the purposes of the road proposed by the special committee in … their report'. This apart, the cost would also be 'less considerable as the ground required for the site of this road is for the most part the property of the Government'. It does not seem that this project ever materialised because there is no indication whatever in subsequent maps of a thoroughfare extending from near the hospital to 'opposite' the South Park Street Cemetery or thereabout, at least in the shape of a single road.

A basic element of any planning exercise is prioritisation, and this is precisely what the special committee on improving the town's environment did with its proposals. It was suggested that of the eleven proposals made, those regarding the road to Garden Reach, the road along Tolly's Nullah, and the development of the area on both sides of Alipore Road be taken up first, special attention being directed to the acquiring of the ground concerned and settling compensation for both landowners and tenants. The committee felt that such an emphasis would be sensible because implementation would not be costly and also because 'the season of the year renders any delay inconvenient'. Regarding the ground south of the hospital, the special committee suggested that convicts should be employed 'as soon as possible to excavate the nullah near the hospital' and that 'a professional gentleman should be desired to report what further assistance may be required of coolies and hackeries for carrying the projected improvement into execution'. On the removal of the native militia cantonment, it said that the proposal could begin to be implemented only after the spot where it would be moved was acquired, which meant it could not be taken up early.[24]

On the two new roads proposed to be built near the hospital, the repair of the road to Russapuglah, and the widening of the road to Beliaghata, the special committee wanted early steps to be taken 'for working out ... the roads ... and forming an estimate of the expenses required' although there could be some delay regarding the latter part of the work. It thought that work on the Beliaghata Road could be suspended 'until the other objects shall have been partly carried into effect'. Regarding the proposal for a 'cut' from Tolly's Nullah 'round the great Circular or Boitaconnah road and of carrying it out to the Salt Water lake', the special committee said it had 'particularly adverted' to the plan because of the advantages flowing from it. However, since it was aware of the 'considerable objections' that could be made to it, it had thought it advisable 'to suspend our judgement upon the point until we shall have been furnished with the report of the special committee for improving the drainage of the town, the two objects being naturally connected with each other'.

Notes

1 The documents are to be found in the Judicial Criminal Proceedings of 25 July 1805.

2 Perhaps William Logan, who in 1793 was reported to be a European resident of Calcutta for eleven years, and is described as 'merchant and agent'. His address then was Old Fort Street ('Families in British India Society' database).

3 Watgunje Street (renamed Kabitirtha Sarani).

4 Proceedings, 29 August 1782.

5 Committee of Revenue Proceedings, 11 November 1782.

6 Committee of Revenue Proceedings, 31 July 1783.

7 Minute of the Governor-General dated 18 August 1800.

8 Thomas Roebuck, *The Annals of the College of Fort William* (Calcutta: Hindoostanee Press, 1819), pp. xxiii, xxiv.

9 Further proof of this is provided by the fact that in September 1795 the secretary of the Military Orphan Society was writing that there was a road 'leading from the south-west corner of the Belvidere bridge along the banks of the nullah' which had been in public use 'for many years past' (Board of Revenue Proceedings, 6 October 1795).

10 What this suggests is that the sepoy cantonments, which had been moved from Chowringhee in the 1780s (see chapter 'Sprucing up Chowringhee'), had been shifted to this area instead of some place on the maidan as was once suggested. It is also clear from the observation made by the special committee that the environs of Alipore Road were gradually becoming a place of resort for genteel people. In other words, Europeans were moving into the area.

11 Judicial Criminal Proceedings, 25 July 1805.

12 The memorandum said the estate belonged to 'Mr Birch'. There were at least two of them in Calcutta at the time, namely, R.C. Birch and J.B. Birch, and it is not clear who among them owned the Russapuglah property.
13 Judicial Civil Proceedings, 31 May and 7 June 1793.
14 But was this 'cut' from Tolly's Nullah made at a later date? Schalch's 1824 map shows just such a formation at the location suggested by the special committee.
15 For the layout of the road network in the area towards the close of the next decade (in 1817) see image 42 on p. 433.
16 Calcutta Committee of Revenue Proceedings, 12 May 1777.
17 Governor-General in Council Proceedings, 14 February 1787.
18 Board of Revenue Proceedings, 16 May and 3 June 1794.
19 Board of Revenue Proceedings, 16 May 1794.
20 Board of Revenue Proceedings, 22 February 1793.
21 Judicial Criminal Proceedings, 21 September 1810.
22 Calcutta Committee of Revenue Proceedings, 18 August 1779.
23 Board of Revenue Proceedings, 20 and 25 January 1790.
24 Schalch's map of 1824 shows that more than two decades later the Calcutta militia lines were still located roughly at the spot where the military command hospital stands today, on Alipore Road.

26

Cleaning up the Town

The previous chapter dealt with problem areas and remedies lying outside the ambit of the town proper. The importance of the report of the special committee 'for considering the nuisances which exist throughout the town of Calcutta', submitted to the Government along with the general committee's comments on 31 August 1804,[1] lies in the fact that it provides an idea about certain topographical aspects of the town itself as it then was. These aspects highlight the point that the facets of town development which had emerged over the previous four decades focusing on the regulation of space were entirely disaggregated and were devoid of any centralised approach to improving conditions within the rapidly growing town. In other words, the report was a first step towards urban planning and the assumption of civic responsibility by those in charge of the town's governance.

The first point noted by the report was 'the rapid descent from the top of the Allipore and Kidderpore bridges' which had led to the occurrence of 'dangerous' accidents. As a remedy, it was suggested that the ground 'on the northern side' of both the bridges be raised 'and that the rail be continued as far as the declivity may extend on each side of the road'. The special committee then talked about the Cooly Bazar area (see image 24 on p. 195) suggesting that only 'tiled houses' should be allowed there and that 'the sheds belonging to the garrison storekeeper and other military officers in the vicinity of the bazaar be [also] tiled'. The committee asked for a survey of the river bank 'between Chandpaul Ghaut and Chitpore' and also a report on 'the sheds and huts which have been erected on the west side of the road running in that direction'[2] as well as on the encroachments made 'and now serve to impede the navigation of the river'. It suggested removal of the huts and the sheds 'improperly situated' in order to 'promote the free navigation of the river and to afford to boats an easy access to the shore at all places'. This probably was among the earliest moves taken by the authorities to clear the riverside of encroachments and obstructions comprehensively, features which had been a part of the scene since the early years of the settlement.

As we have seen earlier,[3] the Dharamtala bazar was situated at the north-east corner of the esplanade, being positively a leftover of the phase of town development from which Calcutta was emerging. The special committee sensed the mismatch and suggested its removal to a spot 'not very remote from that on which it stands at present'. The committee felt that if there was a problem in shifting the bazar then at least the streets could be widened 'and other measures' taken which would render the area 'less offensive than it is at present'. The bazaar was an old one, its ownership having passed through a number of twists and turns over the preceding couple of decades. The special committee said that the 'ill-judged construction of this bazaar, and the consequent uncleanly state of it, added to the central and exposed situation of the place, induce us to represent it a grievous nuisance'. As an alternative site for it, the 'considerable' ground 'to the south-east of the present bazaar' (where Janbazar is now located or its neighbourhood) was suggested, the spot being 'perfectly well-calculated, both by situation and extent, for the erection of a new bazaar, and on which there are no buildings of any consequence at present'.

The general committee agreed with the suggestion stating that not only was the proposed site 'a proper situation' for the bazar but that the ground could be bought for a 'moderate' sum as it was occupied 'by a few scattered houses of a very inferior order ... some

44 A view of Alipur bridge, by William Wood, 1833

45 Kidderpur bridge in 1833, by William Wood

of the huts [being] of little or no value'. It wrote to the Government that the new location of the bazar

> ... would be equally convenient for those who now resort to the present bazaar, and as the space is considerably greater, the new marketplace might be constructed upon a greater scale more suitable to the growing wealth and population of Calcutta, more compatible with comfort, cleanliness and salubrity, and more consistent in point of appearance with the improvements making in that principal quarter of the town.

It was felt that there would be 'little difficulty' in persuading the owner of the bazar to make the shift to the new spot which was not merely 'so eligible and contiguous' but also because of the low cost that would be incurred in moving 'the present materials ... in constructing the new buildings' to a place so close by. Importantly, even in those early days the ground on which the bazaar stood was considered a premium location, the general committee suggesting that since the spot was so 'extremely valuable' and so 'centrally' located with a 'commanding prospect' it would be 'particularly well-adapted for the erection of the Town Hall, or any ornamental building, which Government or the public might have occasion for'.[4]

The special committee then turned its attention to the esplanade beginning with the riverside. The Respondentia Walk was confined mainly to the north of Chandpal Ghat, the Esplanade Row west forming its southern limit.[5] The committee proposed that

> ... the quarter of the esplanade on the riverside adjoining to Chandpaul Ghaut be cleared of the bricks, rubbish, timbers and old guns which are scattered upon it, and that instructions be given to the officers in charge of the Engineer department to level the ground and to keep it in good order for the militia parades and public walks, and that a rail be put upon the east side of the bridge at the water shed[6] to prevent accidents.

The committee also proposed that the 'ditches in the north-east quarter of the esplanade be dressed by sloping the sides, and that the inequalities in the ground in that quarter be filled up'. There was at the time a road through this part of the esplanade which, as the committee saw it, created problems which needed to be tackled. It wrote that the 'diagonal road, which is at present opened through this part of the esplanade, is considered objectionable ... in consequence of the quantity of dust it creates, to the great inconvenience of the inhabitants of Esplanade Row'. Since the road was also objectionable 'upon grounds connected with police considerations', the committee proposed that it be shut down. It suggested a restructuring of the corner where Park Street met Chowringhee Road, a point which had been raised years earlier but which, clearly, had not been attended to. The committee wanted 'the sharp angle formed by Park Street[7] and the Chowrinhghee road, on the south side, [to] be removed' in view of accidents between carriages going in different directions at this point 'in consequence of the view of each other's approach being obstructed by the angle of the compound to the house lately occupied by Colonel Garstin'. Over the past couple of centuries the offending angle has been rounded off, but even today one can envision the problems which arose in the past when both roads—especially Park Street—were far narrower than they are today.

Within twenty years, the road where the second Mrs Warren Hastings lived and where her husband later moved from Buckingham House,[8] which was then the official abode of the Governor-General, had been named Hastings Street. The special committee on 'nuisances' felt that the western end of the road needed cleaning up, its specific suggestion being that 'the range of godowns obstructing the passage from Hastings Street to the river – commonly called Vrignon's godowns – be removed'. Arguing its case the committee said: 'This narrow passage is the principal thoroughfare for goods and passengers proceeding from Chandpaul Ghaut and Kootchagoody Ghaut into the town, and, consequently,

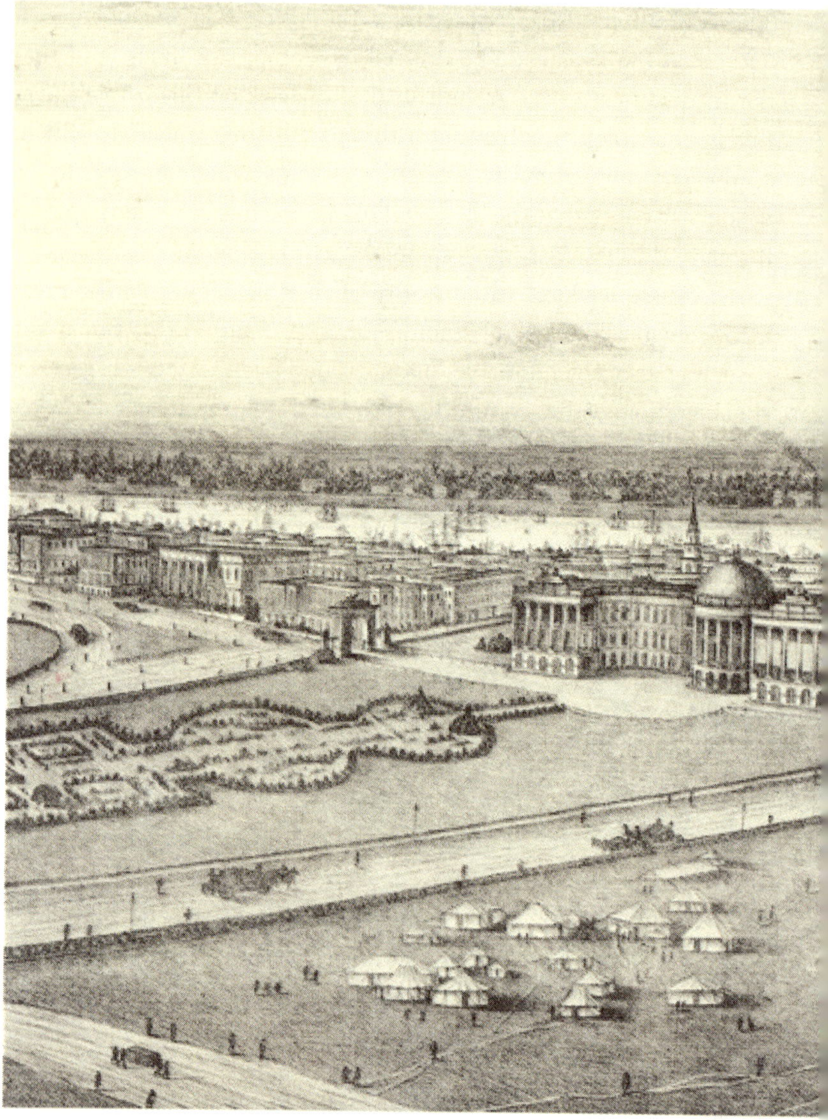

46 A section of Frederick Fiebig's 1847 panorama of the city shows the diagonal road (right) which Lord Wellesley's committee wanted closed

carriages, hackeries and palanquins are frequently interrupted and detained, to the great inconvenience of the inhabitants and obstruction to the commerce of the town'. The committee also noted that a 'similar inconvenience' arose from the 'narrow and irregular passage' between the houses occupied by David Hare, 'the watchmaker'[9] and propagator of the cause of native education,and a Mr Terry contiguous to the Bankshall and proposed that the road be 'widened and that a more regular direction be given to it'. Given the steady increase in trade and commerce, which was enhancing the importance of Cutchagoody ghat, it was but natural that the constriction in the passage of communication to the town posed by Vrignon's godowns would be noticed by the authorities. The general committee fully backed the special

47 The Bankshall Street-Church Lane-Hastings Street area as shown in Upjohn's map of 1792–1793

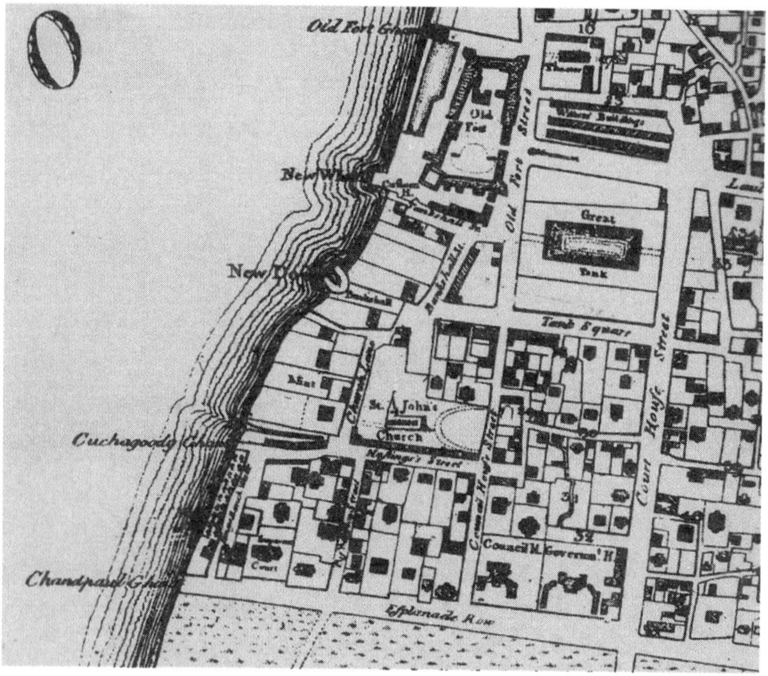

committee's recommendation in this regard. It also agreed with the proposal 'to widen and straighten the road leading from the west end of Hastings Street to the Bankshall'.[10]

The next three proposals related to the closure of three burial grounds not just because they were full but also because they needed to be moved from their existing locations, which at the time they were opened for interments were outside the limits of the town. The first burial ground which the committee wanted closed was the 'English burial ground' (the present-day South Park Street Cemetery), the specific recommendation being that the site for a new one should be 'somewhere between Boitaconnah and the Portuguese burying ground on the east side of Circular road'. The reason given by the special committee for the shift was that it was 'objectionable that the repository of the dead should be in the south-east quarter of the town' and also that it would soon be necessary 'to extend' its limits.

This cemetery was established when, in the mid-1760s, the authorities drew attention to the shortage of burial space, noting on 29 September 1766[11] that

> ... the present Burying Ground [the one which was to the west of St John's church—at that time, cathedral—where the grave of Job Charnock and other members of his family still stands] situate in the middle of the Town is ... very detrimental to the health of the inhabitants and too much confined.

The Secret Department asked the civil architect 'to point out [a] more convenient situation for one to be made of proper dimensions',[12] which finally led to the South Park Street Cemetery becoming the burial ground for the town in the 1760s, the first interment there being of a John Wood, a writer in the Custom House, on 25 August 1767.[13] Thirty years later, it was the turn of the new cemetery to cry out for space, the first move in this direction being made by the chaplains at the presidency, T. Blanshard and D. Brown. They petitioned the Governor-General on 22 April 1796 that since no ground was available for expansion of the cemetery (the 'Presidency Burial Ground') adjacent to it on the southern side of today's Park Street—that is, the ground belonging to W. Camac—'at a reasonable price', they were prepared to settle for land on 'the opposite side of the road adjoining the Mission Burial Ground [which too has given way to the pressures of modern-day town improvement] in which very few people have been interred'. The chaplains felt that this burial ground could be 'converted, when enlarged, to the public use of the Settlement'. In other words, it is yesteryear's north Park Street cemetery that is being talked about here, the ground today housing a school premises. The chaplains informed the Governor-General in Council that the Collector of Calcutta, Francis Gladwin, had told them that 'a few begahs of ground may be had on two sides of the Mission Ground at a moderate price', ground in which the chaplains had an interest provided the collector could supply them with more complete information about the 'practicability of procuring such ground'.[14]

The letter was sent to the Board of Revenue along with the instruction that it call upon the collector 'to report for the information of the Government whether the ground pointed out by the chaplains can be procured by purchase, and at what rate'. Gladwin wrote back to say that 'Subdyall Tehwary, an invalid jemadar of sepoys', possessed five bighas seventeen kathas 'adjoining to the Mission burying ground' which he was willing to sell at Sicca Rs 22 a katha, which came to Rs 2,574 for the entire plot. There was also a 'brick dwelling house' standing on the ground which Tiwary wanted to sell for Rs 400, the total cost adding up to Rs 2,974, which the collector felt was not an over-estimate. The Board of Revenue sent the letter to the Governor-General in Council, which approved the purchase.[15]

Getting back to the report of the special committee, the second burial ground highlighted by it was the 'hospital burial ground', located to the south of the hospital. It was suggested that this ground too would have to be closed, a new site being selected 'at no inconvenient distance from the hospital'. The committee described the burial ground as 'one entire mass of bones', Reverend David Brown[16] testifying that 'one quarter of it has been filled four times over – though the graves have been regularly marked out close to each other – within ... his remembrance'. The third burial ground which the committee also wanted closed was that 'of the Mussulmans', the suggestion being that a new site be granted to them 'in lieu of it on the north side of the Portuguese burying ground'. This place for interment was in a particularly bad shape, the committee describing it as turning into a 'perfect marsh' during the rains. It said the bodies were generally interred 'in a negligent manner, sometimes within two feet of the surface, and the jackalls constantly prowl in the place'.[17]

This burial ground was probably the one at Kassiabagan (see images 34 and 48 on p. 277 and p. 463), to the east of Circular Road. One set of records indicates that the burial ground 'in Chuckerbear' (Chakraberia) was opened in 1792, the ground, measuring forty bighas, being given to the Government 'for the purpose of a burying ground' by a John Revor at Rs 150 a bigha. The antecedents of the land are of some interest because, among other things, it shows the extent of land holdings by Church people at the time. The collector of Calcutta wrote to the Board of Revenue on 6 February 1792 that the land was part of the premises long possessed by the Reverend John William Gerlach in whose name he [Revor] has produced a pottah for 77 begahs 16 ½ cottahs with an assignment to him from the Reverend Thomas Blanchard as administrator to Gerlach deceased. Giving details of the topography of the area, the collector wrote to the Board of Revenue on 12 November 1792 that the boundaries of the burying ground 'had already been fixed by Captain [F. H.] Pearson and are such as to prevent any encroachment'. On the north there was the Birjee Road (today's Circular Road) running east and west 'and its (ditch) of near 30 feet breadth' (the Maratha ditch); on the east there was a ditch thirteen feet broad 'running north and south'; on the south there was nine-feet-wide ditch running east and west 'to the south corner of a tank belonging to Lieutenant

Wilford'; and on the west the ground extended till the bank of a tank, 'as far as the length of the tank towards the northward and a ditch of about 30 feet breadth (till) the north corner of the tank to the ditch (along) Birjee Road'. The collector wrote:

> The measurement was made from the (edge) of the Birjee Road ditch on the north to the outward edge of the ditch on the south – 305 yards; from the bank of the tank on the west to the outward of the ditch on the east – 210 yards. These dimensions give an area of 64,050 square yards which at 1,600 yards to the begah contain 40 begahs and a fractional part of one cottah.[18]

This, however, was not the end of the story as far as the Kassiabagan Muslim burial ground was concerned. In the mid-1870s the Government was keen on resuming the land covered by the burial ground 'to the south of Circular Road', one of the suggested possibilities being to turn it into a 'people's park or [devote] it to some other equally useful purpose' beneficial to the public but not doing anything which would 'be repugnant to the feelings of the Mahomedan community'.[19] In the 1870s, the burial ground had 'long ceased to be used as a place of interment'. Problems arose for the Government in the shape of a claim made by Fazlur Rahman, the 'self-constituted' *mutwali*, that the ground belonged to him, the official view being that he had no right whatever to it, the ground being 'without a proprietor and, therefore, appertains to Government'. Fazlur Rahman's father, Ghulam Rahman, took the story back to 'the time of Mr Martin's [C.F. Martyn] magistracy which closed in 1814', when he (Rahman) had been 'in charge of the burial ground'. Ghulam Rahman said the Muslims 'used *then* to be buried in a spot near the Fort', which was stopped by the authorities. At this point, the Lucknow nawab, Sadaat Ali Khan, 'who was then on a visit to Calcutta', asked the Government on behalf of the Muslim community 'to give up to them as a cemetery the land in Kassiabagan now in question, which had lapsed to

Government as the property of a Mr Johnson who about that time died intestate'. Ghulam Rahman said the request was complied with by the Government 'and an establishment of four *mallies* granted, not by the Newab but by Government, and he, Gholam Rohomon, was put in charge'. All this was stated by Ghulam Rahman in 1853 to W.H. Elliott, the Chief Magistrate of Calcutta, the latter stating that it was 'not far from the truth'.

In an effort to get at the truth, R.C. Sterndale, then vice-chairman of the Suburban Municipality, drew up a memorandum which takes us back to the beginning of the 1780s regarding the ownership of the ground in question. Sterndale wrote:

> The chittahs (of 1200 BS/ 1794) in the collectorate clearly show that the land was originally Government land held by Mr Richard Johnson, and there is a record to the effect that in the chittahs of 1188 BS (1781) the Hon'ble Company resumed 40 biggahs of the holding of Mr Richard Johnson for the purpose of a burial ground for the Mehomedans.

According to Sterndale, Johnson's holding

> ... was in all sixty-four biggahs, and on the Government taking up the larger and presumably the most valuable portion of his holding, he appears to have disposed of the remainder, for I find in an advertisement of 1788 the northern boundary of a certain property (now the London Mission Society's school), described as the new road leading to the ground late the property of Richard Johnson Esq (now known as the Peepulputty Road).

Sterndale said that this disposed of Ghulam Rahman's statement made to Elliott that the land had lapsed to Government as the property of Richard Johnson who had died intestate (Johnson in fact lived 'up to 1804 and perhaps longer'); and also the claim that the land was granted by Government at the request of Sadaat Ali Khan, for the latter 'did not ascend the musnud of Oude until 1798 when, according to the records extant, the burial ground had been in existence for seventeen years', taking the burial ground's existence back to 1781. The vice-chairman concluded his memorandum by stating that the Kassiabagan cemetery had been closed by the Government 'for sanitary reasons' after providing the Muslim community with another ground for interment purposes (where we are not told) and that the courts, including the High Court, had ruled that the Government could put the ground to 'any purpose it sees fitting'.

The finding of the official exercise in the 1870s was that the land forming the Muslim burial ground at Kassiabagan was

> … never … an endowment granted by Nawab Saadut Ali Khan but that [it] was, and is now, Government property and that Fuzlool Rohomun is not, and never was, a mutwallee and has no rights of any kind in the ground known as Kassiabagan and formerly used as a Mehomedan cemetery.

So where does all this leave us with regard to John Revor and his 1791 gesture of giving Government land for a native cemetery, and also the landholding of Reverend Gerlach? In view of the fact that the Board of Revenue records do contain information on the early history of the burial ground, it is a bit surprising that Sterndale should have drawn a blank 'in the office of the Magistrate and Collector of the 24-Parganas'. The vice-chairman says he was specifically informed that, 'with the exception of a file of correspondence, the information contained in which being based on hearsay … there were no records'. It is possible, though improbable, that we are talking about two different spots both covering four bighas and more and being located roughly in the same area. If this was indeed the case, Sterndale would have mentioned it in his note, especially because both the grounds would be located to the south of Circular Road. But there is no reference at all to this in the records. Heysham's map (1856) clearly shows the existence of a 'Mussalman's burial ground' to the east of Circular Road.

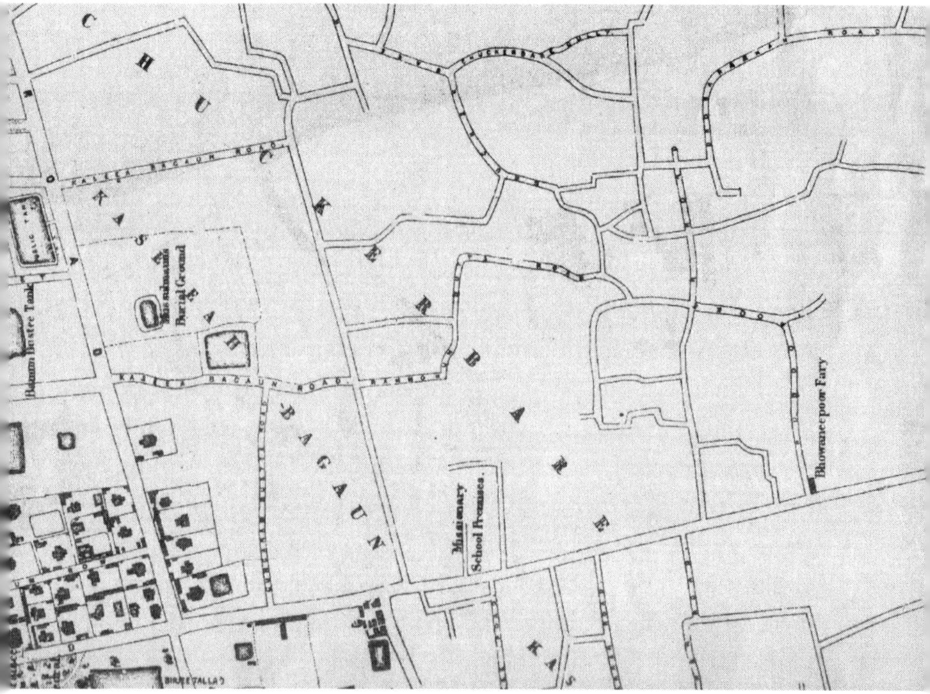

48 W. Heysham's 1856 map showing the location of the Mussalman burial ground at Kassiabagan

49 Thomas Daniell's 1786 rendition of the old fort and Holwell's monument

Returning to the special committee's report, the last four proposals relate to the heart of the English town, that is, the BBD Bagh area of today.

The first object of attention was of course the ruins of the old fort which, even in those early days, must have been an ugly sight in a rapidly expanding town. For Lord Wellesley, who had wasted no time in building the new Government House, it must have been a trial of patience in not being able to do anything quickly to get rid of the ruins of the fort, especially when a new one was already operational. Perhaps, the Governor-General wanted to develop the square around the great tank in an integrated manner with all the different aspects of the scenario being tackled at one and the same time, which is just what his Committee for the Improvement of the Town was engaged in. The special committee on 'nuisances' suggested that a survey be done with the objective of exhausting any possibilities which might have remained of parts of the old fort being repaired and upgraded and put to good use. After all, the fort premises—that is, the parts of it left standing after 1756–1757—were still being used as warehouses for export and import with the Customs people also operating from there. The committee wrote:

> The decayed and ruinous state of that building has attracted the attention of your committee who are of opinion that those high walls, equally useless to the proprietors and disfiguring to the appearance of a principal quarter of the town, serve to obstruct a free circulation of air, and also from their being strongly impregnated with saltpetre and extremely damp, occasion noxious and unwholesome vapours.

Further, the point was also made that the ground on which the ruins stood was 'very valuable', an economic dimension which could not be ignored for long by the authorities.

The general committee agreed with the suggestion of the special committee and wrote to the Government that the 'remaining original buildings of the old fort should be pulled down with all convenient dispatch'. It cited the views of John Taylor, the export warehouse keeper, which had been submitted by the special committee, who

> … from his official situation has been enabled to represent the inutility of those buildings in their present ruinous and decayed state, and also to bring to the notice of Your Excellency in Council an estimate of the heavy annual expense which is incurred by renting store houses for the export and import establishment.

Taylor had suggested that 'the whole of the buildings' be pulled down and that 'a range of spacious godowns' be erected in their place. The 'great additional accommodation' which the godowns would afford would enable the Board of Trade 'considerably to reduce the annual expense incurred from the hire of godowns for the use of the export and import warehouse departments amounting, on an average of the last three years ending 30th April 1804, to nearly 12,000 sicca rupees per annum'.

The special committee then wrote of the marine paymaster's office which was located at a spot south of the old fort and to the west of present-day Bankshall Street. The committee lamented the fact that the house occupied

> ... upwards of three-quarters of [the] ground which formerly constituted the approach to one of the principal ghauts of the town and that, in their judgement, the disuse into which *Kuouillah ghaut* has of late years fallen for commercial purposes may fairly be ascribed to the obstruction occasioned by the encroachment above adverted to.

It said that if the approach to the ghat was widened by the removal of the house, the ghat would 'in consequence of its local advantages become one of the most convenient and popular ghauts in Calcutta'. Taylor, who was asked for his view on this issue as well, agreed that the marine paymaster's house should be pulled down. However, he made the point that 'being contiguous to the bankshall' the location of the house was convenient 'to 150 Europeans and 70 natives employed under the master attendant,[20] who received their wages from the marine department'.[21]

Wellesley had had the northern gate of his Government House positioned in such a way that it opened out on to Wellesley Place (today's Red Cross Place), which in turn was tailored to the aesthetic requirements of the northern facade of Government House. Before Wellesley's time, as indicated by both Wood's map of 1784–1785 and Upjohn's of 1792–1793, north of the spot where Buckingham House was located (where Raj Bhavan now stands) was the tortuous passage known as Corkscrew Lane which wormed its way till Larkins' Lane.[22] Beyond the east-west Larkins' Lane, till the 'great tank' (Laldighi), there was no road. Wellesley cleared up the ground north of his palace and had the wide Wellesley Place made leading directly to the tank, beyond which could be seen the range of buildings which later became the consolidated pile known as Writers' Buildings. The statue of Lord Hastings, originally placed where the mid-twentieth century monstrosity of the Calcutta Telephones building now stands in BBD Bagh, had not yet come up, which means that there would have been an unimpeded view of the buildings to the north of Laldighi from the grand north staircase of Government House.[23] Nothing could be better than to have parks and gardens around Laldighi which could be seen from the steps of the Governor-General's house.[24]

Whether or not the special committee had this in mind is difficult to say, but it did suggest an improvement in the topographical layout of the area. It proposed that the ground 'on all sides adjacent to the great tank be cleared away, and that the present buildings of every description, as well as the gardens on the north side, be removed and measures be taken to prevent future encroachments of like nature'. It further said that

> … a wall, railing and chain similar to those which encompass the south side of the Government House be constructed all around

50 Thomas Daniell's painting of Holwell's Monument, 1798

> the tank, and a spacious gravel walk for public accommodation be made immediately within the enclosure and that handsome, substantial benches or garden chairs be placed in the centre of each of the walks which enclose the great tank.

The last suggestion of the special committee related to the sprucing up of the Holwell's Monument—located at the head of the road leading east from the old fort—which had been put up by Holwell in memory of those who had perished in the 'black hole' incident in 1756. The committee said that the column 'situated at the west end of the Writers' Buildings be thoroughly repaired and handsomely decorated, and that an ornamental iron railing be erected around it'.

Notes

1 Judicial Criminal Proceedings, 25 July 1805.

2 The 'waterside road' to the north which figured in the August 1755 Consultations. See chapter 'The Early Roads'.

3 See chapter 'The Dharamtala Bazar'.

4 Given Wellesley's penchant for putting up grand structures in an effort to recast the shoddy town he had inherited into the 'respectable' capital of a fast-spreading English politico-trading empire, it is not a little surprising that the plans of the Committee for the Improvement of Calcutta regarding the Dharamtala bazar were never implemented. Had the plans been acted upon, the eastern facade of the esplanade at that spot would have undergone a sea change, which probably would have left an indelible mark on the city affecting our own times. Instead, the function of the 'ornamental building' in that part of the city is today performed solely by the majestic pile known as the Metropolitan Building, set up a hundred years later to the south of the bazar. The remaining facade of the line of buildings looking out on what is today known as the 'Metro channel' is decrepit and depressing, three of the four buildings being built in the nineteenth century.

5 See chapter 'The Strand Road'.

6 If this was the watergate of the new fort, it gives us an idea of the extent of the ground to the south which was to be covered by the proposed improvements.

7 Note the name already given to the road which was formerly known as Burial Ground Road. The road had been given the name in view of the extensive park set up on the grounds of the house standing at the southern end of today's Middleton Row, once owned by Henry Vansittart and subsequently the residence of Sir Elijah Impey, Chief Justice of the Supreme Court and a friend of Warren Hastings.

8 Ray Choudhury, *The Lord Sahib's House*, p. 70.

9 After whom Hare Street is named.

10 The language used here suggests that, at this point of time, Hastings Street extended till Church Lane and that it was linked to the river further to the west by a passage through the godowns.

11 Long, *Selections*, p. 603.

12 Ibid., Preface.

13 *The Bengal Obituary*, Calcutta, 1991 reprint (first edition: 1848), p. 69; Cotton, *Calcutta Old and New*, p. 465.

14 To the west of the Mission cemetery, where John Zachariah Kiernander was buried in 1799, was the cemetery later known as the French burial ground, which too has fallen victim to the pressures of urbanisation. This bit of ground was initially bought by Edward Tiretta in March 1797 primarily with the purpose of serving as the new resting place of the remains of his young wife Angelique de Carrion who had died a year earlier and had been buried at the Portuguese cemetery. Tiretta was unhappy with the arrangement because no monument was allowed to be built over the remains at this cemetery, which led him to buy the ground off Park Street which was later passed on to the church (Cotton, *Calcutta Old and New*, p. 464; Robb, *Sex and Sensibility*, pp. 26–28).

15 Board of Revenue Proceedings, 10 May and 3, 17, 22 June 1796.

16 He was chaplain of St John's and was also conducting services at the Old Mission Church (Kiernander's) at this time (*Bengal Past and Present*, vol. 10, 1915, p. 317ff).

17 Judicial Criminal Proceedings, 25 July 1805.

18 Board of Revenue Proceedings, 27 January, 11 June, 28 July and 26 November 1792.

19 Municipal Municipal, File 32A, Proceedings, B 25-27, April 1875.

20 The job of master attendant, whose appointment in the early years had to have the sanction of the Company, entailed 'surveying and sounding the river, laying the buoys, surveying of ships on [a] variety of occasions, reporting the condition of the sloops, making of pilots,

masters, etc, and judging of their qualifications' (Bengal Public Consultations, 29 December 1752).

21 Judicial Criminal Proceedings, 25 July 1805. According to Taylor, the marine paymaster's house was bought by the Government in April 1788 for Sicca Rs 10,000 and an extra Sicca Rs 4,000 was spent afterwards on repairs and on putting up 'an additional upper room to the office'.

22 Named after William Larkins (Cotton, *Calcutta Old and New*, p. 672).

23 John Flaxman's statue of Lord Hastings, erected in 1824, was made a part of the Dalhousie Institute built in 1865, which was demolished in the middle of the twentieth century to make way for the Calcutta Telephones block.

24 See Ray Choudhury, *The Lord Sahib's House,* pp. 337–338.

27

The Lottery Route

When Wellesley formed his Committee for the Improvement of the Town of Calcutta he was aware that whatever had been done for the 'development' of the town before his time had been the handiwork of the magistrates. This may be why he was somewhat apologetic towards them when he set up the committee. After the committee was shelved, it was back to the magistrates. Someone had to continue to look after the immediate 'development' needs of the town and who else but the magistrates were best suited for that role. Not surprisingly, they slipped back into the job almost seamlessly—with, however, one difference. In the light of Wellesley's initiative, the entire exercise of town development had taken on a different hue with the result that the magistrates approached their old job differently than they had done in the past. The obstacle which had halted the Governor-General's committee in its tracks was the issue of funds without which the development of the town could not be carried out. Not only was there a general tightness of the East India Company's budgets at this time, Wellesley himself had come under increasing fire for financial 'irresponsibility'. Following his departure,[1] the subject of funds was quite naturally uppermost in the minds of the magistrates and it is hardly surprising that at the end of December 1806 they were writing to the Governor-General in Council on ways to garner resources to help them get on with their job of 'policing' the town more effectively than before.[2]

The magistrates, C.F. Martyn, W.C. Blaquiere, E. Thoroton and A. Stewart, wrote on 27 December 1806 that while they were fully aware of the importance of raising resources 'for the more complete repair of the roads, and for other objects of [policing] the town of Calcutta', they had offered their views on the subject 'influenced rather by what appears desirable than by what appears to us practicable under the present constitution of the town of Calcutta'. As they saw the problem, while the legislature had indeed vested the Governor-General in Council with the power of passing by-laws for the maintenance of the police of Calcutta, they had considerable doubt whether this could 'be construed to extend to the levy of new taxes, although they should be expressly declared to be intended for the support of the police of the city'. They then went on to list a number of taxes which could be used to raise resources for the general improvement of the town. These were:

> ... a duty on all horses exceeding twelve hands in height at the rate of ten rupees per annum, and on all tattoos and other horses being less than twelve hands in height at the rate of four rupees per annum; a duty of five rupees a year on each wheel of every coach, chariot, berlin landau, phaeton, curricle, buggy, tandem and chaise that shall be kept by any person for his own use or be let out to hire; a duty to be levied on all country-built carriages commonly called khurranchees,[3] including carriages used for children, at the rate of two rupees yearly for each wheel; a tax on all palanqueens at the rate of four rupees per annum.

The magistrates said that if these taxes were implementable they could be extended to cover 'the vicinity of Calcutta beyond the jurisdiction of the Supreme Court of Judicature, which would of course tend considerably to increase their produce'.

Referring to Wellesley's time, the magistrates made the point that the Governor-General in Council, the Supreme Court judges and the public at large had noticed the 'improvements' made 'in the maintenance of the peace of the city', implying that the town had become a safer place to live in. Patting themselves on the back, they said that the benefits were still enjoyed by the community 'in a degree, we believe, not inferior to the advantages experienced from the best regulated police of any town in Europe'.[4] However, they admitted that 'other objects of [the] police intimately connected with the health and convenience of the public have by no means kept pace with the improvements made in the prevention of crimes and offences'. The structural inadequacy of the prevailing system was underscored when they pointed out that the reason for the drawback was 'the want of a fixed revenue exclusively applicable to purposes of that nature'. Echoing the views of the erstwhile committee for the town's improvement, they said that the only source of such funds was the proceeds of the house tax but that tax, far from being able to help out with resources for the town's general improvement, 'is actually insufficient for the ordinary purposes to which it is destined by Act of Parliament, of repairing and watching the streets of Calcutta ...' Admittedly, the Governor-General in Council was empowered to raise the house tax from 5 per cent on annual rent to 7 ½ per cent, but such an increase, if implemented, would raise a howl of protest and be beset by difficulties mainly of a political nature.

The magistrates then listed the problem areas facing the police establishment which required an 'immediate' remedy, and also 'the permanent objects of the police for the maintenance of which a local and ascertained revenue appears to us to be indispensably necessary'. Among the most important problems was the 'defective construction of the drains throughout the old part of the town of Calcutta'. As pointed out by Wellesley in his 1803 Minute, the drains had been constructed on a principle 'so radically defective that they do not answer any one of the purposes for which drains are usually intended'. A fund of not less than Rs 30,000 or Rs 40,000 annually would be needed for making new drains till the replacement of the old drains was completed. A second area requiring urgent attention was the opening of new streets, 'not only for the purpose of facilitating the communication between the different parts of the city but also for the purpose of affording convenient sites for the erection of new houses which are at present greatly wanted, particularly by the European part of the community'. Land would have to be purchased before the new streets could be made for which a 'considerable' sum would be required, as also for making the streets with brick and for constructing the associated drains. An allied, equally important, sphere was the re-making of some of the existing streets within the town with brick in view of the fact that during the rains the people were faced with 'the greatest inconvenience'. Yet another task waiting to be taken in hand was the widening of some of the existing streets and removing houses 'projecting into them which could only be effected by the purchase of the property required from individuals', which again would require substantial resources.

Corrupt as they were,[5] it would appear that even the Calcutta magistrates had been bitten by the planning bug for every one of these ideas was to figure in later years when separate and dedicated committees for the improvement of the town were to take on the responsibility for sprucing up different aspects of the development scenario. They felt that if the proposal to increase taxes was accepted and implemented, a fund of between Rs 1,00,000 and Rs 1,50,000 per annum would be available 'for the removal of existing nuisances and ... the gradual improvement' of the town. In case resources of this magnitude were not forthcoming because of problems with implementing the tax-increase proposal, the magistrates hoped the Government would sanction 'such disbursements as may be required for such of the purposes above noticed as appear to be most urgent and pressing, among which we must necessarily reckon the watering of the streets and the gradual reconstruction of the drains'. Once again having recourse to the loan proposal of the earlier committee for the improvement of the town, the magistrates said that the money thus spent could be treated as an advance to be repaid from the funds 'which may hereafter be raised for local purposes in the town of Calcutta'. On receipt of the above letter, the Government wrote to the advocate-general, Robert Smith, in early 1807 asking him for his views on 'whether any means can be legally adopted for raising taxes' such as those suggested by the magistrates.[6] Smith wrote back on the same day stating that 'such taxes cannot, as the law is at present, be imposed within the limits of Calcutta for the support of the police of the city by any authority in this country'.[7]

Even though Wellesley had left the scene some eighteen months earlier, his vision of a new Calcutta had left a mark on those in Government whom he had left behind. Following the advocate-general's response, Barlow, the Acting Governor-General, could have left the issue at that and told the magistrates that there was no way in which their suggestions could be accepted. But this was not what happened. In its letter[8] to the Court of Directors in London, the Governor-General in Council referred to the letter from the magistrates and said that it was clear that there was an 'urgent necessity' to raise 'additional funds for the removal of public nuisances and for other objects ultimately connected with the convenience and health of the city'. The Governor-General in Council asked for powers to impose taxes of the kind specified by the magistrates and also to increase or reduce the tax rates as required. It informed the Court that discussions had taken place to raise by a 'small' amount the town duties attracted by certain articles of consumption to assist in the funding of the projects concerned. It wrote that by such means 'it is possible (although we are not yet prepared to offer a final opinion on the subject) that funds may be raised sufficient for the purpose of watering the roads in and near the city of Calcutta'. However, it did not entertain 'the smallest hope' that resources raised from such increase would be adequate to ensure the general improvement of the town 'on the plan described in the letter from the magistrates'.

The Court's response was bureaucratic, to say the least. It wrote to the Council on 14 September 1808[9] that it was aware

> ... that no legal authority is rested in you to levy taxes on the inhabitants of Calcutta for any other purpose than that set forth in the clause of the

> Act of the 33rd of the King, Chap 52, Sec 158, and having already fully explained our sentiments as to the fund from whence the expense of watering the roads ought to be defrayed, we have now only to inform you that we shall take into consideration the propriety of applying to Parliament for the necessary authority to enable you to raise funds for the purposes mentioned by the magistrates of Calcutta in their address to your secretary under date the 27th December 1806.

The Government in Calcutta made it clear to the Directors that if the shortage in resources was allowed to persist the unsatisfactory state of affairs would continue, the fear being expressed that there would be no improvement unless 'a fixed local revenue could be raised and applied annually to the gradual improvement of the city'. As regards the Court's suggestion made in April 1806[10] that 'voluntary' contributions from the people could meet the expense on watering of the roads, the Governor-General in Council was firm in its view that this was not feasible. It said that while the 'opulent part of the European residents' in the town could perhaps be persuaded to do their bit in this direction, given the 'general character of the natives' there was no reason to expect that they would 'join in any plan of that nature'. It felt that an arrangement with the focus on voluntary contributions

> ... could only be adopted and carried into effect by the community itself without any interference on the part of Government, and we have not learned that any plan of that kind was in agitation, even when it was supposed that no further expense would be allowed on this account by Government.[11]

In the same letter, Barlow's Government in Calcutta apprised the Court that, despite the talk of a shortage of resources, the total municipal revenue as it existed at the time would allow the annual appropriation of a lakh of rupees to the improvement of the town, the funds being 'now applied to the general exigencies of Government'.

The Council said that from the 'tenure of [the Court's] observations and orders' it appeared that there was inadequate understanding of 'the nature of the municipal revenue of the town of Calcutta and the manner in which that fund has been appropriated'. The Council explained that the assessment or the house tax was levied under a specific statute (33 George III, Chapter 52, Section 158), the proceeds being 'exclusively applicable by law to repairing, watching and cleaning the streets of Calcutta'. Under this particular head, an annual deficiency had existed 'for sometime past' amounting on an average to Rs 27,278 over the three-year period 1804 to 1807. This shortfall—which had been reduced to less than Rs 4,000—was 'according to former usage in the public accounts' met by a loan to the magistrates and had been 'necessarily and unavoidably ... defrayed by Government, the magistrates possessing no funds from which they could by their own authority make good the deficiency'. Importantly, the Council clarified that though a shortfall did exist under the head of 'repairing, watching and cleaning of the streets', the overall municipal accounts was in surplus, 'exceeding a lakh of rupees', which was credited to the Government 'after defraying all expenses attendant on the support of the police of Calcutta, even in its present highly improved state'. Inevitably, the Council argued that, if the whole of the municipal revenue was applied to local purposes, a sum more than a lakh of rupees could be annually appropriated 'to the improvement of the town of Calcutta, which is now applied to the general exigencies of Government'.

Within a few months, a suggestion was made on the arrangement of funds for the town's development which, looking back, may be described as a game-changer. Lord Minto had taken over as Governor-General at the end of July 1807. In early October, George Dowdeswell, the Superintendent-General of the Police and Secretary to the Government, wrote to the Governor-General in Council[12] focusing on the poor state of police functions relating to 'the convenience and health of the inhabitants' as opposed to the 'immediate security of their persons and property'. Dowdeswell

51 Lord Minto in 1813

wrote that performance in this area of administration was so wanting that he had no doubt that 'any plan calculated to remove these inconveniences will appear to the Right Honourable the Governor General in Council to be deserving of full consideration'. Elucidating, he said that all the efforts made in the direction of town-improvement undertaken in recent times had pointed to two things: first, that 'many nuisances at present exist which, in a growing population like that of Calcutta, it is essential to the convenience and health of the inhabitants to remove'; secondly, that no means had as yet been found for 'raising a revenue for the removal of these nuisances and for the general improvement of the city without divesting to local purposes a part of the funds at present applied to the general exigencies of the State'. Wellesley had given priority to the problem of poor drainage in his Minute. Dowdeswell too wrote that the principal problem lay in the faulty drainage of the town, stating that all surveys and reports made till then had pointedly noticed 'the inconvenience arising from the erroneous principle upon which the drains have been constructed', and that it was with the objective of removing this defect that he had taken the initiative to write to the Government.

Dowdeswell then focused on the instrument of lotteries—which were already commonplace for all manner of private and public fund-raising—for generating the funds and referred to the lotteries that were already functioning to raise money for the erection of the Town Hall and 'for the reception, among other objects, of the statues voted to the late Marquis Cornwallis and Marquis Wellesley'.[13] He said three more lotteries were required for the completion of the Town Hall, but the schedule for drawing them had been so arranged that the funds required for the erection of the Town Hall would have been 'completely raised by the expiration of the ensuing year'. The secretary-cum-police chief then suggested that the lottery drawings be continued thereafter, the proceeds being set aside

> ... in the first instance, to the reconstruction of the drains within the town of Calcutta, and afterwards to the construction of some of the streets with brick, which are at present dirty roads or lanes, to the opening of new streets, and to such other objects of public utility as Government may direct.

He urged that if his proposal was accepted the plan should be put to work 'immediately'. He was aware that the lottery proceeds, to be used for improving the town, would not start flowing in till about another eighteen or twenty months (Dowdeswell was writing on 8 October 1807), but the drainage work would take 'some years' to complete, 'and only a limited sum can be annually applied to that purpose'. Following the suggestion made by the Calcutta magistrates in December of the previous year, he said that if the Government could advance 'as much money during the ensuing eighteen or twenty months as may be required for the reconstruction of the drains [his information was that the annual amount would be about Rs 40,000, which would of course be repaid from the lottery proceeds] a great deal of time would be saved without the smallest actual loss to the Company'.

Dowdeswell wanted emphasis laid on two aspects of the project, namely, implementation of the improvements projected for the town and superintendence of the lotteries. As regards the first point, he said that since the magistrates were already so closely associated with improvement work in the town, they should be constituted into a committee

> ... for the superintendence of the execution of the improvements in question, aided by the advice and assistance of one or two professional persons from the Corps of Engineers and of any other persons whom, from general or professional knowledge, Government may also wish to unite with them in that committee.

By these means, the secretary felt the Government would be in full control of the work that would be undertaken to improve the town. Being a civilian, he felt that a revenue officer should be inducted into the committee so that he could assist whenever there was a need to purchase ground 'for the opening of new streets or for other public purposes'. Wellesley had made the surveyor to the magistrates, Richard Blechynden, a member of his committee. Dowdeswell too wanted the surveyor to be involved in the executive part of the work, being the 'person best qualified to undertake it'. Keeping a hawk's eye on the expenditure aspect, he added that Blechynden's additional work would be 'so immediately connected with his ordinary duty that I am not aware that it would be necessary to grant him any additional salary on that account'. The only expense involved, excluding the actual cost of the improvements, would be that incurred on 'a small establishment similar to what was allowed to the secretary to the late Committee for Improving the Town of Calcutta to assist in the conduct of the correspondence'.

As for the superintendence of the lotteries, he suggested the setting up of an office of a separate commissioner to take on the job. The regularity and success with which the present commissioners had done their job naturally pointed towards them as a suitable agency to perform the task. But, as Dowdeswell wrote, in view of the complaints made by some of them regarding 'the interruption which it [the job] occasions to their official duties, some modification may be requisite in the selection of the Commissioners'. He concluded the letter with the remark that the only points on which a decision was required was 'the early commencement of the proposed repairs, the advances requisite for that purpose, and the appointment of persons to conduct that part of the business'.

Notes

1 Cornwallis had taken over for a second stint at the end of July 1805, his tenure being cut short by his death at Ghazipur before three months had passed. The mantle of the Governor-General had then passed temporarily to George Hilaro Barlow, at the time the seniormost civilian on the Supreme Council. He was to rule the roost till the end of July 1807 when Gilbert Lord Minto assumed charge of the East India Company's affairs in the East.

2 Judicial Criminal Proceedings, 29 January 1807. On 7 February 1807, the Governor-General in Council had written to the Court (General Letters to the Court of Directors, Judicial Series, 7 February 1807) that following the receipt of the latter's despatch of 25 April 1805, on the means to be adopted for raising new taxes 'for the improvement of the town of Calcutta, for watering the roads and for other purposes connected with the Police of the metropolis', it had referred the issue to the magistrates 'for their consideration and report'. The letter from the magistrates was the result of that reference.

3 See chapter 'The Dharamtala Bazar', note 15.

4 The magistrates would of course say this about themselves. But contemporary commentators from within the system saw the police office differently. Richard Blechynden's son, Arthur, who later succeeded his father as surveyor of roads, wrote in his diary in 1807 that the magistrates 'were "so slow in their operations, and so lazy and negligent in their duty" that business could hardly be carried on, works

were continually delayed, sure justice was not to be obtained, and bribery was rife' (Robb, *Sentiment and Self*, p. 193).

5 One contemporary described the magistrates as a 'set of extortioners and oppressors' (Robb, *Sentiment and Self*, p. 173).

6 Judicial Criminal Proceedings, 29 January 1807.

7 Ibid.

8 General Letters to the Court of Directors, Judicial Series, 7 February 1807.

9 General Letters from the Court of Directors.

10 General Letters from the Court of Directors, 25 April 1806. See also chapter 'The Stage is Set' for differences between Wellesley and the Court.

11 General Letters to the Court of Directors, Judicial Series, 7 February 1807.

12 Judicial Criminal Proceedings, 16 October 1807.

13 The statues of both Wellesley and Cornwallis are to be found today in the Victoria Memorial Hall. For the story of how they got there, see The Marquis Curzon of Kedleston, *British Government in India*, vol. 1 (London: Cassell and Company, 1925), pp. 87, 95–96.

28

Minto Gives a Push

While Wellesley had fired the first shot in the campaign to begin the era of urban planning in Calcutta, Minto truly set the ball rolling, the work being carried on subsequently by the Earl of Moira (later Lord Hastings) who succeeded him seven years later in October 1813 and remained in the hot seat till January 1823. By this time, the Lottery Committee had begun in right earnest its epochal work of sowing the seeds of modern Calcutta. Following his arrival, Minto had three months to familiarise himself with the problems confronting him among which were those relating to Calcutta. It is only normal to expect that during this period the new Governor-General would have held discussions with a wide range of people, officials and non-officials, including Dowdeswell, who would most certainly have primed him on the issues affecting the town. Conceivably, Minto may himself have suggested that his secretary and police chief put things down on paper.

Presented with Dowdeswell's views on 8 October 1807 on a new executive framework for the attempt to improve conditions in Calcutta, the Governor-General in Council resolved four days later on 12 October that it was 'essential to the health and convenience of the community that the long projected improvements in the town of Calcutta should be commenced without further delay'. It agreed with the plan proposed to defray the expenses of the development work. Importantly, Minto did not wait for the Court's approval of the proposal to have recourse to lotteries for the provision of funds for town-development and, in a manner of speaking, struck out on his own. In its letter to the Court dated 30 January 1808,[1] the Governor-General in Council fully backed Dowdeswell's plan of funding the improvements through lottery funds. It did not seek the Court's approval of Dowdeswell's plan but plainly told London that, in view of 'the urgent necessity which exists for commencing the improvements to which [Dowdeswell's] remarks refer without delay, particularly the construction of the drains and the opening of some new water-courses, we have appointed a committee for superintending the execution of the projected improvements'. It said the decision had been taken

> … to adopt the plan recommended by the Superintendent of Police, of establishing Lotteries, as soon as circumstances would permit for defraying the expense required on that account; and in the meantime to make such advances from the treasury as might be required for the commencement of the improvements in question.

Minto's unilateral initiative became a fait accompli for the Court. In its letter to the Governor-General in Council of 14 February 1812, in reply to the latter's 22 May 1807 missive,[2] the Court said it was 'satisfied' that the 'improvements and repairs' pertaining to the town 'were necessary' and that 'though we are not friendly to Lotteries in general, we are not aware that under the circumstances of the case and the limited extent of your powers as to assessing the inhabitants of Calcutta any [more] preferable mode of providing for the expence could have been resorted to'.[3] The gradual evolution of the Court's response to the use of lottery funds continued. Two years later, on 28 October 1814, on the subject of raising resources from lotteries for the town's development, the Court was writing to the Governor-General[4] that it had stated in former despatches its general objections to the encouragement of lotteries, 'by which we still abide'. However, it added that 'as in the present instance you state the incurred expenses to have been defrayed out of the funds already provided from those resources [lotteries], we are glad to find the community will in any way derive a benefit from their having existed'. In other words, the 'general objections' played second fiddle to the end-result which provided the justification for lottery funds being used for town development.

The new Committee for the Improvement of the Town of Calcutta was appointed having as its members officials and magistrates such as George Dowdeswell, Charles Buller, Captain Thomas Wood, P. Moir, C.F. Martyn, W.C. Blaquiere, A. Stewart and Thomas Charters. The Governor-General in Council laid out the scheme of action to be pursued. Among the 'objects of public and general utility' were, first, the construction of 'drains and watercourses in those streets and places in which works of that description may be requisite'; secondly, the reconstruction 'of such of the existing drains as shall appear to have been originally formed [as is very generally the case] on erroneous principles'; thirdly, the construction of such streets would have to be taken up 'which have not yet been paved with brick or other materials in those parts of the town which, from their extensive population, may appear to require it'; and fourthly, new streets were to be opened up to facilitate 'the communication between the different parts of the city and of affording sites for the erection of new buildings'. On roadmaking, the Governor-General in Council asked the committee to find out whether 'some other materials [could] be obtained for the repair of the streets, of a better and more durable nature than brick'.[5] Pointing to the increasing incidence of fires breaking out in the town between March and May, especially in the native parts, the committee was asked to ascertain the steps that could be taken to prevent such outbreaks. The committee was also asked to communicate to the Government any other aspects of town development other than those listed above which could be taken up for planning and execution.[6]

As regards the funding arrangement, the Governor-General in Council decreed that lotteries would be established 'as soon as circumstances will permit, on account of Government; and that the whole amount of their net produce shall be applied to the purposes in question'. It agreed with Dowdeswell's immediate plan of action regarding the reconstruction of old drains in some of the crowded parts of the town and the construction of new drains 'in certain places', and agreed to advance funds for such works by the Government 'as may be immediately required for those purposes, to be hereafter repaid from the produce of the lotteries'. The committee was asked to get on with such projects and was told—an old theme—that the surveyor to the magistrates would assist it as far as the 'executive part of the business' was concerned, 'under your direction and control'. In other words, what Wellesley had set out to do four years earlier and was thwarted in his attempts by a combative Court of Directors, Minto accomplished at the very beginning of his term, the magistrates offering him a way out regarding the funding problem, a solution which the 'city fathers' continued to rely on till the mid-1830s.

A year passed and the scheme for lotteries took further shape. On 17 October 1808 Dowdeswell wrote[7] to Thomas Brown, the chief secretary, that since the Government had approved the plan to establish lotteries for improvements 'in and near the city of Calcutta', it was time to lay down the arrangements for implementation of the proposal. On the appointment of commissioners for the superintendence of the lottery, he said that some of the 'present commissioners' for improving the town had complained 'of the interruption which it [their job as commissioners] occasioned to their official duties'. Dowdeswell felt the problem was not with 'the general conduct of the business ... but in signing of tickets and in the superintendence of the actual drawing of the lottery'. He said that if these responsibilities were taken care of there would be no problem with the present commissioners accepting the new role. Secondly, he suggested the appointment of a senior official as superintendent of the lotteries (with a salary of Rs 800 per month and a monthly house allowance of Rs 200), a part of whose job would be 'to sign the tickets and superintend the drawings'. Further, the number of commissioners should be reduced to six from the existing sixteen, the higher number being due to the fact that they had to perform 'the embarrassing duties above mentioned'. Imparting the requisite social status and standing to the exercise, Dowdeswell suggested that the lottery commissioners were to be selected 'from among the most respectable of the Company's servants at the Presidency'. He felt that two lotteries should be held each year 'on nearly the scale of those latterly established on account of the Town Hall amounting together to the sum of 14,00,000 or 15,00,000 rupees, estimating the aggregate expenses … at 20,000 or 30,000 rupees per annum'. The secretary wrote that the main reason for his writing to the Government so early was that 'sufficient time would have to be allowed for arranging all the subordinate parts of the plan [previous] to the commencement of the ensuing year'. He proposed the immediate appointment of the commissioners and officers, their new positions taking effect from 1 January 1809. Dowdeswell's scheme was adopted, the following persons being appointed commissioners: J. Fombelle, G. Dowdeswell, J. Thornhill, C. Buller, H. Stone and J.W. Sherer. John Adam was appointed superintendent of the lotteries.[8]

Six years earlier, Wellesley had pointed out in his Minute that an improvement of the town's drainage system was the first job which should be taken up, a priority reiterated by Dowdeswell in his October 1807 letter to Minto. This is the road which the new committee took as it began its work on town improvement. It would, however, be wrong to suggest that in the intervening period no work whatever had been done in this sphere. The town magistrates had in fact continued with their normal work, engaging in disaggregated drainage work if and when the need arose. Thus, their surveyor had routinely engaged in the annual exercise of drawing up a list of projects to be completed in the ensuing twelve months, which was followed up by an action-taken report at the end of the year concerned. At the end of December 1808, Richard Blechynden was writing to the Government[9] that he had

> ... completed all the pucka drains contained in my report of January 27, 1808 with the exception of the one along Esplanade Row, which cannot be made until Colonel Garstin has finished the Town Hall,[10] and another small one in Ranny Moody Gully which must be left in its present state until I can ascertain whether it is not possible to raise the east end of Mr Raban's compound.[11]

Referring to one of the most important drainage improvements in the town, which would mark a break with the 'system' in place over the past decades, Blechynden wrote that 'as many [drains] as possible' mentioned in his January report 'were made to empty themselves into the two main sewers that lead into the river'. However, he felt that as 'all the water to the east of the Loll Bazar must be drained into the Salt Water Lake, there ought in like manner to be a main sewer along the Boitaconnah road, and another along the Durrumtollah road, to collect the water and convey it to the Mahratta ditch'. The surveyor said he was 'afraid' to propose the project, especially the Lalbazar main sewer, 'for the road being more than a mile in length, the cost of this single main drain will be as much as you would wish to devote to the whole of the improvement of the town for an entire year, *vizt* sicca rupees 30,100'. Even so, Blechynden, left no stone unturned in laying stress on the fundamental importance of the project. He wrote that the proposed main sewer was 'of the first necessity' because the consequence of 'making collateral drains without some convenient receptacle to hold the water till it can run off will be inundating the town instead of draining it'. As it was, 'the very road in question, the Boitaconnah road, is for hours under water after heavy rain for want of a receptacle of the kind'. In fact, as early as 1799, Blechynden had posited the idea that the gradual declivity of the town from Chitpur Road was towards the east, which is why he had suggested that the Baitakhana Road (Circular Road) 'which ran along the line of the Maratha ditch ... be made a foot lower than the Chitpur Road'. This would result in rainwater flowing 'away from the river towards the salt lakes – that is, from west to east – and so help reduce flooding in the built-up parts of the settlement'.[12]

Writing to the committee for improving the town on 28 December 1808, the Governor-General in Council backed Blechynden's proposal. It said that, as the 'declivity of the town east of the Cossitollah lies to the eastward, it appears impracticable effectually to drain the town without a principal watercourse in that direction'. Blechynden's fears on the issue of funds were misplaced, for the Council proclaimed that even though the cost of the sewer project was 'considerable' it had no hesitation 'in recommending that the work be undertaken'. On its part, the committee added that it had learnt from its own enquiries that 'whatever partial improvements may be made in the construction of the small drains in other streets', they would have little impact unless 'a principal watercourse [was constructed] to the eastward'. Apart from the main-sewer project, the committee also drew attention to the 'repair or construction of sundry drains on the principle of those which have been recently completed', which means that there would be a continuity of the drainage-improvement schemes begun earlier. Along with the estimate given for the major project, the total expenditure for the drainage schemes for 1809 was estimated to be more than Sicca Rs 50,000, which was approved by the Government.

Getting river water farther into the town which could then be used by *bhistees* to water the streets is something which people in Calcutta remember seeing even in the fifties of the last century. Richard Blechynden[13] may be credited with having first mooted the idea though in a very primitive shape in keeping with the times he was living in. In his 27 December 1808 letter he wrote that while during the course of the year he had been working on the drains taking the water to the river, it had occurred to him that 'every drain that emptied itself into the river might in like manner be supplied with water from it, for watering the roads, and thereby preserve

52 Even as late as the mid-1820s 'bhistees' were drawing water from Laldighi, as is depicted in the 1826 painting of James Baillie Fraser

53 An aqueduct in Old Court House Street, opposite the gate to Laldighi (BBD Bagh tank), from a painting by James Baillie Fraser of the Scotch church (St Andrew's), 1826

a considerable quantity of the Loll Dhiggy water for more useful purposes'. He reported to the committee that, with this scheme in mind, he had taken

> ... special care in the construction of the drains ... and have the pleasure to inform you that, from a simple process[14] ... the drains around Tank Square, in Court House street, Loll Bazar, Mission Row *Taunt Kannah* and Cross street[15] may be filled with river water, so that the *bheesties* have only to dip their *mussucks* into them and have them instantly filled close to the very spot they are to water.

He estimated that the 'great reduction' in the number of bhistees employed for the work of watering the roads would 'more than pay the expense of pumping water at the river side, independent of the great saving of the Loll Dhiggy water, at a time it would not be replenished from the river on account of its brackishness and when a great demand would be made on it for the wants of the shipping of the port'. Blechynden defended himself against the possible charge that he was busy devising ways to reduce the expenditure on bhistees, which was not a part of the town surveyor's job, by saying that he had been led to make the suggestion in view of the constant pressure on him to 'keep up a supply of good water in the Loll Dhiggy'.[16] Given the central importance of supplying water to the principal roads in the town to keep them clean, it was to be expected that with time there would be a continual upgradation in the technology with which this could be done. This is precisely what happened in Calcutta, the different stages being the building of the first aqueducts in 1813 to carry the water from the river (see image 53 on p. 490), the setting up of a mechanical pump at Chandpal Ghat to lift the water into the aqueducts, which was subsequently 'upgraded' to a steam engine the smoking chimney of which can be seen in portrayals of the riverside during the early part of the nineteenth century (see image 54 on p. 492).[17]

On the supply of good water, the Committee for the Improvement of the Town attached early importance to the subject when it wrote to the Government on 28 December 1808[18] that the 'third' project for the ensuing year[19]—apart from the main sewers and work on sundry drains—was an improvement 'of one of the principal watercourses of the city, which runs from the vicinity of the great tank commonly called Loll Dighee to the river'. The committee explained that the objective of this specific project was to have

> ... a perfect facility of filling that reservoir with water from the river when it is not brackish, particularly in the rains, when it is most pure, and of supplying water during the months of March, April and May at little trouble and consequently at reduced expense for watering the streets; and by those means of preserving the water in the Loll Dighee for more essential purposes.

The committee said that the project was 'apparently also connected with the constant supply of good and pure water for the shipping of this port, but on which it is not of course our province to offer any opinion'.

54 The smoking chimney (left) of the steam engine at Chandpal ghat. The Supreme Court building is on the right in the painting, by William Wood, 1833

Calcutta had not yet become a great port servicing the needs of the British empire in the East. Even so, in the early years of the nineteenth century, shipping had become the backbone of the British presence in the city. Not surprisingly, the subject of water for shipping had become important enough to have generated controversy. On 23 September 1805 Blechynden wrote[20] to Captain John Hayes arguing against the setting up of a reservoir filled with 'pure, wholesome water, for the shipping of the port' in the vicinity of Chinsurah. The justification cited for the scheme was that the reservoir would be 'beyond the influence of the flood tide'. The surveyor felt there was no need to go to Chinsurah for this purpose when 'a thousandth part of the expense would provide you your desideratum in the very heart of Calcutta'. He pointed out that the principal objection to the river water 'before Calcutta arises from its being sometimes brackish', but this happened only during March, April and May 'during which period none of it need be pumped into reservoir I allude to'. Blechynden told Hayes that the reservoir was none other than the great tank 'now full of excellent water from the river, and the purity of this water is recommended by the able analysis of Dr William Hunter, the surgeon to the marine to whom you may refer'. He added that since the great tank held 'no less than 1,30,320 tons' of water, there was no fear of a scarcity during the March-May period 'when water will not be pumped into it'. Spelling out how the arrangement for watering the streets would work during this period, Blechynden wrote that the cost would be cut 'by directing the *bheesties* to take the water requisite for the watering the roads from the pucka drain which will still remain full of water, and be supplied by the machinery at the river side, although the channel thence to the tank will be stopped'.

Notes

1 General Letters to the Court, Judicial Series.
2 General Letters from and to the Court of Directors, Judicial Series.
3 The Court made the reference to lotteries despite the fact that the 22 May letter from Calcutta had made no reference to them whatever.
4 General Letters from the Court of Directors, Judicial Series.
5 See Judicial Criminal Proceedings, 6 January 1809 for the surveyor's views on the subject. Three different modes of road-making were examined, the surveyor opting for the 'pucka pavement' variant while the committee for improving the town favoured the 'brick and gravel' method.
6 Judicial Criminal Proceedings, 16 October 1807.
7 Judicial Criminal Proceedings, 21 October 1808.
8 On 14 January 1809 the 'commissioners for superintending the lottery' wrote to the Government that the drawing of the 'present Town Hall lottery being nearly completed' they were submitting the draft

of a scheme for the first lottery for the town's improvement to be drawn on 1 July 1809. The lottery would incorporate some changes compared to the Town Hall lottery. The commissioners (J. Fombelle, G. Dowdeswell and J. Thornhill) proposed limiting the first lottery to 6,000 tickets, or Sicca Rs 6 lakhs, 'instead of continuing the amount at Rs 7,50,000, the standard of the past lotteries'. They felt that the experience of the first lottery would enable them to recommend any changes if necessary for future such exercises. The first prize was fixed at Rs 1 lakh. There were to be two second prizes of Rs 50,000 each, three third prizes of Rs 20,000 each, six fourth prizes of Rs 10,000 each, ten fifth prizes of Rs 5,000 each, fourteen sixth prizes of Rs 1,000 each, and 1,440 seventh prizes of Rs 100 each. Rs 72,000 was set aside for 'the improvement of Calcutta and the expenses of the lottery' yielding a total expenditure of Rs 6 lakhs which was to be collected from the sale of 6,000 tickets. There were other regulations such as that 'the 15th drawn ticket on the last day will be entitled to one of the prizes of Sicca Rs 50,000'; '... the prizes with the exception of the tickets sold at Madras and Bombay will be paid at the Bank of Bengal without deduction thirty days after the drawing shall have been completed. In like manner the prizes drawn amongst tickets sold at Madras and Bombay will be paid by the agents at those Presidencies respectively so soon as the necessary adjustments thereof can be transmitted to the agents.'

The proposed rules also laid down that '... the price of such tickets as may remain unsold on the 28th of June (three days prior to the drawing) will be raised to sicca rupees 110 for each ticket until the period fixed for the commencement of the drawing, when the tickets unsold will be liable to such further progressive increase of price as the commissioners shall judge proper.'

It was proposed that tickets 'signed by John Adam Esq, Superintendent of the Lotteries, will be ready for sale at the Bank of Bengal on the 1st of March 1809', and that 'a supply of tickets will be forwarded to Messrs Harrington and Co. at Madras and to Messrs Forbes and Co. at Bombay as soon as may be practicable, to be sold at those Presidencies'. The proposed scheme was signed by John Adam and dated 20 January 1809. The Governor-General in Council accepted the plan as proposed, decreeing that '... the whole of the funds which may be realised by the above means will be applied to the improvement of the town of Calcutta and its vicinity after defraying the necessary expenses of the lotteries and any deficiency [that] may [arise] in the funds required for the completion of the Town Hall' (Judicial Criminal Proceedings, 20 January 1809).

9 Judicial Criminal Proceedings, 6 January 1809.

10 The decision to build the Town Hall, which has come down to us, was taken in February 1804, Colonel John Garstin of the Engineers having already finalised the design of the building—in Richard Blechynden's judgement, 'with a mixture of arrogance, poor design, miscalculation, and bad execution' (Robb, *Sentiment and Self*, p. 8)—before Wellesley left for home the following year. However, it took eight long years to build, the completion of the edifice being reported in 1813 under Minto (Losty, *Calcutta City of Palaces*, p. 91).

11 Thomas Raban was an attorney in Calcutta at the time. See Robb, *Sentiment and Self*, p. 34.

12 Robb, *Useful Friendship*, p. 132.

13 Blechynden, who arrived in Calcutta in 1782, had long experience with civic work in the town. As early as 1784 he had found employment as 'unofficial assistant' to Edward Tiretta, the town's surveyor of roads, an engagement that lasted till the early 1790s. In 1797 he was appointed officially as Tiretta's assistant, succeeding him as superintendent of roads in 1803. Blechynden remained in this post till his death in February 1822. Peter Robb (ibid., p. xvii) writes that throughout his time in India, Blechynden 'engaged in public infrastructural improvement, as well as private building contracts and surveying for the Supreme Court and others. He was respected generally not only for his work for Calcutta but for his fairness, and hence much employed with powers of attorney, in mediation, and as a legal executor'.

14 The cost of the scheme, including infrastructure, was put at Sicca Rs 4,751-8-0.

15 Cotton (*Calcutta Old and New*, p. 277) says that Barretto's Lane—which today links British Indian Street (Abdul Hamid Street) and Mangoe Lane (Surendro Mohon Ghose Sarani)—is called 'in the maps of 1792 and 1794' Cross Street. This is borne out by both Wood's map of 1784–1785 and Upjohn's map of 1792–1793, the latter however showing another road leading to the river called Barretto's Lane (No. 10 in the map's 'References').

16 At the end of 1809, Blechynden listed among his completed drainage projects the following: 'A large main sewer with a shallow drain on the top extending from the Loll Bazar cross road to the Circular road'

(Judicial Criminal Proceedings, 24 November 1809). The committee for improvement of the town had shot down the surveyor's proposal to build the Dharamtala main sewer, or one 'in any part of the town', on the ground that it would be 'premature' to do so at that juncture (Judicial Criminal Proceedings, 6 January 1809).

17 Judicial Criminal Proceedings, 29 January and 15 April 1814; Lottery Committee Proceedings, 16 July 1818 and 9 December 1819.

18 Judicial Criminal Proceedings, 6 January 1809.

19 The Judicial Criminal Proceedings of 24 November 1809 carried a report by Blechynden which indicated that 'nearly' all the three projects had been completed during the year.

20 Judicial Criminal Proceedings, 6 January 1809.

29

A Flurry of Proposals

Lord Minto ended his Governor-Generalship in early October 1813. Towards the end of his tenure the tempo of work undertaken by the committee for improving the town, whose president at the time was John Eliot, was increasing as is indicated by the flurry of proposals—in the shape of three letters all dated 6 May—it sent to the Governor-General in Council for sanction and eventual implementation.[1] In the first letter, the committee sent a proposal drawn up by one of its members, W. Blaquiere, to increase the supply of 'wholesome water' for the native parts of the town, the estimated cost of which was put at Sicca Rs 7,040, its comment being that it would be 'superfluous to enlarge on the substantial benefits which the community would [derive] from more abundant supplies of wholesome water'. Blaquiere's letter to the committee (of 25 April) said that his proposals were the result of discussions within the committee which laid stress on the point that 'public tanks in different parts of the town would not only add to its improvement but be highly beneficial to the inhabitants who suffer greatly from the want of pure water'. He selected two spots where such tanks could be located, the first an 'old tank' called Neogypukur measuring two bighas four kathas ten chittacks, located to the south of what was then Janbazar Street (today's S.N. Banerjee Road) in the Taltala area, and the second, measuring a bigha and kathas, at 'Durzee

Para in Simleah in a north-west direction [to] Mannictulla in a part of town thronged by inhabitants who suffer much from the scarcity of water'.

The second letter dwelt on extending the supply of river water to the tanks in the event of the rains failing. This was part of a plan presented to the committee for that part of the town 'extending from Chandpaul Ghaut to the south-east gate of the Government House, from thence to the east end of Writers' Buildings and west end of the Durrumtollah'. The estimate submitted for the entire project added up to sicca Rs 60,000 and it included

> ... a road from Chandpaul Ghaut to the south-[east] gate of the Government House, the [road] from the south-east gate of the Government House to the great Circular road [through the maidan?], the road from the west end of the Dhurrumtollah to Bridgeah *Tullao* [Birjee-talao], the road from [that to] the burying ground to the north-east of Mr Middleton's[2] estate, the Court House, the Bow Bazar and round tank square.[3]

The plans were ambitious and the committee was prepared to proceed cautiously. It proposed that only a part of the plan be immediately implemented, leaving open the option of extending it to other parts of the town—for which the estimate had already been drawn up—basing itself on the experience gained from the partial implementation.

The plan also proposed the building of a 'conduit' (an aqueduct) much upon the principle of that already made on the sides of the road over the Course (maidan),

> ... on the side of the principal streets [through] which the water is to be conveyed from Chandpaul Ghaut, and the saving in the [wages] of the *bheesties*, it is supposed, will induce the proprietors of the houses, who now water only a small portion of the streets, to keep the streets well-watered at their own expense.

The committee felt that when the drain was made it would afford a ready supply of water to the engines 'which [in view of] the late conflagrations has been much wanted'. The plan had been authored by H. Wood, who had offered to superintend the works 'free of expense'. His estimate being on the 'lowest scale, such as only to cover the actual expense attending the construction of masonry', the committee asked the Governor-General in Council to advance Sicca Rs 15,000 for the project.

The third letter was more project-specific in that it proposed the leavening of 'an inconvenient and dangerous angle at the junction of Colingah Street with the great Circular road', the cost of which was reckoned to be just Rs 25. However, as much as Rs 2,800 was also sought for the 'reconstruction or enlargement of several bridges in the Esplanade and in different parts of the town', and Rs 40-13-3 for the 'addition to the bridge on the north of Mr Middleton's premises on the burying ground road'. The detailed estimate provided for the work on the bridges shows that the development work was spread across the town, from 'widening the Dum Dum road bridge at Shaum bazar', 'opposite the burying ground road leading to Gurriahut', the Chowringhee and Hospital sorties, to the maidan near the Alipore bridge.

It would be unfair to accuse Minto's committee for improving the town of favouring the development of just the 'white' part of the town at the expense of the sprawling, congested 'native' section, mainly to the north but also to the south. As the saying goes, one swallow does not make a summer, but the flight of even a solitary swallow (which, of course, was not the case here) ought not to be overlooked and ignored because it is after all a welcome harbinger of warmth and sunshine. Take, for example, the case of the road to the Kali temple from the Russapuglah Road[4] which was in bad shape in 1813, and which was improved substantially by John Eliot, the magistrate, who noted its poor condition while passing by the road on his 'constant visits' to the Russapuglah jail. He wrote to the Government on 19 March[5] that he was appalled at the 'shocking state of the cross lane from Russah to the temple at Colly Ghaut', specifically by the sight of women with infants in their arms, their feet

> ... cut in a [fearful?] manner by . . . bricks thrown on this very narrow lane by a person of the name of Fackeerchaund Dutt, who constantly promised to put it in a complete state of repair, from a motive of piety. But with most natives of his description, their penurious disposition ever-prevents the execution and he has since avowed to me that he declined any further repair.

The lane, Eliot wrote, was so narrow that two palanquins could not pass each other, at places 'even one with convenience', let alone a carriage. Respectable natives had frequently brought up the subject with him, the plea always being to improve the condition of a road which was used so greatly by pilgrims 'from all parts of India', on their way to the 'great temple of Cally Takoorany at Cally Ghaut'.[6]

Eliot buckled down to the task of trying to restore 'an old and ancient road from general neglect, long usurped by all'. He expostulated with the 'Bramins of the temple and the zemindars of the place' for having allowed the encroachments which had made passage through the lane so very difficult. He wrote:

> I considered it my duty, as a magistrate, to remove the difficulty of access to the temple, being fully aware how gratifying it would be to the feelings of the Hindoos of every description; and when I considered the then state of this lane, the immense number of pilgrims constantly and daily resorting to this temple of such veneration to the Hindoos, and the suffering of the aged , infirm and particularly the women who all go barefooted, it became an act of humanity after the dreadful sights I personally witnessed.

Eliot reported to the Government that he had been successful in inducing the natives to remove the encroachments and also set their houses back from the road, with the result that it had now been widened to a breadth of twenty-six feet 'to the universal satisfaction of every individual who has the occasion to visit the temple', using even their carriages which was not possible earlier. The magistrate, however, drew attention to the fact that the road was 'only an earthen one, and in the rains is liable to rapid destruction particularly in such a general and constant thoroughfare, and ultimately liable to become again impassable'. He recommended that it be made pucca and that eight bridges be built across it for which Sicca Rs 6,240 would be needed, 'a very small sum considering the utility of this road and its communication with the temple'.

The magistrate had done his job but the Governor-General in Council did not agree with his suggestion regarding funding of the work. It wanted 'the opulent Hindoos ... themselves (to) adopt some means of repairing the roads leading to their places of worship or that they must submit to the inconvenience arising from the want of the necessary repairs'. The question arises: what did repair work on a road have to do with religion? Would the Government have agreed to the repairs if no temple had been located on the road? Incidentally, from the point of improvement *per se*, the denouement was fortunate for Eliot wrote back to the Government[7] informing it that the money required for repairing the road had been collected. He enclosed a letter he had received from Radhamadhub Banerjee, Radhamohun Banerjee and Abhoycharan Banerjee, all 'respectable natives of the town', which read:

> We cannot express the joy you have been good enough to afford us, by obtaining the orders of his Lordship in Council for the erection of our Colly Ghaut Road and in consequence of which we think it quite needless to raise this small sum of money required by Mr Blechynden by subscription for that purpose. We beg leave to furnish you with bank notes for Sicca Rs 6,240 in full of Mr Blechynden's estimate and trust your goodness will order the needful to be done.

It would be unfair to infer from the official stand on the repair of this particular road that, as a matter of policy, the authorities were generally not interested, or hesitant, to develop the native part of the town. Available evidence suggests that the committee for improvement of the town was in fact also working towards bettering the conditions prevailing in the native areas. To take an example, four years earlier, in November 1809, the committee presented to the Governor-General in Council[8] an estimate totalling Sicca Rs 17,187 for 'construction of some of the streets inhabited chiefly by the natives with bricks'. The committee felt that the 'execution of this work, to a far greater extent than that which is in the present instance proposed to be adopted, is essential to the health of the city and, we presume to add, to the credit of the Government'. It added:

> Persons who have only seen the European part (which is probably the case with a great many individuals) have little conception of the state of the remainder of the city. But those who have been led there by their public, or private avocations, will with one voice bear testimony to the disgusting and wretched condition of at least six parts in eight of the town of Calcutta.[9]

A more reliable clue to the committee's attitude towards developing the native areas is to be found in its views on the street-watering issue, a civic responsibility which was gaining in importance with the growth of the town.[10] Prior to October 1802, watering the streets of the town was the responsibility of the Military Board when a proposal was made to transfer the work to 'the police department'.[11] On 15 October of that year the Military Board wrote to the Government that 'the majority' of the members of the board felt that the roads could be watered 'at a less expence by the magistrates of police of the town of Calcutta than by the executive officer of Fort William whose numerous and important avocations leave him but little leisure to attend to the proper and *oeconomick* [emphasis in original] execution of this duty'. Commenting on the Government's order of 10 March 1809 on 'the watering of the streets in and near the city', the committee rued the fact that, given 'the legal difficulties which exist, or rather the absolute impracticability of raising new taxes in the town of Calcutta', the Court of Directors should have prohibited 'the continuance of a plan which certainly contributed essentially to the convenience, and we think to the health of the city'.[12] Under the plan struck down, the committee had suggested that the funds raised in each street could be applied to the watering of that particular street.

Discussing the project further, the committee for improvement of the town pointed out that there were three 'possible means' of raising such funds: first, 'a part of the lottery funds' could be set aside for the purpose; secondly, the rate of assessment could be increased; and thirdly, 'voluntary contributions' could be welcomed. The obvious difficulty with the first point was that a charge on the lottery funds 'would create a considerable reduction of the funds applicable to the construction of new streets and drains and other objects of the first importance to the salubrity of the city'. The committee ruled out this option 'except in case of actual necessity'. The second option would have made sense if the assessment was raised 'in that part of the town occupied chiefly by Europeans without enhancing the rate on the houses of the natives', but this, the committee said, was 'not legally practicable'. As regards raising the assessment across the board, the committee felt that the natives

> ... would have substantial ground for complaint were a tax, which is raised for the express purpose of watching, cleansing and repairing the streets of Calcutta, to be increased while the streets in their own quarter of the town (although well-guarded and watched) are very imperfectly drained, and not at all repaired.

In other words, the principle of equity would have been violated here. The committee was a practitioner of the art of consultation and persuasion as opposed to the peremptory imposition of the official diktat. It wrote: 'Wherever the natives shall have learnt from experience that their convenience is consulted in repairing and draining the streets, the same objections may not occur, as now exist, to raising the assessment'.

But this option belonged to the future and was, therefore, of little use at the time. Of the three paths, therefore, only the third, namely, voluntary contributions, remained, the committee stating that since it had no other option it would traverse it but in the form of an 'experiment'. It told the Government that it was

> … not well-informed with respect to the course pursued on occasions of this nature in the principal cities in England, as noticed by the Honourable Court,[13] but we apprehend that it must at all times be extremely difficult, without the sanction of legal authority, to give consistency and durability to any plan in which the disposition and convenience of the poor and the rich, of Europeans and natives, of the liberal and the parsimonious, are liable to be consulted.[14]

Notes

1 Judicial Criminal Proceedings, 14 May 1813.

2 Which Middleton is this? There was one, a president of the Board of Trade in the 1770s, who once resided in the house which was the garden house of Henry Vansittart, the Governor. This Middleton died in 1775. There was another Samuel Middleton who too belonged to the civil service. Cotton (*Calcutta Old and New*, p. 232) writes that this Middleton, 'who owned considerable property in the neighbourhood [of Park Street] and who flourished in the time of Cornwallis and Wellesley', acted for a time as police magistrate and was appointed 'Commissioner in the Sunderbands for suppressing depredation of dacoits' in 1792. The records also indicate that an S. Middleton was the magistrate in Jessore in August 1804. This Middleton was sacked by the Government, a decision with which the Court of Directors agreed (General Letters from the Court of Directors to the Governor-General, 14 Sepember 1808) because he had been convicted 'of having held an interest in several indigo

works in the district of Jessore contrary to his duty and the terms of his Oath by which he was bound not to be concerned … directly or indirectly in any commercial transaction'. The *Calcutta Municipal Gazette* of 7 August 1982 said that Middleton was 'owner of property measuring 79 bighas south of the Burial Ground Road, by the side of [Charles] Short's lands' (Nair, *A History of Calcutta's Streets*, p. 843). Peter Robb (*Self and Sentiment*, p. 234) provides proof that this Middleton was indeed the Jessore man. He defrauded Richard Blechynden, who he had engaged in his building projects, through his 'procrastination and obfuscation' which ultimately cost Blechynden 'his fee and many of his costs, ending his hope of a return to England'. Middleton re-entered the Company's service following an interview with the then Governor-General, Lord Minto (Robb, *Useful Friendship*, p. 270, note 3).

3 The relevant page of the Proceedings volume at the West Bengal State Archives is torn making decipherment difficult.

4 One here thinks of the Kali Temple Road, but see Nair, *A History of Calcutta's Streets*, pp. 466–467.

5 Judicial Criminal Proceedings, 27 March 1813.

6 The Kalighat temple had been rebuilt by the Sabarna Choudhuries in 1809. See article 'Kalighat and Calcutta' by Gaur Das Bysack in *The Calcutta Review*, vol. XCII, January 1891, pp. 305–327; also Nair, *A History of Calcutta's Streets*, p. 466.

7 Judicial Criminal Proceedings, 17 April 1813.

8 Judicial Criminal Proceedings, 24 November 1809. The committee's letter was signed by G. Dowdeswell, T. Wood, C.F. Martyn, W.C. Blaquiere and R. Fergusson.

9 The surveyor's list of streets in the native part of the town to be made of brick was as follows:

Name of road	Long	Wide	Sq. Ft.	Sicca Rs
Burtollah St	1,200	15	18,000	927-4-0
Burra Bazar High St	1,163	22	25,586	1,421-8-0
-Do- to Dhurrumtollah St	272	15	4.080	210-4-0
-Do- to the eastward	150	15	2,250	115-12-0

-Do- to the south-east	740	14	10,360	575-12-0
-Do- to the west	428	14	5,992	333-0-0
-Do- to Cotton St	426	12	5,112	263-0-0
-Do- to the Armenian Church	450	15	6,750	347-12-0
Cotton St	1,668	16	22,688	1,168-8-0
Dyahattah St	698	15	10,440	580-0-0
From the Jail of the Court of Requests to the Bow Bazar	2,500	15	37,500	2,083-0-0
From the Collootollah to Tantonia Road and filing 2 sides of a large tank 300ft long	3,700	15	55,500	3,383-5-0
Mannuktollah Road from Circular Road to Simlah	4,473	16	71,568	3,976-0-0
North branch of -Do- from Simlah to Chitpore Road	1,234	13	16,042	891-6-0
South branch of -Do-	1,260	13	16,380	910-5-0
TOTAL Sicca Rs				17,187

10 Judicial Criminal Proceedings, 24 November 1809.

11 Judicial Criminal Proceedings, 4 November 1802.

12 Letter from the Court of Directors, Judicial Series, 14 September 1808. See chapter 'The Stage is Set'.

13 See chapter 'The Stage is Set'.

14 A draft notification was prepared by the committee with little expectation that it would be approved by the Government. Among other things, it fixed the rate of contribution by the public 'at the same rate as the monthly tax on houses, it being computed that this rate will in ordinary cases be sufficient to defray the expenses required'. In the event, the Government accepted the proposal along with the committee's suggestion that an European be appointed on a salary of Rs 50 a month, who was to be employed 'under the general control of the surveyor, in adjusting and levying the contributions, in

superintending the persons employed in watering the roads, and in execution of any of the general duties entrusted to Mr Blechynden which may be required of him' (Judicial Criminal Proceedings, 24 November 1809).

30

Birth of a Canal

The implementation of Wellesley's vision to improve the town was beset with problems of his own making, springing mainly from his inclination to be his own master in faraway India. The result was that his effort in this direction had to be put on hold. Such hurdles, however, did not obstruct Minto's path, and it is safe to suggest that the real work of improving Calcutta's basic infrastructure was begun during his time. Some of the benefits resulting from the development work had begun to show during Minto's time itself. Thus, the aligning of the water courses in an east-west direction had led to a remarkable improvement in draining the town east of Chitpur Road, where the gradient of the town was towards the salt water lake. The extent of the improvement which resulted from the step taken is adequately indicated in a letter[1] written by John Eliot, the magistrate of the 24-Parganas, in October 1813.

Eliot told Dowdeswell, who had by then become chief secretary, that there were three clear objectives for the 'straight road' opened by him 'from the grand Circular one bordering the town [Circular Road], to the Salt Water Lake'.[2] The first was the 'attainment of a wish expressed by the principal native inhabitants of the town of Calcutta … presented to me on the bench of the Supreme Court', which was later backed by 'a general representation from the principal European merchants and Captains connected with the shipping of India'. The second was

> … converting the ditches on the two sides by which the road must be formed into water courses to aid the draining of the town from the Chitpore Road and from Matchoah Bazar down Narrain Chattergeah's Street[3] (see PIX 43), which I observed was materially wanted to give [passage] to the water in a direct line, and by which [means] I was convinced from my observations the large lodgement of water between the Chitpore and the Circular Road in that direction could be reduced.

The magistrate wrote that 'on any slight excess of rain', Chitpur Road would be under two to three feet of water. The third objective was the forming of a 'direct and easy communication' with the salt water lake and 'that part of the town'.

Eliot said there was little doubt that the third objective had been 'fully attained' and that the first would be discussed 'on a future occasion in my capacity as town magistrate'. As regards the drainage justification, which is of greater interest to us, he said that the best proof that the objective had been met was provided by a recent 'violent storm' which saw 'no lodgement of water at the Chitpore road' despite the fact that the rain was heavy enough to fill that road, 'and other places of that part of Calcutta', with water at least four-feet deep. The magistrate wrote with satisfaction:

> I purposely went down that road [Chitpore road] at 5 o'clock on the very evening of the storm to observe the effect of the several water courses I had recently formed, and I had the gratification to observe there was not a drop of water lying on any part of the road to Chitpore.

There was of course another reason for Eliot narrating these welcome facts to the Governor-General in Council. The new watercourse had had an adverse impact of its own on people living in the area through which it passed. As the magistrate himself pointed out, the heavy downpour had 'unfortunately … attended with considerable injury to various individuals' with many houses and trees being brought down 'by the immense torrent of water brought down this new [passage] for the water from this part of Calcutta'. Consequently, wooden planks as long as twenty to thirty feet were required for people to commute between the new road and their houses which had been separated by the 'ravine' created by the force of the water hurtling east from the town, a project which would need an expenditure of Rs 500 to 600. Eliot also sought approval for compensation for those whose houses had been 'washed into the water courses', the payment being justified on the ground that the water course was a part of the scheme proposed by him to the Governor-General in Council on 16 December 1811, which was subsequently approved. These were teething problems for the city's development effort and the Government was willing to pay for damage suffered by the people in the course of implementation. The estimated expenditure for the planks as well as the compensation sought for people whose property had been affected 'accidentally' were allowed.

In fact, an east-west waterway near Sealdah was an important drainage course which existed in the area in former times. The proposal to reopen one was a part of the general effort to improve the drainage in the eastern part of the town. As much was mentioned to the Governor-General in Council by the commissioners for improving the town in their very first letter (dated 27 October 1807) to it following Minto's assumption of office.[4] The letter laid emphasis on the 'necessity of *reopening* [emphasis added] a canal which we have reason to believe formerly communicated from the Mahratta Ditch at the east end of the Dhurrumtollah Road with the Salt Water Lake'.[5] The commissioners wrote that because of the 'obstruction of that passage, all the water and filth collected in the Mahratta Ditch from far the greater part of the town becomes stagnant and offensive in the highest degree'. By reopening the canal, which would be about two miles in length, the commissioners said a passage would be formed to the salt water lake, which was necessary for effective drainage. As a first step towards implementation of the proposal, the Government was asked to ascertain whether the ground required for the canal was private or public property, and to purchase such additional ground as would be required to make the canal thirty feet wide. The commissioners sugar-coated the pill with the comment that the expense incurred on the project would be 'little', being restricted to the cost of the ground concerned since labour was to be provided by convicts. The Governor-General in Council approved of the suggestion and asked the Board of Revenue to depute an officer to make the enquiries required and also to draw up an estimate of the cost involved.

John Shakespeare, assistant to the Board of Revenue, was chosen for the job and by January 1808 he had submitted his report on the project. The records[6] indicate that it was Shakespeare who suggested that instead of being a simple drainage project for which a 'small cut' would be adequate—which would be open to 'constant encroachment from the landholders on each bank'—the project be implemented 'on a more extensive scale so as to form a navigable canal for the benefit of the merchants bringing goods to Calcutta from the salt water lake'. The Board thought the idea 'deserving of consideration' but said that a decision on it would have to be taken by the committee for improving the town, which had been appointed in the meantime. On its part, the Government sent the correspondence to the committee for its views.

Shakespeare's report[7] makes interesting reading because, among other things, it throws light on the old east-west water courses in the town, including the old creek running along Hastings Street from the river eastward. Shakespeare wrote that on being given his new job the first thing he did was to institute a search amongst the records of the 24-Parganas Collectorate in an effort 'to discover any papers that might relate to the canal denominated Dinga Banga,[8] which is said to have formerly extended from the Mahratta ditch to the salt lake'. After drawing a blank at the Collectorate, he paid a visit to the area itself with the objective of trying 'to trace the site of the old watercourse', which met with success 'without much difficulty'. For the first quarter of a mile the site was 'very apparent from the remains of old brick bridges, but beyond this no trace of the canal was to be perceived'. He, therefore, thought it advisable 'to insert the pins 30 feet apart in a direct line to the Salt Lake, merely deviating occasionally to avoid high ground, large tanks, etc, etc'. Having plotted the probable course of the water channel, which was 'approved' by Blechynden, Shakespeare did a survey of the proprietorship of the ground which would have to be taken up for the canal. He allowed a ten per cent increase on the original price paid for the ground by the landowners in view of the subsequent increase in the price of land.

Expanding on the suggestion that something more ambitious be aimed at than 'merely repairing the [old] watercourse', Shakespeare revealed that the plan to have a canal in the area was not a new one. He wrote that 'several years ago', a proposal had been made to the Government 'on cutting a navigable canal from the Byttiah Khannah Road to the salt lake in a parallel line with the Balliaghaut Road', the scheme being probably set aside because of the cost involved. Shakespeare said if the watercourse was made into a navigable canal '90 ft would be required for its width and 30 ft on each side to deposit the excavation on – in all 150 ft'. But where the land was cheap more of it could be bought 'as by levelling the excavated earth a considerable rent may be realised from the ryots who would be desirous of occupying the banks of the canal'. Shakespeare estimated the total cost of the project at Sicca Rs 42,034-1-0, which would include everything except 'only the trifling expense of working tools and baskets'. Since convicts would be put to work he did not envisage any labour cost, his information being that 2,000 men working on a daily basis would be able to complete the canal within three months. The principal benefit flowing from the canal would be 'the great facility' it would afford to inland navigation by enabling merchants to bring their goods 'close to the town without the trouble of shifting them into hackeries, or the risk of their being damaged by exposure to the weather'. Since the existing movement of goods was appreciable—around 1,000 hackeries worked daily on the Beliaghata-Calcutta road transporting goods—Shakespeare felt that there would result a 'considerable' toll-revenue from the passage of goods like 'charcoal, rice, sago, jagree, oil, dal, matts, koir … pepper, beetlenut, cloth, chunam … and the chief part of [fire] wood consumed in Calcutta'. He added that opening a navigable canal would probably also lead to the setting up of 'an extensive bazar on [the Baitakhana Road's] western end', making commerce even easier for the merchants concerned. In short, therefore, infrastructure was being provided to meet the growing economic needs of the expanding town.

But this provision of infrastructure had to be an integrated exercise to have the maximum beneficial impact. This is because progress in one area would always have a ripple effect on the other parts of the canvas as it were, more so in areas which were contiguous to the one where development was being initiated. The building of the canal squarely fell into this category. On 22 November 1809[9] the committee for improving the town wrote to the Government that as the canal, 'which had been completed two-thirds or more', did not 'unite with the Boitaconnah road [Circular road] it is necessary for the accommodation of the public to widen some of the avenues from the canal to the city, and to open others'. It wrote that considering the quantity of merchandise which would be imported into Calcutta through the new canal, 'it has appeared to us that different avenues from it into the city would be more convenient than one general road, however large it might have been made'. In order to facilitate the work, a survey of the ground 'lying in the vicinity of [the] western extremity of the canal' was submitted to the Government, which indicated the roads 'proposed to be widened or enlarged' in the area.[10]

The committee for the improvement of the town agreed with Shakespeare's plan to make a navigable canal.[11] No important amendments were suggested apart from the passing thought that, instead of the two bridges suggested by Shakespeare to be built across the canal, one would be enough. The committee put the total cost of the project (with one bridge) at around Rs 50,000, which would include the cost of hired labour at around Rs 16,000. Emphasising the point that the Government would be more than indemnified as far as the project cost was concerned with the help of the tolls based on the model applied to boats passing through Tolly's Nullah, it was urged that construction be taken in hand with the objective of making the canal navigable in 'the present year, if the season will permit of the execution of the work before the commencement of the rains'. If this could not be done, the 'narrow cut' suggested for drainage purposes could be completed, which could be made navigable in the 'ensuing season'. On 4 March 1808 the Governor-General in Council wrote back agreeing with the committee's suggestion to have a 'narrow cut (made) for the purpose of draining the town in the present year ... and to render it navigable the ensuing season'.[12]

Notes

1 Judicial Criminal Proceedings, 13 November 1813.

2 Admittedly, the Beliaghata Road was 'opened' by Eliot, but there is evidence to suggest that there was an effort to make the road a good two decades earlier. In 1790 we read about the problem of finding a place 'for the purpose of making bricks for the road from Balliagaut' (Board of Revenue Proceedings, 25 January 1790). In all probability, from very early on there already was a kutcha road from the vicinity of Sealdah to the eastward serving as a means of communication to the natives bringing fish and other produce to the riverside from the interior.

3 By the 1820s Narayan Chatterjee Street had come to be called Matchua Bazar Street (Schalch's map), subsequent transformations in its name being effected in the twentieth century.

4 Judicial Criminal Proceedings, 30 October 1807.

5 Probably the old course of the creek which ran from the river eastward along the alignment of Hastings Street and down Creek Row.

6 Judicial Criminal Proceedings, 29 January 1808.

7 Judicial Criminal Proceedings, 4 March 1808.

8 Dingabhanga, therefore, is the native name of the creek leading from

the river to the salt water lake. This is confirmed by a letter written by H. Shakespeare to the Lottery Committee on 24 April 1820 (Proceedings of the Lottery Committee). The waterway is known as 'the creek' in the English records.

9 Judicial Criminal Proceedings, 24 November 1809.

10 Very often, it is in the details of policy implementation that the basic quality of governance in terms of accommodation and humaneness is revealed. One such example is provided in the records regarding land-acquisition for the Beliaghata canal and its associated road network, specifically the road leading 'from the Circular road to the new nullah'. A problem appears to have cropped up (Judicial Criminal Proceedings, 29 December 1809) involving a spot of land required for the road project which was not easily available, the matter travelling up to the advocate-general for his opinion. The latter wrote that 'no title can be made to the ground' in question because the owner was 'a minor of eight or nine years of age', the son of a European, the late William Spencer. The advocate-general's view was that if any other piece of ground could be used in place of the Spencer plot 'the purchase of the latter should be given up'. Without much ado, the Government told the committee to choose 'some other bit of ground' other than the Spencer plot for the road project

11 Judicial Criminal Proceedings, 4 March 1808.

12 Ibid.

31

Moira Prepares the Ground

In early October 1813 the Earl of Moira took over the Governor-Generalship and, among other tasks associated with furthering the English power in the East, continued the onerous work of improving the city of Calcutta. His signal contribution was to preside over the work of the reconstituted Lottery Committee in its early years, extending to it all the encouragement needed for it to make headway in the initial years of its work. But even before the revamped Lottery Committee began its work in October 1817, the new Lord Sahib instituted an administrative reform measure and an alteration in the legal framework overseeing the Government's power to implement development work which, as events were to prove, had far-reaching consequences.

The first step was a total revamp of the police system, the suggestion towards this end being first made by the Chief Justice of the Supreme Court, Sir Edward Hyde East.[1] The Chief Justice felt that three magistrates were not enough for the city which he described as 'this extensive metropolis' having a population of 'not less than 700,000 persons'.[2] The Chief Justice suggested that there should be six magistrates instead of just three. The Governor-General accepted the suggestion and named Sir William Rumbold, J.B. East and J.B. Birch as the new Justices of the Peace for the town in addition to Martyn, Blaquiere and Fergusson. The Chief Justice also suggested that despite the fact that the city of London

55 Earl of Moira, later Lord Hastings

had eight police offices with three justices sitting in each besides the ordinary police of the city magistrates,

> … the magistrates in Calcutta should [divide] their sittings only into different chambers of the same building, for the sake of better arranging and dispatching the business before them, and of uniting again in cases which require the presence and judgement of two or more, according to the subject matter, with the additional advantage of conferring together as a body in all matters of moment, or consulting each other on occasional questions [of] difficulty.

In his Minute,[3] Moira said it might be 'convenient' to establish two police offices in Calcutta instead of one, 'on the principle observed in the City of London'. However, the cost of the new arrangement would necessarily be higher because of the increase in the number of offices although some advantages would also arise 'from the union of the magistrates in one house'. Moira said that 'both objects' would be 'best promoted by removing the present police office to a more centrical part of the town', adding that no place could be better suited than 'the spot where the old Court House formerly stood,[4] and which is the immediate property of Government.' He proposed that steps be taken to put up a suitable building on the site which was probably lying vacant at the time. The Governor-General added that the saving that would be effected as house rent for the various police offices spread all over the town would 'nearly counterbalance the expense to which Government will be subject in the erection of the building'.

While the Chief Justice focused on the 'strictness of a judicial nature' as the principal function of the police, Moira took pains to expand the revamp of the police system to include other objects 'which appear to me to require, in an almost equal degree, the consideration of Government'. The most important of these was the

> ... repair and conservation of the public roads, drains, water-courses, and other public works which at present exist, the construction of new roads and other works of that nature for the general convenience of the community; the prevention or removal of nuisances; and the care of the navigation of the river Hooghly in the immediate vicinity of Calcutta.

He argued that these functions could not be 'properly and efficiently performed but by persons who can give almost daily attention to them and who possess the requisite legal means of carrying into effect the plans which it may be resolved with reference to the general powers vested in them by law to adopt'. It is clear that, with the increase in the pressure of work, the need had arisen for quicker and better implementation of the mammoth task of improving conditions in the town, and that the perceived solution lay in having a dedicated group of magistrates and a helpful structure of the magistracy.[5]

The Governor-General suggested that a position of 'first magistrate of Calcutta' be created, to be filled by 'a covenanted servant of experience and capacity' who would work with the other Justices of the Peace. This officer's jurisdiction would cover both the town and the suburbs. He wrote that the improvements which had been begun, 'and which should on every principle be extended', covered partly the city and partly the suburbs. It was, therefore, 'essential that the authority, to which the further prosecution of those works may be confided, should be empowered to act with respect to those objects, both in Calcutta and the places adjacent'. Moira, however, hastened to add that it was not his intention that the first magistrate should be invested 'exclusively with the discharge of the duties above noticed', that in fact the new position should be seen as one being filled by the leader of a team. There would be other magistrates acting as a 'separate board' to deal with such issues, the first magistrate's role being to 'give more than an ordinary share of attention to the digesting of the necessary plans, for the consideration of his colleagues, and, in cases requiring it, for the determination of Government, and in superintending the execution of such works'. Importantly, the Governor-General made it clear that the new arrangement would 'supersede the powers at present vested in the committee for the improvement of Calcutta, which in some instances at least have been obviously confided to persons who cannot, from their other official avocations, give the requisite attention to the business'. Thus, the upshot of the reform was that it was back to the magistracy as far as improving the town was concerned.

Regarding funding of the development projects, the Governor-General pointed to two methods which could be pursued. The first was of course the proceeds of the house tax 'which is appropriable by law … to the cleansing, watering and repairing of the streets of Calcutta', the second being the lottery proceeds. Taking the house-tax funds, he said they were only adequate for payments made to the native establishments of the police 'and the ordinary repair of the roads'. But the lottery proceeds were a different proposition altogether. Exhibiting remarkable prescience, Moira said that, 'if judiciously applied', such funds could result in 'the most substantial improvements in the town of Calcutta and in its vicinity in the course of a very few years'. Being aware of the scourge of 'leakage' of funds, Moira made it clear that no part of the lottery funds was to be spent without the 'express sanction' of the Governor-General in Council, and that 'the accounts of the expenditure should be submitted to the strictest examination previously to being passed by Government'.

The second major reform instituted by Moira was the adoption of the Jury Act[6] which, among other things, was an admission of the fact that the Government was increasingly coming up against obstacles in the implementation of development projects and that the stage had been reached where an enabling institutional framework was required to smoothen things out. The 1814 legislation, however, was not a bolt from the blue. It drew its lineage from the 9 January 1781 'rule, ordinance and regulation' (ROR) effected by the regime of Warren Hastings 'for the good order and civil government of the United Company's Settlement at Fort William in Bengal'. The justification for the new legislation was provided in the preamble itself which said that the 1781 law 'has been rendered in a great measure useless and is not in other respects adapted to the [present] state' of the town. A pressing need had emerged to 'provide for making and opening of highways, roads, streets, lanes and passages' in the town, 'and for the conservation and repair thereof as well as of such as already exists'. The health aspect had also gained in importance, the 1814 law stating that a new measure was needed to improve matters since the health of the inhabitants 'greatly depends upon the proper draining of the said settlement, and the removal of the many annoyances and obstructions which have been, and are, created to, and in, the highways, roads, streets, lanes and passages therein'. A new law was required in view of the 'divers encroachments and public nuisances' made upon these thoroughfares and on the banks of the Hooghly 'to the prejudice of the navigation of the said river, to the injury and obstruction of the anchorage for the shipping, and to the manifest endangering of that part of the said settlement upon and near the banks of the said river'.

Another aspect of town life, long lost to us, needed substantial improvement. As the new law put it, 'great numbers of idle and disorderly persons and others of low condition appear and go armed with swords, spears and other offensive weapons unsuited to their condition by night and by day through the highways-passages [of the town] to the great terror and affright of the peaceable inhabitants'. Coupled with this group was another set of people 'having no ... occupation' who came to the town 'from various places beyond and without Calcutta', who also carried offensive weapons, these people being 'frequently taken [in by] persons and householders ... for the purpose of going with and attending them armed whenever they leave their houses'. This group of armed people, generally, 'caused great affright and terror to the ... peaceful inhabitants of Calcutta and are frequently guilty of great violence to their persons'. Here, the 1814 Act was referring to personal bodyguards and *lathials* employed by native personages and satraps of all sorts who were—perhaps in perfect consonance with the last flicker of the dying embers of a traditional, fractured, feudal society—trying to replicate a social milieu in which they themselves as well as their forefathers had been nurtured, being unaware of the fact that the social function they were providing was, among other things, in direct confrontation with the administrative mores of a rapidly growing European 'corporate imperial' power playing to a totally different set of rules.

Since new tasks were awaiting the town administration, the preamble made it clear that the 1781 law was being annulled and a new set of rules was being put into place to attain the fresh objective of improving the quality of life in Calcutta. The details of the new law may seem tedious to enumerate, but they have been included here in view of the fact that they were of epochal importance to construction activity in the town and its general cleanliness and hygiene, principally when seen in the perspective of a break with the past.

The first regulation (Article 3 of the ROR) aimed at cleaning up the streets of the town. It stated that, after it came into force, if anyone was found to throw

> ... any carrion, dirt, soil, straws or dung or any other filth or rubbish or annoyance whatsoever on any of the roads, streets, ways or public passages, or into any of the drains or sewers, made or to be made within the said settlement, or fix or fasten any scaffolding, bamboos or ropes ...

or leave 'any carriages, bricks, lime or chunam or any other matter or thing for the space of four hours, which may occasion any annoyance, nuisance or obstruction whatever, or stop or obstruct, incommode or endanger any person or carriage', the person concerned would be fined ten sicca rupees 'for every such offence' per day.

The new law made exceptions, for a 'limited' but extendable period not exceeding a year, for

> ... inhabitants or proprietors or owners of lands or houses ... or their builders or workmen to make and keep up ... any enclosure on the highway, before or on the sides of their respective houses or buildings, or before or on the side of any intended houses or buildings, in order to [construct] the building, pulling down or repairing the same , or the appurtenances thereto, and for the laying necessary materials for the same, and the rubbish arising therefrom.

However, the exceptions would have to be described in the licences given for such work. Engaging in a celebration of detail, the new regulation stated that enough road space was to be left for 'carts, coaches and other carriages to pass and repass'. The town was not well-lit at night and it was more than likely that unsuspecting users of roads could run into the enclosures so formed. The new law, therefore, made it mandatory for the licensees to keep a 'lighted candle or lamp in a lantern' marking out such enclosures 'after sunset till daybreak, till such time the enclosures were done away with'.

Anyone extinguishing or concealing such lights would be fined up to twenty sicca rupees for every such offence committed.

Article 4 aimed at tackling 'offensive' building hardware which needed to be removed both to improve the visual aspect of the town and also to make life easier for the people. The stipulation laid down that any two or more Justices of the Peace could issue notices to 'the owner or occupier of any house, building, land, tenement or hereditaments' in the town 'from which any penthouse, bow window, porch, shed, balcony, rail, bulk signpost, spout, gutter or [any] other thing ... overhangs, juts into, or in any way projects or encroaches upon any street, square, lane, or other public passage', to 'take down, remove, alter or regulate such projection or encroachment'. In the case of 'any sign, spout or gutter', these were to be 'either carried away or affixed on the front of the house, shop or building ... in such a manner as not to annoy or incommode the public'. The Justices of the Peace could also issue notices to the occupier of 'any stall, shamble or [booth] standing in, or otherwise encroaching upon, any street, square, lane, or other public passage', to remove them. In the event of refusal to abide by the notice for fourteen days, the regulation stated that any two or more Justices of the Peace could have such encroachments demolished 'in such manner as they shall think proper'. In such cases, the owner or occupier concerned would have to foot the expense of removal and transport and also provide a further sum not exceeding 100 sicca rupees 'in respect of the erection or continuance of the said nuisance'. Drawing a line between tenant and owner, the new act enjoined that 'no occupier of any such house or stall shall be liable to be in any way questioned or drawn into suit by the owners of the same house, stall or premises for any such nuisance abated by the orders of the said Justices'.

Article 5 focused on new offenders regarding the construction of penthouses, balcony, etc., after the regulation went into force, the penalty for such people being a fine not exceeding 100 sicca rupees. As for those putting up stalls, etc., the corresponding fine for every such offence would be a maximum of twenty sicca rupees. For those making encroachments on the banks of the river 'below high watermark', such as 'any projection, pier, buttress', etc., a penalty not exceeding 100 sicca rupees would be levied 'for every day that such projection or encroachment shall continue after notice in writing given to him or her' by the Justices of the Peace. The penalty would also apply to those persisting with the construction of penthouses, balconies, etc. For those involved with stalls, etc., a fine not exceeding ten sicca rupees would be imposed for every day of violation of the notice issued to them.

Article 6 stated:

> No head builder, master carpenter, master mason or other mistry or workman, in rebuilding or new-fronting any old building situate in or near any street, square, lane or public way, shall bring the foundation thereof forward beyond the old foundation so as to encroach upon any such street, square, lane or public way.

Anyone doing so after notice had been served on him would forfeit for every such offence a sum not exceeding 1,000 sicca rupees. The provision was a double-edged one for it also applied to owners of such buildings who would have to pay the same penalty for transgressing the law. The regulation stipulated that any two Justices of the Peace could

> order the same to be taken down, dug up, removed, carried away, altered, or regulated in such manner as they shall think proper; and such owner or occupier shall forfeit a further sum equal to the expenses and charges of abating, throwing down, digging up, removing, altering and regulating such annoyance.

Importantly, the new law gave a reprieve for any 'dwelling house or any wall thereof which shall have been built for more than three months', stating that they would not 'be pulled down or removed, or the owner be in any way affected by virtue of this ROR, although it may be otherwise subject to the law against public nuisances'. The reprieve was probably an admission of the fact that the problem with regard to houses having already violated the specific stipulation was so severe that setting it right would have been an impossible task.

On a positive note, Article 7 gave the Justices of the Peace the power 'to make and complete ... all and every such roads, passages and streets or [drains] or sewers as they ... shall judge convenient and expedient to be made, cut and completed subject to the provisions hereafter ordained'. The next article gave them the power 'to treat and agree with the owners of such lands, houses, tenements and other hereditaments ... as it shall and may be necessary to purchase for the purposes of cutting any drains or sewers and of making and completing such roads, streets and passages'.

The next six sections of the act dealt with the functions and operational features of a jury. Article 9 threw up signposts in cases of disagreement between the Government and the public in the discharge of the above responsibilities. It stipulated that, in case of any refusal on the part of any person to agree with the Justices of the Peace on 'the sale of any such lands, houses, tenements or hereditaments' as mentioned in Article 8, the Justices were to 'cause the value of the said premises to be enquired into, and ascertained, by and on the oath of a jury of twelve indifferent men'. Where the property concerned belonged to a native, the regulation stipulated that the sheriff would have to include in the jury 'natives together with British subjects', 'resident in the same settlement'. The jury was to decide on the damages and compensation to be made to owners and other people involved in the premises concerned, the Justices of the Peace being empowered to help the jury members to examine witnesses and also enable it to visit the site concerned. The Article stated that the Justices of the Peace were to make sure that the 'damages and recompense' settled on by the jury were to be paid to those so named by the jury,

> … such order and adjudication (being) final and conclusive, to all intents and purposes, against all parties and persons whatsoever, claiming in possession, remainder, reversion or otherwise, their heirs, executors or administrators or successors respectively, as well absent as present, infants, … lunatics, idiots and persons under any disability whatsoever, as well as all other person and persons whomsoever.

The next Article stipulated that, following the promulgation of the new law, if any person was entitled

> … either in reversion or remainder, to any such premises, the money so to be awarded as a satisfaction … [would] go and be settled to the same use or uses as the same premises were, for which such money [would] be paid, unless such person, so interested, shall consent to give up such interest, the charge of the conveyance of the same to be defrayed by the said Justices of the Peace from such funds as they may be authorised to apply to the purposes aforesaid.

Article 11 related to disputed premises, the regulation stipulating that wherever such differences arose regarding premises which the Justices of the Peace wanted to purchase for the public purpose, the money to be set aside for the purchase would have to be 'paid into the hands of the Accountant-General of the Supreme Court of Judicature for the use and benefit of such person or persons who shall or may appear entitled thereto by any order, decree or judgement of the said Supreme Court'.

Article 9 had dealt with the method to settle differences arising between owners of premises and the Government, namely, through the appointment of a twelve-member jury. Article 12 laid out the procedure governing the appointment of such a jury. It decreed that the Justices of the Peace were empowered to direct the sheriff 'to empanel, summon and return an indifferent jury of 24 persons … resident in the said town'. Ten days notice would be served on all parties concerned to present themselves before the authorities, the

Justices of the Peace selecting and swearing in twelve out of the twenty-four persons summoned for the purpose of forming the jury. In other words, the Government would be empowered to select jurors to settle disputes in which it itself was a party, immediately casting an unavoidable shadow on the fairness of decisions taken by juries so constituted. The article also laid emphasis on the point that the Justices were not to take possession of any property 'for which such jury shall have ascertained the damages to be sustained and recompence to be given' until the owner of the property had been paid the 'full sum … so assessed'. Further, the regulation stated that all those involved in a dispute could institute 'lawful challenges' against any member of the jury at the time of his swearing-in. In case any person summoned to be on a jury disassociated himself with the body after being sworn in and before any verdict was given, or any person summoned to be a witness did not appear 'or refuses to be examined without any sufficient reason', the Justices of the Peace were empowered to impose a fine on such persons ranging from Rs 20 to Rs 100 sicca rupees. If the fine was not paid on demand, the Justices were empowered 'to levy the same by distress sale of the offender's goods and chattels', returning the excess after the fine is paid to the person whose goods had been subjected to distress sale.

Article 13 stipulated that each jury member on being summoned by the sheriff would be paid three sicca rupees. For 'every return of a jury' sixteen sicca rupees was to be paid; and eighty sicca rupees was to be paid to every jury 'for the attending the said Justices of the Peace on the empanelling'. The fees were to be paid by the Justices from funds placed at their disposal for the purpose. The next article stated that any 'verdict, order and adjudication' given in any case were to be kept by the Clerk of the Peace and had to be 'deposited with and be kept amongst the records of the Quarter Sessions of the Peace and for the Town of Calcutta, and that true copies thereof shall be received and allowed as good evidence in all courts'.

Article 15 dealt with the menace of armed people coming into the town (see above). It laid down that any person 'of low condition' who entered the town 'armed with swords, spears or other offensive weapons made in part or entirely of steel, iron or other metal' would have to deposit the same with 'with the tannahdar of the first tannah at which he shall arrive, which tannahdar shall give a receipt for the same'. On leaving the town, the person concerned could take back his weapon on production of the receipt. Further, the regulation ordained that if any person 'of low condition' was found 'walking, parading or appearing' in the streets of the town 'with a sword, spear or other offensive weapon'

> ... in his hand or exposed to view, whether sheathed or not sheathed, unless he be in the service of some person who shall have obtained the authority of Government at the said settlement to retain and take the person so armed in his or her retinue, or not being in such service shall have obtained a licence to carry the same from any of His Majesty's said Justices of the Peace,

... such arms were to be seized by 'a tannahdar or other officer belonging to the police'. A fine not exceeding twenty sicca rupees would be imposed on the person in whose possession the arms were found. In the absence of the fine being paid, any Justice of the Peace could order the sale of the 'offender's goods and chattel' and have the fine paid from the proceeds of such sale, the surplus being returned to the person concerned.

As with Article 15, the next article also focused on a social problem, namely, the 'enticement' of 'married women and also female children unmarried, such female children unmarried being within the age of 13 years of the Mahomedan and Hindu religion', from 'the protection and possession and against the will of their husbands, parents or guardians, respectively, by the wicked machinations of evil-disposed persons'. The new regulation said that the victims

> ... lived in a state of adultery, or have been sold as common prostitutes, or deflowered, or have been disposed of in marriage against the will

> of their respective husbands, parents or guardians, by those evil-disposed persons or by such as are in combination with them, to the great detriment of public morals and to the injury of the said married women and female children and of their respective husbands, parents, guardians, or other persons having the lawful care of such female children aforesaid.

The point of interest is that, after the new regulation took effect, it would become 'lawful' for the sufferers 'to complain of such injury and offence' to the Justices of the Peace, the latter being given the power to take cognizance of the complaints and proceed against the alleged culprits according to settled legal procedures, leading to their acquittal or conviction. In case of conviction, the persons concerned were to pay a fine not exceeding 200 sicca rupees. If the fine was not paid within a week, they were to be sent 'to the House of Correction to hard labour for any time not exceeding the space of six calendar months'. On the 'forfeitures and penalties' ordered by the new law under different sections, Article 17 made the point that if, after the method laid down in the various articles, the penalties were still not met, the Justices of the Peace were authorised to send such offenders to 'the common Gaol of Calcutta' for a period not exceeding six months.

Notes

1. Judicial Criminal Proceedings, 14 June 1814.
2. In his Minute the Governor-General said the population of the suburbs could not be 'less than one-third' of the city's population, which gives a figure of around 2,30,000, yielding a total of 9,30,000 for the city and the suburbs taken together.
3. Judicial Criminal Proceedings, 14 June 1814.
4. Where St Andrew's Kirk stands now in BBD Bagh.
5. This was the formulation/rationalisation of high policy. There was a definite need for reformation here but implementation of the policy led to its own problems. Thus, at the personal level, the superintendent of roads, Richard Blechynden's salary was reduced by

Rs 300, 'returning it to Rs 700'. Blechynden, therefore, was clearly an aggrieved party and could be expected to be readily critical of those who had effected this downturn in his fortunes. Even so, his critique of the changes is important and cannot easily be dismissed because it referred to facets of implementation which could increase the level of inefficiency of the new system which was being put into place. Peter Robb (*Sentiment and Self*, p. 137) writes: 'It seemed a step backwards from a reasoned and progressive approach to the town's administration and reflected a prolonged period of in-fighting. Blechynden could see why the previous justices, namely Macklew, Blaquiere and Thoroton, had been appointed – they were Persian and Bengali scholars – and even Martyn might have been intended as a kind of moderating influence because of his legal training. Now justices were being appointed, Blechynden complained, to bulk out the "overgrown salaries" of "a greedy phalanx" of men who accompanied the new Governor-General (Lord Moira, or Hastings) and who knew nothing of the "language, habits or customs of the natives".'

6 Judicial Criminal Proceedings, 13 December 1814. Though called the Jury Act, the legislation dealt with a broad array of subjects pertaining to development and the progress of the town generally.

Epilogue

With planning for development having taken wings, the terrain before the planners extended far into the horizon. The work done was substantial, extending from this period till the end of the life of the Lottery Committee in the mid-1830s. What is perhaps more important is to recognise two aspects of this development. Firstly, the schemes drawn up and implemented during this period laid firmly the foundations of modern Calcutta, the last burst of serious town-development work being supervised by the Calcutta Improvement Trust in the early years of the twentieth century. Secondly, that though the time was 'ripe' for the town of Calcutta to break off from its eighteenth century moorings as far as infrastructural facilities were concerned and move on to the next phase of civic progress, the speed at which things moved in the early years of the nineteenth century would not have materialised if people like Wellesley, Minto and Hastings were not present on the scene. More than Wellesley, who had set the ball rolling, it was the encouragement and support given to the 'process' by the two subsequent Governors-General that facilitated greatly the movement of the town into the nineteenth century, helping it to don a garb which would with time enhance its reputation as the 'second city' of the British empire.

In early December 1816, Francis Rawdon-Hastings, the Earl of Moira, was created the Marquis of Hastings. From the point of view of his contribution to Calcutta's development, this elevation of the Governor-General could not have been more deserved or justified although, in point of fact, the city's progress had nothing to do with the bestowal of the additional honour. In fact, if Moira was to have been rewarded in any way for his services to the city's development, it would have to be for his establishment of the revamped Lottery Committee. But the revamp followed his elevation to a Marquisate and did not precede it, the body with new responsibilities being set up on 21 October 1817.

The new body, known to posterity as the Lottery Committee, was officially anointed 'a committee for the purpose of superintending the receipts and disbursements of the lottery funds and generally for purposes connected with the improvements of the town of Calcutta and its vicinity'. As happened during Wellesley's closing months in India, this committee was not set up after a previous one looking after the improvement of the town had been wound up. It was also not the result of a reform of the administrative structure of town development, which was what occurred under Moira in June 1814. The Lottery Committee's establishment was in fact announced in the course of discussions held under the aegis of the Vice-President in Council on the suggestions made by the committee appointed (in March 1817) 'for ascertaining the best means for excavating tanks at convenient places in the town of Calcutta for the accommodation of the inhabitants'.[1]

Almost seamlessly, the new committee took over the job of superintending the development works already set in motion by 'the Commissioners of the Lotteries'. Specifically, it was ordered that the lottery funds be used to meet 'the expense of excavating new tanks and filling up old tanks, of opening new streets or roads, of constructing aqueducts, bridges, ghauts, and other similar works, calculated to improve the health, convenience and comfort of the inhabitants of the city and suburbs'. The committee, however, was asked not to look after the repair of the 'streets, roads, drains or other works above alluded to when finished' and that, generally, no expense was to be charged to the lottery funds 'which can properly be included in the assessment department'. The committee was also given the power to bring to the notice of the town magistrates 'such improvements with regard to the draining of the town and the repairs of the streets' as it thought necessary as well as the 'removal or abatement' of any 'nuisances or encroachments' which was noticed by it.

The first members of the new committee were: John Eliot, the magistrate of the suburbs and the town of Calcutta, C. Trower, the collector of the 24-Parganas, W.B. Bayley, secretary to Government in the Judicial Department, H. Wood, the civil auditor, Captain H.S. Montague, the fort adjutant, G.J. Gordon, one of the commissioners of the Court of Requests, A. Macan and A.J. Colvin, Junior. Arthur Blechynden, the son of Richard Blechynden, was to be 'considered as specially attached to the committee as surveyor'.[2] As the membership of the committee indicates, there were lateral linkages with the Government, the executive administration, the city magistrates and the military authorities, which suggests that the generation of development schemes would have the participation of all the principal agencies concerned which would be involved in final approval of projects and their ultimate implementation. Admittedly, this was nothing new to the scheme of the Company's governance ever since the advent of planned growth of Calcutta began to hold centrestage during the time of Wellesley. The membership of the committees of improvement set up by him will bear this out. The point is that the nature of the composition of the various committees dealing with the city's improvement from Wellesley's time to that of Lord Hastings helped greatly in facilitating quicker approval, which was a critical input in the process which helped to alter substantially the face of the town and also the quality of life of both natives and Europeans.

The aspect of the story played out under the auspices of the Lottery Committee deserves separate treatment if justice is to be done to the scale and content of the changes introduced, which resulted not merely in a decisive break with the past but also set the stage for the growth of the city into the twentieth century and beyond.

Notes

1 Proceedings of the Lottery Committee, 24 November 1817.

2 Ibid. Nearly ten years earlier during the Minto years, Blechynden Senior had tried his utmost to induct Arthur into the surveyor's department attached to the committee for the improvement of the town but had failed possibly because of the stubborn opposition of George Dowdeswell. See Robb, *Sentiment and Self*, pp. 131–134.

Glossary

Amlah	Collective name for the officers of a court or office
Aumeen/amin	Inspector, an officer in a legal investigation; also a land surveyor
Bakshi/buxey	Paymaster
Bermooter/ brahmottor	Land granted rent-free to Brahmins for their support
Besshey/beshy	Extra
Bhistee	Carrier of water for domestic use, or watering the roads or trees
Bigha/bigah/ beegah	Measure of land varying in different places, but usually between half and three-quarters of an acre. In Bengal it was equal to 1,600 square yards
Chittas/chuta	Account, memorandum
Chopper	A thatched roof
Choukey	Any place where a watch is posted; a customs station
Corse/coss	A measure of distance varying in different places but usually one-and-a-half or two miles
Covid	Measure of varying lengths, from fourteen to thirty-six inches
Curtcha wassil backey (baki)	Account showing the details of the revenue to be paid, the instalments discharged and the arrears due
Cutcha/kutcha	Unbaked; the opposite of pucca
Cutcherry/kachari /catcherry	Office of administration, court house

Dacoit/dakait	Member of an armed gang
Dewan	Chief native officer of certain Government establishments
Dewutter	Religious endowment; land granted rent-free for the support of a temple
Doul	Statement of the particulars of the gross revenue collected from an estate or district
Fakir/fakeer/ faqueer/fikkeer	Muslim religious mendicant; also loosely and inaccurately applied to Hindu devotees and naked ascetics
Ganj/gunge	Market
Ghat	Landing place
Golah	Store room, place where grain or salt is kept for a season
Gomastah	Agent of a zamindar who collects the rent
Itmandar/ etmaundar	Person charged with the collection of a stipulated revenue for a certain district
Jemadar/ jemedar	Chief or leader of a group; a designated rank in the native army, the police and customs
Jerib aumeen/ jarib amin/ jurib aumeen	Revenue department officer whose job is to survey land and assess its value
Jumma	Assessed revenue
Jummabandi	Settlement of total assessment of land revenue due for a year or period of years from an estate
Katha/cottah	Land-measure equal to a twentieth part of a Bengal bigha
Khalsa	The office of Government under the Mughal administration in which the business of the revenue department was transacted, and which was continued in the early period of British rule
Khamar/comar	Cultivated land which is not hereditary
Khoa	Kind of concrete made of broken brick, lime, etc.
Laldighi	Red tank

Lathial	Hired person armed with a club
Mahal	Department of miscellaneous revenue derived from a tax on some particular class of things or persons
Maidan	Plain, any large open space
Malguzary	Revenue assessment, or land capable of paying assessment
Mandal/mundle	Village headman
Mistry/mistries	An artisan, mason, bricklayer, mechanic, blacksmith, etc.
Mokorary patta	Permanent deed of lease
Mudi	Grocer
Mussucks	Bag carried by a bhistee, which is made of the entire skin of a large goat, stripped of the hair and dressed
Mutwali/ mutwallee	Warden of a mosque or of an endowment
Naib	Deputy
Negabaun	Guard, watchman; under the Mughal Government of Bengal, an officer who inspected weights and measures and affixed his seal to those which were correct
Nekassie	Outlet, drain
Patta/pottah	Deed of lease
Perwana/ parwana	Written order, licence or pass
Phansi	Noose; (Fancy Lane) spot where criminals were hanged
Phyrmaund/ phirmaund/ firman	A royal mandate, an edict, a charter
Potta neeveez	Writer, scribe or secretary in the patta office
Pucca/pucka/ pukka	Permanent, hence a building made of brick and mortar; the opposite of cutcha
Salami	Gratuity or offering on receiving a lease, or any favour real or implied
Sebayat	Manager of a temple
Sheristah	Office of registry or record; sometimes, not appropriately, used for the officer
Sicca	Silver coin of the standard value in Bengal under the East India Company's administration till it was changed to the Company's rupee. It was introduced

	by the Bengal Government in 1793 and abolished in 1836
Sircar	Someone who keeps the accounts and makes the purchases; also applies to the Government
Sunnud	Government deed assigning or acknowledging rights
Talao	A pond, a reservoir of water
Tauntkhana	Place where coarse canvas, or sackcloth, is made
Tehobazari	Hawker or retailer in a bazar who pays rent for the ground on which his shop or stall is placed
Thannah/tanna	Police station; the term belongs properly to the times when military force was used to keep the peace and to collect revenue
Thanadar/ tannahdar	Head of a police station
Vakil/vakeel	Attorney
Zamindar/ zemidar/ jemindar	Landholder; collector of revenue on behalf of the government under the Mahomedan dispensation
Zamindari	The office and rights of a zamindar; also the tract of land he holds, his estate

Acknowledgements

The author is indebted to the late Professor Barun De for guiding him in the early stages of the research for the volume, his abiding regret being that Professor De did not live to see the work being published. The comments of Professor Peter Robb, Professor Emeritus at the School of Oriental and African Studies, on some of the chapters were also of great help in filling in the gaps in information and interpretation which mark the volume, for which the author is solely responsible. A very large part of the research work was done at the West Bengal State Archives, where Sarmishta De, Bidisha Chakraborty and Madhuri Banik were outstanding in the cooperation they extended to the author. The National Atlas & Thematic Mapping Organisation also needs to be complimented for bringing out the very helpful 'Atlas of the City of Calcutta and its Environs' (2010) from which some of the maps used in the book have been sourced. The editor of Niyogi Books, Sucharita Ghosh, was exemplary in her meticulousness in checking the text, every bit of advice proffered by her being greatly appreciated. Needless to say, the constant encouragement provided by the author's wife Shipra, and by Ayana and Ranadev formed the bedrock of the entire effort.

Selected Bibliography

BOOKS

Atlas of the City of Calcutta and its Environs. Kolkata: National Atlas and Thematic Mapping Organisation, 2010.

Barlow, R. and Henry Yule, eds. *The Diary of William Hedges*. London, 1887.

Bowrey, Thomas. *A Geographical Account of Countries Round the Bay of Bengal, 1669-1679*. Edited by R.C. Temple. Cambridge, 1905.

Buckland, C.E. *Dictionary of Indian Biography*, London: Swan Sonnenschein and Company, 1906.

Busteed, H.E. *Echoes from Old Calcutta*. Shannon: Irish University Press, 1908 (first published 1882).

Butler, Iris. *The Eldest Brother*. London: Hodder & Stoughton, 1973.

Carey, W.H. *The Good Old Days of Honourable John Company*. Simla, 1887.

Chakraborty, Bidisha and Sarmistha De, comps. *Select Documents on Calcutta, 1800-1900*. Calcutta, Directorate of State Archives, 2011.

Chakraborty, Bidisha and Sarmistha De. *Calcutta in the Nineteenth Century*. New Delhi: Niyogi Books, 2013.

Corfield, Wilmot. *Calcutta Faces and Places in Pre-Camera Days*. Calcutta: Thacker, Spink and Co., 1910.

Cotton, H.E.A. *Calcutta Old and New*. Calcutta: General, 1980 (first published 1907).

Danvers, F.C. *Bengal, its Chiefs, Agents, and Governors*. Calcutta, 1888.

Davidson, C.J.C. *Diary of Travels and Adventures in Upper India*. London: Henry Colburn, 1843.

Elton, G.R. *The Practice of History*. Collins-Fontana, 1974.

Guha, Ranajit. *The Small Voice of History*. Edited by Partha Chatterjee. Ranikhet: Permanent Black, 2010.

Hamilton, Alexander. *A New Account of the East Indies.* London, 1744.
Hartly House. Calcutta: Thacker, Spink and Co., 1908.
Holwell, J.Z. *India Tracts.* London, 1764.
Hyde, H.B. *The Parish of Bengal.* Calcutta, 1899.

Kedleston, Marquis Curzon of. *British Government in India.* London: Cassell and Company, 1925.
Kincaid, Dennis. *British Social Life in India, 1608-1937.* London: Routledge & Kegan Paul, 1973.
Kripalani, Krishna. *Dwarkanath Tagore: A Forgotten Pioneer.* New Delhi: National Book Trust, 1981.

List of Documents on Calcutta, 1764-1800. Calcutta: The State Archives of West Bengal, 1990.
Long, James. *Selections from Unpublished Records of Government, 1748 to 1767.* Edited by Mahadevaprasad Saha. Calcutta: Firma K L Mukhopadhyay, 1973 (first published 1869).
Lord Macaulay's Essays and Lays of Ancient Rome, Popular Edition. London: Longmans, Green, and Co., 1899.
Losty, J.P. *Calcutta City of Palaces.* London: The British Library, 1990.

Mitter, Kissory Chaund. *Mutty Lall Seal.* Calcutta: 1993 (first published 1869).
Mookerjee, Amarendranath, ed. *Glimpses of the Olden Times.* Calcutta: Eastlight Book House, 1968.
Moore, Charles. *The Sheriffs of Fort William from 1775 to 1926.* Calcutta: Thacker, Spink & Co., 1926.

Nair, P.T. *A History of Calcutta's Streets.* Calcutta: Firma KLM Pvt Ltd, 1987.
———. *Calcutta in the 17th Century.* Calcutta: Firma KLM Pvt Ltd, 1986.

Partha Chatterjee, *The Black Hole of Empire.* Ranikhet: Permanent Black, 2012.

Ray Choudhury, Ranabir. *The Lord Sahib's House.* Kolkata: Wild Strawberries Books, 2010.
Ray, Alok, ed. *Calcutta Keepsake.* Calcutta: Rddhi-India, 1978.
Robb, Peter. *Sentiment and Self: Richard Blechynden's Calcutta Diaries, 1791-1822.* New Delhi: Oxford University Press, 2011.
———. *Sex and Sensibility: Richard Blechynden's Calcutta Diaries, 1791-1822.* New Delhi: Oxford University Press, 2011.
———. *Useful Friendship: Europeans and Indians in Early Calcutta.* New Delhi: Oxford University Press, 2014.
Roberts, P.E. *History of British India.* Oxford, 1921.
Roebuck, Thomas. *The Annals of the College of Fort William.* Calcutta: Hindoostanee Press, 1819.
Roy, A.K. *A Short History of Calcutta.* Calcutta: Rddhi-India, 1982 (first published in 1902).

Seton-Karr, W.S. *Selections from Calcutta Gazettes*, vols 1 and 2. Calcutta: Government of India, 1864 and 1865.
Sinha, Narendra Krishna, ed. *Fort William India House Correspondence*, vol. 5. Government of India, 1949.
Sinha, Pradip. *Calcutta in Urban History*. Calcutta: Firma KLM Pvt Ltd, 1978.
Spencer, Alfred. *Memoirs of William Hickey*. London.
Sreemani, Soumitra. *Anatomy of a Colonial Town Calcutta, 1756-1794*. Calcutta: Firma KLM Pvt Ltd, 1994.
Srinivasachari, C.S., ed. *Fort William-India House Correspondence,* vol. 4. Delhi: Government of India, 1962.

Temple, R.C., ed. *The Diaries of Streynsham Master, 1675-1680*. London: John Murray, 1911.
The Bengal Obituary. Calcutta: Punthi Pustak, 1991 (first published 1848).
The Statesman An Anthology. Calcutta and New Delhi: The Statesman Ltd, 1975.
Tom Raw, the Griffin, by a Civilian and an Officer of the Bengal Establishment. London: R. Ackermann, 1828.

Valentia, George Viscount. *Voyages and Travels to India, Ceylon, The Red Sea, Abyssinia, and Egypt, in the Years 1802, 1803, 1804, 1805, and 1806*. London: William Miller, 1811.

Whitworth, George Clifford. *An Anglo-Indian Dictionary*. New Delhi: Indian Documentation Service, 1976 (first published 1885).
Wilson, C.R. *Old Fort William in Bengal*. London: John Murray, 1906.
———. *The Early Annals of the English in Bengal*. London: W Thacker & Co., 1895.

Yule, Henry and A.C. Burnell, eds. *Hobson-Jobson*. Calcutta: Rupa, 1986 (first published 1886).

MAPS

A French Map, Theodore Forrestie and John Ollifres Plan of Calcutta, 1742.
Aaron Upjohn's Map of Calcutta and its Environs, 1792-1793.

J.A. Schalch's Map of the City of Calcutta and its Environs, 1824.

Map of the Suburbs of Calcutta, 1817.
Mark Wood's Plan of Calcutta, 1784-1785.

Robert Orme's Plan of the Territory of Calcutta 1743, also showing the Military Operations at the time of the 1756 assault of Nawab Shiraj-ud-Daulah.

The Environs of Fort William in 1756-1757 (reproduced from S.C. Hill, *Bengal in 1756-57*, vol. 1).

W. Heysham's Map of Calcutta showing the latest improvements in 1856.

William Wells' Plan of Fort William and Part of the City of Calcutta, 1753.

MONOGRAPH

The South Park Street Cemetery, brought out in association with the foundation of an Association for the Preservation of Historical Cemeteries in India, Calcutta, 1978.

NEWSPAPERS

Calcutta Christian Observer of September 1833
Calcutta Chronicle of 6 January 1794

Hickey's *Bengal Gazette or Calcutta General Advertiser* of 2-9 September 1780

The Calcutta Monthly Journal of April 1799

OFFICIAL DOCUMENTS

Bengal Public Consultations (India Office Records, British Library).
Board of Revenue Proceedings, West Bengal State Archives (WBSA).
Board of Trade Proceedings (WBSA).

Calcutta Committee of Revenue Proceedings (WBSA).
Committee of Revenue Proceedings (WBSA).

General Letters from the Court of Directors, Judicial Series (WBSA).
General Letters to the Court of Directors, Judicial Series (WBSA).
Governor-General in Council Proceedings, Revenue Department (WBSA).

Judicial Civil Proceedings (WBSA).
Judicial Criminal Proceedings (WBSA).
Judicial Proceedings (WBSA).

Lottery Committee Proceedings (WBSA).

Municipal Municipal Proceedings (WBSA).

Revenue Board Consisting of the Whole Council Proceedings (WBSA).

Superintendent of the Khalsa Records Proceedings (WBSA).

Territorial Revenue Proceedings (WBSA).

PERIODICALS

Bengal Past and Present, volumes 2, 6, 10, 14, 26, 37.

The Asiatic Annual Register, 1807.
The Calcutta Review, volumes 18, 70, 92.

Photo Credits

C.R. Wilson, *Old Fort William* (1906) - pp. 90–91, pp. 94–95

G.F. Grand, *The Narrative of George Francis Grand* (1911) - p. 165, p. 336

H.B. Hyde, *The Parish of Bengal* (1899) - p. 58, p. 181, p. 357

H.E. Busteed, *Echoes from Old Calcutta* (1908) - pp. 86–87

Lord Curzon of Kedleston, *British Government in India* (1925) - p. 478, p. 517

National Atlas & Thematic Mapping Organisation - p. 137, p. 192, pp. 322–323, p. 433, p. 440, p. 463

S.C. Hill, *Bengal in 1756-57* (1905) - pp. 88–89

The British Library - p. 64 (above and below), p. 97, pp. 150-151, p. 166, p. 167, p. 168, p. 180 (above and below), p. 198, p. 221, p. 253, p. 255, p. 264 (above and below), p. 306, p. 450, p. 451, pp. 454–455, p. 464, p. 467, p. 490 (above and below), p. 492

The National Library - p. 130, p. 131, p. 133, p. 135, p. 138, pp. 194-195, p. 216, p. 250, p. 272, p. 277, pp. 344–345, p. 367, p. 456

Index

C

D

E

H

I

J

M

U

V

W

Y

Z